COLUMBIA UNIVERSITY STUDIES IN ENGLISH
AND COMPARATIVE LITERATURE

JOHN BUNYAN

MECHANICK PREACHER

JOHN BUNYAN
MECHANICK PREACHER

BY

WILLIAM YORK TINDALL

NEW YORK
RUSSELL & RUSSELL · INC
1964

FOR MY PARENTS

PREFACE

That John Bunyan was a tinker, a poor man, and a lay preacher has been generally known, but insufficiently pondered. The lay preacher who, while his tongue was employed in pursuit of the sublime, worked with his hands for a living, whether at farming, baking, keeping shop, or mending pots, was called a "mechanick."[1] The purpose of this book is to show that John Bunyan was a typical mechanick preacher and that his writings owe their nature both to the social, economic, and sectarian condition of their author and to the literary conventions of a numerous company of mechanicks.

Of the biographies of John Bunyan, that by the late Rev. John Brown is so far the best that more recent biographers have contented themselves with restating his conclusions in a more agreeable manner. As the earlier biographies suffer from sectarian or political bias, so the later are often injured by sentimentality, by too much reliance upon tradition, or by too little knowledge of the lay preachers. But we know from these biographies the details of Bunyan's life: his grievous imprisonments, his military service, and the amiable deportment of his wives. We also know that his features announced both virtue and intelligence, that his sentiments were generous, and his temper affectionate. His scholarly critics, however, have substituted for the celebration of his character the investigation of his allegorical works and their romantic sources. The two volumes which have been devoted to the study of Bunyan's theological position would be of greater value if their authors had been better acquainted with the obscure and trivial pamphlets of Bunyan's sectarian contemporaries.

We have been permitted by these studies to regard Bunyan, standing with popular romances in his hand, against a remote

[1] The archaic spelling has been retained to distinguish the seventeenth-century usage of the word from our own. In Bunyan's time plowmen, confectioners, rabbit keepers, tailors, cobblers, and others whom we should not call mechanics were distinguished by the term.

and awful background composed of Milton and Cromwell. Since Bunyan is different from Milton, we have received the impression that our author was unique, and that, but for the unhappy want of a faculty of self-regeneration, he was a kind of seventeenth-century Phoenix, surprisingly vocal, and splendidly alone. That a tinker should preach and, what is more, write has been thought extraordinary, and, as the poet Browning observed, so mysterious as to be explained only by the assistance of the Deity. But as the notion of Milton's intellectual isolation has yielded before a growing knowledge of the radical works of his contemporaries, so the idea of Bunyan's peculiarity must be abandoned upon acquaintance with the little-known preachers of the seventeenth century. Bunyan was one of a great number of eloquent tinkers, cobblers, and tailors; he thought what they thought, felt what they felt, and wrote according to their conventions; he was one of hundreds of literary mechanicks, and he can be considered unique only by virtue of his survival to our day as the sole conspicuous representative of a class of men from whom he differed less in kind than in degree.

If we are to understand the meaning of Bunyan's works, we must approach them neither as astonishing departures from the modes of polite or respectable literature, with which we are familiar and by which alone we are tempted to judge them, nor as the products of solitude and the Scriptures, but as representative expressions of Bunyan's inelegant, restless, and now unremembered class. The qualities of style for which Bunyan is esteemed today, his raciness, earthiness, and familiarity, were common to his kind, and are not easily to be distinguished from those of other mechanicks. The characters whom we recall in *Pilgrim's Progress* are portraits of Bunyan's sectarian enemies and friends, and the episodes of their pilgrimage were determined by the social and religious preoccupations of the literary mechanick. Our age, which is partial to subjective analysis, admires Bunyan for his interest in the inner experience, but the other mechanicks were equally attentive to the difficulties within their hearts or souls. We like in the work of Bunyan the characteristics and qualities which he shared with other mechanick preachers. Bunyan has survived, while they have perished, not because he was essentially different from these forgotten men but because his conventional expression was somewhat elevated by his genius. If, therefore, we are to understand Bunyan, we must exhume his contemporaries and read him in the feeble light of their decay.

This book is not another biography but a historical study of several aspects of Bunyan's work, which show him to have been a typical mechanick preacher. The first half of this study is devoted to the demonstration of Bunyan's resemblance to the lay preachers of all the enthusiastic sects; the second half treats more particularly of his resemblance to the other Baptist preachers. The first chapter provides definitions and descriptions of the kinds of lay preachers, and places Bunyan among them as a representative mechanick, itinerant, and enthusiast; the second is concerned with Bunyan's spiritual autobiography, *Grace Abounding,* which is shown to be one of many similar works produced for the guidance of others and for the advertisement of their own conversion, call, and gift by enthusiastic preachers; the third chapter is a discussion of that interest in controversial polemics which Bunyan shared with other lay preachers and with the effect of his sectarian acrimony upon *Pilgrim's Progress,* which is indebted to obscure controversies for the characters of By-ends and Ignorance as well as for many details, such as the incidental verses. The fourth and fifth chapters are social and economic in character: this section deals with the social inferiority of Bunyan and the other mechanicks, their economic discontent, the mockery and abuse to which they were subjected by society for their trade, illiteracy, poverty, and presumption, and their class-conscious campaign of preaching against the rich and the powerful in behalf of the oppressed. Bunyan's position in society and his dislike of the upper classes had considerable effect upon his works. The sixth and seventh chapters concern the millennium or the Fifth Monarchy, that lower-class dream of relief and triumph which occupied the fancies of the theocratic Baptists. Bunyan devoted several tracts and part of his *Holy War* to the expression of the millenarian hopes which he shared with other Baptist preachers. The subjects of the eighth and ninth chapters are more literary in character: the first of these chapters, which treats of the kind of propaganda upon which the Baptist and other lay preachers relied for the accomplishment of their purposes, reveals Bunyan as a self-conscious literary artist, who was as completely aware of his methods as any secular writer, and follows the development of his popular manner to its triumph in those excellent works of sectarian propaganda, his poems and allegories; the second of these chapters concerns Bunyan's conventional claim of inspiration and of freedom from literary influence, demonstrates his indebtedness to the tractarian and other literature of his day, and explains his pretensions to literary innocence as a professional necessity of the enthusiastic preacher. The Appendix contains an account of a lost and hitherto neglected work by Bunyan, a tract upon the Quakers, witches, and horses of Cambridge. Since the point of view, approach, and much of the material of these chapters are new, the present work may serve as a modest supplement to the previous works on John Bunyan.

I have read for the purposes of this historical analysis about two thousand tracts written by the lay preachers of the seventeenth century and by their friends and enemies. These tracts are to be found in the Thomason and the other collections of the British Museum; in the Bodleian Library; in the Friends' House Library in London; and in the McAlpin Collection of the Union Theological Seminary in New York. For guidance I have relied chiefly upon the catalogues of the Thomason and the McAlpin collections, the catalogues of the British Museum and the Bodleian, the Baptist bibliography by Mr. W. T. Whitley, and the Quaker and anti-Quaker bibliographies of Joseph Smith. My conclusions are based upon the sixty works of John Bunyan and upon the tracts of his contemporaries.

Secondary works, such as histories of the sects and modern studies of Bunyan, save for the work of John Brown, I avoided until after the completion of the first draft of this book, when I consulted them, frequently with profit. In an investigation of the godly men of the seventeenth century it is advisable to approach with caution the partisan records of sectarian history; and in a study of Bunyan, it is well to ignore, until one is familiar with the character of his work and with that of his contemporaries, the often partial or improper conclusions of his biographers and critics. The early immunity of the present work from secondary influences has enabled it to escape many of the traditional prejudices and sentiments which surround the examination of Bunyan. The errors and prejudices which may, perhaps, conspire to make this work in turn an imperfect representation of fact are at least such as are native to an independent study, to the fatigues of scholarship, and to the temper of the author.

For many courtesies and privileges I am indebted to the librarians of the British Museum, the Bodleian, the Friends' House, and the Union Theological Seminary. To the Trustees and officers of Columbia University, whose gift of a Cutting Fellowship advanced the completion of this book, I wish to express my warmest thanks. I am deeply grateful to Professors Charles Sears Baldwin, Adriaan J. Barnouw, William Tenney Brewster, Jefferson Butler Fletcher, William Witherle Lawrence, George Clinton Densmore Odell, Hoxie Neale Fairchild, Emery Edward Neff, and Ralph Leslie Rusk, and to Dr. Henry Willis Wells, who read and improved my manuscript, and whose suggestions, criticism, and encouragement were of value to me. To three scholars in particular I owe a large debt. Without the critical understanding and the support of Professor Ernest Hunter

Wright this work would not have been possible. Professor William Haller was lavish of his time at all stages of my investigation, which leans heavily upon his deep knowledge of tractarian literature, and owes much to his formal criticism. It is difficult for me to render adequate thanks to Professor Frank Allen Patterson, the principal begetter of this book, who first suggested the subject, who guided and shaped my work from the beginning, and whose sympathy and scholarship have never failed me.

W. Y. T.

Columbia University,
May 21, 1934

CONTENTS

JOHN BUNYAN
MECHANICK PREACHER

CHAPTER I

HEAVENLY FOOTMEN

For he was of that stubborn crew
Of errant saints, whom all men grant
To be the true church militant.

Hudibras, I, i, 192.

John Bunyan was a lay preacher of the sect known as the Particular Open-communion Baptists.[1] The Baptists or Anabaptists, as they were often called, were distinguished from the other sects of the sixteen forties and fifties not entirely by a detestation of paedobaptism, which some of them could regard with equanimity, but by their preference for dipping rather than sprinkling.[2] A scrupulous concern for the truth led to the separation of the Baptists into two hostile divisions, the General and the Particular. The General Baptists, the earlier but decreasingly important faction, professed the suspicious doctrine of universal redemption; but the more numerous Particular Baptists were orthodox Calvinists, who differed from the Independents only in the practice of baptism and from the Presbyterians in this and in the proprieties of ecclesiastical government. A scrupulous aversion to error led the Particular Baptists to subdivide themselves into three groups, which advanced with violence what they had embraced with love. Of these the Seventh Day Baptists preferred to seek the Lord on Saturday instead of Sunday; but no such Jewish superstition contaminated the Strict-communion and the Open-communion Particular Baptists, the latter of whom differed from the former in their tolerant admission of those paedobaptists who were Calvinists as well as saints to the privileges of worship and to the favor of God. As a Particular Open-communion Baptist, Bunyan believed in Calvin, in the observance of Sunday, in the congregational discipline, and in dipping the adult; but he generously condoned the weakness of Independents for infant sprinkling and invited them to partake of his symbolical supper. The liberality of John Bunyan deserved the indulgent applause of the Independents and the astonishment or censure of the Strict-communion Baptists.

Of the other sects of the period, many of which appear to have existed only in the intolerant fancies of the Presbyterians, we need notice but a few since Bunyan chose to ignore the errors of some, and since the examination of a few will serve for all. The Quakers,[3] who had emancipated themselves from Calvin through a democratic mysticism, and the Ranters,[4] who combined pantheism with antinomian liberties, were the principal non-Calvinistic sects of the sixteen fifties. The Muggletonians, who propounded the doctrine of a material God and freely invoked the awful curse of the Lamb, were curious rather than important.[5] The Fifth Monarchists, who were closely affiliated with the Particular Baptists, endeavored to assist the establishment of the earthly kingdom of Jesus by the destruction of the wicked.[6] The Ranters, the Muggletonians, the more radical Quakers, and many of the Calvinistic Baptists, who laid an unfortunate emphasis upon free grace, were antinomian either in theory or in practice; and antinomianism was in general a symptom of revolt against established society.

The sects of the age of Cromwell fall roughly into two large groups, the radical and the conservative. Most of those saints whose religious discontent was qualified by respectability and position united themselves with the Presbyterians or the Independents, whose affection for God endangered neither society nor the conveniences of wealth. But those saints whose troubles were social and economic as well as religious generally found their way to the company of the radicals, Quakers, Baptists, Fifth Monarchists, or Ranters, who promised a new society. Though, for example, the Baptists and even the Quakers secured the loyalty of some polite and eminent men, they claimed the adherence of innumerable laborers, small farmers, shopkeepers, and artisans. It is improper, therefore, to ignore the social character of the radical sects or to treat purely as a religious and political revolt that which was also social and economic. The rise of the radical sects, which an excellent treatise by Mr. Champlin Burrage describes,[7] gave expression and the hope of relief to men of all classes, but especially to those whose difficulties were social or economic. The sorrow of the lower orders, which finds expression today in the secular creed of Marxism, embraced in the seventeenth century the comforts of radical Christianity, whose banners had sanctified the insurrections of the peasants and the revolt of the masses under John of Leyden at Münster. Accidental distinctions of doctrine have concealed from many historians of religious parties, as they obscured from the saints of the seventeenth century, the identity of the radical sects in both nature and purpose. But to the impartial student of enthusiasm the similarities among these sects are at once more evident and more important than the differences.[8]

The leaders of the radical sects and of the Independents were laymen, who had been elevated to the office of the ministry not by the carnal ceremonies of ordination, the mark and error of the Presbyterian, the Anglican, and the Papist, but by the sublime machinery of their own impulse or the will of God, which was usually detected, confirmed, and applauded by the sagacity of the congregation. Ordinarily these dedicated laymen were disqualified by neither rank nor education from the exercise of a divine profession requiring no human assistance beyond the willingness of an audience and the erection of a tub or pulpit, which, since many of them were carpenters, they could often effect by their own industry; but sometimes they were ex-clergymen who had renounced their ordination and succumbed to piety. The lay preachers of Cromwell's day were not without precedent; for the disciples of the Saviour and the primitive apostles had been laymen; the tenets of Lollardy had been preached by laymen as well as by the ordained; in the sixteenth century lay preachers of the Familists, Brownists, and Barrowists had excited

the anxiety of the government; and from 1611 to 1640 the unordained preachers of the separatists had somewhat enlarged the
province of truth. The Civil Wars permitted and encouraged the
expansion of an existing practice; and the disorder which suddenly multiplied the number of preaching laymen was increased
by their eloquence. In pulpit or market place they directed and
inflamed the passions of the discontented, revealed the corruption of church, society, and state, and extended to the vulgar the
hope of justice or of baptism. As their auditors responded, they
enjoyed the satisfaction of orators, of apostles, and not infrequently of martyrs.

Many lay preachers combined the pursuit of sacred rhetoric
with that of a manual trade by which they maintained the body as
they advanced the soul. These industrious men were distinguished from other preachers by the contemptuous name of
mechanick, which malice applied indifferently both to those
who continued to follow a gainful craft in addition to the ministry, and to those who had abandoned shop or tools for preaching.
But the eloquent cobbler could point to biblical predecessors;
the pious fishmonger could find encouragement in the car-
pentry of Jesus; and the illuminated tent-makers to Cromwell's
army, who celebrated the Sabbath with suitable oratory, could
allege the respectable precedent of the disciples. "Elisha was a
plough-man," said Richard Hubberthorn, the Quaker, "and
when the word of the Lord came to him, he left the plough and
obeyed the Word of the Lord . . . and I do witness the same
Call, who was a Husbandman and had a Vineyard, and gathered
fruit, till the Word of the Lord came and called me from it."[9]
The early separatists of England supplied their successors with
a local and more immediate example of mechanick divinity.
Inspiration, example, and opportunity united after 1640 to call
tradesmen of all radical sects to the ministry of the word, but
Baptist mechanicks were the most conspicuous for number. Of
these gifted men, whose emergence was a sign of social revolution,
Benjamin Keach, the Baptist tailor, is representative. From his

obscure occupation this remarkable man arose, and by the assistance of the Spirit, became so articulate that his sermons, allegories, and poems would fill a shelf of the most commodious Baptist library. The power of his utterance, the severity of his martyrdom, and his sponsorship of sugarplums for children, "which have been found to bring from them many strange and monstrous worms," secured the admiration of the faithful. At Keach's trial for Fifth Monarchy opinions, unlicensed publication, and illicit preaching, the judge said: "this Fellow would have Ministers to be . . . Taylors, Pedlars, and Tinkers, such Fellows as he is."[10] John Bunyan, the Baptist tinker, rivaled Keach in his mechanick occupation, in the number and character of his works, in the excellence of his preaching and martyrdom, and in the applause of the multitude.

As the example of the apostles justified the profession of the mechanick, so the vagrancy of these irreproachable men encouraged and excused the practices of the itinerant.[11] Most Independent and many Baptist preachers were content to remain in their proper congregations, but many and perhaps most preachers of the radical sects discovered in themselves an aversion to sedentary enthusiasm, became itinerants, and wandered homeless from town to town. Some preachers contrived to combine the virtues of the itinerant and the stationary apostle by occasional excursions from a center of light. The itinerant was received, nourished, and heeded by the men of godly districts and permitted to open the word in convenient barns or markets, but elsewhere he was accorded the reception of the vagabond.

Quaker, Ranter, and Baptist itinerants descended upon the land, carrying a message of spirituality and peace often to the accompaniment of tumult, riot, and disorder. The unquiet life of these heavenly footmen is described in the words of Richard Hubberthorn:

In obedience to him who called me did I goe, as I was moved by his eternal Spirit, into severall parts of this Nation, Townes, and Cities, and Countries, in the North and West part of England and Wales,

bearing testimony to the truth, and in some parts sealing the testimony with my bloud, and by imprisonments, in persecution, in
perils, often under tryals of cruel mockings, scourgings, and revilings,
enduring the contradiction of sinners . . . as having nothing, yet
possessing all things, as poor, yet making many rich . . . and by the
Spirit of the Lord was I moved, in obedience to him, to come to this
Town [Cambridge], where some did receive the testimony of the
truth, where I stayed certain dayes, and we had certain meetings pub-
lickly from house to house, and the hands of the persecutors was then
bound by the mighty power of God, and they limited from acting
the persecution which was in their hearts. . . . Then I passed forth
of the Town, as I was moved of the Lord, to another people, till again
I was moved to come into this Town, not knowing when I came in
whether I should stay two dayes in the Town, but waiting in the
will of God, out of my own will, I came, as I was moved, and laboured
in travel night and day in the Lords work and service . . . and in
the morning as I went into the street in the market place, two men
followed me, and commanded me to goe with them two before the
Mayor, who when I came before him, came unto me, & violently took
off my hat & threw it upon the ground and asked me whence I came,
and where I had lived, and of what calling I was, and what I came
thither for? . . . the Mayor said, I have a Law against thee, I will
make thee a wandering person, and a rogue; which I denied.[12]

Edward Burrough, another wandering Quaker, abandoned
himself before the age of twenty to the operation of the Holy
Ghost, received the spirit of prophecy, and thus equipped, took
to the road, slept under hedges, enlightened thousands, disputed
with the clergy, and welcomed the disorder by which truth and
peace were fostered. He preached in English to the astonished
nunneries of France, and was deterred from the conversion of
the Pope only by the greater desire to complete the conversion of
England, where he was abused, beaten, and imprisoned. The
discomforts of Newgate abridged his profitable life soon after the
restoration of the exiled monarch, and provided Burrough with
the crown of martyrdom.[13] Laurence Clarkson's itinerant activities advanced in turn, as his light increased, the doctrines of the
Baptists, the Ranters, and the Muggletonians; and the contribu-

tions of his auditors insured the success of his ministry. That he had dipped many in rivers he was ready to admit and we have no reason to doubt; but that he preferred to dip naked women or that his lustful intimacy with them had been permitted to interrupt the course of the sacrament he was careful to deny.[14] His ministrations seem to have been less adapted to edify than to please his imperfect disciples.

Of the Baptist itinerants, Vavasor Powell, who promoted the truth in Wales, was distinguished by his tirelessness and eminence. This restless shepherd superintended the vagrancy of many subordinate itinerants, twelve in Montgomeryshire alone, "certain Journey-men Pedlers, or Itinerant Tobacco mongers, and other of like quality," as the tongue of envy described them. These "wandring Priests and Gospel Postmasters" rode from parish to parish as their leader or their inspiration directed them. The light of God supplied their deficiencies of learning and ennobled their mechanick occupations. To the carnal criticism[15] of his subordinates, Powell gave an apostolic answer:

But you cry out that we send out, Weavers, Smiths, Cappers, Souldiers. It is true there is one Weaver a blessed understanding man, and one Smith a religious godly man (and one that hath more learning then some of your Curates) & it may be two or three gifted godly tryed and approved men besides, (who may be Souldiers or rather Officers) that goe along with our Preachers, as Fellow-helpers (even as the Apostles & Ministers had in the Primitive times) in the work of God, and God hath made them successful.[16]

It was said by the faithful that the horse of Vavasor Powell had carried his rider to every village, fair, market, hillside, hedge, and parish church in Wales, at each of which, as Powell spoke, the gospel temperature was noticeably increased; for when he preached, "a mist or smoak would issue from his Head, so great an agitation of Spirit he had." Often he traveled a hundred miles in a week, preaching continually, several times a day in several places; he sometimes slept at night in the hovels of the poor, whom he made less miserable by his eloquence; his success in London, where he entertained the godly with millenarian expectations, was so conspicuous as to occasion his arrest. The beatings, mockery, and abuse which he received from the unconvinced, the trials and imprisonments he encountered, were to be expected in "th' Apostolike game, for winning Souls"; and he was sufficiently consoled by the advancement of godliness, by the income of one hundred pounds provided by Parliament, by the free offerings of the saints, and, according to the wicked, by the sequestrated revenue of the clergy. His gifts of evangelism and prophecy were both extinguished and consecrated by his martyrdom in Lambeth prison, where in 1670, though his jailer had shown him many kindnesses and allowed him frequent liberties, he died.[17] What his enemies had called his mechanick presumption, his hatred of the upper classes, and his seditious inclinations, had been recorded in 1654 in a premature epitaph:

> Here Propagation lies, that did aspire,
> Like Phaeton to set the World on fire,
> Cry'd down Order, and Ministerial Call,
> And thought to give this Government a fall:
> She would have caus'd the Gentry flock in Swarms,
> To beg relief like Cripples without Armes;
> And would have made the learned Lawyers plead,
> From door to door (poor Souls) for Crusts of Bread.
> Lament Itinerants! this Trade is gone,
> Take up your Tools, and Occupation;
> Silence in Churches; you have long forgot
> Your first callings, inheritance and lot.[18]

The territory of the itinerant John Bunyan, who resembled Powell in most essentials, embraced Bedfordshire and the neighboring counties of Cambridge, Hertford, Leicester, Huntingdon, Northampton, and Buckingham, as well as London, in his later years. In 1655 when the congregation of Bedford recognized his gift and appointed him to preach both locally and on evangelistic expeditions in the vicinity, as Bunyan informs us in *Grace Abounding*, he was already an itinerant tinker, who, from his base at Elstow and Bedford, wandered about the country, plying his trade at fairs, markets, and farms. To supplement the itinerancy of his occupation with that of the gospel was at once apostolic and convenient. A happier providence than that which directed the sedentary cobbler to presume beyond his last to an abnormal vagrancy, had converted Bunyan by an easy and natural compromise from a merely useful into a sublime itinerant. Until his imprisonment in 1660 he profitably combined the trades of tinkering and evangelism; but during this early period he was only one of the several subordinate itinerants maintained and directed by the meeting at Bedford.

The open-communion meeting at Bedford was closely associated with the congregations of John Gibbs at Newport Pagnell, of John Donne at Pertenhall, of William Wheeler at Cranfield, and of William Dell at Yelden, as well as with many minor outposts which it had either founded or enlarged.[19] Bunyan preached in the hospitable pulpits of these churches, but when no pulpit was available, he opened the word in market places, private houses, fields, or the barns of the devout. He encountered and welcomed contentions and brawls; endured and provoked the taunts and hostility of the local clergy, one of whom had him indicted at the assizes; exchanged insults with the rival itinerants of the Quakers; and contributed to the enlightenment or disorder of those regions of darkness which his pugnacity had led him to penetrate.[20]

The twelve-year martyrdom of John Bunyan was so successful, though perhaps defective in wanting the final crown of death, that upon his enlargement from captivity in 1672 he was elevated by the suffrage of his congregation to the full eminence of the ministry. This office carried with it the privilege of supervising the associated open-communion churches of the district, of applying to the government during the period of toleration for the licenses of their preachers, and with the aid of his own congregation of supplying these flocks with subordinate pastors.[21] The

Baptist "messenger" or district superintendent observed and corrected the ministers of his territory, defended them against opponents, disciplined or excommunicated their willful followers, assisted at the ordination of elders, founded new meetings, and pursued the work of evangelism.[22] This responsible office, which was also that of Vavasor Powell, enlarged Bunyan's reputation, and "some, though in a jeering manner no doubt, gave him the Epethite of Bishop Bunyan."[23] His new and almost episcopal dignity not only failed to impede the itinerancy of John Bunyan but increased it by providing the assistance of a horse, upon whose back he was enabled to ride his regular circuit, to visit remote counties, and to make an annual journey to London, where he preached in open-communion conventicles.[24]

Bunyan supported his triumphs with the patience of a bishop and endured the mockery and slander to which every itinerant was subjected with the philosophy of a saint. He dismissed the accusations of immorality which malice invented, bore the contempt of the educated and the gentle, suffered in silence the insinuations of the wicked, and even in the unfortunate affair of Agnes Beaumont, a handsome girl of his flock, he submitted with a sigh to the suspicion of impropriety.[25] The consciousness of innocence preserved him from the designs of envy and secured his fame from carnal ingenuity; but "O it is hard work," he said, "to pocket up the reproaches of all the foolish people . . . and to suffer all their revilings, lies and slanders, without cursing them."[26]

A powerful impulse at heart and a call extraordinary had induced Bunyan to share with other itinerants the discomforts and delights of martyrdom. Those saints who were in no position to inflict were eager to suffer and even to invite martyrdom; for by their sacrifice they advanced the gospel, encouraged the feeble, and preserved or established their own repute. These considerations, as Bunyan confessed,[27] had led him joyously to accept an imprisonment which he could have avoided but to which he owed no little part of his later influence and fame. Every lay preacher, like every primitive Christian, was covetous of what Bunyan called a special dignity of which few were counted worthy.[28] Each ministerial martyr improved his ordeal by the enlightenment of fellow prisoners and jailers and by the publication of tracts devoted to the injustice of his martyrdom at the hands of the Beast.[29] In accordance with this reasonable custom, which was maintained by both Quakers and Baptists, Bunyan added a long section concerning his trial and imprisonment to *Grace Abounding*,[30] composed with greater detail his *Relation of Imprisonment*,[31] and issued his *Prison Meditations,* a recapitulation in verse of the same material.[32] The applause and the piety of saints at large swelled with each production of those in confinement, whose number taxed the capacity of jails and whose ambitions of martyrdom the often reluctant authorities had been compelled to satisfy.

Not every lay preacher was an itinerant or a mechanick, nor was every itinerant a mechanick, but every itinerant and every mechanick was an enthusiast. The enthusiasts depended upon inspiration and revelation, upon openings, trances, illuminations, visions, and celestial voices for what they did or said. The mysterious direction of God exempted them from dependence on man and lent to their actions and speech an unquestionable authority. If they visited a town, if they preached at a market cross, if they thrust pins through their thumbs, or if they devoured an apple, it was by a heavenly impulse.[33] Inspiration enabled those of meager learning to interpret texts of Scripture which baffled the ingenuity of scholars;[34] the voice of God gave them fine words in the night and directed their controversial pen. Thomas Greene, the Quaker, said, "This is the Word which I received from the Lord, the 24th. of the 12th Month, 1659. in the night season, as I lay upon my Bed, when deep sleep was

upon me, saying, Write my Controversie with the false Pastors."[35]
Notable visions appeared to tailors as they sat at their work; John
Mowlin deposed before the justices that

he being at work on his table, there fell from above (according to
his own phrase) a power upon him, and that he being wel and strong
in his joynts, was cast into a great depth of mourning, in so much
that tears did abundantly gush from him: as he sewed by his wife,
there appeared a Vision before him, of which he was ready to demand
this question, What art thou? but had not strength to bring it forth.
. . . The Vision . . . with a powerfull voice said, I am he that have
holes in my hands and feet.[36]

This portentous and perhaps divine visitant impelled the fortunate tailor to attend a meeting at the residence of Goody Fore-
man, to perform cures of the ailing, and to dip those who desired
this consolation. Prophet Hunt, the rabbit keeper, demanded the
key to the church door upon the strength of a similar enlightenment.[37] Innumerable mechanicks assumed the character and the
prerogatives of prophets. "We received often the pouring down
of the Spirit upon us, and the Gift of God's holy eternal Spirit,
as in the dayes of old . . . and we spake with new Tongues, as
the Lord gave us utterance, and as his Spirit led us, which was
poured down upon us."[38] This enviable privilege of intimacy
with the divine presence was called the gift.[39]

"Enthusiasme," said Henry More in *Enthusiasmus Triumphatus,* "is nothing else but a misconceit of being inspired." The
eminent disciple of Plato traced this sad distemper with its
storms of devotion and zeal, its strange ecstasies and trances,
and the surprising eloquence which attended it, not to supernatural but to natural causes, to melancholy and flatulence.[40]
Though the celebrated Richard Baxter was, according to his
own confession, a sufferer from hypochondriac flatulency, he
decried with a vehemence equal to that of More a pretension to
the gift.[41] The enthusiasts believed, said Daniel Featley, "that
the Scripture is not our onely rule of faith, and manners, but that

God revealeth his will to his children at this day by visions and dreams;"[42] and none, said Bishop Edward Fowler, claimed the gifts of prophecy and evangelism but "wild Enthusiasts, Brain-sick, Melancholy and Hot-headed people, who take their own Fancies and Whims, and the products of an ungoverned imagi-nation for Inspirations." [43] The Presbyterians and Anglicans, whose soberness maintained that the feeling of inspiration was not equivalent to inspiration, denied the continued existence of the once valuable offices of apostle, evangelist, and prophet, which had been rendered unnecessary by Scripture and discipline and by an ordained clergy, who administered the sacraments with distinction and expounded the text with learning.[44] The min-isters of the conservative sects, who claimed only a pastoral dig-nity, suspected the character of prophetical revelation: "I could never read," said George Griffith of Vavasor Powell, "that any having the gift of tongues, spoke false Latin; the immediate works of the Deity are alwayes observed the most excellent in their kind; and indeed, if the matter were from above, God would have assisted the author (though not perhaps to an ele-gant, yet sure) to an intelligible phrase."[45] But the public, impressed by the unmistakable presence of the real thing, and heedless of the warnings and agitation of the uninspired, who beheld with reluctance the incursion and success of the gifted, abandoned the scrannel piping of the clergy for the authentic words of God. The quarrel between the established and the gifted was augmented by public participation; disputes were almost constant;[46] for what was one man's gift was another's poison.

The conduct of the enthusiasts was often extraordinary. Wil-liam Franklin, for example, a respectable rope-maker of forty, by the aid of certain visions in 1649 was enabled to confuse him-self with the Son of God; and Mary Gadbury, a Baptist seller of laces, received a simultaneous illumination, deserted her unen-lightened husband, sold all her effects save for one bed, and went to travel with the Son of God in Hampshire, where they enjoyed considerable popular success.[47] John Robins maintained his wife to be the Virgin Mary and her son the Infant Jesus;[48] James Nayler permitted his Quaker followers to adore him as the Messiah and to sing "holy, holy, holy" before him as he entered Bristol.[49] Several offered themselves as the last witnesses of Revelation, many discarded their clothing in the streets, prophets continually gave advice to Charles and Cromwell, and one of the inspired, whose gift was less social in character, piously counted flies, and thrust his leg into the fire.[50] Some of these men may have been knaves who took advantage of the popular interest in witnesses and prophets; others were merely enthusiasts; but not a few, such as the author of a broadside called *Divine Fire-Works*, appear to have been mad:

> I have seen the Lord. The King;
> Who appeared unto me
> On (Innocents Day) the 28 of the last moneth.
> He spake to me and with me . . .
> Then was I raised to sit up in my bed (in
> my shirt) smoaking like a furnace . . .
> Fear not it is I Blu I.
> Whereupon the Spirit within me (with
> exceeding joy) exceedingly groaned; & with
> a loud voice out-sounded
>   O the Blu! O the Blu! O the Blu!
> And the worm, and no man said, what Blu. . . .[51]

At a time when every godly man of the lower orders was potentially a vessel of the Spirit, it was inevitable that the vagaries of the mentally unsound should have taken a religious direction. The tendency of the age to interpret extravagance as a symptom of divine impulse lent itself to the irregularities of those whom we should confine to institutions. When normal enthusiasts, under the influence of current religious beliefs, acted and talked as if they were mad, it was difficult to distinguish the godly from the insane or the feeble-minded. Incurious of prophetical sanity and incapable of discrimination, the saints sometimes encouraged the village half-wit to mount the pulpit, and went to hear him on Sunday. The saints, however, were not peculiar in their inability to discriminate. The sober critic applied the epithet of enthusiast to mad and sane alike; and since only he was confined, the irreligious occupant of Bedlam gloomily admired the liberty of his religious contemporaries. We may condone but must not share the natural error of these honest men; avoiding the facile explanation of universal holiness or of universal insanity, we must remember that some enthusiasts were sane, others mad, and that though some lay preachers were mad, most of those with whom we shall have to deal were normal or of doubtful character. But the mad differed from the sane only in their exaggeration of a temper common to both. The lay preachers flourished in the baroque age of protestantism when the individuality of the movement had run to floridness and excess; as the poets, painters, and architects of their day reflected the spirit of the age in the extravagance of their decoration, so the lay preachers reflected it in the extravagance of their lives, and, seeking the simplicity of the primitive, achieved an almost fashionable decadence.

England was lighted by the queer radiance of insanity and shaken by the regrettable demonstrations of the inspired. An abnormal atmosphere was the normal medium of the lay preachers, who accepted the theory of inspiration, admired anything, however curious, which they knew to be godly, and arranged their daily lives upon preconceptions which the rational must distrust. Their lives were odd but never uninteresting. Though the inspiration of some preachers, such as Lodowick Muggleton, John Robins, Anna Trapnel, and James Nayler, appeared in the irregularity of their deportment, that of the ordinary enthusiasts, such as Hanserd Knollys, John Simpson, and Henry Jessey, was apparent less in their actions than in their ideas, which can be explained only by the pervasive atmosphere of excess. John

Bunyan was an enthusiast of the latter variety. The kindliness of nature preserved his conduct from enormities, but the consciousness of inspiration lent to his inner life a pleasurable excitement, and though he was sane, sanctioned what must be called insobriety of mind. But even in his millenarian convictions, the antinomian tendencies of his early thought, his attention to voices from heaven, and his devotion to martyrdom, he was among the more moderate enthusiasts. John Bunyan never removed his clothing in public, but the difference between him and those who did was only of degree; for he believed as firmly as they in impulse and the gift.

Bunyan's gift was recognized not only by himself but by the faithful at Bedford, who applauded the Deity for calling and qualifying the mechanick for the exercise of the sublime office to which they raised him.[52] The enthusiasm of John Bunyan is evident in the conviction, which appears throughout his writings, that all true ministers were endowed by heavenly influence. "Gifts make a minister," he said; and by the pouring forth of the Holy Ghost upon him the apostle was supplied with an unearthly virtue, directed in his evangelistic routine, enabled to preach without premeditation, and to know the true from the false. The minister was the preferred and almost peculiar channel through which the influence of God was communicated to the elect. His celestial privilege gave to the minister, though he might be innocent of tongues and the learning of the schools, the ability to discover the meaning of the Scriptures.[53] To the Baptist this ability was of particular value since he depended less upon direct than upon scriptural illumination; whereas the light of the Quaker exempted him from the written word, that of the Baptist fell upon the text. But the direct assistance of the Spirit was not denied to the Baptist, who, upon emergent occasions, received from above an appropriate scripture. At a critical moment of Bunyan's examination by the justices, the Lord provided a text: "I say God brought it, for I thought not on it before:

but as he [the justice] was speaking, it came so fresh into my mind, and was set so evidently before me, as if the Scripture had said, Take me, take me. . . ."[54] During Bunyan's conversion texts darted at him from the sky; in his early years he depended like the Quakers upon visions, dreams, voices; and the impulse of heaven directed his itinerancy.[55] When Bunyan preached, prayed, or wrote, according to his own admission, it was not he who spoke but the Spirit within him;[56] and since neither the word nor the impulse was his own, the gifted man could not be silent.[57] But the spontaneous utterance of the inspired excited the incredulity of the carnal mind; at the judicial trial of John Bunyan it was unkind of the justice to ask: "how should we know, that you do not write out your prayers first, and then read them afterwards to the people?"[58]

Pilgrim's Progress is autobiographical in that it illustrates the life of the enthusiastic itinerant. The details of Bunyan's own itinerant career supplied those of Christian's allegorical journey. Like his creator, Christian traveled alone through the country, seeking shelter at friendly houses, engaging in controversies, meeting obstacles, dangers, and discouragements, but never deviating from the way though it led him, as he had known, to the martyrdom of trial and imprisonment at Vanity Fair, where the mockery and persecution which he encountered were the lot of the average lay preacher. He was directed in his journey by the Bible, by the advice of Evangelist, his ministerial guide, by celestial messengers, by mysterious hands from the sky, and by the timely intervention of angels. This enthusiastic guidance was supplemented by the gifts of prophecy which the Porter, Evangelist, and the Shepherds continually displayed:

> Thus by the Shepherds Secrets are reveal'd.
> Which from all other men are kept conceal'd:
> Come to the Shepherds then, if you would see
> Things deep, things hid, and that mysterious be.[59]

These enthusiasts bear a closer resemblance to the gifted minister than Christian himself, who, despite his itinerancy, was intended for the coming saint rather than the preacher; but it was through his hero that Bunyan presented the difficulties and triumphs of his own wandering ministry. The account of Quaker itinerancy by Edward Burrough will serve to show the fidelity with which *Pilgrim's Progress* represents the life of the restless evangelist:

We went forth as commanded of the Lord, leaving all relations and all things of the world behind us, Rulers and people often imprisoning and abusing and resisting us with violence, banishing us out of towns, and putting us out of our Innes . . . the whole company of rude people in a town, often gathering and besetting a house or Inne about where we were entred to lodge, in our travels; often exposed to dificult and hard travels and journies, giving our selves to the Crosse, to take it up against all earthly, often drinking water, and lying in straw in barnes, after a hard daies journey, and yet for all these things, the power and presence of the Lord was with us, and we were carried on in much boldnesse, and faithfulnesse in courage, and without fear or doubtings, through the often hazard of our lives many waies in uproars by evil men, and in markets, and Steeple-houses, and also in travels by robbers, and every way were we exposed to dangers, and perrils, but through all & over all were carried, and are preserved to this day.[60]

Greatheart, the leader of the travelers of the second part of *Pilgrim's Progress,* embodies the ministerial functions of guide, defender, comforter, interpreter, and prophet.[61] His strength against the giants and ogres of persecution was the virtue of the militant preacher, and the feebleness of his followers that of the congregation. But as we shall see in a later chapter, Greatheart is less the enthusiastic itinerant than the superintending minister; and as Christian and Evangelist represent the early life of John Bunyan, Greatheart reflects the later.

The gifts of providence were various but rarely bestowed in their full variety upon a single man. Vavasor Powell and Edward Burrough were enthusiasts and itinerants but not mechanicks;

Benjamin Keach, the tailor, was infrequently itinerant; and Henry Jessey, the enthusiast, suffered from the disadvantage of learning. But Bunyan, who had received the complete endowment of heaven and was all things to God, united in his person the merits of all these men; for he was an enthusiastic, itinerant, and mechanick lay preacher, whose ignorance presented no impediment to the mechanical operation of the Spirit. Moreover Bunyan possessed the virtues of those exemplary enthusiasts, the Quakers, the Ranters, and the Muggletonians, from whom he differed only in details of theology, in the accident of genius, and in that felicitous restraint which, though it permitted the exhibition of ardor, tempered his holiness and preserved him from excess.

CHAPTER II

GRACE ABOUNDING

Oh, what a-do, as I may say, is here before
one sinner can be eternally saved!
Christ a Complete Saviour, I, 235.

Grace Abounding is divided into two parts, of which the first concerns Bunyan's conversion, the second his call and ministry. This pleasing division must be ascribed not to the demands of order and elegance but to those of enthusiasm; the character and sequence of the separated parts, though apparently insignificant or at most natural, were determined by an apostolic convention. Autobiographies distinguished by this division of matter were produced in great numbers during the seventeenth century by enthusiastic preachers. The delicate surgery of soul for which Bunyan is known was the monotonous exercise of his contemporaries; but what the Spirit was content to inspire, it was unwilling to preserve, and of these almost identical autobiographies *Grace Abounding* alone has survived for the general reader. The conformity of *Grace Abounding* to this ministerial convention makes the task of the commentator agreeable by serving both to explain the nature of the book and to illustrate the enthusiastic character of its author.

The year 1666 was remarkable for the municipal conflagration, the epidemic distemper, the disaster at sea, and the publication of *Grace Abounding*. These judgments which the Deity had been provoked to visit upon an abandoned nation excited the dismay of the profane and the extravagant acclamations of the faithful, who looked with equal favor upon the novel and the customary; for, as they were aware, the fire and the triumph of an alien admiral were almost without example, but the autobiography of John Bunyan had been preceded and, as they might conjecture, was to be followed by similar works, which, indeed, from

1649 to 1700 enthusiasts of the radical sects were inspired to write or to applaud. None but enthusiasts composed these testimonials to their apostolic excellence, and few but members of the mechanick classes published them during their effectual ministry. The ministerial autobiography, issued by the fortunate author at the height of his powers, must be distinguished from those belated and posthumous publications, such as the *Journal* of George Fox or the *Reliquiae* of Richard Baxter, which are memoirs rather than advertisements of the gifts of God.

The year 1649 witnessed the death of a monarch and the birth, or at least the first considerable emergence and multiplication, of the enthusiastic autobiography. But this literary portent had been heralded and remotely anticipated by biographies of preachers or eminent converts and by anatomies of the soul, before, during, and after regeneration, which had been devised during the preceding decades for the further enlightenment of the devout.[1] To these works the autobiography owed in silence a considerable debt; but at the turn of the century as enthusiasm prospered and swelled, its active prophets discovered another and a more illustrious model in chapters nine and twenty-two of the *Acts of the Apostles*. The author of the *Acts*, whose attention to visions, voices, and spastic seizures was indefatigable and exact, devoted these passages to the rebirth, vocation, and ministry of Paul. The potential autobiographer recognized with delight his identity with Paul; and in the record of his own sensations, gifts, and acts, which a miraculous influence immediately compelled him to compose and publish, he piously imitated the history of his celebrated predecessor.[2]

As the road to Damascus had beheld the sublime distractions of an apostolic birth, so the first part of the enthusiastic autobiography bore witness to the raptures and travail of the author, who described with love the vagaries of the ordeal which he had endured with distinction. Custom and enthusiasm combined to convince the immodest prophet that the magnitude of his early sin, that each convulsion, impulse, and voice from heaven, which he had been privileged to know in the pains of regeneration, enlarged his ministerial significance. But the second part of the autobiography was of a character more practical though not less divine; for it was devoted to the summons and to the warrant from God which surpassed as it supplanted ordination by man and to the acts of the new apostle.[3] The injured primate, whose head had been severed from his body, might reprehend from his grave this irregularity of ministerial induction, but the companies of the devout received as true certificates of inhuman ordination the autobiographies which prophets, apostles, and even virgins were moved to utter through the press.

The intention of the ghostly autobiographer is discovered in his own statement. Arise Evans, the gifted tailor, was inspired by the example of Paul to compose an autobiography to announce, and to end misunderstandings of, his apostolic commission:

But I suppose such an account as S. Paul sometime gave to the people, is expected from me, that is in some measure a Narration of my whole life, & specially of my calling to his work, Acts 22. Acts 27. wherein you shall finde Gods special purpose in me, preparing me from my infancy, and also leading me by his special hand, from time to time, and declaring his mind unto me, giving me to understand, wherefore I had my being, shewing special signs upon me, while I was yet an infant, to the admiration of my Parents, and of all my friends and acquaintances, that they were forced to prophesie, and to say that God had appointed me for some great work. . . .[4]

"God's secretary," as Arise Evans was known to himself, suffered the disadvantage of a quiet and almost imperceptible conversion, but his calling was conspicuous; he continually enjoyed the solicitude of the Deity, received angelic visitors in his modest shop, and observed with gratitude that in evidence of his vocation the laws of nature had been conveniently suspended: "And seeing the Sun at its rising, skip, play, dance, and turn about like a wheel, I fell down upon my knees." Though he alone could penetrate the sacred text, many had despised him as an illiterate, he complained; King Charles had neglected his political advice; and his parents, thinking him unwell, had confined him in his chamber for certain days, whereupon he had prophesied. The autobiography of Nicholas Smith, the inspired shoemaker, was designed to profess a gift which revealed itself in voices, a sense of mission, and elaborate revelations of a miraculous character and of an awful significance. The spirit which qualified him for the work of the Lord had come to him, he said, "by touching lightly the haire of my head, so soaking down into my head, it made all my necke and shoulders to rise; after two hours, it entred into my soul."[5] From these and the many similar statements it may be inferred that the purpose of the enthusiastic autobiography was the advertisement of the author's experience and gifts. Not the autobiographical impulse, but the desire to promote for the information of disciples and proselytes the heavenly endowment of the prophet, impelled the preacher to issue the printed account of his conversion, call, and apostolic pursuits. It is notable that most of these works were written in prison, a circumstance which enabled the literary enthusiast to improve the effectiveness of his narrative by the appeal of martyrdom.

A second intention, however, is to be observed in most of these displays of piety: the desire to convert or to guide others enriched advertisement with propaganda for rebirth and gospel holiness. The enthusiasts, who were also evangelists, provided their own example for the imitation of young sinners and directed them through the orthodox agitations of conversion. "My new birth which God hath wrought in me," said Prophet Hunt, the rabbit keeper, "I hope the same will be a plain patterne for all those which shall read my book."[6] Richard Coppin, the Ranter, desired the reader of his book to compare his own conversion with that of the author to see how far each had advanced in the way to God.[7] A third intention, upon which the uncritical might insist, the enhancement of the Lord, is but a variant and more seemly expression of the first, since the powers of the inscrutable were evident only in the gifts and in the experience which the prophet observed within himself and was moved devoutly to celebrate.

Were they Ranter, Baptist, Muggletonian, or Quaker, the ambitious autobiographers carefully followed the pattern for this variety of literature and issued works which by their many similarities to *Grace Abounding* serve to illuminate it. The Quakers, though not the earliest, were easily the most forward of the makers and patrons of the ministerial autobiography. Almost all the primitive apostles of this belligerent society composed and published a *Grace Abounding* in which each recorded his advancement from impiety to outward godliness, to inward, real godliness, and, through a sublime or perhaps subliminal influence, to the ministry of the light. The autobiography of the Quaker is not to be distinguished in general outline and detail from that of the Dipper; but, because of the comparative simplicity of the doctrine upon which they were ordered, the conversions, and hence the histories, of the Friends sometimes failed of the intricacy which a Calvinist might boast.

The Inheritance of Jacob by Francis Howgill and *Jacob found in a desert Land* by George Whitehead,[8] which are representative of the Quaker autobiographies, were dedicated by these imitators of Jacob to the miracles of regeneration and call. The seed sprouted in these commodious vessels after they had ignorantly contained the filth of infancy for twelve discreditable years, and drove them lamenting their sins from a love of games and sports to the delusory refuge of formal religion. As they heeded the carnal words of the clergyman, they had moments of pride in works, and sometimes, of terror. Convictions of hollowness attended Howgill to the doors of the Calvinists, within which, under the uncomfortable doctrine of imputed righteousness, he found that he had sinned the unpardonable sin. The wrath of the Holy Ghost pursued him as he fled without the sensation of peace from Independents to Baptists, and then to antinomians of the most liberal character. His ultimate discovery of the truth and his gradual conversion to Quakerism were accompanied by tumult, convulsion, and illumination; the world reeled, the pillars of heaven appeared to be inadequate, Howgill wept. But the voice within him exclaimed; he was consoled, saved, called, and sent by the providence of the Lord to preach the truth to the unconverted. The experience of George Whitehead, which was almost identical, enabled him to say: "The Lord hath called me from my native Country, and . . . his Spirit which is upon me, and his word which he hath put in my mouth, shall not depart from me from henceforth and for evermore."[9]

The Heart Opened by Christ by Richard Farnworth and the autobiographies of Richard Hubberthorn, George Rofe, Edward Burrough, and many other prophets of the Society of Friends are of equal excellence and notable identity.[10] That of John Crook, the resident apostle of Bedfordshire, though otherwise a close parallel to *Grace Abounding,* was published posthumously like Fox's *Journal,* wants in consequence the motive of useful advertisement, and must be regarded as a memoir.[11] The adolescence of Crook, like that of Bunyan, his neighbor, was made formidable by idle sports and by the temptations of Satan; while enjoying the specious holiness of Anglican asceticism, he also read the life of Francis Spira and suffered the horrors attending that conventional indulgence of pious youth. The virtues of dipping proved to be as carnal as those of independency, but he was preserved, like Bunyan, by the special solicitude of the Deity from the error of the Ranters. That section of his book called *How I came by my Ministry* concerns the descent of the Spirit, the ineffable call which could not be ignored, and the impulsive journeys of the itinerant. The autobiography of Edward Burrough, whose evident commission and antipathy to John Bunyan permitted him to question the gifts of that saint, contains like those of Crook and Bunyan the customary details of regeneration and ministry.[12] This work of 1663 had been issued previously in a less elaborate form in 1654 as an Appendix to the earliest tract of Edward Burrough, who was not unacquainted with the merits of timely advertisement.[13]

The autobiographies of Muggletonians, Ranters, and unattached enthusiasts are often longer, stranger, and, since they are even less restrained, more sublimate than those of the Quakers. Lodowick Muggleton's *Acts of the Witnesses,* which suggests by its title a familiarity with at least two books of the gospel, and Laurence Clarkson's *Lost Sheep Found* are the classics of the enthusiastic autobiography.[14] Clarkson, who had professed the doctrines of the Presbyterians, Independents, Baptists, and Ranters before he discovered finality in the bosom of Muggleton, candidly admitted the error of his earlier ways to magnify the correctness of the later. His autobiographical intention and his literary ambition are conveniently stated by himself:

As I am endued with the height of revelation, that neither angel nor man can take from me, which revelation hath begot most of you into the belief of this Commission, let me tell you . . . I write infalibly, without the help of any, as it flows by inspiration or revelation from my Royal seed-spring, otherways it were no other but reasons imagination.[15]

Lodowick Muggleton, one of the two last witnesses, allowed his envy to suspect the intention of Clarkson, who, he said, "grew so proud, and lording over the Beleivers, saying, That no body could write, now John Reeve was dead, but he: And to that purpose he wrote . . . The lost Sheep found."[16] These Muggletonian effusions are rivaled in excellence by the astonishing autobiographies of the prophets Richard Coppin, George Foster,[17] and Abiezer Coppe, the last of whom will distinguish a page or two of a later chapter, and by the *Heights in Depths and Depths in Heights* of Joseph Salmon, also a Ranter, who described his regeneration in the following words: "I arose and (as it were) shooke of my night dresses, and appeared to my selfe, like the sunn, dawning out its refulgent splendor, from behind the darke canopies of the earth."[18]

The Baptists, whose position was a middle one between those of the radical Quakers or Ranters and the conservative Independents, numbered adherents of various social classes. The most respectable Baptists emulated the Independents in a profound autobiographical silence; the reputable but enthusiastic Baptists frequently composed but rarely published autobiographies; when the enthusiastic Baptists of the mechanick classes wrote these spiritual works, they immediately published them. But comparatively few Baptists exercised the autobiographical muse; and in writing and publishing his life Bunyan followed the practice of the mechanick enthusiasts of the Quakers and Ranters rather than that of men of his own persuasion.

William Kiffin was too substantial a merchant to publish the confession which his senility had inspired. This eminent Baptist devoted his memoir not only to his quiet conversion and call but also to the history of his commercial success, which could afford to want the celebration in print of a supplementary godliness.[19] Those learned Baptists Henry Jessey and Hanserd Knollys also failed to publish the autobiographical products of their enthusiasm, from which, therefore, they could expect only a posthumous fame.[20] Benjamin Keach, who intended to write his autobiography, was prevented from the accomplishment of his design by reasons which we cannot ascertain.[21] Even the gifted Vavasor Powell, whose social position, however, was almost respectable, left his excellent autobiography in manuscript.[22] This saint had suffered during his rebirth the malevolent attentions of Satan, who swept occasionally through the room under the disguise of a cold wind, extinguished the candle, slammed the door, and invented other inconveniences. But the survivor of these evils was comforted by the recognition of heaven: as he was leading a charge of parliamentary horse in the capacity of fighting but still fleshly parson, Vavasor Powell was privileged to hear an unearthly voice which said, "I have chosen thee to preach the Gospel." The favorite of heaven immediately understood his spiritual value, prayed vehemently for preservation from a military death, and was pleased by the sudden response of the Lord, who, averting the head of the impetuous horse, directed both horse and rider from the battle to spread His gospel in Montgomeryshire, where the continued direction of heaven, when, for example, the itinerant had lost his way by night, was always useful.

Francis Bampfield, whose enthusiasm remained untempered by education and imprisonment, not only wrote but published in 1681 an autobiography in which he carefully indicated the parallels between his life and that of St. Paul.[23] Anna Trapnel, who published two autobiographies in 1654,[24] was a virgin of John Simpson's Baptist conventicle in London; and since her ghostly counselor was known to Bunyan, it is probable that the piety of Bedford was elevated by her fame. This extraordinary woman was gifted with the accomplishments of prophecy and song, which she combined in the continual performance of her own melodious compositions. During her martyrdom for disturbance of the peace and for an injudicious promotion of the monarchy of Jesus one of her autobiographies and a collection of letters from confinement were published in the necessary endeavor to clear her prophetic character from scandals and reproaches.

An identity of theological auspices gave to the conversion of Anna Trapnel a likeness to that of Bunyan. Fleeing as a child from sin to legal rectitude, she attended cautionary sermons which failed to remove the burden of the law or to provide the grace which periods of terror and the indignation of the Almighty appeared to recommend. Intermittent ravishings of the spirit were followed by the discouragements peculiar to the chief of sinners, as she called herself, and, after the reception of grace, by a relapse and the knowledge that she alone had sinned the sin against the Holy Ghost. When the wrath of God had somewhat abated, however, she enjoyed the sensations of the disciple, beheld symbolic visions, communed with a variety of angels, and by her openings and trances, became the object of pious interest. Up to this point her story resembles that of Bunyan, but the account of her ministry is marked by a difference which must be ascribed as much to her condition as to the strangeness of her gift. The sickness which fell upon her as upon Bunyan was more sociable than his; for she admitted the public to the infirmary of her body and soul, and displayed her curious motions, delirium, and fits of ravishment and palsy to the fascinated and the devout. The pouring forth of the spirit was such that she prophesied incessantly both day and night with no appearance of fatigue and uttered in bed great quantities of verse, which the faithful recorded. She also exercised her gift of song, continuing without pause for nourishment or repose, until at last, as her autobiography relates, "in the afternoon, while I was singing, they sent the Constable for me."[25]

The genius of John Bunyan, equally informed by his experience and by the autobiographical tradition, inspired a conventional work, which is, however, not only representative but excellent in its kind. *Grace Abounding* is indebted for its arrangement and selection of material to the works of Bunyan's predecessors, and for its substance to the common experience of rebirth and call; but though it deviates in no important particular from the autobiographies of other preachers, it is superior to most in the literary adornment and dramatic presentation of customary details. Other preachers had confessed in their autobiographies to a childish delight in games and sports, but to what they had casually referred, Bunyan gave splendor by art:

As I was in the midst of a game at Cat, and having struck it one blow from the hole, just as I was about to strike it the second time, a voice did suddainly dart from Heaven, into my Soul, which said, "Wilt thou leave thy sins, and go to Heaven; or have thy sins, and go to Hell?" At this I was put to an exceeding maze; wherefore, leaving my Cat upon the ground, I looked up to Heaven, and was as if I had, with the eyes of my understanding, seen the Lord Jesus looking down upon

me, as being very hotly displeased with me, and as if he did severely
threaten me with some grievous punishment for these, and other my
ungodly practices.[26]

This passage, which is perhaps the most familiar of the book, is
an unusually specific elaboration of a conventional detail of the
enthusiastic autobiography. Other preachers had struggled with
Satan and lived to record the bitterness of the contention but
few had been moved to present the habitual conflict in terms of
drama and imagination:

If ever Satan and I did strive for any word of God in all my life, it was
for this good word of Christ; he at one end and I at the other. Oh,
what work did we make! It was for this in John, I say, that we did so
tug and strive: He pulled and I pulled; but God be praised, I got the
better of him, I got some sweetness from it.[27]

The genius of Bunyan accepted but enhanced the conventional;
and it may be suspected that his rebirth and ministry are more
impressive than those of most autobiographers because he was a
greater artist.[28] His poetical imagination represented the ordinary circumstances of his conversion with dramatic intelligence
and perhaps with some improvements.

Grace Abounding is more specific and imaginative than most
of the enthusiastic autobiographies, but it fails to surpass that of
Anna Trapnel in the treatment of emotional aberration; nor is
it remarkably superior in psychopathic detail to the work of
Francis Howgill or to the story of Francis Spira, over which Bunyan pored with anxiety during his regeneration.[29] Indeed, Bunyan appears to have imitated, often without improving, these or
other similar accounts both in the conduct of his rebirth and in
the composition of its history. Both regeneration and the autobiography imposed their conventions upon the susceptible mind,
which was carried through the sequences of conversion by the
example, as well as by the instruction, of predecessors, and which
accepted for the exploitation of its experience the patterns of
selection, emphasis, and arrangement of innumerable autobi-

ographies. The menace to infant holiness in the frolic depravity
of games and sports would not have been apparent to the sensitive youth without the light of a devout tradition, nor would this
unregenerate indulgence have found a place in *Grace Abounding*
without the urgency of an autobiographical convention.

The first part of *Grace Abounding,* which concerns the conversion of John Bunyan, owes its details and character to Calvinism and literary influence. The vanities of his natural state, the
sudden consciousness of sin, and the disagreeable prospect of
hell drove Bunyan to the temporary relief of legal holiness. His
dissatisfaction with Anglican works recommended to the notice
of his distracted mind the merits of the Ranters and the Quakers;
but the adorable influence of heaven, of the Scriptures, and of
the old women of Bedford saved him from error and revealed the
truth. He abandoned the law before his discovery of grace, and
suffered in sequence or in confusion the despairs, ecstasies, sick-
nesses, and illuminations which were common to the yearning
Calvinist. Texts darted at him from the sky, voices disturbed his
repose, and tactile hallucinations were a continual bother; he
suffered from neurasthenia, phobias, and a wasting disease; his
digestion was impaired. Hardly had he tasted the comforts of
grace when his insubstantial felicity was abridged by a backsliding which may be attributed perhaps as much to the demands of
the fashionable conversion as to the malice of Satan. A neurotic
compulsion to blasphemy forced him in vain to cover his mouth
with his hand to contain the insufferable words. He knew that
he had sinned the sin against the Holy Ghost, that it was his
melancholy distinction to be the chief of sinners. But Anna
Trapnel, who had experienced each of these impulses, sensations,
and delights, shared his wicked eminence and might justly have
disputed his claim; what is more, the Quakers, whose journey
often included the provinces of Calvinism, had boasted identical
miseries and equal infamy. The details of Bunyan's conversion
could be supplied by a diligent anthologist from the autobiog-

raphies of other preachers. Even the words "My Grace is sufficient for thee," which the Lord Jesus condescended to direct
through the tiles to the ears of John Bunyan and by which the
salvation of that saint was finally consummated, were the instrument of the orthodox regeneration.[30]

As the conversion of Bunyan conformed to the accepted pattern of orthodoxy, as the account of his conversion reflected the
modes of the ministerial autobiography, so the severity of his
ordeal, as presented in *Grace Abounding,* is explained in part by
the motive and the necessity of prophetical advertisement. From
Grace Abounding we might plausibly conclude that the conversion of John Bunyan was among the most arduous, eminent,
and splendid of his time, equaled only by those of the more literary prophets. But if, as we might surmise, the splendor of this
conversion is an improvement upon nature by the genius or
fancy of Bunyan, we might reasonably attribute to him the
motives of the ambitious apostle, whose blameless exaggeration
an indulgent Deity must have sanctioned or at least condoned.
The justice of this surmise becomes apparent when we examine
the tracts in which Bunyan confessed the merits of the difficult
conversion. Though he admitted for the consolation of the feeble, who were his particular care, that easy conversions were not
altogether to be despised, he made it clear in one of his tracts
that a conversion of unusual frightfulness was an honor of which
few were accounted worthy by the Lord, who tested and purged
the strong but let the feeble lightly off.[31] The distinction of a
notorious rebirth, which secured the local reputation of the
saint, was the necessity of the preacher, who extended his autobiographical talents for the advancement of his regeneration.
Bunyan observed in *The Jerusalem Sinner Saved*[32] that his conversion had been the talk of the envious town, and added that
those who had deserved, by their desperate wickedness, the awful
displeasure of heaven and, by their unexpected rebirth, the ultimate attentions of Satan, which were proportioned in severity to

the importance of their object, were qualified both by their capacity and experience as exceptional guides or ministers. For this reason the evidence which might be expected to prove the pastoral fitness of John Bunyan: the abandonment of his infancy and youth, the wonder and eminence of his conversion, the extremities to which his value drove the disappointed fiend, received the careful embellishment of his fancy. The relapse from grace and the subsequent recovery, by which his salvation had been complicated, required an equal emphasis; for "the returning backslider," said Bunyan, "is a rare man, a man of worth and intelligence, a man to whom the men of the world should flock," a man, he continued, whom the sorrows of his past had made a most dependable counselor, as a depressing experience in the belly of leviathan had made the prophet Jonah a competent authority upon the inner truth.[33]

The second part of *Grace Abounding,* which concerns the call and ministry of John Bunyan, betrays the style and sentiments of the conventional prophet. *A brief Account of the Authors Call to the Work of the Ministry,* as this important section is named, states its theme in the opening sentence: "And now I am speaking my Experience, I will in this place thrust in a word or two concerning my Preaching the Word, and of God's dealing with me in that particular also . . . ."[34] Not God alone, however, but also His conventicle at Bedford must be credited with Bunyan's promotion to a sublime office. After the mechanick had been five or six years renovated, the saints of his community, who recalled with awe the vehemence of his rebirth, observed with interest the mysterious deportment and the irrepressible eloquence which distinguished the eminent convert as the vessel of the gift. They did perceive, said Bunyan, "that God had counted me worthy to understand something of his Will in his holy and blessed Word, and had given me utterance in some measure to express what I saw, to others for edification." The modest enthusiast exercised his heavenly endowment among them for a time, and presently the call of the Lord was democratically confirmed, according to the practice of the Baptists, by the recognition of the conventicle, which raised the gifted tinker to the office of the subordinate apostle. Interpreting his sensations as the impulse of heaven, encouraged by the blessed text, and animated by the applause of the godly, Bunyan suspended his diffidence and accepted with gratitude the gifts of God and the duties and distinction of the prophet and evangelist.

By this Text [I Cor. 16:15, 16] I was made to see that the Holy Ghost never intended that men who have Gifts and Abilities, should bury them in the earth, but rather did command and stir up such to the Exercise of their Gift, and also did commend those that were apt and ready so to do, *"They have addicted themselves to the Ministry of the Saints":* This Scripture in these days did continually run in my mind to incourage me, and strengthen me in this my work for God; I have been also incouraged from several Scriptures and Examples of the Godly, both specified in the Word and other ancient Histories, *Acts* 8.4. and 18. 24, 25. &c. I *Pet.* 4. 10. *Rom.* 12.6. Fox *Acts Mon.*
   Wherefore though of my self, of all the Saints the most unworthy, yet I, but with great fear and trembling at the sight of my own weakness, did set upon the work, and did according to my Faith, Preach that blessed Gospel that God had shewed me in the Holy Word of Truth: Which when the Country understood, they came in to hear by hundreds, and that from all parts. . . .[35]

"God's instrument," as the new apostle now called himself, was pleased by the enthusiasm of his audience and by his evident inspiration: "I have been," he said, ". . . as if an Angel of God had stood by at my back to encourage me; O, it hath been with such Power and heavenly Evidence upon my own Soul. . . ." And he found like the Quakers, who had also experienced this supernatural direction, that when he had a work to do for God in a certain barn or town, he had first "the going of God upon" his spirit to desire he might preach there.[36] The history of his martyrdom, with which Bunyan concluded the account of his ministry, proved his apostolic character and secured the admiration of the Particular Open-communion Baptists.

As we have noted, the advertisement of the power of God or rather of their own conversions and gifts was not the only design of the enthusiastic autobiographers, who also intended the guidance of the simple proselyte. The conversion of the minister provided an irreproachable example for his followers; and since example was the readiest means to secure a desirable orthodoxy, the ministerial autobiography served an important purpose in the evangelistic plan of the enthusiast. The rigid formula of regeneration, which preachers of every sect were eager to illustrate by their own experience, imposed the accepted varieties and sequences of terror, trembling, melancholy, and joy upon those who desired to "come aright."

To satisfy a demand for which they were partly responsible guidebooks to conversion, like grace, abounded. Even those respectable preachers who declined to publish their autobiographies issued collections of the experiences of their converts both to direct others by example and to indicate their evangelistic success. Henry Jessey edited a book concerning the conversion of Sarah Wight, "the chief of sinners," whose exemplary temptations at the age of twelve established her claim upon the envy of every Baptist. Vavasor Powell published an anthology of the conversions of those whom he had saved from Satan. The curious story of John Toldervy was presented under the supervision of John Tombes, George Cockayne, and John Goodwin. The last of these accounts of non-ministerial conversions to appear in the seventeenth century was a collection by Bunyan's friend Charles Doe.[37] This instructive literature appears to have been influenced by the experience-meeting in which members of each congregation were accustomed to relate their conversions, openings, and lapses. Other ministers attempted to appeal to the intellect of the pious by abstract outlines of conversion. Richard Bax-

ter wrote three guidebooks of this austere variety, and similar
works were devised by Anthony Palmer and others.[38] Of the more
attractive popularizations of the process in fiction and verse,
Benjamin Keach's *War with the Devil* is typical.[39] The ministerial
autobiography was only one, but the most important of the instruments at the disposal of the solicitous evangelist.

Grace Abounding was intended in part, as Bunyan observed, to
help others by showing what the Lord had done for him.[40] The
heights and depths of his own experience, though somewhat discouraging by their altitude or profundity to the normal ambition, established for unripened wits the order and perfection to
which they should aspire and the model from which a considerable departure in kind could not but be prejudicial to the coming
soul. But Bunyan's efforts to diffuse the proprieties of regeneration extended, like those of other preachers, beyond the limits
of the exemplary narrative of his own experience. *Grace Abounding* is merely the most complete statement of a theme which per-
vades his other tracts and major works.

The high and mysterious process of conversion provided the
substance of Bunyan's hortatory tracts: *The Heavenly Footman*,
which the author considered "as good as a pair of spurs to prick
thy lumpish heart in this rich voyage,"[41] *Instruction for the
Ignorant, Saved by Grace, Come and Welcome*, and, indeed, most
of his other pamphlets.[42] His guidance of those who were "all on a
flame to be converted" and pliant to the ministerial hand was
occasionally abstract, but more often it took the pleasing form
of brief and allusive summaries of *Grace Abounding*. His exhortations and examples embraced the necessity of despair and prepared the coming soul for backsliding, impulses to blasphemy,
the sin against the Holy Ghost, dreams, visions, voices, and con-
vulsions of ecstasy and dismay, which, Bunyan warned, were
incorrectly interpreted by the carnal as the natural effects of
melancholy, solitude, or indulgence in cabbage. He recommended "strange, passionate, sudden rushings forward after

Jesus," advocated fear, trembling, and smiting on the breast, and predicted the deportment of Satan.[43] This advice left little excuse for any failure of his followers to exhibit the orthodox symptoms in their customary sequence. "There is," said Bunyan, "a heavenly subtilty to be managed in this matter."[44]

The triumphant spirit of John Bunyan, which had flowered under the direction of Luther on the Galatians and Dent's *Plaine Mans Pathway to Heaven,*[45] had faith in the efficacy of the guidebook to conversion. Read about the experience of others, he advised, "and try if thy conversion be like or has a good resemblance or oneness with theirs."[46] The goodness of his heart or the sagacity of his profession had given to Bunyan the desire to make the way of others more apparent than his own had been, to provide histories of earlier adventurers, maps of the intricate journey, and directions over pitfalls. "No man," he warned, "can travel here without a guide."[47]

The generous impulse of guidance, which had led the evangelist to the composition of his autobiography and tracts, reappeared in a more gracious embodiment in those excellent histories of conversion *The Holy War* and *Pilgrim's Progress,* which, like the popular allegories of Benjamin Keach, contain but disguise by their fictional character the materials and the intention of the ministerial autobiography. The principal theme of *The Holy War* is the struggle between God and Satan for the individual soul, and the plot of this confusing work with its double climax and intermediate depression represents the progress of the variety of conversion which Bunyan had experienced and which he was anxious to promote. Under the innocent appearance of fiction Bunyan hoped to attract the interest and to guide the steps of the carnal reader and to supply the knowing reader, who found it agreeable to look back, like Lucretius, upon what he had survived, with the pleasure of recognition. The early adventures of Christian before the fall of his burden at the cross constitute a dramatic outline of rebirth. His conviction of sin in the City of Destruction, his distracted pursuit of salvation, his wretchedness in the Slough of Despond, his reprehensible effort to embrace the law at Mount Sinai, and his discovery of the wicket gate are the episodes and conditions of the average regeneration.[48] His discomfort in the Valley of the Shadow and his encounters with Apollyon and Giant Despair suggest the difficulties to be anticipated after the first reception of grace.[49] For the assistance of the foolish reader, who might be at a loss to determine the meaning of this allegory, or for the purpose of supplementary illustration, Bunyan provided a literal synopsis of *Grace Abounding* in the history of Hopeful's experience.[50] The conversion of this saint, which is modeled closely upon the ministerial autobiography, was exorbitant and correct: he cursed, swore, lied, and violated the Sabbath during the term of his natural infancy; he suffered the pangs of guilt, performed the useless propitiations of the law, but found no peace until Jesus appeared to say, "My Grace is sufficient for thee."

But the careful attention which Bunyan had devoted to evangelistic guidance in the first part of *Pilgrim's Progress* appeared inadequate to Thomas Sherman, who wrote a sequel to that successful work. This captious Baptist permitted himself to say that Bunyan had neglected conversion and the preliminary state of sin, and pretended to improve upon his defective model.[51] To us this criticism is of interest as an indication of the value placed by Baptists even upon the more popular guide to rebirth; but to Bunyan, the evangelist, this criticism appeared too frivolous to deserve the dignity of notice or response. In his own continuation of *Pilgrim's Progress* Bunyan again devoted what seemed to him an adequate, but what may seem to us an excessive, attention to the coming soul, not to the period of sin which he had been accused of slighting, but to the milder varieties of conversion which he considered appropriate to women, children, and the feeble. Under the influence of example or of Greatheart, who directed and consoled his flock, Mercy and the other pilgrims were painlessly regenerated.[52] To support the heavenly calling which he shared with Greatheart, Bunyan indicated the importance of the ministerial superintendent,[53] and in order to promote the exemplary guide, he suggested the necessity of acquaintance with previous conversions: many had been helped, the travelers insisted, by the story of Christian's pilgrimage, which they had gladly received as the model for their own; Matthew observed that the story of Fearing's conversion had entertained his thoughts and assisted his journey; and Honest asked Greatheart to tell them of the profitable things of their predecessors.[54]

Like Greatheart, in whom he presented himself under the character of evangelist and guide, Bunyan enjoyed conspicuous success as a fisher of men. According to the unanimous evidence of his friends and enemies, John Bunyan was noted for the number of conversions at which he had assisted; and according to the immodest evidence of his own approval, his preaching of conversion had been as helpful to innumerable disciples as gratifying to God.[55] "I found," said the eminent evangelist, "my Spirit did lean most after awakening and converting-Work, and the Word that I carried did lean it self most that way also."[56] In one sense, *Grace Abounding,* which carried the exemplary burden of his evangelism, is the most significant book that Bunyan wrote, and his other books for the greater part but variant or ancillary expressions of its theme. The purpose of advertisement, which *Grace Abounding* shared with the other enthusiastic autobiographies, may be regarded as part of a large evangelistic plan; for, the greater the reputation of John Bunyan and the more impressive his conversion and gift, the better the fishing for men.

CHAPTER III

APOSTOLIC BLOWS AND KNOCKS

*Or what relation has debating
Of church-affairs, with bear-baiting?*
Hudibras, I, i, 855.

Not bear baiting, of which they disapproved, but controversy, which combined the pleasures of the arena and the crusade, occupied the pugnacity of the unordained evangelists. Every conventicle delegated and applauded a controversialist whose duty was the confutation of questionable doctrine and the defense of his proselytes. This preacher resorted with piety and zeal to any means, however dubious, which would insure the discomfort of the wicked and the triumph of the Saviour. Controversy was the singular property of no class or faction at this time, but since it was most often the fruit of evangelism and self-defense, the lay preacher, even more commonly than his scholarly betters, was implicated in quarrels.

If his territory was menaced by the invasion of misguided itinerants, or if the local clergyman displayed a proud intolerance of his activities, the enthusiast found in controversial acrimony the most reliable support for his evangelism. But when the enthusiast was also a man of no learning or a mechanick, he was compelled to defend himself against the contempt of the learned and the polite. Oral disputes of this latter variety, such as that between Dr. George Griffith and Vavasor Powell, which, because of its popular appeal, no barn in the vicinity was able to accommodate,[1] ordinarily deviated from angry discussions of grammar and logic into the difficult problem of the layman's right to preach. Disputes between the equally ignorant, as when two itinerants met, were of a more elevated character; for in these encounters insults were often accompanied by discussions of the ordinances and even of doctrine. The severity of the disputants was the occasion of universal interest; and, as it swelled, the ardor of the principals not infrequently invited the participation of the audience and the breaking of heads. From fields, market places, and steeple houses the noise of combat arose; and the press was never still.

For Bunyan as for the other mechanick enthusiasts it is difficult to overestimate the importance of controversy. By his position as by his inclination he was drawn throughout his blameless career into a sequence of disputes often so extreme as to excite the surprise of those who are ignorant of enthusiasm. As an evangelist, solicitous for his threatened flock, he constantly lent his passions to oral and pamphlet controversies; and as a mechanick he was often compelled by disagreeable contact with the learned to defend not only the freedom of grace but his ignorance and his authority to preach. In his capacity of evangelist and mechanick, and delegated by his conventicle to defend the truth, Bunyan was prodigal of his talent for controversy; for in addition to the eight or nine tracts which are exclusively contentious, most of his works reveal disputative passages, and his oral debates appear to have been innumerable.

Bunyan's addiction to the controversial habits of his class would be too remote from our values to appear even odd were it not that Bunyan's mechanick enthusiasm, though indifferent of itself, is a means to the understanding of his major works. As it was through his enthusiastic evangelism that we were enabled to determine the nature of *Grace Abounding* and to appreciate the place of *Pilgrim's Progress* in his design, so it is only through a review of his disputes that we shall be able to perceive that *Pilgrim's Progress* was to Bunyan and his readers not merely a popular guidebook to rebirth but a controversial pamphlet. We have seen that this celebrated work is in some part a reflection of Bunyan's life as an itinerant, evangelist, and convert, and we shall see its autobiographical significance to be equally great in its embodiment of forgotten disputes. In this book Bunyan continued and

gave literary finality to what may appear undeserving of com-
memoration, his obscure quarrels with Baptists and Anglicans,
who supplied material as well as heat for the creation of By-ends,
for example, and Ignorance. With the ultimate discovery of these
curious and not uninteresting details in view, we must descend
into what Samuel Butler invidiously called the mystical bear
gardens.

But before making this irrevocable descent, we must pause for
one cautionary note. Because of Bunyan's concern with controversy, it might be thought that he would dignify his interest with
an unqualified approval, but this is not so. In our confusion it
would be difficult to imagine what perverse modesty or deliberate
obliquity lay behind the expression in *Grace Abounding* of a
distaste for combat,[2] did we not remember that it was the custom
of most preachers benevolently to express pacific principles while
they devoted themselves to war.[3] Their interest in peace was like
their hatred of sectarianism. Preferring, in accordance with this
pleasant usage, to call himself a Christian or Congregationalist,
Bunyan the Baptist could not contain his sorrow over sectarians
who deviated willfully from the truth as represented by himself
and the hero of his book;[4] yet no sectarian but considered himself
alone the Christian among mistaken sectarians, and none but
would have named his hero Christian to point this obvious distinction.[5] Since we can safely ignore Bunyan's profession of paci-
fism and nonsectarian Christianity as both harmless and conventional, we may address ourselves without more ado to a survey of
his forgotten quarrels, which, if not unmistakably Christian,
were at least entirely sectarian.

Bunyan's introduction to heresy occurred around the year
1650, before his enlightenment, but though he met Ranters in
the period of their malignancy, and read their books without
understanding a word, he was able to resist them, discouraged,
perhaps, by what he could observe of a systematic antinomianism
to which, before enlightenment, he could not hope to aspire.[6]

The Ranters succeeded, however, in making a lasting impression upon the sensitive youth, a kind of trauma, which he found useful in later years as a means to the understanding and insulting[7] of those more insidious mystics the Quakers, who in 1654 and 1655 descended in hordes upon Bedfordshire. These evangelists effected the conviction and spiritual enlargement of many, including Bunyan, who arrived by their aid at a clearer understanding of the Scriptures,[8] and who found in their dangerous absurdity the occasion for his first literary work. While the Quakers were thus engaged, agitated Baptists, upon whose converts the new itinerants had designs, were hastening to the defense of their flocks or becoming Quakers. Of the countless disputes which were engendered by the efforts of both parties, that between Jeremiah Ives, once a maker of boxes and a cheesemonger, and the messianic James Nayler was typical.[9] Though he had nothing to offer in the way of logic or learning to compare with that of Ives, and though a novice at preaching, Bunyan was commissioned by the desperate elders of his meeting to preserve the integrity of a county menaced by Crook, Fox, and Dewsbury.[10] In 1656, in convenient market places and steeple houses, Bunyan, together with Fenn, Child, Spencly, and brother Burton, disputed with the Quakers, who blasphemed "with a grinning countenance," especially with the itinerant Anne Blackly, whose manners were insufferable.[11] To mitigate the ineffectuality of these intimacies, Bunyan followed his Baptist colleagues into print in the effort to preserve the wavering and to recover those who had been dipped in vain:

We desire through grace, if at any time we chance to see any of Christ's lambs in the teeth of any wolf or bear be they never so terrible in appearance; I say, we desire, we labour, we strive, and lay ourselves out, if it be possible to recover the same, though with the hazard of our lives, or whatsoever may befal us in doing our duty.[12]

Some Gospel Truths Opened, 1656, Bunyan's provocative attack upon the evangelistic Quakers, added nothing new to the arguments of his Baptist predecessors, whom he had evidently read with attention, but it contributed to the accumulating abuse of "Ranters, Quakers, drunkards, and the like." Revolted like any decent Calvinist by the mysticism of the Quakers, who proposed a questionable salvation by the light within, Bunyan destroyed this error and added luster to the truth of justification by imputed righteousness. His tract was but another of the Christ-within-Christ-without debates, which for the preceding three years had depended upon argument and sometimes logic to settle a matter of temperament and individual taste.

By the customary questionnaire at the end of his tract Bunyan had both invited and anticipated retaliation, which came in renewed crossroad controversy and in a formidable pamphlet from London by Edward Burrough, a veteran of many encounters with Magog's army.[13] Burrough was animated by a profound distaste for Calvinism and dipping. He directed his notice to the "blind Sot" of Bedfordshire, who by misunderstanding the light within had proved himself to be of the tribe of priests, and whose devotion to free grace was little short of antinomian. After an interval for recovery, Bunyan issued a vindication[14] in which with animosity he repeated his opinion of the light within, compared the natures of Quaker and Ranter to the discredit of each, and answered point by point the strictures of Burrough, who complicated the verbal cross-purposes of the debate by an antidote in February, 1657 to "John Bunions foule dirty lyes and slanders" and to the venom which Bunyan had spat like a viper.[15] With the feeling, perhaps, that Bedfordshire had been sufficiently saved, Bunyan left this intemperate tract unanswered. Bunyan may not have realized as completely as he could have wished his object of securing the county for Baptist evangelism; but it is probable, in view of the popular interest in these quarrels, that the people of the vicinity had followed the redundancies of the dispute with awe and had been swayed one way or the other as their previous convictions had inclined them.

The Quakers, who were unwilling to let the matter drop,

returned, however, to the attack in December, 1658 in that impressive compendium of argument, George Fox's *The Great Mistery of the Great Whore Unfolded*, prefaced by Edward Burrough.[16] Fox in turn belittled Bunyan's two tracts, as well as those of all other enemies of the truth, and, stopping at nothing, cast doubt upon Bunyan's inspiration and capability as a preacher. Bunyan's opportunity for reprisal came the following summer in Cambridge where he became involved in that deplorable affair of the Quakers, horses, and witches, to the little-known history of which we have devoted the Appendix. This unfortunate gratification appears to have pacified Bunyan's resentment against the Quakers. His abhorrence of the inner light entered subsequently upon a decline from which it never completely recovered, although for brief moments, as in his allusions to the heresies of William Penn's *Sandy Foundation Shaken*, 1668, it showed that it was not dead.[17]

Bunyan was equally resolute in his contacts with the clergy of the neighborhood, who had greeted his primitive evangelism with a distaste which had secured, on one occasion, his indictment at a local assize.[18] Mindful of the reputation of the Saviour and of the possibility of converts, Bunyan had been accustomed to penetrate the "darkest places," where he is said to have convinced one skeptical Cambridge scholar and to have silenced another, accomplishments which, if the report is true, testify alike to his evangelistic skill and to his controversial dexterity.[19] These encounters with the learned and the established differed from those with the obscure Quakers in that, being of superior position, the clergy objected not only to his evangelistic encroachments, but to his mechanick character. Both these objections entered into his dispute with the Rev. Thomas Smith, M.A., B.D., vicar of the parish of Caldecote, Cambridgeshire, keeper of the university library, lecturer in rhetoric in Christ's College, and most alarming of all, student of Arabic and collaborator in Walton's *Polyglot Bible*.[20]

Bunyan had been led by the Spirit or by the policy of his conventicle to the depths of Cambridgeshire, where he devoted himself to the exposure of Quaker witches, to the establishment of outposts for the Bedford meeting, and to the mending of local pots. Upon Bunyan's appearance as preacher in the barn of Daniel Angier in Toft, Cambridgeshire, in May, 1659, Thomas Smith, who had been attracted by the sound of devotion, was unable to contain his displeasure.[21] Smith abridged the process of salvation by the vehemence of his reproaches, and disturbed, without convincing the congregation by the charges of enthusiasm, melancholy, and madness which he leveled both at Bunyan and at his followers.[22] Moreover, he increased the gravity of his censure by questioning the right and qualification of a tinker to preach.[23] But Bunyan, who was accustomed to this variety of annoyance, remained unabashed. He resorted to invective, calling Smith "fool and giddy pated fellow, &c," and objected to Smith's academic mannerisms and usages, especially to those "hell-bred" syllogisms with which Smith had confused the Quakers and hoped to confound him. The pamphlet which Smith devoted to an account of this dispute records his dislike of the itinerancy of evangelistic mechanicks: "One that thrusts himself in to preach in another mans parish against his consent is reckoned by the H. Ghost among no honester men then a Thief and a Murderer," and contains what we can only trust but can never know to be a slander:

But all this your T[inker] hath been guilty of, and much more. For he hath not only intruded into Pulpits in these parts, and caused the people of your Town to hate their lawful Minister, (Mr. John Ellis sen) (as he told me) encouraged them to proceed so far as to cudgel him, and break open the Church doors by violence. I wonder what example or precept in Scripture he hath for this.

Bunyan saw himself accused of illicit and violent trespass, like that for which he had resented the Quakers, and classed with these wandering mystics, upon whom, with a curious but customary display of academic agility, Smith expended his syllogisms in vain throughout that summer.[24] Smith's ungenerous remarks upon Whitehead, Fox, Allen, Blackley, and Bunyan provoked reply from Henry Denne, General Baptist minister in that county, whose considerable learning had been tempered by his fellowship with the devout and by his unhappy experiences in the army with the Levellers.[25] In *The Quaker No Papist* [26] Denne defended lay preaching, Bunyan, and the Quakers from the aspersions of Smith. The response of Smith, *A Gagg for the Quakers*, with an appendix by the heresiographer Richard Blome, virtually ignored Bunyan in favor of Denne and the Quakers, and called for support upon the names of Lord Falkland, Chillingworth, and Jeremy Taylor.[27] Wisely retreating from his first contact with the liberal and amiable Cambridge school of divinity, Bunyan allowed this unpleasant quarrel to expire in the hands of Smith, Denne, and the Quakers.

The tiresome distractions of imprisonment and the tranquillity of other pursuits diverted Bunyan for a number of years from the interests which had enlivened his earlier ministry.[28] He was finally stirred from this virtual retirement, however, to a long period of controversial warmth by another divine whose relationship with the Cambridge group was intimate and tender. Bunyan saw in the Rev. Edward Fowler's *Design of Christianity,* 1671, a fresh insolence of impiety and a splendid opportunity both to destroy a horrible error and to save Bedfordshire.

Edward Fowler, rector of Northill in Bedfordshire, and later bishop of Gloucester,[29] was an eminent man in his day, yet one whose claim to distinction in ours must rest upon the use which Bunyan made of him in *Pilgrim's Progress*. Fowler's abandonment of nonconformity for the established church and his advancement after this step bore witness to his practical disposition. This reasonable man had appeared in 1670 as the popularizer of the latitudinarian point of view in his *Principles and Practices of Certain Moderate Divines*.[30] A moderate in that he tried in his theology to maintain a middle course between Calvinism and

Arminianism, offending both extremes, he is to be numbered with both the latitudinarians and the disciples of the Cambridge Platonists.[31] Though Fowler was never of the inner circles of the Cambridge group, he admired John Smith, expounded his ideas with ease and elegance, edited several of the works of John Worthington, and corresponded with Henry More on witches.

The Design of Christianity,[32] which Fowler intended as a further statement of his latitudinarian beliefs, maintains that the aim of Christianity was the establishment of a holy, moral life of which the first principles were written in the hearts of all men, heathen and Christian, and corroborated by Scripture. To establish these first principles, made known by "Revelation, Nature, or the use of Reason," had been the chief end of the Saviour, who had promoted holiness by example rather than by expiation. From the works of Mede, Chillingworth, Taylor, Plato, Epictetus, Cicero, and especially Hierocles and John Smith, the Cambridge Platonist, Fowler adduced support for his rationalism and morality. That a defense of decent morality should be necessary at this time was evident, he said, from the prevalence of superstition, fanaticism, and enthusiasm, which peevishly decried good works in favor of antinomian free grace.

Bunyan heard in his prison that Fowler's book had given "just offence to Christian ears." Aware that God had chosen him to defend the truth, he finally procured a copy of the dangerous work on February 13, 1672, and on March 27 finished his reply *A Defence of the Doctrine of Justification by Faith*. Since Bunyan was conspicuous among the enthusiastic advocates of free grace whom Fowler had deplored, it was natural that he should object to the idea of good works. In answer to Fowler's pagan insistence upon the exemplary function of Christ, Bunyan affirmed the Saviour's propitiatory sacrifice; in answer to Fowler's corrupt notion of the purity of human nature, Bunyan affirmed the pure truth of the filthiness of man; and in answer to Fowler's foolish reliance upon reason, Bunyan affirmed the wisdom of implicit faith. In a word, as the title of his work suggests, Bunyan defended the doctrine of salvation by faith and imputed righteousness against the humanistic belief in salvation by common morality.

To Bunyan, who had some evidence for his belief in Fowler's citations, Fowler was a pagan philosopher rather than a Christian divine, a "glorious Latitudinarian," who preferred Plato and John Smith to Jesus. Once, said Bunyan, referring to Fowler's appeal for conformity to the custom of the country as both expedient and reasonable, he had heard a ranting latitudinarian preacher say: "If the devil should preach, I would hear him, before I would suffer Persecution."[33] The conviction that latitudinarianism menaced both strictness and orthodoxy, and a profound distaste for the heathen and enlightened tone of one who, in the "rottenness" of his heart, preferred the "snivel" of his own brains to Jesus, led Bunyan to describe and dismiss Fowler's belief as "Papistical Quakerism." Only the seriousness of Fowler's error can excuse the intemperateness of Bunyan's language.

Less moderate in his passions than in his principles, Fowler answered Bunyan in a pamphlet called *Dirt wip't off*,[34] a work devoid of urbanity and distinguished by the unfriendliness of its argument. The quarrel between these two excellent men was really one between two temperaments and two social orders; it is, therefore, to the credit of Fowler's ingenuousness that he penetrated at once through the irrelevancies of doctrine to the fundamentals of malice and abuse. Bunyan, he said, was an ignorant, rude, fanatic zealot, who condemned what he could not understand, and who, by his unfortunate ardor for grace, proved himself an antinomian Ranter,[35] an enemy to the virtue of the community. Hinting at enormities of vice beneath Bunyan's pharisaical smugness, Fowler urged the people of Bedfordshire to shun the guidance of the impure, and, invoking irony, he recommended to Bunyan a catechism for children which he was editing for a departed friend.[36] He also advised Bunyan to learn a little divinity from Richard Baxter, whose careful criticism had dignified *The Design of Christianity,* and in whose opinion he knew himself to be sober, wise, and good.[37]

In his *Advice to Sufferers* Bunyan held it proper for saints to submit in silence to vilification and abuse.[38] This pious consideration or the pressure of a new dispute in which he was presently embroiled prevented an immediate and direct response to Fowler's pamphlet. But although he did not answer directly, Bunyan never forgot Fowler and the latitudinarians, against whom to the end of his days he maintained a tractarian warfare. His dislike of Fowler explains many of the otherwise obscure passages in his later pamphlets and in *Pilgrim's Progress.*

Two of these pamphlets in particular contain material directed against Fowler and his views, *Light for Them that Sit in Darkness,* 1675, and *Israel's Hope Encouraged,* 1692, written probably in 1685-88. In order, as he said in the preface, to preserve his flock from the depredations of false pastors, who lay in wait to poison them, Bunyan sketched again in *Light for Them* the doctrine of justification by imputed righteousness, and attacked those divines who insisted that the theory of Christ's assumption of sin was unbecoming to His dignity, and those who considered the Saviour an example rather than a sacrifice. Bunyan defended his sect from charges of antinomianism by the opinion that true holiness was fostered by free grace, showed anger at the revilings which "abominable children of Hell let fall in their pamphlets" in support of good deeds and a holy life, proved that blood and faith alone could save, and after reducing reason to absurdity, asserted the filthiness of human nature. "No philosopher, tyrant, or devil," he said, had been able, for all their insidious attempts, to destroy the doctrine of grace.[39] Despite the opinion of Offor that this tract referred to the Quakers,[40] it is apparent that Bunyan was directing his attack against Fowler. The allusions to philosophers, holiness, reason, and the arguments on grace and filth place the reference of this work beyond question. *Israel's Hope* also indicates that Fowler's ungracious sentiments could still provoke the passions of John Bunyan. Here Bunyan admonished those who belched out their "frumps, their taunts, their scoffs and their scorns" against free grace, who, casting off the doctrine of propitiation, had lapsed into "Gentilism, Paganism, Heathenism" with a noise of morality and government, and who, upholding carnal reason, rebuked the saints for dwelling upon their sins and the pollution of human nature.[41]

But now "the men of his confederacy" rather than they will submit to the righteousness of God, will lay odiums and scandals upon them that preach they should. Not forsooth, if you will believe them, but that they are highly for the righteousness of God, let it be that which they count so; but then to be sure it shall never be the personal performances of Christ, by which they that believe in him are justified from all things, but that which they call "first principles," "dictates of human nature," "obedience to a moral precept," followed and done as they have Christ for an example; not understanding, that Christ, in his own doings, is the end of all these things to every one that believeth. But if it be urged, that Gentiles and Pagans are possessed with those very principles, only they have not got the art as our men have, to cover them with the name of Christ and principles of Christianity, they fall to commending the Heathens and their philosophers, and the natural motives and principles by which they were actuated; preferring of them much before what by others are called the graces of the Spirit, and principles upon what the doctrine of the free grace and mercy of God by Christ are grounded. But, as I said, all the good that such preachers can do as to the next world, is, to draw the people away from their ensign and their standard, and so lead them among the Gentiles and infidels, to seek by their rules the way to this unspeakable mercy of God. Wherefore their state being thus deplorable, and their spirits incorrigible, they must be pitied, and left, and fled from, if we would live.[42]

The tracts of these later years contain many other references to temporizing latitudinarians, freewillers, the opponents of enthusiasm, and to skeptics, atheists, and doubters, by whom Bunyan meant those who doubted free grace.[43] Within all these infamous categories Bunyan placed Fowler, who had made so profound an impression upon his mind and whose reappearance in the tracts from 1675 to 1688 is so frequent that there is little cause for disquietude over his emergence in *Pilgrim's Progress.*

In the spring of 1672, before the first heat of his indignation over Fowler had expired, Bunyan found himself in another controversy, his first with those whom he admitted to be saints. While still in prison he had composed a tract of innocent appearance, *A Confession of My Faith, and A Reason of My Practice,* a kind of work which it was customary for both individuals and churches to issue in explanation of their prejudices.[44] This work contained, besides a statement of his theology, a long discussion of that dangerous and controversial matter the ordinance of baptism, which served both to explain his views and to involve him in a tractarian dispute with the orthodox Baptists. As an Open-communion Baptist, one who, though a believer in dipping, saw no objection to pious intercourse with certain paedobaptists,[45] Bunyan was less exclusive than the stricter Baptists toward other Calvinist saints; his quarrel with the Baptists, however, was not one between liberalism and formalism but between degrees of intolerance. Bunyan believed that the symbolic rite of dipping, though holy, and good for those who could endure it, as he could, was nevertheless not to be made the necessary initiating ordinance of the church.[46] Admission to the supper was to be determined by saintliness or orthodox Calvinism, by the true baptism of the spirit, rather than by an outward ceremony. Only a saint could be baptized, he said, but baptism did not make a saint. Bunyan gladly dipped those who wanted to be dipped, but he tolerated those who did not care for immersion. Pleading for unity and peace, and filled with resentment against those who had menaced both by carnal insistence upon a symbolic form, Bunyan became involved in a war to end wars, which was not unlike other wars of this character.

The provocation, which had compelled the peaceful man to

assume in place of his usual calm and gay demeanor a ferocity appropriate to war, was extreme. For sixteen years, Bunyan said, the brethren of the baptized way had sent agents to his meeting and to those of the district in the attempt to undermine their open-communion integrity, and, by the suborning of Christ's witnesses, to end a deviation from the orthodox.[47] They had even interviewed Bunyan himself in the strange hope of altering his opinions. Against these impious attempts, which had resulted in strife and debate and in the subversion of some who were now "a stink and reproach to religion," Bunyan had been forced at last to have recourse to the only defensive weapon at his command, publicity.[48] Bunyan's resort to the pamphlet, after the refusal of a challenge to oral dispute with some of the most illustrious Baptists of London, was a cause for both rage and chagrin on the part of the orthodox in that metropolis, who saw in his step the exposure of Baptist vitals to the misunderstandings of the profane.[49] Bunyan answered their attack with indignation, but the evasiveness of his reply, which professed a desire for peace and the uninterrupted enjoyment of his proselytes, equaled the gravity of their insinuations.[50]

The appearance of his *Confession of Faith* had terminated the long incubation of this quarrel:

At this Mr. William Kiffin, Mr. Thomas Paul, and Mr. Henry D'Anvers, and Mr. Denne fell with might and main upon me; some comparing me to the devil, others to a bedlam, others to a sot, and the like, for my seeking peace and truth among the godly.[51]

That these sober Baptists should have been moved to such enormities of comparison by a truthful and pacific book is evidence alike of the long and obscure conflict which had preceded it, and of the importance of Bunyan, who, as leader of one of the principal groups of open-communion churches, had succeeded after the death of Henry Jessey to his honors as the most conspicuous professor of this persuasion.

William Kiffin, whose double eminence as minister of an

important London congregation and as a merchant had earned
him the name of "broker of the word," collaborated in the first
of the replies to Bunyan's *Confession* with Thomas Paul, about
whom nothing is known. Their tract *Some Serious Reflections*,[52]
an expression of the conservative Baptist point of view, characterized Bunyan as a dirt-throwing scholar of Machiavel, a turbu-
lent and mutineering spirit, who preferred peace in the church
to truth, and who in despising baptism despised Christ. Bunyan
answered in his *Differences in Judgment About Baptism, No Bar
to Communion*, 1673, in which he denied that he was an enemy
of dipping as they had claimed, and restated his plea for toleration of those weak brethren who had no light in this uncertain
matter. To support his argument he quoted the opinion of the
late Henry Jessey, his open-communion predecessor.[53] In the
meantime, John Denne, the son of Henry Denne, who had
defended Bunyan fourteen years earlier, added his abuse to that
of Kiffin and Paul.[54] Paul appears to have replied to Bunyan's
second book in a pamphlet now lost,[55] and Henry Danvers did
reply in a postscript to his monumental *Treatise of Baptism*.[56]
Bunyan's *Peaceable Principles and True*, 1673, in answer to Paul
and Danvers, was designed to put a stop to their "artificial squib-
bling."[57] Like his debate with Fowler, this more elaborate one
survived in Bunyan's mind to embitter his later tracts and to
color certain passages of *Pilgrim's Progress*.[58] His statement in
Grace Abounding [59] that he never cared to meddle with things
controverted among the saints is curious rather than true.

The fact that Bunyan's infrequent disputes from this time on
involved matters controverted among the saints indicates that
the attention of his later years was directed to internal polity and
the consolidation of his achievements rather than to the heresies
which had troubled his youth.[60] In 1683 a feminist movement in
his conventicle infringed upon his ministerial prerogatives by
the demand for women's right to hold separate meetings for
prayer. "To keep them in their place," as he expressed it, Bunyan

wrote *A Case of Conscience Resolved,* the immediate occasion of which had been the interference of a mysterious Mr. K., who, by circulating a paper among Bunyan's followers, had caused this female revolt.[61] Bunyan contended that Mr. K.'s intrusion was monstrous and unscriptural, and that since only the gifted were capable of conducting a meeting, his women folk, mindful of Eve and the shame of their sex, should depend upon their minister. He consoled the women, whom he had treated with not unmerited abruptness, with the promise that at a future time he would say something else about them.[62] He was to fulfill this promise in the second part of *Pilgrim's Progress.* The Seventh Day Baptists, who succeeded these women in Bunyan's notice, and who were reasonable in all but their peculiar insist-ence upon the Jewish Sabbath, had long been the object of orthodox expostulation. The possible occasion of his interest in this rather unattractive error was his preaching at Pinners' Hall in London where Francis Bampfield, one of the leading Sabbatarians, also preached, and where friction between the two would have been natural.[63] Like the many pamphleteers who had preceded him on this subject, Bunyan demonstrated in his *Questions about the Nature and Perpetuity of the Seventh-Day Sabbath,* 1685, the unmistakable merits of Sunday as compared to Saturday.

This tedious and discouraging history should reveal the extent and the depth of Bunyan's preoccupation with controversy. But however extensive, deep, or uninteresting his controversial life, it was no more so than that of most enthusiastic lay preachers, in whose company Bunyan's place is assured by his attention to dispute on the grounds of evangelism and mechanick self-defense, if not by the conventionality of his martial practices, which were common to all the ministry, enthusiastic or otherwise. The redundancy and vituperation, which Bunyan affected to convince an audience immune from logic, were the ordinary instruments of ministerial wrath, as was the banality of the point-by-point method of refutation by which, as every minister was aware, Satan's spirit was broken. Equally traditional were the disarming professions of peace, injured innocence, and disinclination to dispute, which if uttered with blandness, imparted an air of reluctance to the militant saint and magnified the infamy of the foe. These characteristics he shared with all preachers, but like the other enthusiastic preachers, who found encouragement in the familiarity of their daily intercourse with the unknowable, Bunyan found in "the pouring forth of the Holy Ghost" within him the courage and skill to attack adversaries at once learned, eloquent, and ripe of parts. And though as a semiliterate mechanick he had all the apparent disadvantage on his side, he was inspired by the consciousness of his gift, as Charles Doe said, and by the immediate assistance of the Holy Spirit to what could not but be victory.[64]

Like his fellows he had discovered in controversy an avenue to fame and repute, and though the desire for applause and a name may not have entered as deeply into his readiness for dispute as Thomas Paul suggested, he had become conspicuous by this means long before he achieved his more durable reputation as a writer. And beyond any doubt his militant activities had had the effect of developing and limbering that style of colloquial and earthy vigor for which he is now justly known. Controversy was both his nursery and his school, and the triumph of *Pilgrim's Progress* was made possible on the playing fields of dissent.

Bunyan's controversial activities are valuable for our purposes in supplying further proof that he was a typical enthusiast and mechanick, but they have a better claim to our attention in their hitherto undetected influence upon *Pilgrim's Progress*. To Bunyan and his sectarian contemporaries this work was an agreeable kind of tract whose value lay in its popular approach to doctrine and ideal, its directions to sound conversion, and its dramatic exposure of the ways and tenets of their enemies. Perceiving in this tract the opportunity of continuing those controversies which had engaged his mind, Bunyan provided his characters with the natures and opinions of some of his opponents. To us By-ends, for example, is a familiar and tiresome character without eminent singularity, but to Bunyan By-ends was a theological and personal enemy whose sentiments could excite the dismay, whose perdition, the complacency of saints.

The Strait Gate, 1676, a tract upon which Bunyan is generally supposed to have been at work when the idea for *Pilgrim's Progress* came to him, contains a list of those false professors who came a long way on the road, who imitated the real thing, but who failed to get to heaven.[65] In this, his *Gangraena,* his *Heresiography,* Bunyan included Talkers, who believed that glibness would avail; Opinionists, whose religion lay in circumstantials; Formalists and Legalists; Libertines or antinomians; Temporizing Latitudinarians; the willfully Ignorant; the Comparative Professor, who judged himself by others; the expedient conformist who changed company with the times; and Freewillers, Socinians, and Quakers. This was Bunyan's first sketch for the controversial material of *Pilgrim's Progress.* Two other tracts, *Come and Welcome,* 1678, and *The Heavenly Footman,* 1692, are also of interest in this connection. In the first of these he spoke of the erroneous opinions which beset one who was coming along the way,[66] and in the second he described the bypaths which are a feature of his pilgrimage. These crooked little paths leading into and out of the way of salvation and upon which Quakers, Ranters, and many others wandered, stumbled, and fell, represented, he said, sectarian error. Most of these paths were characterized by moral righteousness; whereas the main way represented imputed righteousness.[67] By the aid of these supplementary tracts it is easy to apprehend the controversial import of the paths and characters of *Pilgrim's Progress.* It is also evident from his list of errors that the characters are sometimes embodiments of sectarian errors rather than sketches of personified sects. Several sects, for example, were distinguished in Bunyan's opinion by legalism and superficial profession or talkativeness.

Though Bunyan was campaigning in the *Progress* against error as well as sects, it is significant that in *The Strait Gate* he placed particular emphasis upon one sect, the latitudinarians, with whom in the person of Edward Fowler he had recently been at odds. In *Pilgrim's Progress* is a character who is definitely a man of latitude. This excellent flowering from the muck of controversy is By-ends, who represents at once the person of Fowler and the heresy of the latitudinarians.[68]

In his *Design of Christianity* Fowler had deprecated those champions of free grace who felt that if holiness was a design of Christianity, "it was at best but a Bye-one, and that some other matters were much more in his Eye."[69] It is probable that this passage served to suggest the name of By-ends to Bunyan as a suitable *tu-quoque*. To Bunyan the name By-ends connoted ends other than that of salvation by imputed righteousness, and it was of special significance as an allusion to the error implicit in Fowler's title *The Design of Christianity*. It will be recalled that because of Fowler's recommendation of expedient conformity to the trend of the times,[70] Bunyan had called him "a glorious Latitudinarian, that can, as to religion, turn and twist like an eel on the angle, or rather like the weather-cock on the steeple," and one who would approve of hopping from a Presbyterian to a prelatical mode with the trend of the times and back again if need be.[71] Indeed, Fowler had changed from the Presbyterian to the prelatical mode shortly after the Restoration. To By-ends Bunyan gave Fowler's principle of politic conformity, his weathercock spirit, which struggled against neither wind nor tide but took the path of least resistance, the way of credit and esteem in the community.[72] By-ends is made to say:

They are for hazarding all for God at a clap, and I am for taking all advantages to secure my Life and Estate. They are for holding their notions though all other men be against them, but I am for Religion in what, and so far as the times, and my safety will bear it. They are for Religion, when in rags and contempt, but I am for him when he walks in his golden Slippers in the Sun-shine, and with applause.[73]

The defense by By-ends of the right of the clergy to run after great benefices, appears to refer to Fowler's already notorious advancement in the church from one lucrative benefice to a better. It is in reflection of Bunyan's idea of the Anglican concern with filthy lucre, which he had assailed in his first attack upon Fowler,[74] that By-ends perished for the sake of that commodity in Demas's silver mine, where he stumbled and fell and came short of heaven, as Bunyan had warned Fowler those would do who thought like him that they were possessed of righteousness.[75] Fowler and By-ends agreed in their disapproval of strict sectarians for rigidness, over-righteousness, uncharitableness, and intolerance; and both advanced the merits of reason as well as of Scripture. Since with these views it would have been impossible for By-ends to have entered the wicket gate, he had obviously come down a bypath or crept through the hedge, like Fowler, who, Bunyan had said, was among those who were not coming in the right way.[76] Bunyan made By-ends the representative of social eminence, describing him as a gentleman related to lords, parsons, and the rich, in allusion to Fowler's connections among the great, and in reference to the emphasis upon class distinction which, as we shall see in the next chapter, had made of Fowler's attack upon Bunyan a social rather than a religious matter.

It appears certain from these similarities between the persons, ideas, and careers of Fowler and By-ends that Bunyan intended this character to represent the latitudinarians and Fowler in particular. By-ends is the product of the resentment against the Anglicans of an enthusiastic evangelist and a despised mechanick. But in the character of Ignorance, Bunyan also embodied those errors of the Anglicans which had disturbed him in his debate with Fowler.[77]

The miniature controversy between Christian and Hopeful on the one hand and Ignorance on the other is the literary duplication of Bunyan's pamphlet dispute with Fowler on good works. By means of these debates in the *Progress* Bunyan elevated controversy to an ideal plane where he could control both sides of the argument, inconvenience his opponent, and have the last word. Bunyan's fortunate discovery that through these controlled debates between his hero and the caricatured projections of his actual enemies he could experience the pleasures of combat without the complications of reality, invests *Pilgrim's Progress* with the character of a controversial Utopia. The devil's advocate in this encounter with Christian, Ignorance, who had come illicitly down a little crooked lane, was a believer in salvation by good works, almsgiving, prayer, and personal righteousness. As Christian called Ignorance a thief and a robber for coming in the wrong way, so Bunyan had called Fowler a thief for clambering in the wrong way.[78] Like Fowler, Ignorance maintained the purity of human nature against the godly idea of man's filthiness. Recapitulating the arguments of Fowler, Ignorance asserted a belief in salvation by Christ as well as by his own virtue;[79] but, detecting the reliance upon individual merit in this specious credo, Christian outlined the substance of Bunyan's *Defence of the Doctrine of Justification by Faith* for the correction of his virtuous opponent. The reply of Ignorance to this was like that of Fowler:

What! would you have us trust to what Christ in his own person has done without us? This conceit would loosen the reins of our lust, and tolerate us to live as we list. For what matter how we live if we may be justified by Christ's personal righteousness from all, when we believe it?[80]

Fortifying this implication of antinomianism by the usual charge of enthusiasm, Ignorance followed Fowler in his censure of reliance upon direct revelation from heaven as fanatical and the fruit of distracted brains. At the end of this exchange, which conforms to the course of that between Bunyan and Fowler, the two saints left Ignorance to cherish his error, and shortly after had the exquisite pleasure, while those in Paradise were singing without intermission "holy, holy, holy," of beholding certain Shining Ones take Ignorance, bind him, and bear him off to hell.[81]

Whereas By-ends resembles Fowler in both person and doctrine, Ignorance possesses only a theological similarity. Much more generally than either of these, three other characters of *Pilgrim's Progress* owe their natures to Bunyan's quarrel with the Anglicans. These are Mr. Worldly Wiseman, Formalist, and Hypocrisie, all of whom were "gentlemen," all of whom had failed to enter the wicket gate, and all of whom sought salvation by works instead of grace. Mr. Worldly Wiseman[82] directed Christian to the Village of Morality where Legality would help him to find peace and see that he lived in credit and good fashion, but happily Evangelist appeared in time to expound the truth of law and grace and to save Christian from legal heresy. Both Formalist and Hypocrisie pleaded custom and tradition for their similar short cut to heaven.[83]

In the light of Bunyan's tractarian interest at this time in his recent dispute with the Anglicans, it is not surprising that he devoted little attention in the *Progress* to the Quakers, in whom his interest had diminished. The men who lay dashed to pieces at the foot of the Hill of Error for denying the resurrection of the body are probably of that sect, as are those hypocrites who had entered the byway to hell as a result of blaspheming the gospel.[84] As for the other characters, Mr. Self-will, who appears in the second part,[85] is apparently an antinomian, possibly a Ranter, who followed his lusts, believing that if he imitated the vices as well as the virtues of pilgrims he should certainly be saved. Citing the example of Solomon, he contended that in polygamy there was grace. It was opinions like this, observed Honest, that made going on pilgrimage of so little esteem.

Always ready to disown antinomian opinions, of which he had been so frequently accused, Bunyan was attempting once more to anticipate criticism by condemning that error. Talkative, who, since his verbal orthodoxy is unquestionable, has little controversial significance, represents the hypocritical professor within the Calvinist church, the kind of unworthy communicant of whom, as his pamphlets of the seventies and the eighties and the records of the *Church Book* show, Bunyan was endeavoring to purge his meeting.[86] In the characters of Mr. Turn-away and Temporary,[87] backsliders, there is allusion to people like John Child, Bunyan's former colleague, who, under the pressure of persecution, were conforming.[88] And the Flatterer, the man of black flesh concealed by a white robe,[89] who is characterized as "a false Apostle, that hath transformed himself into an Angel of Light," though intended perhaps for a Quaker, is Bunyan's idea of all rival ministers.

Bunyan devoted the first part of the *Progress* principally to the Anglicans, but he turned in the second part, as he said in its Preface, to matters neglected in the first.[90] That these previously slighted matters were products of his quarrel with the strict Baptists is evident from the contents of this work, which includes both a restatement of his position on baptism and his reaction to the theological and ecclesiastical innuendoes of T.S., the General Baptist.

Bunyan's emphasis upon the individual saint and his neglect of church discipline and the ordinances, as well as his treatment of rebirth, had provoked a continuation of *Pilgrim's Progress* in 1682 by T.S., who remedied Bunyan's lapses by dwelling upon the organized church, its sacraments, and the general rather than the particular call.[91] In response to these implications of inadequacy, Bunyan described in his own second part the conduct of a church under Greatheart, and gave his attention to the discipline and sacraments which distinguished it as Baptist. The feast at the Porter's lodge,[92] at which communicants piously consumed "Lamb with the accustomed Sauce belonging thereto," was a concession to T.S., as were the allegorical communions suggested by the pills compounded "ex Carne et Sanguine Christi" and the meal at the house of Gaius.[93] Before having been admitted to the eucharist, some of the original group had benefited by an initiating bath of sanctification at the Interpreter's House, and had been sealed into the fellowship of the traveling conventicle.[94] And apparently in answer to T.S.'s advocacy of the general call, Christiana received an individual letter from God, "smelling after the manner of the best Perfume," and asking her particularly to set out.[95]

Although Bunyan's second part was influenced by his reactions to T.S., it was complicated, in certain allegorical passages which have not been sufficiently understood, by his old dispute with the strict Baptists. His attention in the first part to fundamentals of doctrine and his failure to emphasize matters peculiar to the Baptists had indicated his open-communion position. But in the second part his treatment of this dispute was far from negative. By introducing the bath, Bunyan affirmed what the strict Baptists had claimed he despised, the initiatory rite of dipping. But to counteract the effect of this affirmation, Bunyan introduced open-communion propaganda by admitting to his traveling church members who had not been dipped with the original group, and whose weakness in this circumstance the saints had overlooked. In his *Confession of Faith* Bunyan had pleaded for those who through weakness and feebleness did not have light in the ordinance of baptism, and had urged the church to communicate with the "weak and feeble";[96] and in his *Differences in Judgment,* another tract of the Baptist dispute, he had recurred to this point.[97] Mr. Feeblemind in the second part, who embodies this idea of communication with the feeble, had not been baptized with the others, but he was godly. So weak as to be "offended with that which others have a liberty to do," he had found none willing to go so softly as he was forced to go until Greatheart welcomed him into his open-communion meeting, and promised to avoid for his sake opinionative and doubtful disputes upon non-essentials.[98] After other feeble souls, Mr. Ready-to-hault, Mr. Despondency, and Mr. Much-Afraid, had also been added to the tolerant company, the Shepherds blessed with their approval this open-communion practice.[99]

Bunyan's emphasis upon women and children in this book may be explained in part by his concern over those women whom he had chided in his *Case of Conscience* the year before, whose despair he had promised to remedy, and whose position in the church he hoped to redefine. As a gentle lesson to them he pointed to the submission of matrons and virgins to the leadership of Greatheart; and to placate and correct them he put into the mouth of Gaius a eulogy of women and a statement of their proper servility.[100]

The vexed problem of church singing supplied further controversial detail to *Pilgrim's Progress*. Together with those equally significant questions of anointing with oil and the laying on of hands, the ordinance of singing psalms and hymns had been agitated for years in Baptist circles. Foreseeing difficulties, Gifford had recorded in the *Church Book* a letter of warning against internal division on these grounds; yet in Bunyan's meeting there had arisen over the matter of singing two factions, which fretted unostentatiously together. Until after Bunyan's death, as the *Church Book* indicates,[101] the antipsalmists had been powerful enough to prevent the introduction of singing, but around 1691 they yielded, and singing was permitted with the understanding that the conscientious, whose spirits were wounded by the levity of song, could remain silent or wait in the vestibule until the psalm was done. Baptist bards like Keach and Powell had campaigned for years for the approval of their harmonious produce, and the poet Bunyan also regarded with favor the toleration of the Muses. In several of his tracts as well as in *Pilgrim's Progress* he notified the reluctant of his partiality for song.[102]

But the *Progress* afforded Bunyan an opportunity, which he embraced with enthusiasm, of enlightening the conservative by the introduction of occasional verses, many of them in hymn meter. These songs of *Pilgrim's Progress,* one of the most apparent features of the book, are to be interpreted not as the overflow of literary high spirits but as propaganda for church singing. The significant circumstance that several of these songs have been used for purposes of devotion in Baptist churches [103] supplies additional evidence of their purpose.

It is apparent that controversy, which played so considerable a part in Bunyan's career as an enthusiastic lay preacher, left its mark upon his greatest work, which is in many ways the concluding episode of these obscure battles. In this book is a curious emblem of a man in white upon whom certain villains were occupied in casting dirt, which would not stick.[104] *Pilgrim's Progress* was in part an effort, rather unnecessary since defilement had not defiled, to see the dirt wiped off.

CHAPTER IV

TRADERS IN MANNA

When tinkers bawl'd aloud to settle
Church-discipline, for patching kettle;
No sow-gelder did blow his horn
To geld a cat, but cry'd Reform.
Hudibras, I, ii, 535.

The contempt which men of elegance and wit condescended to cast upon preaching tradesmen served only to inflame the perseverance of these gifted mechanicks. Though embittered by the scorn of those who were kept by custom or intelligence from a conception of the sublime, Samuel How, the preaching cobbler, John Spencer, the preaching horse-rubber, and John Bunyan, the preaching tinker, gloried in their shame. Up to this point we have been concerned with Bunyan's participation in the normal pursuits of enthusiasm, but our task now will be different. To provide some account of the rise of enthusiastic mechanicks in a class-conscious society, to explain the attitude of the conservative toward the presumption of the pious and contemptible, and to illustrate the response of Bunyan and the other mechanicks to the severities of social humiliation, is the design of the present chapter.

From the days of the Lollards England had experienced without becoming reconciled to the presence of preaching mechanicks, but during the ferment of the Civil Wars it beheld with anxiety the multiplication of these men, who abandoned shops and trades for the eminence of tub and pulpit. According to Daniel Featley, D.D., church notices at this time read: "On such a day such a Brewers Clerk Exerciseth, Such a Taylor Expoundeth,"[1] and according to the exaggeration of another observer:

Transported with this fancie, a zealous Taylor hideth his sheares and yard in some privy corner . . . he imitateth an austere garbe, looketh passing grave and sowrely, and is as melancholike as a leane judge . . . inviteth two or three couple of his own Hall, with their doxies, to his house . . . (saying he is called of God) and by revelation am informed, that I should no more ascend my shop-board, to fit garments for mens bodies, but for the future to cloath their soules with the warme woollen of the Word.[2]

Tradesmen of all the radical sects felt the impulse of the Spirit, but since the Baptists were among the earliest to appear as well as the most conspicuous by their numbers, it was they who endured the severest animadversions of established society.

The mechanick preachers carried to its logical extreme the protestant assumption of the priesthood of all believers. Since every Baptist was at least potentially a minister,[3] subject always to a manifest gift and usually to the approval of his conventicle, the circumstance that most of the Baptists were of the lower and the lower middle classes had its effect upon the character of their ministry.[4] From the reports of informers it is possible to gather an idea of the quality of both preacher and communicant of the average Baptist meeting. A raid on a meeting in 1681, for example, disclosed "about one hundred and fifty poor mechanical fellows, and the preacher was like them."[5] A report to Sheldon in 1669 upon the congregation of Bunyan's friend John Gibbs at Newport Pagnell described it as consisting of "inferior tradesmen and mechanical people; led by Mr. Gibbs, one Breedon, and James Rogers, lace buyers, and one Fenne, a hatter."[6] Sheldon's informers characterized the Bedford meeting, of which Bunyan was a member, as of "the meanest sort," headed by John Fenne, hatter, Thomas Honylove, cobbler, and Thomas Cooper, heel-maker.[7] This conventicle, which was representative, numbered among its adherents, grocers, servants, laborers, shoemakers, a cutler, a draper, a tanner, a baker, a blacksmith, a pipemaker, a gardener, a wagoner, a weaver, one well-to-do maltster, and one gentlewoman.[8] As for the preachers of the Baptists, about twenty at this time were ex-clergymen, whose enthusiasm had

caused them to desert their kind, but the rest, as might be supposed from the character of the congregations, were for the most
part mechanicks or ex-mechanicks like John Belcher, the brick-
layer, Samuel Oates, the weaver, Jonathan Jennings, the cheesemonger, and Benjamin Keach, the tailor. The theory of the priesthood of all believers, which had appealed primarily to the lower
classes, enabled the sect and its ministry by a kind of happy anticipation to epitomize the future nation of shopkeepers.

Then even more than now England was a class-conscious land.
Beholding the unrest of the lower orders, the entrenched not
only exclaimed their dismay, but interpreted often without cause
every appearance of discontent as the symptom of popular insurrection. Though the Civil Wars were by no means a struggle
between the upper and lower classes, the conservative liked to
believe that they were, and constant in their superciliousness,
they insisted with distaste that Colonel Pride had been a dray-
man, they called Lilburne a soap-boiler, and they tried to con-
nect Cromwell with the trades.[9] Naturally the prophetical ambition of real mechanicks alienated the sympathies of the refined,
who could not but regard it as incorrect:

> These kind of Vermin swarm like Caterpillars
> And hold Conventicles in Barnes and Sellars
> Some preach (or prate) in Woods, in fields, in stables,
> In hollow trees, in tubs, on tops of tables.[10]

While the clergy uttered solemn and agitated expostulations,
journalists and pamphleteers covered the upstart preaching
tailors and stableboys with abuse, ridicule, and loathing. Their
offense in the eyes of the conservative was not so much against
the apostolic succession as against the system of caste, which had
been designed to defend the privileges of those who had them,
and to keep tradesmen and laborers in their proper place. Consequently while men of position deplored the ecclesiastical error
of unordained preaching, they emphasized the social presumption of intruding upon the preserves of those who were learned

and well-born. And on their side, the mechanicks discovered their sense of mission to be complicated by some purely social resentment.

The consolations of martyrdom were needed by the mechanick who was literate or worldly enough to read the newspapers or the pamphlets of his social superiors and their venal supporters. These works of Satan's party gave voice with various emphasis to three objections to mechanicks: their want of ordination, their illiteracy, and their lowly social position. Concentrating upon these objections, the mechanicks and their friends met attack with attack: they assailed ordination as antichristian, they decried learning as an impediment to inspiration, and they made of social obscurity a virtue; for the Almighty, as Scripture affirms, had chosen not the proud and the noble but the poor and the low.

Among those who presumed to scorn the inscrutable dispensations of God were journalists, who filled their prejudiced pages with accounts of mechanick excess,[11] and pamphleteers, who from 1640, the year of the first considerable appearance of the preaching tradesmen, called upon ridicule to rid the country of what in their darkness they considered a social anomaly. To the gross apprehensions of the author of *New Preachers New*, 1641,[12] Greene, the pious felt-maker, and Spencer, the godly horse-rubber, were presumptuous rather than admirable, though it had been at the suggestion of the Lord that in the morning they made a hat or rubbed a horse and in the afternoon preached a sermon. Directories like *The Brownists Synagogue*, 1641, and *Tub-preachers overturn'd*, 1647, exposed to an unsympathetic public the pretensions of enlightened porters, smiths, and box-makers.[13] John Taylor, although himself a waterman, ridiculed Spilsbury, the Anabaptist hay-weigher, who had dipped Eaton, "a zealous Button Maker, grave and wise."[14] Some, like the author of *A New Directory*, 1647,[15] discovered a profane delight in burlesquing the sermons of godly illiterates such as Ford, the trumpeter, and Dupper, the cow keeper; or, like Nathaniel Ward, indulged a perverse humor in mock encomia of soap-boilers, and lavished preposterous advice upon preaching confectioners:

> Then if in Manna you will trade,
> You must boyle no more Marmolade.[16]

Prominent mechanicks like Praise-God Barebones, the leather seller, were often singled out;[17] but the illustrious Samuel How, the cobbler, even after his untimely death, was accorded, by virtue of his early eminence, the greatest attention. The bestial John Taylor described with prejudice a sermon preached by How at the Nag's Head near to Coleman Street:[18]

> A Preachers work is not to gelde a Sowe,
> Unseemly 'tis a Judge should milk a Cowe:
> A Cobler to a Pulpit should not mount,
> Nor can an Asse cast up a true account.
>
> . . . .
>
> A worthy brother gave the Text, and than
> The Cobler (How) his preachment strait began
> Extemp'ry without any meditation,
> But only by the Spirits revelation,
> He went through-stitch, now hither, & now thither,
> And tooke great paines to draw both ends together:
> For (like a man inspir'd from Amsterdam)
> He scorn'd Ne sutor ultra crepidam;
> His Text he clouted, and his Sermon welted,
> His audience (with devotion) almost melted,
> His speech was neither studied, chew'd or champ'd,
> Or ruminated, but most neatly vamp'd.
>
> . . . .
>
> He fell couragiously upon the Beast,
> And very daintily the Text did wrest;
> His audience wondered what strange power did guide him,
> 'Tis thought no man can do the like beside him.
>
> . . . .
>
> 'Gainst Schooles, and learning he exclaim'd amain,
> Tongues, Science, Logick, Rhetorick, all are vain,

And wisdom much unfitting for a Preacher,
Because the Spirit is the only teacher,
For Christ chose not the Rabines of the Jewes,
No Doctors, Scribes, or Pharisees did chuse:
The poore unlearned simple Fisherman,
The poling, strict tole-gathering Publican,
Tent-makers, and poore men of meane desart,
Such as knew no degrees, or grounds of Art;
And God still being God (as he was then)
Still gives his Spirit to unlearned men,
Such as are Barbers, Mealmen, Brewers, Bakers,
Religious Sowgelders, and Button-makers,
Coopers, and Coblers, Tinkers, Pedlers, Weavers,
And Chimney sweepers. . . .

. . . .

The Latine is the language of the Beast. . . . .
Then since it is the Romish tongue, therefore
Let us that doe not Antichrist adore,
Leave it to Lawyers, Gentlemen, and such
Whose studies in the Scriptures are not much.

This disagreeable report reveals the main contentions of the mechanick preachers, who were forced by the attitude of society to attack learning, lawyers, and gentlemen, and to affirm the preference of the Saviour for apostolic tradesmen. And in the postscript Taylor's verses plead the contention of the Beast, the sanctity of the estates:

Let tradesmen use their trades, let all men be
Imploy'd in what is fitting their degree.

But as they flourished beneath this abuse, the mechanicks were encouraged, if they were aware of them, by defenders like Milton, Walwyn, and Roger Williams, whose godliness or reason was able to detect the truth and the privilege of all men of what rank soever to be prophets and witnesses of Christ.[19] As Roger Williams defended the despised Samuel How,[20] so William Dell, Master of Gonvil and Caius College, and ex-preacher of the word to the army, in which he had deserved his reputation for excess,[21] issued from his academic halls a denunciation of learning in support of illiterate mechanicks. In his *Stumbling Stone,* 1653,[22] Dell maintained the efficacy of the gift, whose luster was most visibly impaired by the contamination of Plato and Aristotle, "wretched heathens, dead and damned many hundred years ago," and commended simple tradesmen, who, though they disrupted society and caused riot and tumult, resembled the Saviour, Himself a mechanick without ordination or degrees, who had chosen mechanicks like Himself for disciples.[23] But the consideration that universities had a kind of secular utility led this master of a college reluctantly to concede their toleration. The answer of Joseph Sedgwick, M.A., to this strange tract, if less godly, had the merit of reasonableness: "Of all things I can least indure Enthusiasme, unlesse it be in brave lofty and Romantick lines. Then methinks it sounds rarely and turned into Latine Verse, might be bound up with Ovid's Metamorphosis."[24] Dell's espousal of the mechanick cause had been noted with equal derision in 1649 by the *Mercurius Elencticus,*[25] which said:

> The graver Cobler shall expound,
> And quote them Dell and Peters. . . .

Since this good though learned man had said that he would "rather chuse to be in fellowship with poor plain Husbandmen and Tradesmen, who believe in Christ, and have received his Spirit, then with the Heads of Universities, and highest, and stateliest of the Clergy,"[26] it was not unnatural for him to approve of John Bunyan. Indeed, it was at the invitation of its pious incumbent that Bunyan preached in Dell's pulpit at Yelden, Bedfordshire, on December 25, 1659. But the reluctant audience, less liberal than their guide and shocked at this mechanick invasion, complained to the House of Lords the following year that not only had Dell stated a preference for preaching plowmen, fresh from the plow, but that he had imposed his curious taste upon them: "Upon Christmas Day last one Bunyan, a tinker, was countenanced and suffered to speak in his pulpit to the congregation, and no orthodox minister did officiate in the church that day."²⁷

By 1659, since for several years he had been opening the word and exercising his humble craft in the vicinity as the Lord directed him, Bunyan had become habituated to congregational intolerance. It was unfortunate for his peace of mind and for his reputation among the polite that of all the mechanick arts he should have professed that of mending kettles; for the tinker was invariably despised, when he could not be ignored, as the most unseemly of artisans, and was selected by satiric malice as the symbol of disreputability and the type of all baseness. We have observed the cruel partiality of Samuel Butler, who made his Ralpho a tailor but his less estimable Magnano a tinker,²⁸ and who, when he would epitomize mechanick presumption, chose for his wicked amusement a professor of this art. But in the writings of the other satirists of this period the tinker had been elevated to an equally conspicuous position as the representative but least respectable variety of mechanick enthusiast.²⁹

While it is known that Bunyan exercised both his tinkering and his preaching until 1660, it is not certain whether, after he became the leader of his congregation in 1672, he continued to ply his worldly trade. After 1672 he almost certainly received enough money from the voluntary contributions of his flock, if not from his writings, to render a secular occupation unnecessary, but he is described in licenses and documents of this date and later as a "brazier";³⁰ whether out of a social inertia that made a man once a tinker always a tinker for purposes of classification and record, or whether because he was still a practicing tinker, it is difficult to determine. The evidence of his own words and the often unreliable statements of his contemporary biographers incline us to the belief that upon his assumption of leadership he ceased his professional labors: "sequestering himself from all secular imployments, to follow that of his Call to the Ministry."[31] But if he did continue his worldly occupation for additional income or to maintain a mechanick status, so useful for his ministry, his trade must have been but a minor part of his activities.[32] At all events, he was known throughout his lifetime as the tinker both by his friends, who used the term as one of apostolic distinction, and by his enemies, who used it as one of reproach.

In order to understand the quality of Bunyan's reception by the conservative it is necessary to consult the records of controversial animosity; for in the hostilities of debate with social superiors the mechanick position by virtue of which Bunyan was valuable in the eyes of the Lord and His saints, became the object of carnal distaste. For many years the clergy, both Anglican and Presbyterian, had found in theological dispute the opportunity to point with aversion to the social infirmities of their more godly opponents. For example, when Thomas Hall, Presbyterian, disputed in 1651 with several Baptist preachers, Lawrence Williams, a nailer, Thomas Palmer, a baker, Thomas Hinde, a plow-wright, Henry Oakes, a weaver, and Humphrey Rogers, lately a baker's boy, he led the argument from the question of ordination to that of logic and learning, which the mechanicks decried, and to summarize his social objection, he said: "Superiors must govern; Inferiours Obey, and be Governed; Ministers must study and Preach; People must hear and obey . . . Baking and Preaching, Nayling and Preaching, Patching and Preaching, and that by men of little abilities, will not hold."[33] In his dispute with Thomas Collier, the Baptist, Hall insisted that this enemy of learning, whom Edwards had called a "mechanicall fellow," was an ex-husbandman, who, he trusted, had better skill in plowing than in preaching.[34] That same year the indefatigable Hall debated with two butchers and a weaver.[35] Conspicuous among the defenders of the mechanicks, Edmund Chillenden, the Baptist, issued his conclusive *Preaching Without Ordination*,[36] which if the enemy had pondered, they had remained silent and abashed; for Chillenden mentioned Jesus, the carpenter, and told how He like more recent mechanicks had been spat upon by Jews:

And seeing God is no respecter of persons, but gives his guifts by his spirit to whom he pleaseth, where by all men that partake of those guifts, are inabled to prophesie or preach, though not ordained what should hinder them from being Prophets and Preachers, and that of the Lords own making, by the free guift of his spirit, seeing it bloweth where it listeth, assoone upon a Cobler, Tinker, Chimney sweeper, Plowman, or any other Tradseman, as to the greatest learnedst Doctors in the world, Then I here demand the reason, why he namely the Cobler, Tincker, &c. may not be permitted to manifest the gifts and graces of God in him, by Preaching and declaring the Gospel as the other: to wit the Learned man. . . .[37]

Like the butchers, weavers, and ex-baker's boys, whose rank Hall had indicated with detestation, Bunyan suffered annoyances during his frequent engagements with the learned and the clerical. When brought for examination before Justice Wingate, he was asked why he did not content himself with following his calling since it was in violation of the law that such as he should preach.[38] As Bunyan was assuring the judge that he could follow his calling and preach the word without confusion, Dr. Lindale, a clergyman of Hitchin, entered and, after taunting the mechanick, requested him to prove that it was lawful for him to preach. From Scripture Bunyan took his answer, "As every man hath received the gift, even so let him minister the same," but Lindale replied: "Indeed I do remember that I have read of one Alexander a Coppersmith, who did much oppose, and disturb the Apostles." Conscious of the implication of this reference to an earlier mechanick, Bunyan added an explanatory parenthesis to his report: "Aiming 'tis like at me, because I was a Tinker."[39] Mr. Foster, who was present, and with whom Bunyan had also debated the matter of his lawful calling, thought Bunyan to be incapacitated by his ignorance of the original Greek from an understanding of the Scriptures:

> To whom I said, that if that was his opinion, that none could understand the Scriptures, but those that had the original Greek, &c. then but a very few of the poorest sort should be saved, (this is harsh) yet the scripture saith, That God hides his things from the wise and prudent, (that is from the learned of the world) and reveals them to babes and sucklings.[40]

During Bunyan's trial, which was characterized by equal social tension and by similar arguments over his authority to preach, Justice Keeling made the point raised by all enemies of the mechanicks:

> He said, let me a little open the Scripture to you. As every man hath received the gift; that is, said he, as every man hath received a trade, so let him follow it. If any man hath received a gift of tinkering; as thou hast done, let him follow his tinkering. And so other men their trades. And the divine his calling, &c.[41]

The arguments of these men of learning and position were repeated by all of Bunyan's controversial opponents, with the exception of the Quakers,[42] who, since they were equally disreputable, could only join Bunyan in the traditional responses of mechanick resentment. Bunyan's unfriendly exchange with Thomas Smith of Cambridge involved on both sides the customary objections: on the part of Smith, to Bunyan's position, authority, and ignorance; and on the part of Bunyan, to Smith's learning and logic: "A way (quoth he) to Oxford with your hell bred Logick."[43] Far from being common to all the vulgar, Smith said, the ministry was reserved for the few, who were set apart to study and preach, "others to plow, and sow, and harrow the ground, and use other lawfull trades, working with their hands." But the nicety of this distinction flattered as it wounded the understanding of its object, whom Smith had described as a "wandering preaching Tinker . . . the meanest of all the vulgar in the Country."[44] Bunyan's supporter, Henry Denne, was reputed to have had a sense of apostolic conduct so correct that he himself, without the excuse of necessity, had taken to trade: "Mr. Den is turned Carter and goes to Cart, (holding that Erroneous opinion) that Ministers must work with their hands, and follow some worldy calling."[45] Although it was to be expected that so excellent a saint should come to the defense of a mechanick, the reasonableness which distinguished Denne's reply to Smith could not have been anticipated: "You seem to be angry with the Tinker, because he strives to mend Souls as well as Kettles and Pans."[46]

The insolence with which Fowler noticed the lowliness and illiteracy of his opponent has few parallels in the controversial literature of the time.[47] "For such a *thing* as he to disgrace either the writing or Person of *Mr. F.* by all his railings," was as impossible, said Fowler, "as it is for the little rude creatures to eclipse the Moon by barking at her, or to make Palaces contemptible by their lifting up their legs against them." Like all the quarrels between scholars and mechanicks, this one embraced not only the matter of social baseness, which occupied much of Fowler's attention, but the usual questions of ignorance and learning. In answer to Bunyan's attack upon his learning and his citation of authorities, Fowler expressed his astonishment that one so brutish and illiterate as Bunyan could have found the words and material for a pamphlet.

Between the upper and lower strata of the Baptists was a social chasm, ordinarily obscured by brotherly love, but revealed by the reply of William Kiffin and Thomas Paul to Bunyan's *Confession of Faith*.[48] To Paul's brief and mild allusion to his social rank Bunyan's reaction was so furious, disproportionate, and indicative of sensitivity, that it can be explained, in view of his silence under the controversial depravities of Smith and Fowler, only as the resentment of such criticism from one of his own sect:

I have read and considered, and have weighed them [your reflections] so well as my rank and abilities will admit me to do. . . . But before I enter the body of your book, give me leave a little to discourse you about your preamble to the same, wherein are two miscarriages unworthy your pretended seriousness, because void of love and humility. The first is, In that you closely disdain my person because of my low descent among men, stigmatizing me for a person of THAT rank, that need not to be heeded or attended unto. p. 1.

Answ. What it is that gives a man reverence with you, I know not; but for certain, He that despiseth the poor reproacheth his Maker; yet, "a poor man is better than a liar." To have gay clothing, or gold rings, or the persons that wear them in admiration; or to be partial in your judgment, or respects, for the sake, or upon the account of, flesh and blood, doubtless convinceth you to be of the law a transgressor, and not without partiality, &c., in the midst of your seeming sanctity.

Again, you say, "I had not meddled with the controversy at all, had I found any of parts that would divert themselves to take notice of YOU." p. 2.

Answ. What need you, before you have shewed one syllable of a reasonable argument in opposition to what I assert, thus trample my person, my gifts, and grace, have I any, so disdainfully under your feet? (Read Ps. i. 1. 2.) What kind of a YOU am I? And why is MY rank so mean, that the most gracious and godly among you, may not duly and soberly consider of what I have said? Was it not the art of the false apostles of old to say thus? To bespatter a man, that his doctrine might be disregarded. "Is not this the carpenter?" And, "His bodily presence is weak and his speech contemptible," 1 Co. x. 10, did not use to be in the mouths of the saints; for they knew that "the wind bloweth, where it listeth." Jn. iii. 8. Neither is it high birth, worldly breeding, or wealth; but the electing love, grace, and the wisdom that comes from heaven, that those who strive for strictness of order in the things and kingdom of Christ, should have in regard and esteem. Ja. iii. 17. Need I read you a lecture? "Hath not God chosen the foolish,-the weak,-the base, yea, and things which are not, to bring to nought things that are?" 1 Co. i. 27, 28. Why then do you despise my rank, my state, and quality in the world? [49]

Since the ignorance and social inferiority of the mechanick were at once the objects of hostile scorn and friendly congratulation, Bunyan's supporters as well as his enemies, though for a different reason, called attention to them. Esteeming what was almost universally despised, they experienced, nevertheless, like the mechanicks themselves, a strange mingling of the emotions of pride and shame. Typical of the apologies for Bunyan was that by his friend Charles Doe, comb-maker, who after dwelling upon the poverty, worldly inconsequence, and mechanick character of the eminent preacher, remarked upon the discrimination of the Lord, who habitually selected such men as the recipients of His gift. Bunyan, he said,

preached about the Country . . . and worked at his tinkering Trade for a Livelihood, whereby the reigning Grace of God appeared the more Sovreign and Glorious in this choice, even as it shone in the choice of Peter a Fisherman, and the rest of the Apostles, and other of the eminent Saints of old, most of them Tradesmen, and of whom most excellent things are spoken.[50]

Yet God's adversaries, he continued, who had the corrupt notion that only those with learning could preach the gospel, failed to recognize the ineffable source of mechanick eloquence. Bunyan's successor, the learned Ebenezer Chandler, open-communion Independent, made much the same complaint:

It's evident, that many in his Life-time did despise him, and all done by him, for the meanness of his Education, and Calling that he was instructed in, and did in the Morning of his dayes follow, as if no good thing could come out of Nazareth; and it's probable some may still be ready to have mean and contemptible Thoughts of his Works, for that reason; as also because he had not that acquired Learning, that others have.[51]

But the prefaces with which Burton and Gibbs hesitantly introduced Bunyan's early tracts to the censorious public afford better evidence of that mingling of pride and apology so common in mechanick defenses. John Burton, minister at Bedford, wrote the Preface to *Some Gospel Truths Opened*, 1656:

Therefore pray, that thou mayest receive this word which is according to the scriptures in faith and love, not as the word of man, but as the word of God, without respect of persons, and be not offended because Christ holds forth the glorious treasure of the gospel to thee

in a poor earthen vessel, by one who hath neither the greatness nor
the wisdom of this world to commend him to thee; for as the scripture, saith Christ, (who was low and contemptible in the world himself) ordinarily chooseth such for himself, and for the doing of his
work. 1 Cor. i. 26-28. Not many wise men after the flesh, not many
mighty, not many noble are called: But God hath chosen the foolish
things of the world, &c. This man is not chosen out of an earthly, but
out of the heavenly university, the church of Christ, which church, as
furnished with the Spirit, gifts, and graces of Christ, was in the beginning, and still is, and will be to the end of the world, that out of
which the word of the Lord, and so all true gospel ministers must
proceed, whether learned or unlearned as to human learning 1 Cor.
xii. 27, 28. And though this man hath not the learning or wisdom of
man, yet through Grace he hath received the teaching of God, and
the learning of the Spirit of Christ, which is the thing that makes a
man both a Christian and a minister of the gospel. "The Lord God
hath given me the tongue of the learned," &c. Is. l. 4, compared with
Lu. iv. 18 where Christ, as man, saith "The Spirit of the Lord is upon
me because he hath anointed me to preach the gospel to the poor,"
&c. He hath, through grace taken these three heavenly degrees, to wit,
union with Christ, the anointing of the Spirit, and experience of the
temptations of Satan, which do more fit a man for that mighty work
of preaching the gospel than all university learning and degrees that
can be had.[52]

The belief that inspiration could compensate for lowliness and
ignorance was restated by John Gibbs, minister at Newport
Pagnell, who wrote the Introduction to Bunyan's *A Few Sighs
from Hell,* 1658.[53] Though a university man, Gibbs suffered from
the misfortune of mechanick parentage, upon which Richard
Carpenter concentrated his attention in *The Anabaptist Washt
and washt, and shrunk in the washing,* 1653.[54] In this work Carpenter alluded frequently to the shame of the family, saying
disingenuously: "I despise no man whose father is a Cooper; but
if such a one as he shall undertake to Hoope-bind his Hogsheads,
or Bucking-Tubs, and not perform it strongly; I shall merrily tell
him of it." Hence Gibbs was in a position to offer sympathy to
Bunyan, the victim of even more pitiless censures, but who, as

Gibbs noted, though his condition and employment were mean and his learning small, had been accounted worthy of enlightenment:

And yet surely if thou shalt (notwithstanding this) stumble at his meanness and want of human learning, thou wilt declare thine unacquaintance with God's declared method, who to perfect his own praise, and to still the enemy and avenger makes choice of babes and sucklings. . . . Cast thine eye back to the beginning of the gospel dispensation (which, surely, if at any time, should have come forth in the wisdom and glory of the world) and thou shalt see what method the Lord did take at the first to exalt his son Jesus: he goes not amongst the Jewish rabbies, nor to the schools of learning, to fetch out his gospel preachers, but to the trades and those most contemptible too. . . .[55]

The apologists for Bunyan, as for the other mechanicks, found justification in the scriptural assurance that few of the mighty and noble had been called, discovered in the gift a substitute for worldly acquirements, and extracted comfort out of his resemblance to the apostles. But their praise was tempered by an awareness of almost universal disdain; and diffidence over the judgment of society was implicit in their words, which have an air at once proud, defensive, and apologetic. To their Christian premise of the worth of ignorance and humbleness, the objections of the profane gave an exaggerated vitality, and provided the mechanicks themselves, if not their apologists, with the motive for counterattacks upon learning and position. The social consciousness of the mechanicks was heightened though not created by the attitude of their superiors, and while the social atmosphere does not account for the premises of the mechanicks and their defenders, it does explain the direction, quality, and emphasis of their reactions.

Their class resentment encouraged, but not wholly inspired, by the scorn of the established caste, the mechanick preachers availed themselves of two defenses, obscurantism or the systematic enhancement of ignorance at the expense of learning, and the elevation of inferiority to a virtue. Though obscurantism was common, it was habitually denied by the more literate defenders of inspiration, like Chandler and Gibbs, both of whom, while pleading the privileges of the ignorant, deplored the excesses of those who were too extreme in their enmity to learning.[56] These two men endeavored to protect Bunyan from the imputation of hatred as well as ignorance of the learning of the schools, as in his defense of Samuel How, the learned Roger Williams had attempted a similar exculpation, claiming that the gifted cobbler honored learning in its place.[57] The works of both How and Bunyan, however, reveal the frivolity of these well-intentioned efforts.

In his versified account of the sermon at Coleman Street, John Taylor presented the substance of Samuel How's celebrated work *The Sufficiencie of the Spirits Teaching*,[58] which for many years remained secure in the esteem of saints as the definitive expression of obscurantism. Defending the weak and contemptible, whose message was "not beautified with the excellencie of speech, and swelling words of mans wisdom, which is enmity to God," How exposed the hollowness of Plato and Aristotle, of rhetoric and logic, and calling attention to the Saviour, who had been unsullied by human learning, he concluded that, though learning might be useful for lawyers and gentlemen in their profane concerns, it was an impediment to true wisdom and the influence of the Spirit. Identical arguments demonstrated the godliness of *A Short Treatise Concerning the lawfullnesse of every mans exercising his gift*[59] by John Spencer, the Baptist horse-rubber.

Bunyan did not devote an entire tract to the expression of his similar prejudices, but it is possible to gather an idea of their character from his frequent emphasis upon the gift and from his insistence that it remain free from the contamination of human learning. Like most of the lowly at this time, he vented his dislike of Satan's wisdom upon Plato and Aristotle, the symbolic objects of mechanick attack. He shared the common assumption that the gift was a substitute for scholarship: "for though I am not skilled in the Hebrew tongue, yet through grace, I am enlightened into the scriptures. . . ."[60] His consistent pretensions to freedom from literary influence, as we shall see in a later chapter, were symptoms of mechanick obscurantism. And his defiant admissions of ignorance and illiteracy, as shown in the boast that he knew neither the figure nor form of a syllogism,[61] and in the proud humility of his marginal note, "The Latine I borrow,"[62] are of similar significance.

If thou do find this empty of fantastical expressions, and without light, vain, whimsical, scholarlike terms, thou must understand it is because I never went to school, to Aristotle, or Plato, but was brought up at my father's house, in a very mean condition, among a company of poor countrymen. But if thou do find a parcel of plain, yet sound, true and home sayings, attribute that to the Lord Jesus's gifts and abilities, which he hath bestowed upon such a poor creature as I am, and have been.[63]

Bunyan's epistle to the reader in *The Holy City* expresses that enmity between grace and learning which had become the favorite antithesis of godly argument:

I. To the Godly Reader.
Friend, - Though the men of this world, at the sight of this book, will not only deride, but laugh in conceit, to consider that one so low, contemptible, and inconsiderable as I, should busy myself in such sort, as to meddle with the exposition of so hard and knotty a Scripture as here they find the subject matter of this little book; yet do thou remember that "God hath chosen the foolish things of the world to confound the wise, and things which are not, to bring to nought things that are." 1 Co. i. 27, 28. Consider also, that even of old it hath been his pleasure to "hide these things from the wise and prudent, and to reveal them unto babes." Mat. xi. 25; xxi. 15, 16. I tell you that the operation of the Word and Spirit of God, without depending upon that idol, so much adored, [i.e., learning] is sufficient of itself to search out "all things, even the deep things of God." 1 Co. ii. 10. . . .

II. To the Learned Reader.

Sir, - I suppose, in your reading of this discourse, you will be apt to blame me for two things: First, Because I have not so beautified my matter with acuteness of language as you could wish or desire. Secondly, Because also I have not given you, either in the line or in the margent, a cloud of sentences from the learned fathers, that have, according to their wisdom, possibly, handled these matters long before me . . . I do find in most such a spirit of whoredom and idolatry concerning the learning of this world, and wisdom of the flesh, and God's glory so much stained and diminished thereby; that had I all their aid and assistance at command, I durst not make use of ought thereof, and that for fear lest that grace, and these gifts that the Lord hath given me, should be attributed to their wits, rather than the light of the Word and Spirit of God . . . Wherefore seeing, though I am without their learned lines, yet well furnished with the words of God, I mean the Bible, I have contented myself with what I there have found. . . .[64]

In this customary statement, with its admixture of pride and diffidence, defiance and uneasiness, Bunyan shared with John Spencer and Samuel How the attitude and arguments of the obscurantist, who deprecated the learning of the world either as unessential in view of the descent of wisdom from above, or as fatal to the reception of this adorable influence.

To their solicitous cultivation of ignorance the mechanicks added a revaluation of inferiority, and in order to justify the ways of God, they pretended to discover the favor of heaven in the disdain of the world. Their consciousness of class distinctions was increased and their ideas of the social hierarchy were inverted from the accepted order by the hostility of their superiors; they sought in their Bibles the assurance that God esteemed the poor and the low while He neglected, except for the bother of damning, those whom the world admired. Since the rich and carnal were dull of hearing, said Samuel How in the pamphlet which we have already noticed, God had chosen the poor and exalted the man of low degree, but Satan, who preferred like Dives the wise, the rich, the noble, and the learned, despised the chosen people.

"If a Man have the Spirit of God, though he be a Pedler, Tinker, Chimney-sweeper, or Cobbler, he may by the helpe of Gods Spirit, give a more publique [i.e., authentic] interpretation, then they all."

That Bunyan's affinity with this enlightened cobbler was noticed by his admirers is clear from the advertisement of his works and a brief history of his mechanick career, appended to the 1692 edition of How's *Sufficiencie of the Spirits Teaching*,[65] and from the fact that Bunyan preached in How's church at the invitation of Stephen More, How's successor in the pastoral cure.[66] In its church book this congregation lamented the attitude which the world had displayed toward its mechanick ministry, who were "falsly represented & brought into contempt as dangerous Persons & of no Account & reproached by calling the eminent Servants of God in ye Days past: Billy ye Bellows Mender, Tom ye Taylor, Simon ye Cobler, Tinker, & I know not what names."[67]

To cast luster upon his mechanick position and social inferiority, Bunyan followed the others of his kind in calling attention to the meanness of the Saviour's person and trade and to the humble condition of the apostles.[68] "When he was born, he made himself, as he saith, a worm, or one of no reputation; he became the reproach and bye-word of the people; he was born in a stable, laid in a manger, earned his bread with his labour, being by trade a carpenter."[69] Of his own similar estate Bunyan could speak with a grandeur imparted by the consciousness of apostolic and messianic precedent: "for though I be poor, and of no repute in the world, as to outward things; yet through grace I have learned by the example of the apostle to preach the truth; and also to work with my hands, both for mine own living, and for those that are with me."[70]

Bunyan's habitual emphasis upon his lowliness appears to be the product of an exaggerated modesty until its adherence to the practice of the devout makes it evident that, far from being modest, it was at once boastful, in its implication of divine preference, and defiant, in reaction against worldly disdain. When on the scaffold before his execution for seditious activities, John James, the Baptist weaver-preacher, boasted that he was but a man of weak parts, neither learned nor knowing:

> I am born of very mean Parents, and I may say as Gideon did, Judges 6. 15. Behold my Family is poor, and I am the least in my Fathers House: I came indeed of a mean Family, the meanest that I know among the people of God, but my Parents were very careful to have me brought up in the fear of God.[71]

An equally class-conscious expression of the virtues of the humble lot is to be found in the biography of Abraham Cheare, the Baptist fuller-preacher:

> He was born at Plymouth, of mean yet honest Parentage, is not by Kindred or any Alliance related to any Person or Family of any Note at all, was not bred up to Learning at any University, or sent any where to Travel for Education, or Experience; but contrariwise, brought up and kept diligently by his parents to Work, in the poor yet honest Trade of a Fuller. . . .[72]

The familiar account in *Grace Abounding* of Bunyan's admirable obscurity is one with those of James and Cheare, and can be understood only as a symptom of mechanick consciousness of class:

> For my Descent then, It was, as is well known by many, of a low and inconsiderable generation; my father's house being of that rank that is meanest, and most despised of all the families in the Land. Wherefore I have not here, as others, to boast of Noble Blood, or of an high-born state according to the flesh; though all things considered, I magnifie the heavenly Majesty, for that by this door he brought me into this World, to partake of the Grace and Life that is in Christ by the Gospel.
>
> But yet, notwithstanding the meanness and inconsiderableness of my Parents, it pleased God to put it into their hearts, to put me to School, to learn both to read and write; the which I also attained, according to the rate of other poor men's children. . . .[73]

Though he resented Thomas Paul's reference to his rank, Bunyan also found it to be a cause for pride, since by the standards of heaven the low became the high. As he professed, Bunyan called attention to his pedigree in this passage of *Grace Abounding* in order to increase the glory of God, but until it is understood that by this he meant God's glory through His choice and afflation of a mechanick instrument, the full significance is not clear. When, in his Preface to *A Few Sighs from Hell,* Bunyan said: "I am thine, if thou be not ashamed to own me, because of my low and contemptible descent in the world;" and when in the second edition he changed this to: "I am thine to serve in the Lord Jesus," he meant according to his social philosophy the same thing.[74] It was this attitude of defiant pride which made Bunyan describe himself as "that poor and contemptible creature John Bunyan of Bedford,"[75] and which actuated his patterned description of the saints as a people "despised and contemptible in the eyes of the world," an expression equally common in the mouths of the Quakers.[76] The admission of lowliness in defiance of the standards of the world had become a boast of excellence; and it is only through a consideration of their class-conditioned mentality that we can comprehend the uses of apparent self-abasement to which the mechanicks were habitually addicted.

But the proud abasement to which, even without the disdain of society, the principles of Christianity would have inclined them was complicated by a shame for which society was entirely responsible. So great an odium attached through their mechanick character to the more popular sects that many found it difficult, even after enlightenment, to reconcile themselves to the ignominy of their new association. John Crook, the Quaker, called this ordeal his crucifixion,[77] and Thomas Lamb, who deserted the more reputable Independents for the Baptists, made it clear that no worldly considerations had prompted his descent:

Alas, alas, I considered beforehand, that this way is every where spoken against, and the generality of the Professors of it of small esteem, for learning, parts, or any thing that commendeth men to the world: their garb and cast that of the Disciples, Luke 6. 20. *Blessed be ye poor:* Now, that they were exclaimed on by the learned in their writings, and frequently in Pulpits at this day, their name cast out as evil, and hated in a manner of all men, that if times of persecution for conscience come, they are like to be the first sufferers: So that I had many struglings and wrestlings with the flesh, before I could get the victory to submit to it; nay, the truth is, had not the truth concerning it struck my conscience, and the light shone into my judgement with that clearness, that I could by no means avoid it with peace, I had never forsaken my old standing, which was more honourable, easie, and every way more acceptable to the outward man.[78]

Shame haunted the way and dogged the traces of the godly mechanick, and as Bunyan complained, had turned many a delicate soul from the path.[79] Its painful effect upon the sensitive is illustrated in the experience of Faithful in the Valley of Humiliation, through which like Bunyan, the mechanick, he was forced to pass.[80] In this unhappy place Shame accosted the saint and insinuated that religion was a pitiful, low, sneaking business for a man to mind, a thing that sundered him from brave spirits and exposed him to the ridicule of society. Since few of the mighty, rich, or noble were of Faithful's opinion, Shame persisted, it was clear that religion meant fellowship with the lowly and estrangement from the great: he "objected the base and low estate and condition of those that were chiefly the Pilgrims of the times in which they lived: also their Ignorance and want of understanding in all natural Science." Profoundly moved by this conspiracy to put him to blush before all men, Faithful was able to comfort himself, however, with the thought that "the poor man that loveth Christ, is richer than the greatest man in the World that hates him." With this consolation and not a little pride he resigned himself to the difficulties of his journey, and even sang, as he paced this inelegant valley.

CHAPTER V

A FEW SIGHS FROM HELL

. . . frogs and toads, that croak'd the Jews
From Pharaoh and his brick-kilns loose,
And flies and mange, that set them free
From task-masters and slavery,
Were likelier to do the feat,
In any indifferent man's conceit.

Hudibras, III, ii, 1221.

To the bewilderment of the comfortably fed, the obscure and the hungry appeared to be discontented with their portion. Burdened by what they presumed to call economic injustice, saddened by social inequality, and animated by the favor of heaven, the vulgar relieved their passions in occasional riots, which were carefully suppressed, but chiefly in those conventional sighs which their leaders and agitators, the lay preachers, formulated and vented for the satisfaction of the inarticulate. Their own position had prejudiced these preachers against rank and learning, as we have observed, and as leaders of the people they made the troubles of the oppressed their own. They adopted for the expression of a common complaint the symbols and patterns which an old tradition conveniently provided. But since in substance and manner their complaint resembled that of the friars, the Lollards, and the German Anabaptists, the alarm of the conservative knew no bounds; for they saw the menace of a new Münster in the preaching of inspired cobblers and tinkers, who, like John of Leyden, made a religious issue of a fancied trouble and held forth the dangerous hope of a heaven on earth. These fears were idle; the energies of the oppressed dissipated into ineffectual mutterings against the rich and the mighty, and the propaganda of the preachers is of significance today not as the incentive to a historic insurrection but as the monument over their hopes. Our patient archaeology must discover the nature, and our attentive scrutiny the meaning, of this monument.

The economic condition of the mechanick classes after 1640 was a reason for their discontent. The Civil Wars had bettered the situation of the landed and mercantile classes in whose economic, political, and religious interests they were waged, but they had failed to remedy the plight of the laborers, artisans, farmers, and small tradesmen, who found the burdens of inclosures and tithes augmented by higher prices and taxes. The poor had been made worse able to live than before, as Winstanley pointed out,[1] and a cynical pamphleteer of 1647 asked: "Is not all the Controversie Whose Slaves the poore shall bee?"[2] From 1640 to 1688 prices were generally high; whereas the income of the lower classes was meager, often below the level of subsistence.[3] The substantial classes, the landlords, merchants, lawyers, gentry, and clergy, lived in comparative luxury, but the laborers found their 4*d* to 10*d* a day sufficient only for the nourishment of gloom.

The accounts of these conditions by humanitarians like John Cook and Peter Chamberlen reveal the extremity of the poor,[4] and the excellent advice of Richard Baxter to rack-renting landlords and discouraged laborers also has this value. While he urged upon the starving tenant the necessity of Christian patience, Baxter counseled the landlord to moderate his rapacity lest the desperation of the poor lead them to fanatical violence and to the destruction of privilege and culture: "If any would raise an Army to extirpate knowledge and religion [i.e., Presbyterianism], the Tinkers and Sowgawters and cratecarryers and beggars and bargemen and all the rabble that cannot reade . . . will be the forwardest to come in to such a militia."[5] A landed proprietor himself, Baxter expressed the conservative fear of a confusion of economics and godliness in a new Münster. Though the poor did not rise in armed revolt, their starvation was seasoned with resentment, and to the alarm of their oppressors, it was evident that they were ill content to lead the life of quiet desperation.

"Their poverty carrying them out to unseemly expression of those in Authority,"[6] men of low and mean callings issued petitions like *The Husbandmans Plea Against Tithes,* 1647,[7] with apparent faith in the utility of protests against profiteering, hoarding, taxes, tithes, free-quarter, inclosures, and rack rents. "Our Flesh," one broadside petitioner complained, "is that whereupon you Rich men live, and wherewith you decke and adorne your selves . . . Necessity dissolves all Lawes and Government, and Hunger will breake through stone Walls."[8] The author of *Englands Troublers Troubled,* 1648,[9] detected a confederacy of the rich and potent to enslave the poor:

Ye insolent and deceitful men . . . ye have by corruption in government, by unjust and unequall lawes, by fraud, cousenage, tyranny and oppression gotten most of the land of this distressed and enslaved nation into your ravenous clawes, ye have by monopolies, usuries & combinations engrossed all the wealth, monies and houses into your possessions, yea and inclosed our commons in most Counties. . . . How excessively and unconscionably have ye advanced your land rents in the Country, and house and shop rents in the City within these fourty years? How many families have ye eaten out at doores and made beggers, some with racke rents, and others with engrossing of leases, and monopolizing of trades?

With the ill-fated attempt of the Diggers in 1649 under Gerrard Winstanley, who had been driven out of trade by the rich and powerful, this dominantly secular kind of protest against economic injustice attained its climax and end.[10] To Winstanley's proclamation that "the earth was not made purposely for you to be Lords of it, and we to be your Slaves, Servants, and Beggers; But it was to be a common Livelihood to all, without respect of persons," the Norman landlords had replied by a resort to violence and by the confiscation of his cows.

After 1650 the discontent of the oppressed was usually sponsored by the sects, and though this disguise made social dissatisfaction no more acceptable to Cromwell[11] and the landlords than the more secular complaint of Winstanley, it was better suited to the taste of the devout. The secularity of the Levellers and Diggers had alienated most of the saints, who preferred, like many earlier Christians, to maintain religious appearances in their economic, social, and political protests.[12] For the saints the class struggle needed the dignity of divine auspices, and as the miserable of today look for their sanction to Karl Marx and *The Communist Manifesto,* their seventeenth-century predecessors looked to Jesus and the Bible.[13]

The religious man may remain only half aware, or by virtue of a rationalization, quite unaware of the social or economic motives which determine his sectarian adherence. In the seventeenth century religion at once gave the masses a voice and obscured their vision. However deep his social and economic trouble, the sectarian made of it even to himself a religious trouble, and confused by his own translation, failed to comprehend the original. Once transformed into Dives, the rich oppressor of the poor became a religious portent, impending over hell, rather than the neighboring landlord, who gave to the symbol of Dives its relevance.

Religious symbolism provided the sectarian with the most natural, the most passionate, and the best available medium for the expression of all things. And since the imagery of the Bible was the work of the socially minded prophets and apostles, it was well enough suited to the needs of later malcontents. The biblical quarrel with the rich and the mighty lent the weight of divine approval to subsequent protest; and the tradition which came to the seventeenth century from the friars and peasants established the propriety of biblical symbols for the uses of social complaint.[14]

Even the comparatively secular protests of the Levellers and Diggers, however, were less of an aberration from the religious mode of the time than is at first apparent. Both parties grew out of the religious ferment, employed religious terminology in their earlier and even in their later tracts, and appear to have subsided after their failure into the consolation of the sects.[15] Revelation had dictated a social plan to Winstanley, who called Jesus Christ the head Leveller,[16] and who expressed his quarrel with society first in the imagery of the Scriptures, and only later, by an unusual clarification, directly in social and economic terms. The upper classes appeared as the Beast and the Whore in the millenarian imagery of his early works, and their oppression of the poor as the forty-two months of prostration and the slaying of the witnesses; Winstanley's indictment of Adam's covetousness gave devious expression to his economic ideas.[17] Without the symbolic indirection of these early tracts, Winstanley's later writings said essentially the same things: the oppression of the witnesses by the Beast had become the Norman landlord's domination of the poor, and the covetousness of Adam the economic selfishness of the upper classes. Through this instructive evolution in Winstanley's terminology much that would be obscure in the work of the lay preachers is made clear.

Where the Diggers abandoned the preaching of social injustice and Utopian dream, the new guides of the submerged, the lay preachers, took up the work. The discontent was the same, but the idiom differed. Of the new preachers of an old dissatisfaction, the Quakers, who appeared as the Diggers subsided, were the most conspicuous, but Ranters, Muggletonians, Baptists, and others of the godly were of this fellowship, and of this fellowship John Bunyan was one.

Many of these enthusiasts knew themselves to have been commissioned by God to preach for the poor against the rich, and by their propaganda to create enmity toward the upper classes out of the discontent of the lower. When on trial in Cambridge in 1654 as a vagabond husbandman-servant, Richard Hubberthorn, the Quaker, said that he had been sent by the Lord to declare against all unrighteousness and

against all those who lay heavie burthens upon the poor by deceipt and oppression, and against all who live in pride, and idleness, and fulnesse of bread, by whom the creation is devoured, and many made poor by your meanes, and you who are rich, who live at ease,

and in pleasure, you live upon the labours of the poor, and lay
heavie burthens upon them, grievous to be born, and you may the
poor complain of, but they who doe receive our testimony there is
the heavie burthens taken off, and the poor is eased, and whosoever
do receive the truth in the love of it, which we freely declare from the
Lord, and hath this worlds good, he cannot see the poor in need nor
want, nor beg their bread, but the truth where it is received opens
the bowles of compassion, and takes off oppression and the heavie
burthen which the poor groans under.[18]

Filled with the generous impulses of settlement-house workers,
a few moralistic humanitarians, like Peter Chamberlen, Samuel
Richardson, and Richard Baxter, also noticed the state of the
poor. But Baxter was so fearful of being associated, by virtue of
his appeal for the poor, with their own enthusiastic spokesmen,
that he took care to forestall suspicion: "You think that this doctrine savours of the Levellers or Quakers," he said to the landlords, and you may say that "all this is but from the Levelling
Spirit of Popularity and by lifting up the vulgar to take down the
nobility and gentry. . . ."[19] His meticulous disclaimer indicates
the reputation of the enthusiastic preachers, who appeared to the
conservative as nothing less than an itinerant order of Johns of
Leyden.

The antinomian Ranters devoutly assumed in 1649 and 1650
the cause of the oppressed. Actuated by a superiority to the
accepted moral laws and by a democratic conviction of the brotherhood of man, the antinomians assailed, when they could not
avoid, the distinctions and ways of society. The reputed sexual
orgies of the Ranters scandalized the good and the pure, and
testified to a sharp severance from the uses of respectability. By
their wild emergences from a proper obscurity into the streets of
the metropolis, shouting their bold class hatreds, they added
anxiety to the disgust of the delicately bred, who unwillingly
beheld but by no means condoned their excesses. They deserved
the stern reprobation of the moralist as of the orthodox divine;

and the charge of economic radicalism was not idle: "They taught," said a journalist, "that it was quite contrary to the end of the Creation, to Appropriate any thing to any Man or Woman; but that there ought to be a Community of all things."[20]

Early in 1650 London became aware of Abiezer Coppe, once an indefatigable dipper,[21] but now a Ranter, who bore an earnest message. His *Fiery Flying Roll*,[22] which was published in two parts in that year, told his story, constituted his manifesto, and by its high rhapsodic style testified to his inspiration. This double tract was, he said, the fruit of a complicated vision in which he had been privileged to hear celestial voices and to receive from an unearthly hand a roll of paper, which, after he had piously devoured it, broiled in his stomach, and came forth in the shape of this tract to level the rich and the mighty. Through Coppe the Lord said, "Howl, howl, ye nobles, howl honourable, howl ye rich men . . . bow downe, bow downe . . . before those poore, nasty, lousie, ragged wretches. . . ." You have feared sword-levelling, and man-levelling, but now you will be levelled by me, the Lord, the real Leveller. "The plague of God is in your purses, barns, houses, ye fat swine of the earth." You shall give your gold and chattles to the poor and hold all things in common; for the day is at hand when "guts will be let out, womens bellies ripped, especially Gammer Demases."

For twelve days Coppe had been hasting about the London streets, but his reception had been cold, especially by the Baptists, who, considering him mad or drunk, he complained, had refused him the use of their meeting-houses in which to prophesy. Denied this innocent exercise, he went about, he said,

charging many Coaches, many hundreds of men and women of the greater rank, in the open streets, with my hand stretched out, my hat cock't up, staring on them as if I would look through them, gnashing with my teeth at some of them, and day and night with a huge loud voice proclaiming the day of the Lord throughout London and Southwark.[23]

But custom dulls the edge of interest, and London and Southwark appear to have remained calm, even when Coppe, weary of
baffling the rich, demonstrated, like the blessed St. Francis, the
proper attitude toward the poor by embracing the more interest-
ingly loathsome. He fondled one, he said, "who had no more nose
on his face, then I have on the back of my hánd, (but only two
little holes in the place where the nose used to stand) . And no
more eyes to be seen then on the back of my hand."[24] This Christian act made it manifest that the Lord had chosen things that
are not to bring to nought things that are.

Exasperation and fatigue moved Parliament in February, 1650,
after a month of this, to order the burning of Coppe's books for
their many "horrid blasphemies and damnable and detestable
opinions,"[25] and Coppe, now under detention, was noticed by
the newspapers. *The Weekly Intelligencer* mentioned

the arrogant and wild deportment of Mr. Copp the great Ranter,
who made the Fiery Roll, who being lately brought before the Committee of Examinations, refused to be uncovered, and disguised himself into a madnesse, flinging Apples and Pears about the roome,
whereupon the Committee returned him to Newgate from whence
he came.[26]

All passions spent in the damps of Newgate, Coppe uttered during the following year a recantation.[27] In this way the authorities
discouraged the spokesmen of the people, whose aspirations and
complaint, even when sanctioned by the Lord, failed to penetrate
a skeptical obstinacy.

The other Ranters, for the most part mechanicks,[28] shared
Coppe's social opinions. Their understandings enlarged by their
own social and economic distress, these enthusiasts spoke for
their class with an emotion born of experience. Joseph Salmon
had urged those of inferior rank to destroy gentry and nobility,
but he was also imprisoned, forced to recant and to retire to
mystical contemplation in the country.[29] Jacob Bauthumley was
obsessed by the inferiority of mechanicks,[30] and Richard Coppin,

whom Coppe had proudly described as an illiterate, demanded for the downtrodden an equal division of the spoil of the wars, and looked to Jesus as the restorer of popular rights.[31] That "despised instrument," George Foster, or Jacob Israel as he called himself, was subject to trances in which he saw the evil of the rich, the bondage of the poor, and the activities of God, "the mighty Leveller," who reduced mountains to the level of the plains.[32] In one of these visions he beheld a man with a sword on a white apocalyptical horse, "cutting down all men and women, that he met with, that were higher then the midle sort, and raised up those that were lower then the midle sort and made them all Equal, and cried out, equalitie, equalitie, in that I have now made all men alike."[33] T. Tany, a goldsmith to the carnal apprehensions of the world, but known to the Lord as Theaurau-john, high priest of the Jews, was illiterate, poor, and also addicted to the cause of the oppressed.[34] Edward Ellis, long a servant to great persons, turned on his former masters to defend the interests of Christ's poor against the rich.[35] This popular dislike of the rich, the honorable, and the learned was shared by Lodowick Muggleton, a tailor and one of the two last witnesses mentioned in Scripture;[36] and his difficult adherent, Laurence Clarkson, formerly a Baptist and a Ranter, who signed himself "a friend of the inslaved Communality," approved of Winstanley's digging and abhorred the landlord and the broker.[37]

There was reason for the confusion of Quaker with Ranter because, except for their tiresome theological and ethical differences, the two sects had much in common to the casual eye: both were prone to enormities of conduct and to the rudest excesses of enthusiasm, and both preached the cause of the oppressed against the mighty of the world.[38] But before respectability overtook them the Quakers were devoted almost as a sect, not as individuals, to social propaganda. Organized society recoiled with distaste from the unseemly ways and message of the early Quaker itinerants, who were thought to menace decency, government,

and the home.[39] By their social meanness, by the boisterous violence of their demonstrations, by their disconcerting habit of
going about naked in public, by their practice of entering
churches and defiling the formal worship of God with riot and
tumult, by their ostentatious indifference to the amenities, and
by their disreputable vagrancy, society was perturbed. The religious sentiments of the conservative were troubled by the theological eccentricity of the Quakers, but their social sensibilities
were more deeply wounded. They beheld a social danger in the
Quakers, and by a triumph of indirection, they arrested them for
heresy, blasphemy, vagrancy, disturbance of the peace, and for
impersonating the Saviour. Desperately they locked the Quakers
in disagreeable jails, but insistent upon martyrdom, the Quakers
liked it. Cromwell and the other authorities, who were ready to
tolerate only quiet discontent, were able by their ceaseless diligence only to mitigate but not to remove the threat of a larger
disturbance. Until the Restoration the undiscouraged Friends
persisted in the usages of peace and love, flourishing under universal disapprobation, hated by other radicals and by conservatives alike, by the Baptists for doctrinal reasons, and by more
respectable believers for reasons both doctrinal and social. As
Edward Burrough said, during the course of an attack upon the
Norman oppressors of the poor, the Quaker preacher was considered "a sower of sedition, or a subverter of the Laws, a turner
of the World up-side down, a pestilent fellow."[40]

Their ranks recruited largely from the radical antinomians,
who had substituted for their disappointed hopes in the army the
pleasures of violent mysticism, and from men of advanced political opinions like Lilburne,[41] the Quakers became in the fifties
a center of social and economic extremism, and continued in
their peculiar and spiritual way the work of the earlier radicals.
Like their godly predecessors, they had been sent by the Lord
to testify against oppression, but they carried their symbolic
demonstrations to levels of studied dramatic effectiveness to

which only the more talented among the Ranters could by a solitary genius attain. They ordinarily directed their propaganda against what they called respect of persons and the grinding of the poor.

Those irregularities of conduct and acts of boorishness by which the Quakers at once injured their reputation in the world and advanced it in heaven, were committed with premeditation in their campaign against respect of persons, which they saw in all the distinctions, politeness, titles of honor, dress, and ceremonies of society. Their pious enmity to all that demonstrated the inequality of man appeared conspicuously in their symbolic refusal to remove their hats and to use the formal modes of direct address. For an inquisitive justice during one of his many martyrdoms, James Nayler biblically defined respect of persons as class distinction: "If I see one in goodly apparel and a gold Ring and see one in poor and vile Raiment and say to him in fine apparel, Sit thou in a higher place then the poor, I am partial."[42] And James Parnell said: "We are accused to be destructive to all Superiority and Honour, Breeding and Manners, because we cannot put off our hats, nor follow the fashions of the world, nor respect any Persons, but speakes the plain word to any one, Rich or Poor."[43] The Quakers, he continued, could not conform to usages by which Satan had confirmed an unnatural inequality among men and fostered all tyranny and oppression.

For amongst the Great and Rich ones of the earth, they will either *thou* or *you* one another if they be of equal degree, as they call it; but if a man of low degree in the earth come to speak to any of them then he must *you* the rich man, but the Rich man will *thou* him. . . . If a poor Labouring man come before one that you call a Minister, he must also show respect by *youing* him, whereas the priest *thous* him.[44]

From their obstinate disinclination to remove their hats before magistrates, and from their refusal to use titles of honor or even the accepted nomenclature of the world, it was natural for their observers to conclude that the Quakers "levelled all conditions and relations, making all things common upon this accompt."[45]

The Quaker addiction to nakedness, a source of endless scandal, was, like their stubbornness about hats, but another of their symbolic messages to society. In Richard Farnworth's *The Pure Language of the Spirit*,[46] a work largely devoted to *thee* and *thou*, the grammar of leveling, there is a note on this extraordinary custom. The Lord had sent some of His children to remove their garments in public as a sign "that so should all the pride and glory of the world and of the pomp and Egyptian craft be cast off and layd aside." Hence, aside from the simple gratification of exhibitionism, these harmless people experienced the pleasures of the social propagandist.

Like the tracts of the Baptist mechanicks, those of the Quakers are full of asperity toward the learning of the world in which they saw not only an infringement upon the purity of inspiration but a further mark of class distinction.[47] Occasionally the impulse of the Spirit led them to demonstrate against the learned as when two Quaker women appeared in Oxford to denounce the pride, covetousness, and popishness of the students.[48] But they were put under the pump and their clothing dirtied in the gutters, a treatment so discourteous as to make untenable their contention that the amenities were peculiar to the upper classes.

Against the grinding of the poor by the wealthy, and by lawyers, clerics, and governors, who had gained riches, influence, and carnal glory by covetousness, the Quakers were equally vehement.[49] Nayler asked:

Was the creature made for that end, to set your hearts upon them; to heape together, out of the reach of the poore and needy; and he who can get the greatest share, should become the greatest man; and all that have little, shall bow downe and worship him . . . Are you not fallen from the estate wherein you was Created? for it was not so from the beginning; for he who made all things good, made all men of one mold, and one blood, to dwell on the face of the Earth; and gave them power over the works of his hands, not to heape together,

to set your hearts upon them: but to use them in his service . . .
You that live in your pride, painting your selves in your costly Apparrell, in venting new wayes and fashions, to make you seem glorious in
the carnall eyes of others, that they may worship you . . . You lustful ones, which lives of the fat of the Earth, whose care is onely to
satisfie the Flesh, and the Lusts thereof, your curious devised dishes,
Dives-like . . . the cryes of the poore which you have oppressed,
whose labours you have spent upon your lusts, the Rust of your Gold
and Silver doth bear witnesse against you. Repent, repent, cast off
your gorgious Apparrell, and guird you with mourning; Let your
Songs of Musicke be turned into howling; your Banqueting and
Feasting, into Fasting, for the Lord is wrath with you, and the Fire
is begun allready.[50]

General attacks upon the rich oppressor, of which the above is a
fair specimen, were supplemented by more specific arraignments
of landlords for their racking of rents, their pride and covetousness. In these economic and moral protestations the Quakers
resembled not only Winstanley but the friars of the fourteenth
century from whom the tradition and pattern of this kind of
social complaint appear to have been handed down by the lower
ministry through the intervening years.[51]

Woe, woe, woe, to the oppressors of the Earth, who grind the faces
of the poor, who rack & stretch out their Rents till the poor with all
the sweat of their brows and hard labour can scarce get Bread to eat,
and Raiment to put on, while they for the satisfying of their gulf of
pride, and delicacies, and gluttony, and drunkenness . . . stil cry
give, give, and there is no end to their covetousness nor no natural
affection to their oppressed Brother. These are the Pharoah's, the
Task-Masters of the Earth, who cause the peoples hearts to cry and
groan under the heavy yoke of their oppression; and God will in
time hear the groanings of the whole Creation, and then wo, wo, wo,
to you who have been such oppressors and hard-hearted Task-
Masters.[52]

While the Quaker itinerants were bringing the word of release
and encouragement to the oppressed, some of the Baptists, a sect
harboring both conservatives and radicals and men of the middle

as well as the lower classes, were spreading in their less ostentatious way a similar social doctrine. The Quakers and the radical Baptists of the lower and the enthusiastic classes were brothers beneath the theology.[53] As we have observed, the tracts of Samuel How and John Spencer were dedicated to the warfare of the classes, and Benjamin Keach, the literary tailor, had much to say against riches, covetousness, and honor.[54] Among the Baptist Fifth Monarchy men, as we shall see in the next chapter, social problems were accorded an attention almost equal to that of the equally radical Quakers. And enthusiasts like Vavasor Powell and John Gibbs were accused of animosity toward gentry, lawyers, and the learned.[55] William Erbury, M.A., the Baptist-Seeker, devoted himself with passion to the cause of the small farmer, laborer, and tradesman, for whom he preached against the wealthy a series of sermons on appropriate texts from Isaiah and the Psalms: "Upon this God began . . . to roar in my Spirit, and I to hear nothing within me but the cry of the oppressed . . . 'twas told me both waking and sleeping that God would break in pieces the oppressor."[56] And the radical William Dell, perhaps more a Seeker than a Baptist, lent his enthusiasm to the defense of the poor.[57] But because few of the Baptist mechanicks were as lavishly addicted to print as the Quakers, most of their social preaching was lost with the winds to which they had intrusted it. Of these mechanicks Bunyan was one of the most prolific writers, and perhaps because of this, it is chiefly in his works that the social contentions, which had occupied Ranters and Quakers, may be traced.

Both because he had been subjected to similar conditions and because as a suggestible reader he was aware of the current patterns for the expression of discontent, Bunyan wrote about the unpleasantness of society in the manner of the Ranters and Quakers, whom, for doctrinal reasons, he particularly disliked. In his early work *A Few Sighs from Hell*, 1658, Bunyan said what the Quakers had said about the riches, selfishness, and pride of the gentry; and occasional references to the mighty and the poor and low impart color and social heat to many of his later works, especially the major ones, for the understanding of which some knowledge of his attitude is necessary. As the humbleness of his early career was succeeded by an agreeable prosperity, his treatment of social problems became less like that of the Quakers, however, and more like that of the moralistic humanitarians such as Baxter. But while the consolation of increasing respectability removed from the work of this pleasant period much of the asperity that he had once shared with the Quakers, a resentment born of unfortunate experience was carried over from his youth to add a more than humanitarian vehemence to his later writings. Inclining at successive periods toward the radical and the humanitarian modes, Bunyan occupies a middle position among the champions of the poor, and a definite but not too conspicuous place in the history of the religious expression of social discontent.

Bunyan's early writings were indebted for much of their character to the economic and social inferiority of their author, an itinerant and indigent tinker, "the Son of an honest poor Labouring Man, who, like Adam Unparadiced, had all the World before him to get his Bread in."[58] His income was undoubtedly irregular and insignificant when in 1660 the appeal of martyrdom became of greater weight than the needs of his wife and children, who were left to the charity of neighbors, while with the spiritual elevation peculiar to incarcerated piety, Bunyan tagged laces and composed poetical effusions for the customary but small reward given to these products of industry. Together with economic distress, which imprisonment aggravated, Bunyan had experienced the social disdain with which mechanicks were received; and from his social and economic discomfort he formed conclusions about the injustice of a social system in which tinkers found it difficult to prosper. His wife, whose opinion Bunyan shared and reported, said to Justice Hales: "because he is a Tinker, and a poor man; therefore he is despised, and cannot have justice."[59] It was natural for a man indicted as a preaching laborer and described in court as "a pestilent fellow"[60] to resent the class system to which his troubles were to be traced, and to look, like his wife, for vengeance at the coming of the Lord.[61] But after 1672 in his time of greater prosperity, "though his Earthly Treasures swelled not to excess; he always had sufficient, to live decently and credibly. . . ."[62] No longer afflicted with the pains of poverty, he felt, however, a sympathy for the poor, and out of his earlier sufferings at the hands of the covetous, he appears to have formulated a conscientious objection to money as the root of evil. This medieval moral principle led him to refuse "a more plentiful Income to keep his Station,"[63] and to decline all other opportunities of material advantage.[64]

The year 1658, when Bunyan wrote *A Few Sighs from Hell,* was one of high prices and low wages,[65] which, together with the poverty and position of the author, account for the nature of this tract. By means of this exposition of Luke, chapter 16, the parable of Lazarus and Dives or the rich man and the beggar, Bunyan expressed, in accordance with the symbolic usages of the sects, his hatred of the upper classes. "For Jesus Christ's sake," he said, "do not slight the truth, because it is discovered in a parable."[66] There was no reason, however, to anticipate either the neglect or the misunderstanding of an audience accustomed to the discovery of radical social and economic meaning in every allusion to Lazarus and Dives. Quakers, Ranters, Diggers, and many others had used Dives and Lazarus so habitually in their religious discussions of economics and society that a tractarian reference to rich oppressors and their victims without the invocation of these useful symbols was almost unthinkable.[67] The expository value of this parable was recognized by all godly economists; but to the mechanick classes, whose pleasantly heated fancies were captivated by their own elevation with Lazarus to Abraham's capacious bosom and by the uncomfortable fate of Dives and his kind, the value of this parable was also consolatory, as Benjamin Harris implied in his excellent verses on the subject:

> Poor men rejoyce whilst rich men houl and cry,
> Such is the pleasure of the Deity.
> Then cease thy tears, poor wretched soul, and lend
> An ear unto poor Lazarus thy friend.[68]

The value of Dives and Lazarus to Bunyan was at once expository and consolatory. In these symbols he saw the opportunity both to express his sorrow and rage over the treatment of mechanicks and to indicate the damnation which the wealthy deserved for their possession of riches and for their grinding of the poor. Of his Lazarus, who represents both the poor man and the mechanick preacher, and whose lowly virtues were enriched by didactic impulses of which Dives would have none, Bunyan said:

Take notice of this, you that are despisers of the least of the Lazaruses of our Lord Jesus Christ; it may be now you are loth to receive these little ones of his, because they are not gentlemen, because they cannot, with Pontius Pilate, speak Hebrew, Greek, and Latin. Nay, they must not, shall not speak to them to admonish them, and all because of this. Though now the gospel of the Lord Jes. Christ may be preached to them freely, and for nothing . . . though now they will not own, regard, or embrace these Christian proffers of the glorious truth of Jesus, because they came out of some of the basest earthen vessels; yet the time is coming, when they will both sigh and cry.[69]

Dives would regret in hell his rejection of this poor but blessed man, and for all his wealth, fine houses, dainty dishes, pleasures, and prosperous companions, and for all his worldly greatness and influence, would find his torment made more exquisite by an ingenious device of the Lord's, an enforced and miserable contemplation of Lazarus amid the baroque felicities of Bunyan's heaven. Then to the amusement of the fortunate participants in a patriarchal refreshment the rich man would say: "O how loth am I, to burn and fry in hell, while you are singing in heaven."[70]

It was natural for Bunyan to proceed beyond the difficulties of
the mechanick preacher to the usual sectarian conclusions about
the economic and social system under which the oppressed
emitted their sighs. Although he handsomely conceded that not
all rich men were bad nor all poor men good,[71] his assumption is
that the upper classes were to be damned for their ways and for
rejecting the gospel which the poor generally received; and the
significance of the word *rich* in this tract is literal: "had not God
given such a discovery of the sad condition of those that are for
the most part rich men, we should have concluded absolutely
that the rich are the blessed men."[72] To Bunyan as to the Quakers
the important sins of Dives, the rich man, were two, pride and
covetousness.[73]

By pride Bunyan intended what the Quakers called respect of
person, the evils of the class system, distinctions in dress, food,
and deportment, especially the haughtiness which distinguished
the well-born:

Methinks to see how the great ones of the world will go strutting up
and down the streets sometimes, it makes me wonder. Surely they look
upon themselves to be the only happy men; but it is because they judge
according to outward appearance . . . "Not many wise men after
the flesh, not many mighty, not many noble are called," 1 Co. i. 26.[74]

Splendid in their new suits, sated with delicious fare, and wanton
in their sports, the rich consorted with the wicked and went to the
other side of the hedge in their ostentatious avoidance of the low
and godly.[75] The image with which George Fox and the author
of *Englands Troublers Troubled* expressed a similar resentment[76] recurred significantly in Bunyan's complaint that the
rich preferred the society of their dogs to that of the saints.

In the accumulation of money "by hook and by crook, as we
say, by swearing, lying, cozening, stealing, covetousness, extor-
tion,"[77] Bunyan saw the cause of oppression, by which the poor
were ground, of profligacy, by which they were annoyed, and of
moral and religious obliquity, by which they were martyred.

How many pounds do some men spend in a year on their dogs, when in the meanwhile the poor saints of God may starve for hunger? They will build houses for their dogs, when the saints must be glad to wander, and lodge in dens and caves of the earth, He. xi. 38. and if they be in any of their houses for the hire, they will warn them out or eject them, or pull down the house over their heads, rather than not rid themselves of such tenants.[78]

Some landlords may have had so great an intolerance of sectarians as to dispossess them upon discovery of their pious inclination, but it is more likely that Bunyan had made a religious issue out of an economic problem, and that he contemplated the progress of inclosures and rack-renting through eyes colored by a warm enthusiasm. Landlords, who were both covetous and sensible, demolished houses and evicted tenants to inclose lands, not as an unprofitable gesture against piety. In neighboring Leicestershire there had been recent riots against inclosure,[79] and feeling against landlords was high throughout the entire country. In a Bedfordshire petition of 1659, the year after Bunyan wrote this tract, the economic background of his complaint is apparent. Parliament was asked to remove the Norman yoke, to

take some effectual course for the alteration of Coppy-hold tenures (as great a mark of Tyranny) that the poor Tenants thereof may not be left to the mercy of the Lords of such Mannors (whilst great men are made free) but may all have a proportionable taste (in their capacities) of the benefit of a Commonwealths freedom.[80]

But to Bunyan the oppressing landlord was the persecuting landlord, as to him the poor man was godly, the rich man impious. On each recurrence of the tenant-landlord problem in this tract, Bunyan translated it into the province of religion:

Oh what red lines will those be against those ungodly landlords, that so keep under their poor tenants that they dare not go out to hear the word, for fear their rent should be raised, or they turned out of their houses. What sayest thou, landlord, will it not cut thy soul when thou shalt see that thou couldst not be content to miss of heaven thyself, but thou must labour to hinder others also?[81]

The wealth and position upon which the landlord relied secured rather than tempered his condemnation before the tribunal of class antipathy and economic discomfort. Dives lay deep in Bunyan's hell, but this simple remedy for the injustice of pride and covetousness, while excellent in the next world, was ineffectual in this. Hence, though Bunyan did not intend it so, the title of his tract might be taken as an allusion not to the fate of the rich oppressor, but to the unremedied condition of the saint, to whom John Gibbs said in his Preface, "Thou hast all thy hell here."[82]

Dives and Lazarus reappeared to illustrate the social implication of many of Bunyan's other tracts,[83] notably *The Heavenly Footman,* in which the author mentioned his *Few Sighs from Hell* and expressed his view of society, clearly, but with that moderation which served to distinguish him from the Ranter:

It may be the servants of some men, as the horsekeeper, ploughman, scullion, &c., are more looking after heaven than their masters. I am apt to think sometimes, that more servants than masters, that more tenants than landlords, will inherit the kingdom of heaven.[84]

It is also this greater moderation which distinguishes *A Few Sighs from Hell* from its two closest parallels, James Parnell's *The Trumpet of the Lord Blowne,* 1655, and Laurence Clarkson's *The Right Devil Discovered,* 1659.[85] The first of these is a Quaker commentary upon the sixteenth chapter of Luke from which the author drew conclusions which, by their similarity, cast light upon Bunyan's meaning:

Woe unto you that are called Lords, Ladies, Knights, Gentlemen, and Gentlewomen, in respect to your persons, who are exalted in the earth, who are proud, and high, and lofty, who are called of men Master, and Sir, and Mistris, and Madam, in respect to your persons, because of your gay Cloathing, because of your much earth, which by fraud, deceit, and oppression you have gotten together, you are exalted above your fellow creatures, and grind the faces of the poore, and they are as slaves under you, and must labour and toyle under you, and you must live at ease, sporting in day time, and spending your time in pleasures, and Chambring, and wantonness . . . and all your dainty dishes . . . and you have your fine attire, and all manner of new fashions, Silk and velvet, and purple, Gold and Silver, and you have your waiting-men, and waiting-maids under you to wait upon you, and your Coaches to ride, and your high and lofty horses is like yourselves, according to your lofty minds, and you sit at ease, Dives like, devouring the Creation . . . and your fellow-creatures must labour like slaves under you, and works for all this, when you are at your pleasures, they must be at work and labour, that must Hunger and thirst and labour, when you are eating, and drinking, and sleeping, and here like Dives you sit at ease, and poor Lazarus lyes starving without, and here you are Lords over your fellow-Creatures, and they must bow and crouch to you or else, they must bee hated, and punished, and put out from your presence, and be scoffed and scorned. . . .

Clarkson used Cain instead of Dives to symbolize the proud and the rich in a tract devoted to the discovery that these and no others were the right devils.

Bunyan's social and economic troubles, which inclined the complaint of his youth toward the modes of Quaker radicalism, were succeeded, as we have noted, by a happier economic lot, which imparted to his later expression a more disinterested character. His treatment of economic matters in *Mr. Badman,* 1680, has something of that moral tone which comes of sympathy with the oppressed rather than of immediate suffering. But as he came to resemble humanitarians like Baxter more closely, he retained much of his earlier kinship with Winstanley and the Quakers, and the discussions in *Mr. Badman* fall between the radical and the conservative extremes. Like the men of both extremes, John Bunyan exposed in the manner of the medieval friars the evils of buying and selling, covetousness, false weights and measures, and the grinding of the faces of the poor by sharp commercial practice.[86] Grotesquely inappropriate in the age of mercantilism, long after the new ethics of commercial expediency had superseded those of medieval Christianity,[87] the economic opinions of Bunyan, Baxter, and the Quakers were the last moral vestiges of the Middle Ages. While the new middle classes unscrupulously flourished, preachers of the lower classes and conservative moralists uttered their traditional and outmoded deprecation.

Though Bunyan and Baxter expressed themselves by means of the same medieval moral formula, Bunyan was animated, like the Quakers, by a class antipathy in which Baxter had no share. Baxter attacked commercial greed with the antiquated morality of the conservative clergyman; Bunyan attacked it as the spokesman of the lower classes, who had partaken neither of the fruits of the new prosperity nor of its ethics. His hatred of buying and selling was directed less against the sin of covetousness than against the classes to whom this sin was peculiar. In the person of Mr. Badman, who though not rich, wanted to be, and spoke even on his deathbed of property and great titles,[88] Bunyan found the opportunity to display and rebuke the practices and natures of the covetous. The phraseology of Amos provided that of Bunyan's attack upon false weights and measures by which the poor were cheated,[89] and his own observation supplied the substance of his arraignment of landlords, who took petty advantage of the necessities of the poor:

As for Example: There is a poor body that dwells, we will suppose, so many miles from the Market; and this man wants a Bushel of Grist, a pound of Butter, or a Cheese for himself, his wife and poor children: But dwelling so far from the Market, if he goes thither, he shall lose his dayes work, which will be eight pence or ten pence dammage to him, and that is something to a poor man. So he goeth to one of his Masters or Dames for what he wanteth, and asks them to help him with such a thing: Yes, say they, you may have it; but withall they give him a gripe, perhaps make him pay as much (or more) for it at home, as they can get when they have carryed it five miles to a Market, yea and that too for the Refuse of their Commodity.[90]

Bunyan's indignation embraced usurers;[91] profiteers, who made of buying and selling an instrument of oppression: "I mean such who buy up Butter, Cheese, Eggs, Bacon, &c. by whole sale, and sell it again (as they call it) by penny worths . . . to the poor, all the week after the market is past";[92] and hoarders of grain, who cried scarcity to advance the prices: "Now that God may shew his dislike against this, he doth, as it were, license the people to curse such an hoarder up. He that withholdeth corn, the people shall curse him. . . ."[93]

Many of them *bite* and *pinch* the poor by this kind of evil dealing. These destroy the poor because he is poor, and that is a grievous sin. *He that oppresseth the poor to increase his riches, and that giveth to the rich, shall surely come to want.* Therefore he saith again, *Rob not the poor because he is poor, neither oppress the afflicted in the gate; for the Lord will plead their cause, and spoil the soul of them that spoile them.* Oh that he that gripeth and grindeth the face of the poor, would take notice of these two Scriptures.[94]

A Few Sighs from Hell and *Mr. Badman* contain the most elaborate statements of Bunyan's social and economic opinions, but hidden away in his other tracts are many briefer passages, often single sentences or texts, which might escape the notice of one unfamiliar with the devious habits of preachers, but clear enough to their subtle audience. He alluded to the oppression of poor laborers by wicked masters, whose unjust profits he called to the notice of the Lord.[95] He saw in property, wealth, and covetousness the cause of all worldly evil, and in eminence and prosperity the ruin of the soul.[96] So conscientious was his objection to money, that although John Burton of Bedford had been supported by a benefice, Bunyan never wearied of deploring the covetousness of the ministry.[97] "Behold," Bunyan quoted from the psalmist, "these are the ungodly that prosper in the world, they increase in riches."[98]

Bunyan's aversion to wealth, which appears intermittently throughout his tracts, also colors his great allegories. In *The Holy War*, in order to further his design of weakening and destroying Mansoul by wealth and prosperity, Lucifer sent Mr. Penniwise-Pound-Foolish and Mr. Prodigality, together with other ostentatious and voluptuous men, to undermine municipal innocence; and his trusted ally Lord Covetousness, "that horrible villain," lurked in the town.[99] Quoting in his margin Luke on the deceitfulness of riches, Bunyan called Lucifer's endeavor to choke men with the good things of the world a masterpiece of hell.[100] In *Pilgrim's Progress* Vanity Fair is the place where houses, lands, honors, preferments, titles, and the like, are bartered.[101] Demas, the proprietor of the silver mine where By-ends expired, had figured in many economic discussions of the day like Dives as the symbol of the rich man.[102] Madam Bubble, who was ever fingering her money and who laughed poor pilgrims to scorn while commending the rich, was the mistress of the Enchanted Ground or worldly security and delight.[103] The celebrated Muck-raker, who could look no way but downwards though one above his head offered him a crown, is symbolic of the rich man as Christiana knowingly surmised. Her prayer against the muckrake, "give me not riches," deserved the applause of the Interpreter, who considered it a rare prayer indeed.[104] Bunyan's resentment of riches had become with the years an attenuated but chronic principle; and in his mind to the end of his days the wicked and the rich remained inseparably linked. Though he often perceived the hand of God in both successes and failures, Bunyan never considered worldly affluence a sign of God's approval.[105] His use of that prerogative of the pious to interpret all things according to their knowledge of the Lord's intentions was plebeian rather than bourgeois. He was too fresh from the ranks of the economically oppressed, and too sincere a champion of his less fortunate followers, to perceive that alliance between holiness and prosperity which his complacent successors were to detect and which Benjamin Franklin was to record for the use of the good and the industrious.

In the last chapter we observed that class antagonism was to be attributed in part to the social, and in this, to the economic inferiority of the saints. We have seen, moreover, that expressions of this antagonism belong to a tradition of social preaching of which the Quakers were the most conspicuous exponents. Bun-yan's class hatred is to be explained, therefore, as the fruit both of his social and economic position and of his conformity as a preacher to the tradition of propaganda against the rich and the mighty.

Like the Quaker and Ranter propagandists Bunyan was accus-tomed to cite those texts of Scripture which bore the comforting assurance that God had chosen the poor and the low but had sent the rich men empty away.[106] The social and economic sig-nificance of these citations was as apparent to the saints as it appears remote and trivial to us. And like the Quakers Bunyan esteemed for its social implications the biblical imagery of moun-tains, valleys, and waters, of which Laurence Clarkson said: "If you could understand the Scriptures, you shall read it calleth rich wicked men Mountains, and poor believing men Valleys."[107] High mountains were to Bunyan an appetite and a feeling, but not a love; in the geographical and hydraulic symbolism of his *Water of Life* he followed the usages of contemporary social propaganda:

Water naturally descends to and abides in low places, in valleys and places which are undermost; and the grace of God and the Spirit of grace is of that nature also; the hills and lofty mountains have not the rivers running over the tops of them; no though they may run "among them." But they run among the valleys: and "God resisteth the proud, and giveth grace unto the humble," "to the lowly." Ja. iv. 6. 1 Pe. v.5. Pr. iii. 34. . . . . Though a river, in the streams of it, is common, yet a river, as it passes through a country or province, will choose its own way, it will run in the valleys, in the plains, not over steeples and hills. . . . The grace of God is compared to a river, perhaps to show of what a low esteem it is with the rich and the full. . . . It is therefore, for the poor and needy. . . .[108]

Against pride, to which in Dives and Mr. Badman, he had devoted his pained attention, Bunyan inveighed like a Quaker.[109] Pride was the motive "when you slight this or that person, though gracious; that is look over them, and shun them

for their poverty in this world, and choose rather to have converse
with others, that possibly are less gracious, because of their greatness in this world."[110] Bunyan detested those symptoms of pride,
"the beggarly art of complimenting," manners, civility, and fine
apparel;[111] and he deplored the wanton interest of the upper
classes in playhouses and sports.[112] Much that we have been
accustomed to set down to the score of Puritanism should be
ascribed equally to the social prejudices of the saints. The moral
commentaries of *Mr. Badman,* like that Gomorrhean pillar of
salt, are petrifications of backward glances at the evils of strati-
fied society.

To rank, good birth, tender breeding, and gentility Bunyan
maintained an unabating and Quakerish opposition;[113] for,
according to his simple criteria, not birth but rebirth was important. Bunyan's enmity toward the refined and the polite appears
in his allegories in which the villains are gentlemen, noblemen,
or ladies. By-ends was a "gentleman of good quality," connected
by birth with many rich and important people, Lord Turn-
about, Lord Time-server, Mr. Anything, Parson Two-tongues,
and other latitudinarian conformists, who dwelt with him in
the town of Fair-speech, "a very wealthy place," where few good
people lived. By-ends had a wife, Lady Faining's daughter, who
had arrived at such a pitch of breeding that she knew how to
carry it to all, even to prince and peasant. When By-ends met
Mr. Hold-the-world, Mr. Money-love, and Mr. Save-all, old
schoolfellows of his under Mr. Gripe-man, schoolmaster of Love-
gain in the county of Coveting, he bowed and composed compli-
ments. Later he perished in that silver mine near the hill called
Lucre where Demas stood "gentlemanlike."[114] In By-ends Bunyan concentrated his detestation of the theology, riches, gentility, learning, and politeness of the upper classes. Before that
wicked nobleman of Vanity Fair, Lord Hate-good, Faithful was
brought to trial for having slandered several of the nobility,
including Lord Luxurious, Lord Desire of vain glory, Old Lord
Letchery, and Sir Having Greedy, and during the course of the

inquisition, was called by Mr. High Mind "a sorry scrub."[115] Bunyan's choice of noblemen to represent sins in his moral allegory indicates his conviction that it was chiefly the upper classes who possessed the qualities of vainglory, wantonness, and covetousness. Mrs. Wanton, "an admirably well-bred gentlewoman," had entertained Mr. Lechery and Mr. Filth with music and dancing;[116] and Formalist, Hypocrisie, and Mr. Worldly Wiseman, who recommended civility and good fashion, are all described as gentlemen. In *The Holy War* Bunyan's devils were invariably polite, called each other gentlemen, and when they met, spoke only after "a Diabolonian Ceremony or two" or with a "low congy."[117] Although Bunyan did use the term gentleman in this book occasionally to describe good, or partly good, people,[118] his villains are invariably of the gentry. Ill-pause is "the old gentleman," Old Inquisitive is "a mean man of estate," Messrs Deceit, Profane, Carnal Security, and Evil Questioning are all called gentlemen.[119] Lord Willbewill, in the days when he was free and evil, was "another of the gentry," a freeholder, proud of his estate and privileges, who went over to Diabolus to become a magistrate and one of his great ones.[120] Mr. Desires-awake, on the other hand, was a poor godly man who "dwelt in a very mean cottage."[121] When brought before the jury of saints, Mr. Lustings said, "I am a man of high birth, and have been used to pleasures and pastimes of greatness," but according to a witness for the prosecution, he was even greater in wickedness than in pedigree.[122]

Bunyan's refusal, despite his greater prosperity, to abandon his campaign against the rich, the proud, and the potent, suggests that he wrote in these later years less as a discontented mechanick than as a spokesman and comforter of the oppressed. Like the Quaker preachers, but in his less immoderate way, he was a social propagandist, who expressed the complaint of his followers and directed their aspirations toward heaven for relief and toward the earthly kingdom of Jesus. As one of his elegists said, Bunyan was "a leader of the people."[123]

CHAPTER VI

THE HOLY CITY

He knew the seat of paradise,
Could tell in what degree it lies;
And, as he was dispos'd could prove it
Below the moon, or else above it.
                    Hudibras, I, i, 175.

That excellent witty invention, the Fifth Monarchy, opened a door of hope to the oppressed, and contributed to the innocent pleasure of the godly; but the wicked could not regard it with composure. Not content with the insubstantial felicity of heaven, the saints also desired the empire of the earth, and at the suggestion of certain dark texts of Scripture they imagined a temporal kingdom of the devout, in which, under the government of Jesus, His favorites should flourish and abase the profane by the equitable laws of Moses.[1] The millennium had inflamed the fancies of the more imaginative Jews; it had solaced the obscurity of the early Christians; and it had served to encourage the German Anabaptists, whose experimental temper was favored by opportunity and rewarded by the conspicuous advancement of the Saviour at Münster.[2] Cromwell's England was pervaded by millenarian hopes, so general before 1653 that few of the godly escaped them, but after 1653 so extreme among the Fifth Monarchy men and other theocratic Calvinists as to alienate the cautious.[3] Lay preachers of the enthusiastic sects, especially the Baptists, animated the oppressed with a zealous anticipation of relief and vengeance under the government of Jesus and His saints. As one of these guides to the submerged, John Bunyan preached the millennium, issued useful prospectuses of the kingdom of Jesus, and devoted his *Holy War* to the description of heaven on earth.

The Fifth Monarchy movement cannot be considered pri-

marily a stirring of the vulgar, but after the end of the Saints'
Parliament in 1653, except for a few cultured enthusiasts, most
of the active millenarians were mechanicks, of whom Venner,
the wine-cooper, John James, the weaver, and Belcher, the brick-
layer, were representative. Thurloe described the generality of
Fifth Monarchy agents as grocers, watchmakers, weavers, bakers,
shopkeepers, or tailors, and characterized the millenarian insur-
rectionists of 1657 as "inconsiderable and despicable" persons
of mean quality.[4] Many of the oppressed were attracted by the
prospect of an economic, social, and political revolution under
Jesus, who dignified their ambitions by the flavor of unmistakable piety. Their manifesto, *A Standard Set up,* translated into
millenarian terms the political desires of the Levellers and the
social and economic contentions of the Diggers and Quakers;[5]
and that accurately named pamphlet, *A Door of Hope,* held forth
to the despised and discontented the certainty of temporal relief
from the injustice of landlords, rich men, and the mighty and
the prospect of dominion over Babylon: "As Christ was a tender
Plant and Root out of dry ground; so may his Kingdom arise
out of a poor, obscure, illitterate, and (such as the world calls)
Fanatick People."[6]

The ambiguous scriptures, upon which these uncomfortable
people based their hope, offered no impediment to pious subtlety and penetration. Daniel's account of the four beasts, the
ten horns, the little horn, Nebuchadnezzar's strange dream, the
stone cut without hands, and the entire seventh chapter of this
prophet, appeared significant to the devout.[7] Daniel was corroborated and complicated by the Revelation of St. John, whose
introduction of the figures 1,260, 3½, and 42 challenged but could
not puzzle the wits of pious mathematicians. The beast with seven
heads, who was to rule for forty-two months, the slaying and
resurrection of the witnesses, the seven angels, the vials, and
above all the account of the Holy City (Revelation, Chapter 21)
were observed to be a chronicle of the past, an elegant allusion

to the present, and a prophecy of the immediate future. The prophets Isaiah, Malachi, Zechariah, Zephaniah, and the psalmist added weight and necessity to millenarian conclusions.[8] But candor must admit the uncertainty of these conclusions; and many commentators of the time maintained that reason and sobriety counseled a wise indecision.

The orthodox interpretation of these texts is evidence of millenarian leanings. The godly agreed that Daniel's four beasts represented the four monarchies of the world, Babylonian, Persian, Greek, and Roman, that the ten horns upon the brow of the fourth were the remaining kingdoms, and that the little horn, whose premature decay signified the approach of Jesus, was either Charles or Cromwell.[9] Unlike the respectable critics, who thought that the second coming of Jesus was His coming to judgment and that the prophecy of Revelation referred to a past or present spiritual revival, the millenarians unanimously insisted that the second coming was to inaugurate His rule on earth for one thousand years. They agreed upon the temporal elements of the prophecy, the 1,260 years of the Beast, the torpor for three and a half years of the witnesses, and their resurrection for one thousand years.[10] But there was an unfortunate discrepancy in the initial point of their computations, some preferring the conversion of Constantine, some advancing other arbitrary dates according to their light. Consequently they set various times for Christ's appearance: some preferred 1651, others 1655, 1657, 1666, 1673, or 1688;[11] but after 1660 many abandoned mathematical calculation for indeterminate hopes. The surprise is not that the millenarians disagreed over certain details, but that there should have been substantial agreement.

According to some millenarians, Christ would appear in person to assume the crown, but others held that His coming was to be in spirit within His militant saints, through whom He would subdue and govern the wicked by proxy. Some early commentators, who believed in His personal appearance, advised the saints to prepare the way for the kingdom by the slaughter of the wicked.[12] In view of this delegation of Christ's proper work to the saints, who could not hope like their master to conclude it instantly, these men believed that the conquest of Babylon could not but be gradual. The later commentators generally maintained that both conquest and sovereignty were to rest with the saints, whom the Lord would direct not with His bodily presence but with an appropriate influence. Docile saints relied for the success of the Fifth Monarchy upon endurance, prayer, testimony against the Beast, and the preaching of the millennium; and many professed their hope of a gradual millenarian reformation of the state through the inspired instrumentality of Parliament, Cromwell, or even a regenerated Charles.[13] But the impatient and high spirited, who doubted the efficacy of repose, advocated and attempted armed insurrection to establish the truth of the Scriptures, to destroy the wicked, and to encourage Jesus, whose inexplicable delay was a matter of concern.[14]

In 1651 the Fifth Monarchy men, a religio-political faction, numbering many Baptists, began at the church of Allhallows in London to consider ways of advancing Christ's kingdom.[15] After the failure of the one attempt at parliamentary government by the devout in 1653, Christopher Feake, John Rogers, John Simpson, and the other men of this persuasion, convinced that Cromwell had removed the crown from the head of King Jesus and set it impiously upon his own, testified against the government and plotted the return of Jesus to power. Vavasor Powell conducted an itinerant campaign against the Beast in Wales; Venner's despised remnant resorted to arms in 1657; and Feake preached incendiary sermons in city pulpits. Cromwell considered the activities and expressions of these men so seditious as to necessitate their confinement. The remaining witnesses, however, continued to testify.

Cromwell's antipathy to that "seraphical notion,"[16] the Fifth Monarchy, was that of the other less vehement saints, who distrusted the possibilities of government according to inspiration and the laws of Moses, and who contemplated with reluctance their own slaughter even in an irreproachable cause by their passionate brethren. The assurances of the millenarians were insufficient to quiet fears of another Münster and wild rumors of violence.[17] At Tiverton in Devon in 1659 a night alarm "that Fifth Monarchyemen, Anabaptists and Quakers were joyned together" to disembowel the profane, interrupted the slumber of the inhabitants.[18] But the conduct of Venner's followers in January, 1661 occasioned greater apprehension. Entering St. Paul's, these petulant men asked the first comer for whom he was; upon his reply that he was for King Charles, they responded, "We are for King Jesus," and intolerantly shot him dead.[19] This incident marked the beginning of two days of armed rioting in the streets during which about twenty of the intemperate followers of Jesus were destroyed by troopers and agitated citizens, and many more sent to Newgate. Their unhappy excess prejudiced the designs of the Saviour and created that fear of sectarian insurrection which for over twenty years made the authorities regard every conventicle with distrust and suspicion. Thereafter, despite the immediate disclaimers issued by frightened Baptists, Independents, and Quakers,[20] both public and government were always finding Fifth Monarchy men under the bed.

There is little reason for the common idea that with Venner's failure the millenarian ambitions of the saints instantly declined.[21] Though projects of revolt became fewer and less significant, the expectation of Christ's coming continued without abatement. With 1661 the golden age of millenarian speculation and activity ended, to be followed, however, by the attenuated silver age, during which, down to 1688, successive persecutions stimulated rather than dampened the desire for Christ's kingdom. In 1650 most saints, even reasonable men like Owen, had looked to the millennium with impatient expectancy; by 1661 the conduct of the Fifth Monarchy men had alienated the prudent and left the advancement of the cause to the enthusiasts. In 1665, however, even Lodowick Muggleton, who greedily embraced the outrageous, failed to draw millenarian conclusions from Revelation.[22] The opinion shared by Knollys, Danvers, and Bunyan was almost peculiar to Baptist enthusiasts. That apocalyptical scholar, Henry More, whose learned analysis of Revelation was "diametrically opposite to this Enthusiastick Phrensie," derided not only the orthodox Fifth Monarchy interpretation but the surviving "mock prophets" who presumed to preach it.[23] And Richard Baxter, who attacked More and Thomas Beverley for claiming Revelation to be intelligible, disposed contemptuously of the Fifth Monarchy: "Very many of the Antinomian, and Separating Opinion, that least understand it, lay much of their Religion on it."[24] Persistent amid the disdain of scholar and saint alike, the Baptists maintained their belated chiliasm; and their deductions from Revelation, unlike the academic exercises of Dent, Brightman, Mede, and More,[25] were the wild stuff of dreams. Government spies reported, with possible exaggeration, the continued vitality of radical Fifth Monarchists in Baptist conventicles.[26] But the infrequent pamphlets, if not the sermons, of these agitators were necessarily moderate in tone and carefully ambiguous.[27]

Mildness characterized the works of the foremost Baptist millenarian, Hanserd Knollys, who had been suspected of complicity in Venner's insurrection, who had been placed in Newgate where he was reported to be plotting revolt, and who was said by an informer to have preached in September, 1661 at Allhallows, the Fifth Monarchy center.[28] His better energies were devoted, however, to the tracts in which he expounded Revelation in the manner of his millenarian predecessors but with the customary Baptist insistence upon passive obedience to the government of the Beast and upon the peacefulness of the saints.[29] According to Knollys, Christ's descent in 1688 was to occur in spirit within the saints, who could further the establishment of the kingdom only by their spiritual activity. *Theopolis, or the City of God New Jerusalem,* 1672, by Henry Danvers resembles the tracts of Knollys in idea, treatment, and moderation.[30] For twenty years after the Restoration Danvers was involved in most of the plots against the government. His arrests were frequent; spies reported him to have preached sedition; and as late as 1682 an informer found Danvers entertaining a congregation of seven hundred Fifth Monarchy men at Houndsditch.[31] The harmless sentiments of this eminent Baptist afford a pleasing contrast to his dubious history.

John Bunyan's interest in the millennium after 1660, when it suffered the neglect of the sober and the fashionable, may be explained by his enthusiastic inclination, by the oppression and persecution to which he was subjected, and by the influence of his friends and acquaintances. Like Danvers and Knollys, Bunyan was moderate in his millenarian professions; but his familiarity with the activities of the extremists is clear from his *Relation of Imprisonment.* He had been placed in confinement by the order of a justice, who, even before Venner, had suspected Bunyan of intending under the innocent pretext of illegal worship "some fearful business, to the destruction of the country."[32] And on April 3, 1661, when the memory of Venner was fresh, Cobb, who visited Bunyan in prison, received his conventional repudiation of disloyalty with skepticism:

Cobb: Every one will say the same, said he; you see the late insurrection at London, under what glorious pretences they went, and yet indeed they intended no less than the ruin of the kingdom and commonwealth.
Bun: That practice of theirs, I abhor, said I; yet it doth not follow, that because they did so, therefore all others will do so. I look upon it as my duty to behave myself under the King's government, both as becomes a man and a christian; and if an occasion was offered me, I should willingly manifest my loyalty to my Prince, both by word and deed.[33]

When in the autumn of 1661 the indifference of his jailer permitted Bunyan to visit London, where he had opportunity in
the conventicles of his friends to absorb millenarian ideas, he
was accused again of sedition: "They charged me also, that I
went thither to plot and raise division, and make insurrection,
which, God knows, was a slander."[34] In 1661, therefore, Bunyan
was suspected of and exposed to Fifth Monarchy ideas; but it is
not necessary to seek the origin of his preoccupation with the
kingdom of saints in his casual contacts. He was acquainted more
or less intimately with Henry Jessey, John Simpson, George Cockayne, Vavasor Powell, Henry Danvers, Hanserd Knollys, John
Okey, Benjamin Keach, John Owen, and William Dell, all of
whom professed millenarian opinions, some radical, some moderate.

According to their *Church Book,* the saints of Bedford maintained a familiar yet respectful relationship with "Mr. Simson,
Mr. Jesse and Mr. Cockin," to whom they looked for advice in
November, 1659 and on many other occasions.[35] The cautious
temper of John Simpson, who carefully abstained from publishing his theories, did not secure his fame from the imputation of
desperate millenarianism by Thurloe and the informers.[36] Simpson and Feake were rebuked by Arise Evans in 1654 for their
Fifth Monarchy radicalism;[37] members of Simpson's church as
well as some from those of Jessey, Knollys, and Feake signed a
millenarian manifesto that same year;[38] and Anna Trapnel, who
diffusely proclaimed the approach of Jesus in 990 double-col-
umned folio pages of extempore verse, received the eucharist at
Simpson's conventicle.[39] Simpson was an advocate of violence
before 1654, when the authorities found it convenient to incar-
cerate him, but from 1656 to 1660 he discovered the less dangerous merits of passive expectancy. The Restoration, however,
appears to have revived his spirit: a warrant for his arrest in
November, 1661 followed upon the report that together with
Jessey and Knollys at Allhallows he had seditiously urged a resort

to arms against the government of the Beast.[40] His death in 1662 suddenly abridged his usefulness to the Baptists.

George Cockayne, an Independent with Bedfordshire connections, mentioned his long friendship with Bunyan in the obituary notice which he contributed to Bunyan's *Acceptable Sacrifice,* 1688. In 1648 Cockayne composed a mildly millenarian tract,[41] but his other surviving works provide no evidence that his interests extended beyond a continual celebration of the funerals of eminent grocers. Yet he had attended the early Fifth Monarchy meetings,[42] and with Feake and Simpson he had been associated in a joint preface to Joseph Kellet's book against the Quakers.[43] Erbury reported having heard Cockayne, Simpson, and Feake preaching radically at Allhallows in 1652;[44] and from 1664 to 1678 excited informers reported Fifth Monarchy conventicles at the residence of this "fanatic" in Soper Lane, and expressed a lively concern over the nature of his opinions.[45]

Bunyan's tracts and the *Church Book* record his friendship with Henry Jessey,[46] a dependable and untiring supporter of the Saviour's monarchical interests.[47] Jessey and Feake wrote sympathetic Prefaces to Mary Cary's *The Little Horns Doom & Downfall,* 1651; Jessey, Powell, and Danvers signed a Fifth Monarchy manifesto in 1659;[48] and in 1661 Jessey was implicated, together with Cockayne, in the publication of the seditious *Mirabilis Annus,*[49] a book devoted to signs of the fall of the present government and to the approach of Jesus. In 1660 he was reported to be conspiring against the state; and his deathbed exhortation in 1663 to assist the coming revolt for Jesus, as well as the consequent animation of the vulgar, who attended his obsequies in multitudes, were the occasion of official anxiety.[50] But the last words of this illustrious Baptist appear to have no millenarian significance: he exclaimed, "more Julip, more Julip," and immediately expired.[51]

Bunyan is known to have possessed a copy of the *Concordance,* 1673, by Vavasor Powell, who was described in 1668 by an informer as "the great metropolitan fifth monarchy preacher."[52] This useful work, which contains a collection of "those Scripture Prophesies which relate to the Call of the Jews, and the Glory that shall be in the latter Days," was of value to all millenarians, who could find therein a convenient classification of most of the texts upon which their hope of a New Jerusalem rested.[53] Powell's Fifth Monarchy activities had perturbed Cromwell; and the State Papers describe him as factious and dangerous.[54] The Preface to Powell's *Concordance* was supplied by Bunyan's friend John Owen, who from 1649 to 1652 had believed that the "only important design in the world is setting up the kingdom of Christ."[55] But Owen's moderate millenarianism was succeeded by comparative neglect after the excesses of the Fifth Monarchists had offended his intelligence. Like Owen, Bunyan's friend William Dell expressed chiliastic convictions of a harmless variety.[56] As we have observed, Bunyan knew Henry Danvers; he must have known Hanserd Knollys, who also preached at Pinners' Hall and who was on familiar terms with Jessey; and he must have heard of John Canne, the eminent Fifth Monarchist and biblical commentator, who had been connected with both Jessey and Stephen More.[57] Benjamin Keach, Bunyan's rival and also a friend of John Child, was imprisoned and pilloried in 1664 for having suggested the Fifth Monarchy to the tender intellects of the young; but undiscouraged by martyrdom, he continued the millenarian education of children and, in his more elevated pamphlets, of adults.[58]

Although its *Church Book* preserved a discreet silence about the kingdom of Jesus, Bunyan's meeting had not remained unaffected by the imminence of His coming.[59] Several members of this society, notably John Fenn, signed *The Humble and Serious Testimony*, April 14, 1657, which owed its form and substance to the piety of William Dell and John Donne.[60] The millenarian implications of this petition against Cromwell's intended acceptance of a crown which should be reserved for

Jesus are made more apparent by the similarity of contempora-
neous protests by millenarians like Jessey and Knollys.[61] While it
is not known whether Bunyan signed this petition, which occasioned an official inquiry, it is evident that he knew of it since
several of his friends and neighbors were involved. Among the
latter was Colonel John Okey of Leighton Buzzard near Bedford,
who, one month later in May, 1657, was dangerously implicated
in Venner's first insurrection.[62] In 1661 Okey's fame was such
that, although he was not in England, it was confidently affirmed
by distracted witnesses of Venner's second attempt that he was
among its leaders; and in June, 1661 he was reported to be
plotting with Danvers.[63]

Undoubtedly influenced by friends and acquaintances of this
character, and provided with a motive by the persecution of the
Beast, Bunyan issued from prison in 1665 his first unmistakable
pronouncements upon the Fifth Monarchy.[64] In his *Prison Meditations,* a poetical fruit of that year, Bunyan alluded felicitously
to "Christ that king potent," and said:

> Just thus it is, we suffer here
>   For him a little pain,
> Who, when he doth again appear,
>   Will with him let us reign.[65]

And before the ambitious martyrs of Bedford jail, Bunyan
preached on Revelation, Chapter 21 a sermon which the applause
of the hopeful led him to print for their use.[66] This sermon,
The Holy City: Or The New Jerusalem, was alleged by its author
to be devoid of indebtedness to man,[67] but it is impossible to be
satisfied with the doubtful evidence of his own assurances. Inspiration or the unassisted contemplation of the Scriptures, though
excellent, must strike the judicious critic as incapable of produc-
ing a commentary upon Chapter 21 of Revelation so orthodox
as to conform in detail to the arbitrary interpretation of the chil-
iasts. Since this text contains the climax of the millenarian prophecies, it had been favored by Fifth Monarchists for many

years; each had made the same commentary, and each the same
conclusion. Revelation, Chapter 21 was to supply Danvers with
the subject for his *Theopolis, or the City of God New Jerusalem,*
and Knollys with an opportunity for similar deductions.[68] Far
from demonstrating his inspiration, which is widely recognized,
however, by many respectable judges, *The Holy City* serves only
to prove Bunyan's familiarity with the Fifth Monarchy tradition.

That mysterious scripture, Revelation 21: 10-27; 22: 1-4,[69]
which Bunyan chose for his consolatory tract, concerns what
Baxter was to call the unintelligible, but what millenarians professed to be the earthly kingdom of the saints and the destruction
of the Beast. Like its numerous parallels, *The Holy City* is a
verse-by-verse commentary upon the symbolism of St. John,
whose picture of the municipal enlargement of the righteous
was taken both literally and figuratively as tradition or inspiration demanded. Bunyan devoted a meticulous attention to the
significance of the walls, battlements, foundations, gates, and
towers of the New Jerusalem. This pious exercise was to become
useful as well as comforting to him years later in the composition
of *The Holy War,* for which the tract before us is a kind of study.

With the assistance of texts from Daniel, Isaiah, and Zechariah,
whom the Fifth Monarchists habitually cited, Bunyan described
in his *Holy City* the agreeable prosperity of the church, released
from the power of Antichrist, and restored in the present world
to a primitive luster:

For observe it, Christ hath not only obtained the kingdom of heaven
for those that are his, when this world is ended, but hath also, as a
reward for his sufferings, the whole world given into his hand; wherefore, as all the kings, and princes, and powers of this world have had
their time to reign, and have glory in this world in the face of all, so
Christ will have his time at this day, to show who is "the only Potentate - and Lord of lords." 1 Ti. vi. 15. At which day he will not only
set up his kingdom in the midst of their kingdoms, as he doth now,
but will set it up even upon the top of their kingdoms; at which day
there will not be a nation in the world but must bend to Jerusalem

or perish. Is. lx. 12. For "the kingdom and dominion, and the greatness of the kingdom under the heaven, shall be given to the people
of the saints of the Most High, whose kingdom is an everlasting
kingdom, and all dominions shall serve and obey him." Da. vii. 27.
"And his dominion shall be from sea to sea, and from the river to
the ends of the earth." Zec. ix. 10. O holiness, how shall it shine in
kings and nations, when God doth this![70]

The governors of this contemplated theocracy were to be saints,
who for one thousand years would expand in the pleasant consciousness of absolute authority over such of the wicked as had
not been removed.[71] Much of Bunyan's apparent delight in the
prospect of this revolution came from the certainty of vengeance
upon the oppressor, the "high ones, lofty ones, and the proud,"
whose sudden departure from saintly indignation into the dens
and holes of the earth, whence they could behold the honor and
glory of the new governors, occurred pleasurably to his fancy.[72]
" 'The sons also of them that afflicted thee shall come bending
unto thee, and all they that despised thee shall fall down at the
soles of thy feet.' Is. lx. 14."[73] The thought of the Fifth Monarchy was especially gratifying, he said, "to such men that have for
several years been held in the chains of affliction."[74]

Bunyan's millennium was of the later Baptist variety. Like
Danvers and Knollys he deplored the carnal belief in the Saviour's personal presence in the City of God and the equally perverse notion of an immediate and almost ignoble retirement to
heaven without the benefits of a triumph on earth:

Some conceiving that this city will not be built until the Lord comes
from heaven in person; others again concluding that when he comes,
then there shall be no longer tarrying here, but that all shall forth-
with, even all the godly, be taken up into heaven: with divers other
opinions in these matters.[75]

The spirit of God[76] could be trusted, however, to establish a
substantial empire through the instrumentality of the saints,
whose eagerness, commendably tempered by sobriety, declined
the material sword in favor of evangelism, church discipline, and

the preaching of the word. The triumph of theocracy was anticipated in the separation from the world of "a select company of
visible believers."[77] But the industry of lay preachers was of
greater importance; for by their diligence and propaganda the
city would be won, defended, and governed.[78] Since their millenarian success depended upon appropriate exclusiveness, discipline, and preaching, the journey of the church from Babylon
to the New Jerusalem was to be deliberate and gradual.[79] Need-
ing the impulse of saintly effort, the mechanism of the seven
vials awaited that perfection of ministerial activity upon which
its operation was contingent.

But endeavors to substitute the monarchy of Jesus for that of
Charles even by the sword of the word were the cause of official
anxiety and suspicion. The memory of Venner was still fresh
in 1665; Keach had been arrested in 1664 for millenarian opinions no more insidious than Bunyan's; and the expressions of
loyalty which came from the millenarians were both necessary
and futile. Bunyan's statement of innocence in this tract was
as politic as customary. The city

meddleth not with any man's matters but her own; she comes all
along by the King's highway; that is, alone by the rules that her Lord
hath prescribed for her in his testament. The governors of this world
need not at all fear a disturbance from her, or a diminishing of ought
they have. She will not meddle with their fields nor vineyards. . . . It
is a false report then that the governors of the nations have received
against the city, this New Jerusalem, if they believe, that according to
the tale that is told them, she is and hath been of old a rebellious
city, and destructive to kings, and a diminisher of their revenues
. . . Her glory is spiritual and heavenly, and she is satisfied with
what is her own. It is true, the kings and nations of this world shall
one day bring their glory and honour to this city; but yet not by
outward force or compulsion; none shall constrain them but the love
of Christ and the beauty of this city. . . . If any shall, out of mistrust or enmity against this city and her prosperity, bend themselves
to disappoint the designs of the eternal God concerning her building
and glory, then they must take what followeth.[80]

But the implacable malice of worldly monarchs toward their heavenly successor menaced, if it did not destroy, Bunyan's loyalty. As the holy city took shape, Bunyan said, "most of the kings and great ones of the earth will be found employed in another work, than to fall in love with Mount Zion. . . . They will be found in love with Mistress Babylon. . . ."[81] He conceded the possible conversion and assistance of some, but looked with complacency upon the eventual humiliation of the rest.[82]

Oral sermons at this period were generally more extreme than tracts, which, though by radicals, were distinguished by the moderation of their sentiments. For want of other records, we must judge of Bunyan's position by the evidence of his printed works, which reveal a mild and sedentary chiliasm. Though Bunyan professed conventional Fifth Monarchy opinions, he favored the word, not the sword. We can only admire the restraint which preserved the tracts of Danvers, Knollys, and Bunyan from the alarming and unambiguous militancy of earlier Baptist publications.

The profound silence in which Bunyan contemplated the approach of the millennium from 1666 to 1682 may be attributed to his failure to publish anything from 1666 to 1672 and to his subsequent preoccupation with controversy and popular literature.[83] Our impatience over his neglect, however, cannot but be followed by a grateful surprise upon discovery of the millenarian richness of his later works.

Allusions without bitterness to the problem of time in several of these later tracts illustrate our author's inflexible resignation to the tiresome delay of the Saviour:

This therefore calls for faith and patience in saints and by this he also tries the world; so that they, in mocking manner, begin to say already, "Where is the promise of his coming?" 2 Pe. iii. 4. But I say again, We must look and wait. If the people waited for Zacharias, and wondered that he staid so long, because he staid in the holy place somewhat longer than they expected, no marvel if the faith of the world about Christ's coming is fled and gone long ago, yea, and that the children also are put to it to wait, since a scripture "little while" doth prove so long. For that which the apostle saith, "yet a little while" doth prove to some to be a very long little. Jn. xvi. 16. He. x. 37.[84]

The disappointment of so many prophets was Bunyan's opportunity to discourage the setting of times for the celestial monarch, whose millenarian schedule, if not intention, was properly inscrutable, and to deprecate those mathematical speculations to which his own literary genius had never inclined him:

I shall not therefore meddle with the times and seasons which the Father hath put in his own power; no, though they as to Antichrist's ruin are revealed; because by the Holy Ghost there is a challenge made, notwithstanding the time is set, and by the word related to the man of wisdom, to find it out if he can. Re. xiii. 18.[85]

Prudence led Bunyan in the effort to quiet the fears of the magistrates to a seeming inconsistency in *The House of the Forest of Lebanon,* a pamphlet published posthumously in 1692; but this apparent repudiation of the millennium is observed on closer study to be a simple restatement of his moderate and pacific views:

I know there are extravagant opinions in the world about the kingdom of Christ, as if it consisted in temporal glory in part, and as if he would take it to him by carnal weapons, and so maintain it in its greatness and grandeur; but I confess myself an alien to these notions, and believe and profess the quite contrary, and look for the coming of Christ to judgment personally, and betwixt this and that, for his coming in Spirit, and in the power of his word to destroy Antichrist, to inform kings, and so give quietness to his church on earth; which shall gradually be accomplished, when the reign of the beast, the whore, the false prophet, and of the man of sin is out. 2 Thes. ii. 8. Is. xlix. 23. lii. 15. lx. 3, 10, 11, 16; lxii. 2. Re. xxi. 24.[86]

The prospect of the Saviour's theoretical presence had always served to satisfy the demands of Bunyan's modest chiliasm; his sorrow over the violence of some millenarians had always equaled his delight in the gradual propagation of the word; and his superiority to temporal pomp, which would in any case follow upon the establishment of the Fifth Monarchy, was nicely calculated for the distraction of magistrates.

That exercise in veiled sedition, *An Exposition of the First Ten Chapters of Genesis,* also published in 1692, resolves all possible doubts about the orthodoxy of Bunyan's millenarian beliefs. In Adam's reign and in the first sabbath Bunyan discovered proof of the millennial resurrection of the saints, the chaining of the dragon, the decline of the four great monarchies of the world, and "the glory that the church shall have in the latter day, even in the seventh thousand years of the world, that sabbath when Christ shall set up his kingdom on earth, according to that which is written, 'They lived and reigned with Christ a thousand years.' Re. xx. 1-4."[87] "The world," he concluded, "is therefore in our hand, and disposed by our doctrine, by our faith and prayers, although they think far otherwise, and shall one day feel their judgments are according."[88] The Fifth Monarchy was so imminent in his opinion that some of the present saints would live to enjoy the fruits of their hopes, sufferings, and endeavors.[89]

Bunyan's dedication to the millennium of an entire tract, *Of Antichrist and His Ruin: and of the Slaying of the Witnesses,* 1692, brought his concern with the earthly kingdom to a climax and, since he died shortly after its composition, to an end:

God will have his primitive church state set up in the world, (even where Antichrist has set up his;) wherefore, in order to this, Antichrist must be pulled down, down stick and stone; and then they that live to see it, will behold the new Jerusalem come down from heaven, as a bride adorned for her husband.[90]

With painful exactitude Bunyan described the nature of Antichrist, the time, causes, signs, and means of his ruin, and the splendor to be when the saints " 'shall take them captives whose captives they were; and they shall rule over their oppressors.'

Isa. 14.2."[91] For the first time he expounded the texts concerning the testifying of the witnesses for 1,260 days, their slaughter at the hands of the Beast, and their lifeless prostration for 3½ days in the streets.[92] In the violence of persecution, the weakness and degeneracy of God's church, and the powerlessness of preachers he saw, as impatient observers had for thirty years, the encouraging signs of the end.[93] He anticipated with pleasure the gradual decay of the ten horns, the operation of the seven vials, and the decline of Babylon and the Whore.[94] Again he looked for the fall of Antichrist to the reformation of the church and to the preaching of its ministry,[95] whose millenarian importance indicates their value in Bunyan's eyes. The surprising novelty of this tract, however, lies in the emphasis upon the function of earthly kings, who, while the preacher killed the soul, were to kill the body of Antichrist. In order to secure their requisite forbearance, Bunyan provided for the conversion, evidently by the propaganda of the minister, of kings, who, when aware of their idolatrous subservience to the harlot, would abandon her to the ferocity of the magistrate. Hence, Bunyan advocated patience under the persecution of kings, whom he pitied rather than blamed.[96] His fulsome exculpation of monarch and magistrate appears to owe more to necessity, however, than to pity or love: "I only drop this, because I would shew my brethren that I also am one of them; and to set them right that have wrong thoughts of me, as to so weighty matters as these."[97]

Before we ponder the millenarian significance of *The Holy War* it would be improper to avoid a further exploration of Bunyan's attitude toward the magistrates and the king of England. In the light of Bunyan's attacks upon persecutors, informers, and the established church,[98] his insistence in several of the later tracts upon loyalty to the king and the magistrates, who acted "beyond measure, cruelly," and his advice to saints to "kiss the rod, and love it," are curious: "Let us take heed of admitting the least thought in our minds of evil, against God, the king,

or them that are under them in employ. . . ."[99] But for a persecuted sectarian, to whom the king meant imprisonment, the
cry for God, for country, and for jail involved a marriage of loy-
alties so dubious as to amount to miscegenation. Bunyan's customary denials of sedition, his defenses of the saints, "a base
people charged with fearful crimes," who were, however, as
innocent of faction as Paul or Jesus, and his claim that he had
never preached rebellion cannot be considered unambiguous.[100] To kiss with love the rod that smites one is sound Christian theory, but unless it is the effect of masochism, it is not
natural.

The explanation is simple: Bunyan's expressions of loyalty
were dictated by judgment, policy, and the practice of the Baptists, who refused to admit their occasional interest in sedition.
This reasonable disinclination may be noted in the denial by
Vavasor Powell's followers of their leader's Fifth Monarchy activities at a time when his antipathy toward the government was
so notorious as to necessitate his confinement.[101] Neither the biographies nor the autobiographies of Powell, Knollys, and Jessey
mention the millenarian and sometimes treasonable designs of
these men. A wise suppression of dangerous facts served for
official purposes to establish conformity to that article of the Baptist confessions of faith which demanded obedience to the magistracy as a divine precept;[102] and a Baptist statement of loyalty
usually reflected an unselfish subordination of the truth to a
commendable orthodoxy. Henry Danvers found a pious sub-
scription to the Baptist credo to be convenient before plotting
treason. And John Bunyan, whose *Confession of Faith* contained
a statement of the official Baptist attitude toward the magistrate,[103] also saw the virtues of regularity. But the profession of
loyalty was not only good Baptist policy, it was good policy.

Had the Baptist confessions of faith been deficient in loyalty,
policy would have secured Bunyan's ostensible devotion to king
and state; for his judgment, which improved with age, and twelve

years of imprisonment had attenuated his earlier ardor for martyrdom. A sober appreciation of his usefulness to the community
enabled him to decline the pleasures of injured innocence. The
cultivation of the expedient, the secrecy of his preaching, and the
agility with which he eluded constables [104] account for his continued enjoyment of liberty at a time when many saints were
languishing in prison. Bunyan's contemporary biographers mention his "wariness" and "caution" in dealing with the authorities,[105] and Bunyan himself said, "I am not for running myself
into sufferings."[106] Moreover, that sense of responsibility, so
correct in a leader of the people, softened his public pronouncements in the hope of quieting "the looser sort of Christians,"
whose useless display of antimonarchical vehemence might prejudice the cause: "I speak not these things, as knowing any that
are disaffected to the government. . . . But because I appear thus
in public, and know not into whose hands these lines may come,
therefore thus I write."[107]

That Bunyan cherished a deep and natural hatred of both
king and government, like any normal Baptist of the time,[108] is
apparent from remarks scattered throughout his tracts, often next
to professions of loyalty, which served to hide his real opinion
from all but the elect and the inquisitive. The premise of his
millenarian tracts, in which he wisely expressed his love for the
government, was the corruption and enmity of the Beast or the
rulers of the world. His hope of the conversion of some kings
did not lessen his belief in their present wickedness: he saw and
detested the injustice of laws, jails, magistrates, and governors,
between whom and the saints was a perpetual war.[109] His denial
of sedition was a denial of violence, not of propaganda against
the government.

Additional evidence of Bunyan's distrust of the government,
as well as of his refusal to coöperate with it, is furnished by his
early biographers, who reported his detection of James's motives
in respect of the test act, his wary campaign against the new-

modeling of corporations, and his refusal of a conciliatory offer of public office:

During these things there were Regulators sent in to all Cities and Towns corporate, to new model the Government in the Magistracy. &c. by turning out some, and putting in others; against this, Mr. Bunyan, expressed his Zeal with some weariness [wariness], as foreseeing the bad consequence that would attend it, and laboured with his Congregation, to prevent their being imposed on in this kind, and when a great man in those days coming to Bedford, upon some such Errand, sent for him, as 'tis supposed to give him a place of publick Trust; he would by no means come at him, but sent his Excuse.[110]

Members of Bunyan's congregation and many of his friends were conspicuous in their enmity to secular kings. A letter from Bedfordshire to Cromwell, May 13, 1653, on the selection of members for the Saints' Parliament,[111] expressed approval of a theocratic government and condemnation of kingly oppression. This letter was signed by Bunyan's friends, John Eston, John Gifford, John Gibbs, William Dell, John Donne, and by Bunyan himself.[112] The 1657 petition against kingship and for a holy commonwealth, *The Humble and Serious Testimony,* which we have already noticed, was signed by John Fenn, Richard Cooper, Robert Grew, John Eston, William Dell, and John Donne, all of whom Bunyan knew.[113] They had fought, they said, for civil and religious liberty, and had no intention of permitting the return of monarchy even under Cromwell; until Christ should be pleased to set up His kingdom on earth, they were resolved upon faithfulness to the good old cause. For further indication of their attitude the authors referred to a London petition,[114] which was even less reticent about the virtues of republicanism and the dangers of arbitrary secular government. Similar petitions against the return of earthly kings came in the next few years from Henry Jessey and Henry Danvers as well as from many other Baptists. Paul Hobson, whose preaching Bunyan must have heard at Newport Pagnell, was a determined

enemy of kings, as was William Dell; Bunyan's friend John Gibbs
had assisted at the capture of an eminent royalist in 1659; and
Henry Denne had been an active Leveller.[115] Few except the most
respectable Baptists accepted with equanimity the return of the
Beast after 1660.[116] In 1669 the Bedford meeting was accused of
rebellious designs by an embittered backslider, and its resentment of governmental persecution is apparent in *A true and
Impartial Narrative,* 1670.[117] After 1688, when the necessity of
politic restraint was less, Baptists openly referred to the Stuart
governments as tyrannical, popish, and oppressive.[118]

Bunyan's detestation of the government is apparent, as we
have observed, not in his official and conciliatory gestures, but
rather in scattered and inconspicuous references to the rule of
the wicked. But for the full expression of his opinions he discovered the values of obliquity, and said what he thought under
the cover of allegory or of biblical exegesis. Indirection relieved
his feelings, communicated his ideas to the saints, and hid them
from all but the closest scrutiny of the authorities. Both his
Exposition of Genesis and *The Holy War* are excellent examples
of this indirection.

This kind of politic duplicity was common among the saints.
Benjamin Keach combined in *The Travels of True Godliness*
an open profession of loyalty with an allegorical attack upon the
government. His complaint about charges of sedition and his
insistence upon the patriotism of the saints were invalidated both
by the preceding story of a visit to an imaginary island where
lords and princes, one of whom had been deprived of his head,
conspired against true godliness, and by the subsequent account
of the fall of Babylon and the approach of Jesus.[119] As early as
1655 Richard Coppin, whose theological eccentricity had made
him detestable, said that, since God's truth was often observed
to be contrary to the law of man, the author was "forced to appear
in the clouds, and speak something darkly, and under parables."[120] And John Rogers, the Fifth Monarchy man, deplored

with rhetorical splendor the necessity which forced the saints
to hide their thoughts under metaphors: "Must we counterfeit
with you? and come to you with Pythanology? must we either
speak in Tropes and Figures? or else in Ropes and Faggots? or
imprisonment at least?"[121]

But even indirection was unsafe as appears from the sad fortune of Richard Baxter, a man whom respectability had preserved from treasonable warmth, but whom prominence had
exposed to unusual notice. The eight mildly seditious allusions
to persecutors and to the established church, which Baxter had
made in his innocent *Paraphrase on the New Testament,* failed
to escape the vigilance of Roger L'Estrange and the severe censure of Judge Jeffreys, who, in 1685, sentenced the unfortunate
and senile man to prison.[122] Baxter resented the sentence,
objected to the accusation, as any sectarian would, and claimed
with reason that by L'Estrange's methods the Lord's prayer could
be proved seditious: "By that measure, no Minister must speak
against any Sin, till he be sure that the Rulers are neither guilty,
nor defamed of it, lest he be thought to mean them." But
L'Estrange had equal reason for his distrust of separatists, who, in
fear of the law, were "forc'd to cover their Meaning under Ambi-
guities, and Hints, to the greater Hazzard of the Libeller than of
the Publique."[123]

Officials rarely troubled their wits over the allegories of the
humble, however, and, despite his comparative celebrity among
them, Bunyan was fairly secure in his practices. The noise of
Baxter's misfortune, however, may have prompted Bunyan's
introduction of those assurances of loyalty which distinguish his
later works and may account for his failure to publish the tracts
to which he had given this doubtful protection. But *An Exposition of the First Ten Chapters of Genesis,* 1692, one of these posthumous publications, and written like the rest in 1683 or later
under the ferocity of the persecutors, is free from the dilution
of a specious loyalty. Under the disarming guise of a sober exege-

sis of that irrelevant book of the Scriptures, Bunyan offered to the subtlety of the elect and to the anticipated incomprehension or negligence of the wicked an elaborate commentary upon persecution and government. His scriptural wisdom enabled him to see that the book of Genesis was a prophetical allegory of seventeenth-century politics.[124]

The Holy Ghost, as Bunyan and every reputable Baptist, Fifth Monarchy man, and Quaker knew, had intended Cain and Nimrod as the types of all kings and tyrants.[125] In the history of Cain and Abel Bunyan beheld the struggle between the wicked and the pious, the oppressor and the oppressed, and the ruler and the subject: "It is the lot of Cain's brood, to be lords and rulers first, while Abel and his generation have their necks under persecution." Cain represented the honorable, the wealthy, the mighty, and those princes and potentates who, with "the hellish rage of tyrants," were intent upon the destruction of the low and the godly. The ancient enmity between Cain and Abel explained the impossibility of obedience to the present government of Cain's successors.[126] Without equivocation Bunyan referred to kings as tyrants, nor did he attempt to conceal, save by the obscurity of his project, his idea of the open war between saint and ruler. In the history of Noah's flood, Bunyan found further reference to persecution[127] and the lesson that saints should not look to the mountains [kings] for safety, but to God. This idea, which is antithetical to the conciliatory reliance upon kings in *Of Antichrist and His Ruin,* explains Bunyan's rejection of all official overtures. In the giants of Genesis, Bunyan again saw persecutors, armed with reasons of state, against whom Enos, the lay preacher, "a man that was miserable in this world, for the sake of God," maintained an untiring fight,[128] like that of Greatheart against Giants Grim, Maul, and Slaygood, the allegorical persecutors in *Pilgrim's Progress.*[129] In Nimrod Bunyan saw the abuses of absolutism: "I am apt to think he was the first that in this new world sought after absolute monarchy."[130]

This characterization of their notorious predecessor permits no uncertainty about Bunyan's opinion of the Stuarts:

. . . through the pride of his countenance, [Nimrod] did scorn that others, or any, should be his equal; nay, could not be content till all made obeisance to him. He therefore would needs be the author and master of what religion he pleased; and would also subject the rest of his brethren thereto, by what ways his lusts thought best. Wherefore he began a fresh persecution. That sin therefore which the other world was drowned for was again revived by this cursed man, even to lord it over the sons of God, and to enforce idolatry and superstition upon them and hence he is called the "mighty hunter."[131]

The inquisitive official might suspect but could not prove the seditious implications of Bunyan's Nimrod, the tyrant and the persecutor of saints. For this reason the exposition of allegory was the best available medium, save allegory itself, for the expression of a holy commonwealthsman.

But the saint might justly quarrel with the imputation of treason since what was seditious to the carnal understanding of the official was godly in the eyes of the elect, who recognized allegiance to no king but Jesus. A variety of definition gave to the men of either side the pleasing consciousness of rectitude. Bunyan denied sedition in the interests not only of expediency but of truth; for in his opinion the pursuit of a higher loyalty to God did not admit of the secular charge of treason. Noah, he said in his *Exposition of Genesis*, was excused of treason or rebellion because he had followed the word of God; and Paul, though offensive to ungodly men, was correct in his denial of sedition because he had been directed by a celestial impulse:

Hence note, that a man is not to be counted an offender, how contrary soever he lieth, either in doctrine or practice, to men, &c. if both have the command of God, and are surely grounded upon the words of his mouth. This made Jeremiah, though he preached, That the city of Jerusalem should be burnt with fire, the king and people should go into captivity; yet stand upon his own vindication before his enemies, and plead his innocency against them that persecuted him.

Je. xxvi. 10-15. Daniel also, though he did openly break the king's decree, and refused to stoop to his idolatrous and devilish demand; yet purged himself of both treason and sedition, and justifies his act as innocent and harmless even in the sight of God.[132]

Political antinomianism preserved the integrity of Bunyan's conscience. His devotion to a higher law permitted the virtuous infraction of a lower and dignified with the odor of heaven the politic darkness of exegesis and allegory.

THE HOLY WAR

These reasons may perhaps look oddly
To the wicked, though they evince the godly.
Hudibras, II, ii, 381.

Concerning the holy war "made by Shaddai upon Diabolus for
the regaining of the metropolis of the world": its object was millenarian, its scene the Holy City, which in 1665 had achieved
its insubstantial destiny in the vehemence of Bunyan's applause.
The Holy War is an allegory of conversion, but to indulge the
more sedentary Baptists, whose displeasure with the Fourth
equaled their delight in the Fifth Monarchy, Bunyan followed
the progress of rebirth in the imagery of the millennium. By
this pleasing device he expressed at once his opinions of state
and soul, flattered the grateful understandings of his audience,
elevated the new life to the dignity of his allegorical vehicle,
and added splendor to the designs of the church by the analogy
of individual salvation. The blameless character of his theme
gave him security and freedom to reveal, by the arts of metaphor and allusion, the truth about the empires of Jesus and the
Beast.

It is a great pity that the ingenuity of our author and the
lamentable passage of time have conspired to hide his double
intention from the pious reader of later years. The origin of
the celebrated city of Mansoul, however, has secured and war-
ranted the notice of serious critics, whose speculations have been
numerous, subtle, and vain. In 1897 Richard Heath, an authority on John of Leyden, supposed from his knowledge of the six-
teenth-century Anabaptists that *The Holy War* owed its nature
to a conjectural tradition of Münster still current among the
English Baptists.[1] Though his acuteness was correct in detecting
the resemblance between the millenarian kingdoms of Münster

and Mansoul, his unfamiliarity with the Fifth Monarchy movement in the seventeenth century prevented the suggestion of a
likelier and contemporary source. Moreover, he was not aware
that the relationship between the German Anabaptists and the
English Baptists was too remote to permit the survival of an
oral tradition; and that no seventeenth-century Baptist willingly
admitted or even contemplated the resemblance of his millenarian designs to those of Münster. That excellent biographer,
John Brown, conjectured that the fortifications of Mansoul were
indebted to Bunyan's military observations at Newport Pagnell
and Leicester during the war.[2] But Bunyan's presence at
Leicester remains doubtful, and the fortifications of Newport
Pagnell, which consisted of trenches and earthworks, were an
imperfect model for the elaborate battlements of Mansoul. Mr.
Gerald R. Owst recently advanced the notion that Bunyan's fortified inclosure was that of the medieval psychomachia, which
the rhetorical conservatism of preachers had preserved by way
of illustration in sermons of later times.[3] It may be granted that
this tradition served to confirm Bunyan in his choice of imagery,
but the psychomachia alone cannot account for the character of
his city. As Thomas Sherman suggested in 1682, as Dr. James
Blanton Wharey discovered in 1904, and as our ignorance of
their work enabled us to find independently in 1932, Bunyan
owed much to Richard Bernard's allegory, *The Isle of Man*.[4]
But though he took the names of characters, certain other details,
and perhaps the idea of psychological allegory from Bernard,
Bunyan could not have been deeply influenced or even pleased
by Bernard's vague and negligent treatment of municipal structure. The walled city of Mansoul came not from Bunyan's own
military experience nor from his perusal of Bernard but from
the Fifth Monarchy tradition of his day, immediately from his
own *Holy City*, and ultimately from the book of Revelation.

The imagery of the fortified town is that which Bunyan was
accustomed to use in his descriptions of the militant church both

in the present under persecution and in the future under the kindly government of Jesus. He employed the military and municipal metaphors of *The Holy War* in his verses *Of the Building . . . of the House of God,* 1688, to indicate the present condition of the church, whose foes, he said, could not

> Destroy her battlements, or ground-work shake.
> Here's God the Lord encamping round about
> His dwelling place . . .
> The holy watchers at her gates do stand,
> With their destroying weapons in their hand.

Jesus, the Holy Ghost, and the ministers of God were the governors of this theocratic community as of the city of Mansoul or the Holy City, the church triumphant on earth.[5]

The military, architectural, and governmental imagery of *The Holy City* is the source and explanation of Mansoul, whose walls and gates had also been defaced by Antichrist, whose "captain-general" was also Jesus, and whose thoroughfares were also made respectable by the residence of the Holy Ghost.[6] The presence in Mansoul of that noble vegetable the tree of life (Revelation 22: 2), whose flourishing was peculiar to the Holy City, makes it difficult to avoid the conclusion that Mansoul was the city of the millennium.[7] Since robes of a chaste and immaculate whiteness were the livery of the Holy City, the ceremonious embellishment of the citizens of Mansoul in garments of this kind, as prescribed by Revelation 19: 8; 7: 13-17 and by the universal concurrence of Fifth Monarchy commentators, confirms the millenarian character of this municipal corporation.[8] The absence of facilities for regular and decent worship in Mansoul, as Bunyan pointed out in *The Holy City,* was characteristic of the millennium.[9]

The bold imitation of Bunyan's *Holy War* by Benjamin Keach in his *Progress of Sin,* 1684, serves both to degrade his originality and to illuminate the millenarian nature of his model, the implications of which, like many imitators, he exaggerated.[10] It was clear to Keach, as it must have been to all of Bunyan's Baptist readers, that the history of Mansoul was not only that of the individual but also that of the church of God in persecution and triumph. Accordingly Keach emphasized the millenarian character of Bunyan's town by citing appropriate texts from Revelation and by calling it "the Holy City" and the "City of God."

To the profane the plot of Bunyan's *Holy War* may appear to be simple. The walled city of Mansoul, founded by Shaddai, was captured by Diabolus, who subjected it to the pleasures for many years, until its rescue by Emanuel, who set up a government under which the town improved in virtue. Gradually, however, the imperfect corporation grew weary of holiness and became so tepid in its adulation that Emanuel abandoned it; whereupon Diabolus renewed his siege against the now penitent inhabitants, whose reluctant bodies he finally secured but whose awakened souls he found it impossible to seduce. After a suitable period of neglect Emanuel returned to expel the bad intruder and to reëstablish a kingdom which was, he hoped, to endure until the last judgment.

Bunyan intended this allegory to provide a convenient history of the successive victories and defeats of good and evil in the soul during conversion, but *The Holy War,* like other more illustrious allegories, has several layers of meaning. Though its main allegorical subject is conversion, that mysterious and, in the light of foreknowledge and election, perhaps unnecessary struggle between God and Satan for the individual soul, this ambitious work admits of several other interpretations both allegorical and literal: the ecclesiastical, the political, and the millenarian.

That Bunyan was accustomed to a variety of meaning is evident from his interpretations of Scripture, in which, like Henry Jessey, he delighted to discover the literal and the several allegorical implications of a text. In *The Holy City* he ingeniously observed three layers of significance in the scriptural word *sun,*

and in his *Exposition of Genesis* he commended the divine
Author of the Scriptures for enriching the story of Noah's flood
not only with a literal but with three allegorical meanings.[11]
"In the interpretations of Scripture," said Henry Jessey, "the
literal sense of the matter and words is alwaies first to be taken."[12]
And in the interpretation of *The Holy War,* which is based
upon current modes of scriptural exegesis and upon what Bunyan considered the literary practice of the Spirit, it would be
incorrect to ignore the several strata of meaning.

The secret of the comparative failure of this work lies, perhaps, in Bunyan's inability to pursue with success a complication
beyond his gifts. The several inconsistencies of *The Holy War*
must be ascribed to the infringement of one of the contrapuntal
meanings upon another. Because of Bunyan's professional interest in conversion, the other allegorical and literal layers sometimes suffered considerable distortion; and his unrelenting antipathy to the great and the mighty sometimes caused an emphasis
of the secondary meanings at the expense of evangelism.[13] At any
given point of the book one layer is usually predominant; for,
attempting to express the many, Bunyan was compelled by the
limitations of his genius to slight the one. The envious Benjamin
Keach experienced the same difficulty in his *Progress of Sin.*[14]

In addition to the dominant theme of conversion Bunyan presented the biblical narrative of the fall and salvation of man
together with the history of the church, which merges in the
beginning with biblical, in the end with millennial, and throughout with the political history of his own times. The story of the
fall of Mansoul, tempted to eat of the tree of knowledge by
Diabolus, its subsequent degeneration as described in Genesis,
and its salvation by the coming of Emanuel, who substituted
grace for law, is told at the beginning of the book. The later
purity of the primitive church, its backsliding under the Beast,
and its final and future glory at the return of Emanuel occupy
the middle and end. During his accounts of the degeneration of

the church in Noah's day and later in that of the Beast, Bunyan
introduced the political conditions of his own day. Secured from
the notice of the wicked by the darkness of allegory, he recorded
his unamiable interpretation of the ways of the arbitrary and
persecuting Stuarts.

The new-modeling of Mansoul by Diabolus, who provided a
new charter and installed new officers subservient to his desires,[15]
reflects the new-modeling of English towns and cities by Charles
II, against whose efforts to substitute the rule of the wicked in
Bedford Bunyan was reported to be firm.[16] John Brown's assumption, however, that this passage in *The Holy War* is based upon
Charles's conduct toward Bedford[17] cannot be corroborated by
the evidence of history, which reveals only the preliminary questioning in December, 1681 of the recorder of Bedford before the
publication in February, 1682 of *The Holy War*. The removal
of the recorder and the naming of new burgesses for Bedford
did not occur until October, 1683 and the new charter did not
arrive until January, 1684.[18] Bunyan appears to have based his
account upon current rumors of the contemplated change in
Bedford or upon the new-modeling of other towns, which had
suffered this indignity earlier, and whose experience might serve
as a warning to the elect of Bedford or as a spur to their indignation. This passage in *The Holy War,* therefore, is significant not
as local history but as propaganda against the arbitrary designs
of a government for which Bunyan had no love.

After new-modeling the town of Mansoul, Diabolus proceeded
to corrupt all laws both civil and moral, to encourage worldliness
and impiety, and to set a bad example for the common people:
"For who doth not perceive but when those that sit aloft, are
vile, and corrupt themselves; they corrupt the whole Region and
Country where they are." The wicked governor imposed an oath
of allegiance to win for himself a loyalty owed to God (Isaiah
28: 15) ; he enslaved his subjects by "Priviledges, Grants, Immu-
nities, Profits, and honours"; and he worked so insidiously upon

their passions that the imbruted citizens, sedulously hymning the praises of a tyrant, neglected and finally forgot the claims of Emanuel, their rightful king. "And let this serve," Bunyan said with pleasing irony, "to give a taste to them that love to hear tell of what is done beyond their knowledge, a far off in other Countries."[19] The reference to Restoration England in this allegorical history is apparent and illustrative of Bunyan's undivided loyalty to Jesus, who received the devotion which an earthly tyrant impiously demanded. And the allusion in what follows to the antimillenarian activities of the Stuart government is equally apparent. Diabolus improved his resemblance to Charles, the patron of Sir Roger L'Estrange, by appointing as licenser of the press a certain Mr. Filth, an abandoned man, whose encouragement of polite at the expense of godly literature was intended to embarrass the designs of Emanuel; for, as the cause of Diabolus was promoted by the liberal publication of "Odious Atheistical Pamphlets and filthy Ballads & Romances full of baldry," that of his celestial competitor was injured by the proscription of those tracts in which his coming had received a decorous publicity. Diabolus undertook the destruction of all books which referred to the coming, of all plotters, whose pugnacity required their active assistance in the work of preparation, and of all the pious remnant "that shall prate of what by Shaddai and Emanuel is intended." Not even the Bible, with its dangerous suggestions of a new dynasty, nor gospel preachers, with their illicit mutterings in secret places of a messianic succession, escaped the notice of the apprehensive monarch, whose nights like those of Charles were not a little disturbed by the prospect of theocracy.[20]

The millenarian significance of Emanuel's coming is made more apparent by the connotation of his illustrious name; for Emmanuel or Emanuel, as Bunyan has it, was the king under whom Isaiah had predicted the success of the chiliad. Since this reputable prophet used the name at the beginning of a passage to which millenarians referred with a profound emotion, and since the Fifth Monarchists made frequent and professional reference to this name, it is clear that to a sectarian of Bunyan's time Emanuel meant Jesus in His capacity of governor of the world.[21] The choice of Shaddai for God is of equal appropriateness in a millenarian context, but it is less certain where Bunyan found the word, since it occurs in neither the King James nor the Genevan translations. His acquaintance with this mysterious appellation must be explained conjecturally by his friendship with scholars like Jessey, Dell, and Owen or else by the assistance of a biblical commentary. Shaddai is the Hebrew God of power and vengeance.[22]

The millenarian resolution of Bunyan's Emanuel demonstrates the felicity of his name. Noting with concern the occupation of the Holy City of Mansoul by Diabolus or the Beast, who had control of castle, hold, and walls,[23] Emanuel resolved to secure for himself the enjoyment of an earthly "Crown and Dignity," (Isaiah 49: 5) , and to make his intention clear, immediately issued the Scriptures.[24] Since the millenarian theme of *The Holy War* is imposed at this point upon that of the redemption, Emanuel's statement implies his mission both as Saviour by the covenant of grace and as governor of the world:

I am sent by my Father to possess it [the town] my self, and to guide it by the skilfulness of my hands into such a conformity to him as shall be pleasing in his sight. I will therefore possess it my self, I will dispossess and cast thee [Diabolus] out: I will set up mine own standard in the midst of them: I will also govern them by new Laws, new Officers, new motives, and new ways: Yea, I will pull down this Town, and build it again, and it shall be as though it had not been, and it shall then be the glory of the whole Universe [the earth].[25]

Upon Emanuel's military victory, Diabolus was bound in chains, according to millenarian plan, sent to wander in the parched places of the earth, and thence despatched to the pit where he disconsolately endured the period of Emanuel's earthly rule.[26]

The pompous entry and the sublime deportment of King Emanuel were designed to be pleasing to the orthodox. Surpassing in his glory the "great ones of the world," the new monarch, whose splendor exceeded even that of his gilded chariot, quartered his troops upon the fickle inhabitants, who prayed that victor and army might remain perpetually to govern the earth and to impose celestial laws upon them. Emanuel condescended to reply: "I will possess my self of your Castle of Mansoul, and will set my Souldiers over you; yea I will yet do things in Mansoul that cannot be parallel'd in any Nation, Country or Kingdom under Heaven." The happy government of this potentate, who in turn new-modeled the town into "such a condition as might be most pleasing to him," deserved the benevolent interest of Bunyan, whose citation of Revelation 22: 4, a text concerning the New Jerusalem, confirms the millenarian significance of Emanuel's kingdom. Emanuel prudently supervised the militia, the police, and the law, but left the immediate administration of his ordinances to subordinates, for whose guidance he recommended a daily consultation of "the Revelation of Mysteries."[27] We must regard with respectful awe the wisdom of regulating a state by that excellent treatise of government, the Revelation of St. John.

The new charter, which Emanuel provided for this enviable community, is at once the covenant of grace and of earthly dominion:

I do give, grant and bestow upon them freely the world, and what is therein for their good, and they shall have that power over them, as shall stand with the honour of my Father, my glory, and their comfort, yea, I grant them the benefits of life and death, and of things present, and things to come. This priviledg, no other City, Town or Corporation shall have but my Mansoul only.

This grant of terrestrial supremacy was made more pleasant by the exclusion of all but visible saints. And to maintain the provisions of his charter Emanuel founded a ministry, God's "vicegerent on Earth," with power to establish theocratic conformity by force.[28] The earthly happiness of the white-robed subjects of Emanuel's monarchy "lasted all that Summer."[29]

But the benefits of theocracy were not to endure, and, corrupted from within, the town declined. The presence within the walls of disguised Diabolonians was required both by Bunyan's idea of the depravity of human nature and by his opinion of the nature of the millennium, during which, he had said in *The Holy City*, it would still be difficult for saints, who had to judge by outward appearance, to discriminate between the elect and the hypocritical.[30] One of these subverters of the holy state, Mr. Carnal Security, was the cause of the backsliding, essential to Bunyan's scheme of conversion, and corresponding to what most commentators called the lukewarm or the Laodicean period of the church.[31] Bunyan had predicted this millenarian defection in *The Holy City*:

Now the reason why she lost the title of city at her going into captivity is, because then she lost her situation and strength; she followed others than Christ, wherefore he suffered her enemies to scale her walls, to break her battlements; he suffered, as you see here, the great red dragon, and beast with seven heads and ten horns, to get into her vinyard, who made most fearful work both with her and all her friends; her gates also were now either broken down or shut up, so that none could, according to her laws and statutes enter into her; her charter also, even the Bible itself, was most grossly abused and corrupted. . . .[32]

According to the best millenarian calculations this backsliding was to occur in the latter days of the Fifth Monarchy when Gog and Magog, as prophesied in Revelation, and as described in *The Holy City*, were to descend upon the New Jerusalem:

. . . she will yet once again be beset with raging Gog and Magog, which enemies will, after the long safety and tranquility of this city, through the instigation of the devil come upon the breadth of the earth, and encamp about this holy city. Eze. xxviii, xxix. But behold in the midst of this intention to swallow her up, the Lord rains fire and brimstone from heaven and destroys them all.[33]

A curious statement in another tract deals with this belated attack and illuminates the motives of the Lord: "God will get himself great glory by permitting the . . . dragon, to revel it in the church of God."[34] The attack by Gog and Magog, therefore, may account in part for the temporary return of Diabolus.

The first coming of Emanuel conforms to the plan of the millennium, but there is also evidence for a millenarian interpretation of his second coming. Diabolus had reëstablished himself by an army of Doubters or latitudinarian skeptics, among whom the election Doubters or Arminians bore the scutcheon of the Red Dragon of Revelation, the beast with seven heads and ten horns, inimical to saints.[35] The political subjection of the town by these Restoration persecutors, whose vain songs and blasphemous stories were an offense to piety, was so complete that none in the streets now looked like a religious man. But from the castle the stubborn saints ineffectually testified against their oppressors for about two and a half years. With the addition of the time consumed in the subsequent negotiations with Emanuel, this period may indicate the death of the witnesses for three and a half days. But the addition of a theoretical year is unnecessary in that Bunyan, who had never shown a taste for the mystical mathematics of heaven, refused to commit himself in his millenarian tracts to prophecies of time. Since Bunyan said that he was unaware how long the figurative death or political subjection of the witnesses would actually last,[36] and since the condition of the saints in Mansoul was that of the witnesses, this passage may reasonably be taken to allude to the millenarian prophecy of their death. Emanuel's letter, which promised his appearance "upon the third day," seems to have little significance.[37] But the predicted resurrection of the witnesses is indicated by the revival of the townsmen, who, upon news of Emanuel's coming, were "like men raised from the dead."[38] This resurrection was the official prelude to the millennium, to the period of which Emanuel referred in his inaugural address:

he intended to leave Mansoul in the world for a time, he said, and then to translate it to heaven where it would see wonders it could never see "shouldst thou live in Universe [the world] the space of a thousand years."[39]

But even after the reëstablishment of Emanuel's earthly kingdom, the town was assaulted by another force, which consisted of Bloodmen or persecutors, in the attempt to accomplish by violence what had proved impossible by doubt. "Their implacable malice remained," as Bunyan said in *Of Antichrist and His Ruin,* "when their church-state was gone; wherefore they will now at last make another attempt upon the men that had been the instruments in Christ's hand. . . ." And in this same tract Bunyan foresaw two final wars against the resurrected witnesses, the first against their faith, the attack by Doubters, and the second against their bodies, the attack by Bloodmen.[40] It was a commonplace of millenarian speculation that even after Christ's coming the Pope and other willful men would remain to be subdued.[41] Among the captains of the Bloodmen were Cain, Nimrod, and Pope, who were held, upon their capture by Emanuel, for the "great and general Assizes" at the end of the millennium.[42]

Of the two monarchies of Emanuel the first is more elaborately described, but the millenarian character of both is at once obvious and perplexing. Orthodoxy demands one Fifth Monarchy, not two; the claims of art are better satisfied with one; and the joy of our discovery must be qualified by the misfortune of finding two kingdoms where one might be expected. The excess of Bunyan's Emanuel, who came twice to establish his kingdom, compares unfortunately with the restraint of his celestial prototype, who was to have been contented with a single appearance. To impose order upon a millenarian irregularity, when the negligent or too zealous author perhaps intended none, calls for scholarship of the sort expended upon Shakespeare by those who think him Bacon. To insist upon one explanation of this pleonasm would be to value ingenuity at too high a rate. But as the sober historian must scrupulously avoid, the speculative scholar may tentatively suggest, the possible. The plot of *The Holy War* lends itself to three possible interpretations.

According to the first of these, the initial reign of Diabolus is the 1,260 days of the Beast; the first appearance of Emanuel is the Fifth Monarchy; the decline of Mansoul and the attack by Diabolus are explained by the predicted assault by Gog and Magog; and the return of Emanuel is the resumption of the Fifth Monarchy until the last judgment. By this interpretation the episodes of *The Holy War* conform to the accepted history of the Holy City; but the conscription of Gog and Magog relies upon the evidence of Bunyan's tracts rather than upon internal clews, and the slaying of the witnesses occurs improperly in the sequence of events.

According to the second, Emanuel's first coming marks the foundation of the primitive church, the ideal state, which, as every saint was aware, the Fifth Monarchy was to restore with more grandeur.[43] The degeneration of the town is the 1,260 days of the Beast, ending with the slaying of the witnesses or the complete subjection of the town by Diabolus; and the second appearance of Emanuel is the beginning of the real Fifth Monarchy. This explanation is agreeable to the theme of church history; it accounts for the millenarian preliminaries of the second coming; but the first kingdom of Emanuel is almost too millenarian in character to represent the primitive church.

According to the third, the plot of *The Holy War* takes its shape from the political sequences of Bunyan's own time. The first reign of Diabolus is the government of Charles I; the first appearance of Emanuel is the rule of the saints from 1649 to 1653; the decline of the town is the defection of Cromwell; and the return of Diabolus is the Restoration. The second kingdom of Emanuel becomes the real Fifth Monarchy of which the interregnum rule of the saints had been a foretaste. This interpretation affords a gratifying explanation of the political elements of the book, and though it is open to the same objection as the second, it deserves further study.

Restoration intolerance is accurately described in the activities of the Doubters and Bloodmen, but we at once encounter a difficulty in that the moral abandonment, censorship, and anti-millenarian zealousness of the first kingdom of Diabolus also reflect the period of Charles II. However, if Bunyan intended the first reign of Diabolus to be the England of Charles I, it is likely that he would employ to describe it the moral and political details of the reign of Charles II as more familiar both to himself and to his reader. Since *The Holy War* is propaganda rather than history, Bunyan's purpose would be served better by a description of contemporary conditions than by historical verisimilitude. Nor need antiquarian consistency be required in the matter of these almost identical reigns of the horned Beast. But Bunyan did provide for his account of Emanuel's first appearance military details which are drawn historically from the period of the Civil Wars. Although Bunyan had not served in the New Model army but in a county garrison at Newport Pagnell, he attributed to Emanuel's troops, and also occasionally to those of Diabolus, the practices of Cromwell's army. Reference to C. H. Firth's *Cromwell's Army* establishes the Cromwellian deportment of Emanuel's troops, whose systematic iconoclasm, exemplary conduct, councils of war, emblematic banners, passwords, arms, equipment, and maneuvers, disciplinary punishments, preaching captains, and millenarian convictions are those of the New Model army.[44] The use of terms such as "forlorn hope" for advance squad, and "reformades" for superfluous officers, indicates the period of the Civil Wars.[45] While it is possible that Bunyan intended no historical implication, it is equally possible that he meant these Cromwellian practices to suggest a chronological period in his plot.

Our conjecture that the first rule of Emanuel corresponds

to the triumph of the English saints, which culminated in the short parliament of 1653,[46] is supported by the interest of Bunyan and his community in that adventure in government by the righteous, as shown in their letter of 1653 to Cromwell. Cromwell's prorogation of this millenarian parliament, however, marked in the eyes of the pious the beginning of a saintly decline which resulted in the carnal offer of the crown to Cromwell in 1657,[47] and eventually in the Restoration. The sorrowful testimony of the saints records their conviction of this backsliding from millenarian ideals. Jessey, Knollys, and most Baptist millenarians were unable to contain their chagrin. Feake, Rogers, and the other Fifth Monarchy men looked sternly upon Cromwell and indicated the apostasy of their lost leader; their Moses, as Spittlehouse had prematurely hailed him,[48] had become intimate with the harlot, and they loved him this side adultery. The Bedford meeting, whose *Church Book* reveals a similar apprehension of the increasing worldliness of Cromwell, deplored in *The Humble and Serious Testimony*, 1657, a "defection" from the "Cause of Christ" on the part of those who had been "chief Instruments in it." And in his first work, *Some Gospel Truths*, 1656, Bunyan bewailed the backsliding and coldness of those who had been hot two or three years before.[49] This pious conviction appears to be reflected in the decay of Mansoul under Mr. Carnal Security, who abridged the promise of an auspicious beginning, as Cromwell had done from 1653 to his death. The feeble protests of the preachers of Mansoul were those of the commonwealth millenarians, whose admonitions were an insufficient antidote to the poison of carnal security.[50] As the Saints' Parliament was a tantalizing sample of the millennium, doomed to failure by the carnality of former saints, whose increasing conservatism was responsible for the Restoration, so the first kingdom of Emanuel was an abortive chiliad, condemned by carnal decay to be succeeded by the incursion of Diabolus. During the time of the Bloodmen and the Doubters the saints of

Mansoul maintained like their Restoration brethren a verbal campaign against the infidel.[51] These activities of the witnesses and their subjection for a time to the Beast suggest those Restoration conditions which were interpreted by Bunyan as signs of Christ's coming,[52] to which after 1660 the hopeful Baptists still looked. Emanuel's second appearance, therefore, is this expected coming, the actual as contrasted with the provisional monarchy of Jesus.

Candor must admit and doubt must applaud a careful hesitancy over the application of any of these three hypothetical outlines to the work of one who may have declined a consistent for a loose and ancillary exploitation of millenarian materials. Our speculations, for each of which there is both favorable and unfavorable evidence, may have served only to animate the disgust of the severe or the amusement of the generous reader. The one conclusion which we may draw from this confusing book is that Bunyan had the millennium in mind when he wrote it, and that the idea of the Holy City, as well as the political conditions of his time, supplied much of the imagery and action of his allegory. The plot may or may not involve an unsuccessful attempt at a consistent history of the millennium and its preliminaries. Since Bunyan found difficulty in the coördination of his several themes, it is probable, however, that the necessities of his allegory of conversion, which demanded a period of backsliding, rather than any of our questionable suggestions, explain the irregular conduct of Emanuel. Bunyan's only intention in respect of the millennium would appear to have been to suggest it and to employ it as the vehicle for his allegory of rebirth for which it has an undeniable appropriateness. The imagery of the kingdom of Jesus, which the godly reader would immediately detect, was at once an agreeable means of evangelistic instruction and a stimulant to millenarian ambitions.

These ambitions were reflected in the constitution and procedure of the dissenting churches, which were regarded and conducted by their inmates as little theocracies.[53] The Bedford meeting regulated the lives of its members by the laws of God, ordered their social behavior, sternly supervised the tenderest intimacies of the chamber, and by the awful weapon of excommunication, disciplined its candidates for the coming dictatorship of the godly, under which they were to impose their own celestial severity upon the profane and the unwilling.[54] Their dreams of power and heavenly discipline happily anticipated the establishment of godly inquisitions to control the world as they controlled themselves when the expansion of their little theocracy by divine assistance and by the industry of the elect had embraced the nations of the earth. Christopher Feake, the Fifth Monarchy man, said:

A Glorious Evangelical inquisition shall be set up in due time, and the Ministers of the Gospel shall be Gospel-inquisitors (I speak in allusion to the Spanish Popish Inquisition) . . . we shall have recourse to the word of Christ and what is found opposite or contradictory thereto, we shall discover it and reveal it openly.[55]

William Aspinwall, the millenarian Baptist, who dreamed of death penalties for Sabbath breaking, said: "The Saints sitting in Counsel, shall bring those Beasts to a judiciall Triall."[56] Aware of the inconveniences which might be expected to attend the triumph of theocracy, Henry Cromwell had written to Thurloe of the Baptists in 1655: "I shall be carefull to keep them from power, whoe, if they hade it in their power, would express little tenderness to those, that would not submitt to their way."[57] A normal Baptist in all but his liberal attitude toward sprinkling, Bunyan shared the simple desires of his fellows, and contrived for their entertainment the millenarian kingdoms of Emanuel, which faithfully represented their expectations of theocracy. The godly reader of *The Holy War*, like the reader of Richard Baxter's *Holy Commonwealth*, could discover and admire his Utopia in action, and though his satisfaction was literary, it was nevertheless profound, for in Bunyan's excellent book he could contemplate with delight the strictness of the coming tribunal of saints and the discouragement of the ungodly by gibbet and cross.

The trials of the wicked by a judge and jury of saints during the happy reigns of Emanuel conform to the judicial practice of the millennium as conceived by Feake and Aspinwall; they have, however, a double significance, allegorical and literal. Like the trial scenes of Bernard's *Isle of Man,* those of *The Holy War* concern the mortification of sin, but they also reflect a popular literary tradition in which the device of a trial by jury was used literally against religious and political enemies, such as the Papist, the Presbyterian, or the Good Old Cause.[58] Though Bunyan's millenarian assizes have a moral significance in his allegory of conversion, they have a literal meaning in his subordinate themes.[59] That the intended recipients of these inquisitorial attentions took them seriously and literally is evident from the reaction of James Park, a Quaker, to the trial scene of Benjamin Keach's *Progress of Sin:* "It may be easily seen, what this Baptist Teacher would be doing (had he power in his hands) . . . ."[60]

Unregenerate England, which had observed the theocracy of Massachusetts and the punishment of James Nayler by a committee of parliamentary saints, had reason to fear the success of King Jesus. And before their enlightenment the inhabitants of Mansoul had distrusted the possibilities of Emanuel's "unlimited power." [61] But the merits of his Utopian severity were apparent to those champions of toleration who had endured and profitably studied the judicial practices of Vanity Fair. Upon the first victory of Emanuel those of the ungodly who had survived the immediate slaughter were seized and confined by the orthodox constabulary. The credulous prisoners prayed Emanuel not to destroy them, but when he remained unmoved by their piteous cries and when his justice was observed to proceed without abatement, they were covered with confusion. Accused of

profanity, lying, skepticism, fornication, impenitency, Sabbath
breaking, and cheerfulness, they were brought to trial before
an inquisition of saints, among whom were Mr. Zealforgod and
Mr. Heavenlimind. "When all such beasts as these are cast out
of Mansoul," said the latter, "what a goodly Town will it be
then." Since judicial wisdom limited the witnesses to those for
the prosecution, and since the holiness of the jury was greater
than their benevolence, the offenders were condemned to suffer
the pains of crucifixion. The less obviously wicked, whose looks
alone were insufficient to accuse them, were discovered by the
diligence of spies and informers. That "Christian act," the crucifixion of Harmless mirth, Jolley, and Griggish, for toying with
the girls and for other impieties, was followed by the trial and
condemnation to death of heretics, whose opinions of grace,
election, and vocation were uncalvinistic and detestable. The
virtuous citizens piously brained several Diabolonians in the
streets, and, appropriating the wealth of others, they gave it to
the godly poor.[62]

For the eventual triumph of this millenarian Utopia Bunyan
relied, as we have noted in our review of *The Holy City,* not
only upon the discipline of the church but upon the activities
of the lay preachers, to whose important work he also devoted
a conspicuous part of *The Holy War.* His ministers, who had
functions to perform in both the evangelistic and the millenarian
plots of this celebrated book, are sometimes treated literally
as ministers or captains and sometimes allegorically as graces.
The propaganda of these preachers—for Bunyan was always the
literary man—was the one weapon of this holy war.[63] The first
army which Shaddai sent against Mansoul was directed by those
four preaching captains, Boanerges, Conviction, Judgment, and
Execution. Boanerges or Son of Thunder (Mark 3: 17), was a
name commonly selected by the redeemed for the description
of favorite preachers; and the citation of I Thessalonians 2: 7-11
and Luke 10: 5 indicates the ministerial character of these war-

riors, whose army of forty thousand represents the Bible as well as the church. These preachers, who held commissions from God, not man, conducted their troops with discipline and decorum; for the world, as Bunyan said in the margin, "are convinced by the well-ordered life of the godly." [64]

In the futile effort to defend himself, Diabolus prohibited all preaching and news of Emanuel's coming, encouraged license and folly as proper antidotes to discipline, and issued frivolous counter-propaganda. Moreover, he insidiously informed his subjects that "the Ministers of the Word" had come as enemies to destroy the town, not to save it; and he appeared to be gratified by the obedient response of the ignorant, who exclaimed: "The men that turn the World upside down are come . . . the destroyers of our peace." The refusal of the inhabitants to listen to their preaching provoked from the captains the threat of force by which they alluded allegorically to a redoubled vehemency of preaching appropriate to the ears of the reluctant, who persisted, however, in describing the effusions of piety as an insufferable and hideous noise. The indignant ministers added, in words which Bunyan had used in his *Holy City,* that the wicked must listen or "take what follows"; for they had come as agents of the Lord to free the poor from a "cruel Tyranny." [65]

The colloquy between the ministerial invaders and the wicked proprietors of Mansoul follows the course of Bunyan's debates with the neighboring clergy, against whose pastoral privileges his campaign would appear from this to have had a millenarian as well as an evangelistic intention. To a supercilious query about his right to preach, Boanerges answered that he and his fellows were "ambassadors for Christ," (II Corinthians 5: 20), commissioned by God, in whose name he proceeded to utter intimations of the fury of their hastening master. Ill-pause, Satan's orator, doubtless a clergyman, and Lord Incredulity returned to the question of laymen's authority to preach and accused the captains of disturbance of the peace. At the instigation of their leaders, the townsmen "despised" the persons and message of the preachers of Shaddai's army, deeming them "some Vagabond Runagate Crew . . . gotten together in tumultuous manner" and disreputably itinerant.[66] These sneers and the rage of the captains inspired an attack upon Eargate, against which the invaders directed their artillery or the power of the word.[67] Throughout that winter they delivered orthodox sermons without intermission, and by the assistance of the Spirit became so tiresome that the inhabitants all but perished of fatigue. At last this ingenious campaign had its intended effect: the desperate townsmen mutinied, dissension grew, and riot completed what boredom had begun.[68] The incessant oratory of the captains and the clamor of their prayers were heard not only in Mansoul, where none could endure them, but in heaven, whence they decided Emanuel to descend, presumably in spirit, with a formidable armament of forty-four battering rams and twelve slings. Invigorated by the knowledge of his presence, Emanuel's militia plied the sword of the word and the sling with such effect that Eargate opened to them, but not without a dismal exchange in which Captain Conviction was wounded appropriately in the mouth.[69]

The Holy City had been secured, as Bunyan predicted in his tracts, by the preaching and prayer of the ministry, by the discipline of the saints, and by the spiritual assistance of Jesus, but without the conversion of earthly rulers, who had remained immune from fatigue or truth.[70] The new governors, as was proper in a theocracy, were ministers, who ruled, advised, exhorted, and defended the heavenly corporation. Their rule could not but be correct because it was their privilege to hold daily communion with Emanuel and they enjoyed the advice and the applause of the resident Spirit. That extraordinary and irresistible instrument which Emanuel devised for Mouthgate was the ministerial voice, which was not only to take but to defend the New Jerusalem. During the period of decline, the cautionary exhortations of ministers sent the townsmen home "sermon smitten" and occasionally, when the word was very powerful, "sermon sick." And to insure the menaced exclusiveness of the city, the preachers examined all who wished to enter. They never tired of annoying the surrounding Diabolonians with the sword of the word, they issued innumerable sermons to oppress the wicked, and when the enemy resorted to blasphemy, they replied with prayers, psalms, and more sermons. Their hopeful predictions of an ultimate victory, which they were enabled to foresee by the clever interpretation of texts, heartened the godly. But their fortitude was ignorantly ascribed by the Bloodmen to enthusiasm or "the extravagance of their wild and foolish fancies." [71]

For the success of the holy war Bunyan relied upon the work of the enthusiastic lay preachers, whose sermons and prayers turned the obstinacy of the profane into a wearied acquiescence and charmed the susceptible into the way of truth. The spiritual descent of Jesus to assume the crown, which, in His physical absence, the ministry could be relied upon to support over the throne at a suitable elevation, depended upon ministerial propaganda and awaited the triumph of the preacher, who controlled by divine assistance the sword of the word.

CHAPTER VIII

THE COMPLETE ANGLER

Art thou a fish, O man, art thou a fish?
Water of Life, III, 544.

The sword of the word is a very pretty instrument, which can annoy the wicked without wounding the tenderest sentiments of a saint; and when it is bent conveniently into a hook, it is useful for angling. Since engine and bait were metaphorical and the fish were men, the pious were much attracted to the sport and assiduously practiced it, less for entertainment, however, than for use, under the impression that the cause of their Saviour was at stake. To fish for men by words, to lure them into an agreeable captivity for the advancement of heaven on earth, was the principal occupation and delight of the lay preachers. These virtuous men had reduced their piscatory pursuits to a conscious and elaborate art, of which they were able to speak with great authority. John Bunyan devoted considerable attention to the capture of fishes, and by the more knowing of his admirers he was said to be adept at this elegant accomplishment.

The popular style of preaching and writing, to which Bunyan and many of his fellows looked for the establishment of Christ's earthly kingdom, was simple, colloquial, redundant, and conspicuously metaphorical. From the friars of the Middle Ages, who had availed themselves of *exemplum* and anecdote for the greater conviction of the poor, this variety of ministerial blandishment had descended by the obscure channels of apostolic succession to the humble preachers of the seventeenth century.[1] These successful propagandists also addressed the "mean and poorer sort of men"[2] in language and imagery which their hearers understood, and they adopted every traditional device of vulgar rhetoric to achieve the color, simplicity, and vehemence by which laborers and farmers were pleased. Sometimes from necessity but more often by design the lay preachers employed the idiom of their social class; they avoided, even when they were capable of, the scholarly allusions, the Ciceronian schemes and tropes, and the witty conceits of the clergy;[3] they drew their metaphors and analogies from the Bible and from the common life about them; and some of them, like Bunyan, cultivated a racy colloquialism with full awareness of its effect. The popular style had been developed in the early years of the Civil Wars by radicals who found in the rhetoric of Martin Marprelate and ultimately of the friars a means of disconcerting the Presbyterians and of stealing their audience.[4] The careful perfection of this popular mode accounts for the great difference between the sermons of lay preachers and those of the clergy, who declined to abate their gentility by stooping to the methods of the demagogue. It is not surprising that the vulgar preferred the attractive rhetoric of barn and hedge to the chill and academic cadences of the established pulpit. The loose and inviting style of the lay preachers was so inimical to the reputations and prejudicial to the interests of the clergy that it could not but be considered a menace to respectability and the state. Accordingly, when Roger L'Estrange issued his proposals for licensing the press, he urged the authorities to regard with displeasure and to destroy with care the tracts of "great Masters of the Popular Stile . . . [who] strike home to the Capacity and Humour of the Multitude."[5]

Few of the clergy saw the wisdom of humoring the incapacity of the multitude, but Richard Baxter, that eminent though godly man, condescended in 1674 to attempt "the language of the Vulgar" in order to win the attention of the obscure for whom he had designed a useful tract, *The Poor Man's Family Book.* But his inability to reconcile his conscience to the pursuit of a diffuse and degrading manner and the consideration that "riper Christians need not so loose a stile or method as the ignorant and vulgar do" made him abandon in disgust the usages of popularity.[6] The envious clergy were compelled to deplore what they were unable to emulate, but Praise-God Barebones, the pious leather seller, consciously affected the style of which Baxter was incapable. If by chance his tract should fall into the hands of the learned, he said,

I desire they would take no exception at any Tottologie or want of Art they shall find in it, for the Author professeth it not, and did applie himselfe to weaker capacities, and so went over things the ofter that they might the lesse mistake or mis-construe his meaning.[7]

When the clergy, who were insufficiently covetous of popular approval to learn of Barebones, indulged their rhetorical inclinations, they generally employed a style of pedantic wit, euphuism, and classical elegance, which in the mouth of a Thomas Fuller appealed to a sophisticated and courtly audience but held little attraction for the simple. And the colorless and intellectual clarity favored by the Anglicans of Restoration times[8] was neither diffuse nor amusing enough to be popular.

In 1656, however, a certain Abraham Wright issued a collection of five model sermons from the polite pulpit with the purpose of proving the inability of popular and the ability of cultivated preachers to adapt their method to an audience of any description.[9] To discredit mechanicks, who had convinced a lewd public that they alone were the "God-amighties of the Pulpit . . . because somewhat more forward then the rest of their Brethren in a popular way of preaching," Wright offered to the admiration of his readers the resources of style and manner at the command of Anglicans, Presbyterians, and Independents:

For when they shall clearly see, that any one of any Trade, and he too sometimes very deboist and vicious, can serve the turn of the Pulpit, they will then begin also to know, that it is not Gifts, but impudence, not the Spirit of God, but a frontlesse ignorance that calls out these men to Humor, and in humoring to divide and confound the people.

His hopeful sponsorship of the intellectual subtlety of Bishop Andrewes, the baroque ornamentation of Cartwright, and the unadorned precision of an Independent preacher before a substantial city audience, however, was imperfectly calculated to please the lower orders, who were better amused by their own preachers. The popular method could be counteracted neither by the exposure of the intellectual meagerness of mechanicks nor by a display of the scholarly devices of the educated but only by the adoption of a popular method.

Unwilling or unable to condescend, the conservative ministry sadly beheld the success of their popular rivals, whose vulgarity was superior to scorn and contempt. Even John Tombes, the respectable Baptist, deprecated those preachers who invented "sublimate conceites to fit the desires of the people," and the fickleness of the mob, who avoided dull in order to embrace popular preachers, "as if no teaching were wholesome meate, but such as is wet with their affected Teachers spittle, I meane his phrase, method, action, elocution."[10] But the successful preacher, whose unseemly deportment, enthusiastic heat, and colloquial speech were objects of clerical derision, was content to be scorned; for he won and amused new lambs for the Lord. If the inflexible clergy looked down their noses at him as an indecorous buffoon, he had the consolation of the evangelist and the showman in the grateful applause of the vulgar.

The rhetorical practice and the malicious deprecation of Vavasor Powell will serve to illustrate the problem of the popular preacher. An irritated clergyman complained that this itinerant was accustomed to appeal to the passions of the base by the use of homely analogies such as that of two horses, which, having met on the road, refused to part, a commonplace of bestial intimacy, from which Powell absurdly drew a lesson.[11] But the biographer of Vavasor Powell commended what the clergyman had condemned; the Welsh evangelist, he said, opened the word

to the meanest capacity, and still endeavoured to suit his discourse to the occasion and condition of the Hearers . . . he was very excellent in the illustrating of his doctrine by familiar Comparisons,

Parables, and Similitudes which used to be very profitable to the hearers, tending greatly to imprint the truth in their minds.[12]

When, at the commencement of his career, from both inclination and policy Bunyan adopted this method of preaching, he also received the abuse or the apology of the learned and the admiration of the good. That godly graduate of Cambridge, John Gibbs, who had preserved a suspicious remnant of delicacy, expressed the fear in his Introduction to Bunyan's *A Few Sighs from Hell* that some readers might be offended by the "plain and downright language" of the author, and that "the manner of delivery" might prejudice those who were "nice and curious."[13] The audience for which Bunyan had designed this excellent tract, however, required no apology for its popular style since he had given them not only the best his early talents afforded but what his readers desired. His followers were devoted to the plainness which Gibbs had hesitantly observed, and they expressed with no little vehemence their satisfaction with Bunyan's familiar manner, his use of similitudes, and the emotional depth of his preaching. Remarking upon the fertility of his invention, Ebenezer Chandler and John Wilson said that Bunyan possessed "a Peculiar Phrase to himself in expressing the Conceptions of his Mind," and had the art of saying with liveliness "deep things brought into a familiar Phrase" and "cloathed in a familiar Style."[14] To the testimony of these men, who had heard him preach, should be added that of Charles Doe, who had been taken by Bunyan's analogies and by the artfulness of his delivery:

. . . me thought all his Sermons were adapted to my Condition, and had apt Similitudes, being full of the Love of God, and the manner of its secret working upon the Soul, and of the Soul under the sense of it, that I could weep for Joy most part of his Sermons.[15]

Even more impressive of Bunyan's emotional profundity is the statement of an elegist, who lent to admiration the sublime assistance of poetry:

When for conviction, on the law he fell,
You'd think you heard the damned's groans in hell:
And then almost at every word he spake,
Mens lips would quiver and their hearts wou'd ach:
But when he came to speak t'a doubting soul,
His very bowels would within him roul.[16]

From another comment it appears that while many were attracted to Bunyan's sermons by the passionate simplicity of the man, whom the seasonable interference of the Spirit had filled with pleasing words, or by their anticipation of similitudes and pious insobriety, others came to hear him to be amused, as "meer Spectators for novelty sake, rather than to edifie and be improved."[17] The eloquent mechanick was compelled to suffer the attention of those whose carnal delight in his popular methods was equal only to their wonder that a tinker could preach. But Bunyan seems to have welcomed this adventitious interest and to have turned it to the advantage of the Lord by converting the curious as he trod with dexterity that perilous line between edification and amusement.[18]

He from above had gain'd that heavenly art,
To captivate the stoutest sinner's heart.[19]

The heavenly art of this ornament of his profession was of two varieties: a direct and simple prose, suitable for the conviction of the mature, and a familiar prose or verse, abounding in anecdote and metaphor, which he designed for the captivation of obstinate or difficult men, and for the enticement of children, females, and the feeble-minded. He discovered both varieties of method and all varieties of convert to be of value for the foundation of Christ's kingdom. On the evangelistic and controversial front he employed that straight and simple weapon the sword of the word, whose spiritual carnage conspicuously enlarged the province of the Lord; but for the capture and preparation of future theocrats, whose immaturity made the

sword unchivalrous or inexpedient, he wisely preferred to angle
with a bent and subtle instrument. Throughout the course of
this study we have met with examples of Bunyan's direct method;
therefore we shall now devote ourselves to the illustration of the
familiar and metaphorical art which occupied his ripest powers
in the decade before his death and to the evidence for considering him a conscious propagandist.

Bunyan made use of similitudes of the kind which had
imparted substance and color to the message of medieval
preachers; but he surpassed most of the popular preachers of
his generation in the quality of homeliness which his encomiasts
observed and which he appears to have cultivated. Bunyan's published sermons are distinguished by an agreeable incongruity,
common enough in the oral though not in the printed effusions
of lay preachers, a suggestion of the barnyard amid the auster-
ities of the temple, a fruitful but morganatic marriage of the
spiritual and the earthy, having the virtue of the conceit but even
more repugnant to decorum. That extraordinary sermon *The
Jerusalem Sinner Saved* was calculated to the meridian of popular taste and adapted to the edification of those who were enam-
ored of the exorbitant:

For example, though I shall give you but a *homely* one; suppose a
family to be very lousy, and one or two of the family to be in chief the
breeders, the way, the quickest way to clear that family, or at least
to weaken the so swarming of those vermin, is, in the first place, to
sweeten the skin, head, and clothes of the chief breeders; and then,
though all the family should be apt to breed them, the number of
them, and so the greatness of that plague there, will be the more
impaired. Why, there are some people that are in chief the devil's
sin-breeders in the towns and places where they live. The place, town,
or family where they live, must needs be horribly lousy, as it were,
eaten up with vermin. Now, let the Lord Jesus, in the first place,
cleanse these great breeders, and there will be given a nip to those
swarms of sins that used to be committed in such places throughout
the town, house, or family, where such sin-breeding persons used
to be.

I speak by experience. I was one of these lousy ones, one of these great sin-breeders; I infected all the youth of the town where I was born, with all manner of youthful vanities.[20]

The critical italics of the author and his rhetorical question in *Solomon's Temple:* "But why, may some say, do you make so homely a comparison?"[21] reveal an awareness of the character of his work. Bunyan fostered this congenial homeliness which experience had proved to be of value for the promotion of the Lord. In the pious endeavor to maintain the legend, which he had found so profitable, of being the simple and gifted laborer, Bunyan deliberately preached like one long after he had become acquainted with tedious and respectable English. His earliest sermons want the earthiness of the later; for when he was a practicing tinker, he had worn Sunday clothes, which the wisdom of maturity and the expectations of his audience were subsequently to make him discard. He had found the homely manner to be a splendid approach both to the understandings of the vulgar, whom he met upon a comfortable footing of social ease, and to the favor of superiors, the less delicate of whom were attracted by the informality of his preaching. Like Dupper, the cow keeper, and the other early mechanicks, if we may credit the parodies of their sermons,[22] and like Mr. Will Rogers of our own day, Bunyan capitalized the flavor of his inconsiderable origin.

Austerity, which had been foreign to the practice of Christ, was useless for the evangelist, whom Bunyan urged to handle the less obstinately wicked in the manner of the Saviour, to "be familiar with them for their good."[23] The personal anecdotes in Bunyan's sermons illustrate his practical application of the familiarity which he advocated:

I remember we had in our town, some time since, a little girl, that loved to eat the heads of foul tobacco-pipes, and neither rod nor good words could reclaim her, and make her leave them. So her father takes advice of a doctor, to wean her from them; and it was this: Take, saith he, a great many of the foulest tobacco-pipe heads you can get, and boil them in milk, and make a posset of that milk, and make your daughter drink the posset-drink up. He did so, and gave his girl it, and made her drink it up; the which became so irksome and nauseous to her stomach, and made her so sick, that she could never abide to meddle with tobacco-pipe heads any more, and so was cured of that disease.

Thou lovest thy sin, and neither rod nor good words will as yet reclaim thee. Well, take heed; if thou wilt not be reclaimed, God will make thee a posset of them. . . .[24]

Of his odd comparison of God to a thief and cheater Bunyan said: "I know the comparison is odious, yet such have been made by a holier mouth than mine, and as the case may be, they may be aptest of all to illustrate that which a man is about to explain."[25] The common analogy of broken bones and wounds was a favorite with him; he introduced the tender and the pathetic by instances drawn from courtship, marriage, the home, and the amiable conduct of the young;[26] and metaphors gleaned from the harvest and from the constabulary activities of the village lend the familiarity of barns and bailiffs to the mysterious work of the Lord:

If thou hast some beginnings that look like good, and death should overtake thee before those beginnings are ripe, thy fruit will wither, and thou wilt fall short of being gathered into God's barn. Some men are cut off like the tops of the ears of corn, and some are even nipped by death in the very bud of their spring; but the safety is when a man is ripe, and shall be gathered to his grave, as a shock of corn to the barn in its season, Job. xxiv. 20-24; v. 26 . . . Death is God's sergeant, God's bailiff, and he arrests in God's name when he comes, but seldom gives warning before he clappeth us on the shoulder; and when he arrests us, though he may stay a little while, and give us leave to pant, and tumble, and toss ourselves for a while upon a bed of languishing, yet at last he will prick our bladder, and let out our life, and then our soul will be poured upon the ground. . . .[27]

"Let me illustrate this truth unto you by this familiar similitude," said Bunyan as if in comment upon his general rather than upon a specific example of his practice.[28] Even when he drew his illustrations from the Scriptures, he made them homely and familiar:

Here is sudden work for sufferers; here is no intimation beforehand. The executioner comes to John; now, whether he was at dinner, or asleep, or whatever he was about, the bloody man bolts in upon him, and the first word he salutes him with is, Sir, strip, lay down your neck, for I am come to take away your head. But hold, stay; wherefore? pray let me commit my soul to God. No. I must not stay; I am in haste: slap, says his sword, and off falls the good man's head. This is sudden work.[29]

Age and sobriety had the effect of increasing both the number and the metaphorical richness of Bunyan's sermons. Two of these works of his mellower years are elaborations of single metaphors, conceits of the kind that Thomas Fuller had been accustomed to pursue intricately from page to page.[30] Bunyan's adoption of this practice may have been the fruit of his long preoccupation with analogy or of his belated imitation of a style which was growing unfashionable in the decent pulpit. The word "advocate," which Paul had used, gave Bunyan the opportunity, in his *Work of Jesus Christ as an Advocate,* 1688, to treat the mediation of the Saviour in the imagery of a court of law before which he pictured the celestial barrister pleading in language above legal reproach. Although he observed that "Similitudes must not be strained too far," nor must metaphors be followed too closely,[31] Bunyan was remorselessly consistent in the pursuit of this questionable image. Even more elaborate, his *Water of Life,* 1688, is a discussion of grace under the metaphor of a medicinal water. "If thou wilt," he said in the Preface, "call this book Bunyan's Bill of his Master's Water of Life." Take a dram of this potation, he advised, in parody of the medical advertisements of his day; it is a specific for all diseases; it will cure melancholy, dissolve doubts, stimulate the appetite, and gently purge a churlish humor. It may be taken with profit at the third, sixth, ninth, or eleventh hour; "Fill the water-pots, saith Christ, up to the brim." At the end he added:

"If any ask why I thus allegorize, I answer, the text doth lead me to it." [32] Elevated above the criticism of man by the example and provocation of the Bible, Bunyan had become a crier of nostrums, a medicine man for the inscrutable. This undignified sermon, enlivened as it undoubtedly was by appropriate gestures and by the professional intonations of the barber-surgeon, delighted and edified its numerous auditors. As the writer of Bunyan's epitaph justly observed, "In types and shadows he'd a mighty reach." [33]

The colloquial flavor and the dramatic interludes of Bunyan's sermons [34] imparted to the interests of the Lord the informality of the village green. The evangelists of our own day, the late Alexander Dowie, the Rev. William Ashley Sunday, and Mrs. Aimee Semple McPherson Hutton, have also been addicted to a wise familiarity. But Bunyan was conspicuous neither for his method nor for his deportment among the lay preachers of his generation.

Bunyan's critical commentaries upon his own practice were less customary. Throughout his sermons Bunyan was careful to scatter casual remarks upon his method, which appears from these passages to have been deliberate and conscious. His self-criticism deserves comparison with that of the educated ministry, which was aware of its literary devices, and with that of Benjamin Keach, the Baptist rhetorician. We have already noticed Bunyan's occasional observations upon his familiarity and homeliness, but he also had much to say about metaphor, style, biblical precedent, and the art of preaching.

He defined the value of metaphor for the uses of the pulpit in *The Water of Life;* [35] and after his employment of several similes in *The Desire of the Righteous*: "as the child is lapped up in its father's skirts, or as the chicken is covered with the feathers of the hen," Bunyan added: "I make use of all these similitudes, thereby to inform you of my meaning." [36] Most of these brief comments reveal an appreciation of the similitude as an expository device particularly useful for "weak capacities."[37] "O! What speaking things are types, shadows, and parables. . . ."[38] He invariably justified his practice by the example of the Bible; and occasionally, as in the following passage, he elevated the dignity of the higher criticism by his poetical rage:

> Indeed the holy Scriptures do make use
> Of many metaphors, that do conduce
> Much to the symbolizing of the place,
> Unto our apprehension. . . .[39]

In the rhetorical splendor of the Holy Ghost, whom he flattered with his imitation and gratified with his applause, Bunyan found scriptural justification for an art which might otherwise have been considered dubious if not carnal.[40] But that devout tailor, Benjamin Keach, had devoted a whole volume, *Tropologia: A Key to open Scripture-Metaphors,* to the admiration and classification of the metaphors of the Holy Ghost. This effort in folio to assist his less literate colleagues to a comprehension of unacademic and biblical rhetoric contains sections devoted to Christ as an advocate, Christ as a physician, and the Spirit as a virtuous water.[41] Bunyan's study of scriptural similitudes, however, needed neither the guidance nor the stimulation of Keach; and though Bunyan's critical commentaries are less formal and systematic than those of Keach, the metaphorical richness of his sermons is far more impressive.[42]

Bunyan was no less articulate about the merits of simplicity, which he advocated as suitable for a pious audience. He would speak, he said in *The Saint's Knowledge,* "not in a nice distinction of words but in a plain and familiar discourse."[43] By nice distinctions he referred to the academic style of the clergy, who, he said, played with words, affected uncouth expressions, and indulged their profane fancies with metaphysical wit. Benjamin Keach was equally hostile to the vain and flesh-pleasing rhetoric of the schools, to witty or learned turns and florid orations, and equally partial to godly plainness.[44]

A conviction that preaching was an art, which merited the study and care of the ministry, served to heighten and complicate Bunyan's practice. In his *Book for Boys and Girls* he compared the preacher to a skillful player on an instrument;[45] and in *Grace Abounding* he recorded his endless pursuit of the effective word, his diligent endeavor "to find out such a word as might, if God would bless, lay hold of and awaken conscience," and his effort "so to speak the Word, as that thereby (if it were possible) the sin and Person guilty might be particularized by it."[46] He labored to make his preaching concrete, personal, and attractive; and ever sensitive to the effect of his words, he noted their reception:

I have observed, that a Word cast in by the by, hath done more execution in a Sermon, than all that was spoken besides: sometimes also when I have thought I did no good, then I did most of all; and at other times when I thought I should catch fish, I have fished for nothing.[47]

Of the excellent art of fishing Bunyan was accustomed to speak with candor and sentiment; for as Scripture intimates, the fisher of men professed a craft, notable for its subtlety, exigent of skill, and distinguished by its sublime intention. The temple of Solomon provided for Bunyan's critical penetration the significant ornaments of nets and pomegranates:

These nets were they which shewed for what intent the apostolical office was ordained; namely, that by their preaching they might bring many souls to God. And hence Christ calls them fishermen, saying, "Ye shall catch men." . . . Pomegranates, you know, are beautiful to look on, pleasant to the palate, comfortable to the stomach, and cheering by their juice. . . . And this was to show that the net of the gospel . . . is sufficiently baited with such varieties as are apt to allure the world to be catched by them. . . . No wonder, then if, when men of skill did cast this net into the sea, such numbers of fish have been catched, even by one sermon. They baited their nets with *taking* things, things taking to the eye and taste. . . . No marvel, then, if men are so glad, and that for gladness they leap like fishes in a net, when they see themselves catched in this drag of the holy gospel.[48]

The sensuous bait of the Scriptures and the art of the Holy Ghost furnished Bunyan with material and instruction; and the aptness of the pupil gave him the hope of future achievements:

I have found, through God's grace, good success in preaching upon this subject, and perhaps so I may by my writing upon it too. I have, as you see, let down this net for a draught. The Lord catch some great fishes by it, for the magnifying of his truth.[49]

That *Pilgrim's Progress* was but another though a more ambitious, subtle, and unusual piscatory exercise is apparent from the poetical effusion with which Bunyan prefaced that instructive work:

> You see the ways the Fisher-man doth take
> To catch the Fish; what Engines doth he make?
> Behold! How he engageth all his wits;
> Also his snares, lines, angles, hooks, and nets:
> Yet Fish there be, that neither Hook nor Line,
> Nor Snare, nor Net, nor Engine can make thine:
> They must be grop'd for, and be tickled too,
> Or they will not be catcht, what e'er you do.[50]

The sermon was the engine of Bunyan's conventional angling; but when the capture of more difficult fish demanded the almost incredible method of tickling, Bunyan abandoned himself without hesitation to this unorthodox pursuit and produced *Pilgrim's Progress*. This work and the others for which Bunyan is now remembered were "tracts," as Bunyan's contemporaries correctly described them,[51] both in that they were composed with the purpose of his sermons, and in that they were logical extensions of the art of familiar preaching. By the promotion of the similitudes and the other popular devices which he had developed in his sermons from an incidental to an essential function Bunyan sought to catch the fancy and effect the salvation of a wider audience. Those who were immune from the occasional embellishment of the obvious tract might succumb to a more generous bait, a gilded engine, and a seductive manipulation.

Though Bunyan wanted the inclination and the accomplishments of the theologian, he possessed those of the popularizer. By the arts of metaphor, allegory, and colloquial speech and by the ingratiating disguise of verse or fiction, he adorned Calvin, yet made him familiar, concealed him without impropriety, yet introduced him to the curiosity and the favor of the public. As Charles Doe observed of that ingenious enhancement of Calvinism, *Pilgrim's Progress,* "it wins . . . smoothly upon their affections, and so insensibly distills the Gospel into them."[52] For over two hundred years this useful work has been the favorite resort of missionary and Sunday-school superintendent alike in their delicate task of enlightening without antagonizing the untutored mind.

The invocation of the Muses for the enlargement of piety was the almost inevitable consequence, as it was the extension, of Bunyan's art of popular preaching; but his interest in poetry and fiction may also be traced to a literary tradition then current among the Baptists and other dissenters, whose pleasing tracts inspired his emulation. In the early years of the century the Puritan Arthur Dent, whose popular manner Baxter attempted in vain to imitate, had employed the graces of dialogue "for the better understanding of the simple" and for the instruction of "the meaner capacity." Dent's *Plaine Mans Pathway to Heaven,* which Bunyan had thoughtfully perused, was an effort to popularize the fundamentals, as were his familiar dialogues on predestination for the use of the young.[53] The example of Dent and that of Richard Bernard, who had used allegory for the same purpose, were influential. Among the Baptists to follow this practice were Benjamin Keach, Thomas Sherman, and William Balmford, who had published virtuous dramas and allegorical verses before Bunyan turned his serious attention to the lighter evangelism.[54] Though Bunyan had found encouragement in the example of his predecessors, he succeeded more conspicuously than they; and the popularity of his works not only occasioned in turn the imitation of others, among whom were both Keach and Sherman, but served to establish the propriety of the familiar method. The Preface to Sherman's *Second Part of The Pilgrim's Progress* contains a statement of Bunyan's repute, intention, and indebtedness to the tradition of Bernard and his followers, who deplored but turned to their own advantage the debauchery of an age which could be contented only with novels, romances, and plays to the neglect of divinity and to the peril of the soul:

The observation whereof put some eminent and ingenious persons upon writing some Religious Discourses, which they designed for a General Use in such kind of methods as might incline many to read them, for the methods sake, which otherwise would never have been persuaded to have perused them, as Bernard's Isle of Man, Gentile Sinner, &c. Hoping that the Power of those plain Truths which they thereby delivered in so much plainess and familiarity, that made them the more easly to be understood, by most illiterate persons, and meanest capacities; and yet afford pleasure, delight and satisfaction to the most Judicious, Learned and Knowing Reader. And this consideration was the Motive which put the Author of the First Part of the Pilgrims Progress, upon composing and publishing that necessary and useful Tract, which hath deservedly obtained such an Universal esteem and commendation. And this Consideration likewise, together with the importunity of others, was the Motive that prevailed with me, to compose and publish the following Meditations in such a method as might serve as a Supplement, or a Second Part to it. . . .[55]

As Sherman prefaced this work with a critical discussion of his artistic and his ulterior motives, so Benjamin Keach and John Bunyan habitually devoted their introductions to the criticism and justification of their methods. For each of his more popular books Bunyan composed a preface wherein he declared and defended his literary and evangelistic principles. More elaborate than the incidental criticism, which we have noticed, these formal commentaries upon his aim, method, and scriptural precedent also testify to his thorough consciousness of the arts which he employed, and by their apologetic tone indicate the conservative hostility of some readers to the use of those popular devices by which alone others were to be taken. Though it is probable that these introductions were occasioned rather by the necessity of defense than by an impulse toward analysis, they are, nevertheless, Bunyan's essays in criticism, which differ from Dryden's less in kind than in magnitude and importance, and which reveal both deliberation of method and awareness of effect.

The first of these prefaces is to be found in *Profitable Meditations,* 1661, a small volume of verse, written for the most part in the ancient tradition of the poetical debate, and devoted to the harmonious advancement of truth. Bunyan had been moved to venture from the ways of prosaic evangelism into the gracious purlieus of poetry by the conviction that rhyme had power to seduce the obstinate and to confirm the pliable:

> Men's heart is apt in Meeter to delight,
> Also in that to bear away the more:
> This is the cause I hear in Verses write,
> Therefore affect this Book, and read it o're.
>
> When Doctors give their Physick to the Sick,
> They make it pleasing with some other thing:
> Truth also by this means is very quick,
> When men by Faith it in their hearts do sing.[56]

The variety of metaphors at Bunyan's command permitted this surprising deviation from the imagery of fishing to that of physic, which was, however, of equal merit for the discovery of his intention. His poetical preface was not limited to the subtleties of practical medicine but also embraced the more specious province of propriety. The generous influence of nature, and possibly of grace, had reconciled Bunyan to the assistance of the carnal arts; but no influence had power to abate the scrupulous antipathy of many Baptists to this almost idolatrous employment of the Muses. Before the stern tribunal of the pious, whose disinclination to countenance the questionable delights of poetry was as great an impediment to popular evangelism as to the singing of hymns,

Bunyan was constrained by necessity and hope to plead his justification by an ingenious apology:

> Take none offence, Friend, at my method here,
> Cause thou in Verses simple Truth dost see:
> But to them soberly incline thine ear,
> And with the Truth it self affected be.
>
> 'Tis not the Method, but the Truth alone
> Should please a Saint, and mollifie his heart:
> Truth in or out of Meeter is but one;
> And this thou knowst, if thou a Christian art.[57]

In the need for extreme methods to attract the immature and the aesthetic and in the illiberal displeasure of the conservative lay the dilemma of the Baptist poet. But undismayed by the misunderstanding of his excellent purpose, Bunyan continued the melodious celebration of sublimity and truth by suitable numbers, and eventually by works of fiction, for which he also provided prefaces of explanation and defense. The apologetic evangelist enjoyed the gratifications of art and the consciousness of virtue.

Bunyan devoted the Preface to the first part of *Pilgrim's Progress* to an apology for fiction, allegory, and the popular method. He had offered his manuscript to the judgment of the godly, some of whom said, "John, Print it; others said, not so"; but the encouragement of the former had more effect with the liberal author than the obduracy of the latter, with whom he took this prefatory occasion to expostulate:

> May I not write in such a style as this?
> In such a Method too, and yet not miss
> My end, thy good? why may it not be done?

For the enlightenment of those who maintained that his book was obscure, insubstantial, and giddy, Bunyan called attention to the example and implication of the Scriptures, whose irreproachable protagonists, the prophets, the apostles, and the Saviour had known and practiced the arts of metaphor, allegory, and obscurity.[58] Inspired and justified by the parables, types, and shadows of his heavenly model, Bunyan had piously adopted the metaphorical craft, to which he had also been attracted by the consideration that "Truth within a Fable" was more memorable and more solacious than doctrine unadorned:

> Come, Truth, altho in Swadling-clouts, I find,
> Informs the Judgment, rectifies the Mind;
> Pleases the Understanding, makes the Will
> Submit; The Memory too it doth fill
> With what doth our Imaginations please;
> Likewise, it tends our Troubles to appease.

The advantages of allegory also claimed Bunyan's attention in the Preface to the second part of *Pilgrim's Progress*:

> I also know, a dark Similitude
> Will on the Fancie more it self intrude,
> And Will stick faster in the Heart and Head,
> Than things from Similies not borrowed.[59]

Though Bunyan had said of the first part of this illustrious work, "It seems a Novelty," it was hardly one; for many writers such as Keach and Bernard had made use of dialogue and allegory to sweeten their message. The objection which Bunyan encountered was occasioned not only by his use of allegory, to which many of his readers were accustomed, but by his familiarity, his homeliness, and his want of proper dignity. If Bunyan had presented his similitudes with the sobriety of Keach or Patrick, he would have escaped the condemnation of the solemn; but he had introduced to fiction the agreeable familiarity of his preaching, and what had been and continued to be the cause of his success was now the occasion of reproach. The anticipation of this danger had made Bunyan warn the reader of *Pilgrim's Progress* to beware lest the levity of this book excite unseemly laughter;[60] and the grounds of his fear may be observed in the Preface to Sherman's continuation of his allegory. In order to rectify the blemishes of

Bunyan's frivolous work, Sherman had "endeavoured to deliver the whole in such serious and spiritual phrases, that may prevent that lightness and laughter, which the reading some passages therein, occasion in some vain and frothy minds."[61] His own allegory, Sherman claimed with pride, was so free from excitements to laughter as to be suitable for a gift at funerals. It is difficult for us to understand how Bunyan's pilgrim could have occasioned improper amusement, but the saints appear to have been delicately attuned to the risible. "Some there be that say he laughs too loud," Bunyan admitted in the Preface to the second part, but this laughter, he reminded the reader, had a serious purpose and a heavenly character. Since the objection to his familiar and homely style—

> This Book is writ in such a Dialect,
> As may the minds of listless Men affect.[62]

—had not prevented the success of his work, Bunyan ignored the captious, who confused the solemn with the profound, and despised the imitator, who was incapable of the gospel mode which "no man now useth, nor with ease dissemble can." The extravagant acclamation of the public encouraged the hesitant author and vindicated in his own eyes the employment in fiction of the homeliness of his tracts. The second part of the *Progress* is racier than the first; and his subsequent writings increasingly abounded in that familiarity whose virtue his triumph had proved.

The confident Preface to the second part of *Pilgrim's Progress* is not an apology. To those who objected he could now say that their dislike of his method was an unfortunate peculiarity of the sort which keeps some from the wholesome enjoyment of cheese, fish, or swine. Though the Prefaces of *Mr. Badman* and *The Holy War* contain less of a critical nature, they advance the claim of realism, repeat the theory of instruction through amusement, and justify the author's use of dialogue by his own convenience and the pleasure of the reader. It was Bunyan's growing assurance which enabled him to say in *Mr. Badman*: "Why I have handled the matter in this method, is best known to my self."[63]

Before we investigate the last and most extraordinary example of Bunyan's popular manner, we must pause to inquire into the natures and the prefaces of those less ingratiating works which Bunyan intended for men of riper parts. As we have observed, Bunyan had two styles: the popular for the immature; and the simple and direct for the knowing. His serious propaganda, he implied, was meat for the strong, and his familiar verses and allegories milk for the feeble.[64] Accordingly Bunyan advised those readers who were desirous of milk and incapable of meat to avoid *The Holy City* in which he had treated without frivolity a subject worthy of the interest of men. The Preface, which contains this advice, expresses some apprehension lest the learned and the exacting should despise his plain and homely manner, but the emphasis is upon the plain, and the homeliness is not that of his familiar tracts. Throughout this Preface he professed an intentional simplicity and indicated his avoidance of "high swelling words of vanity" in favor of "pure and naked truth" as appropriate to his noble purpose and serious audience. Simplicity had also recommended itself to Bunyan as suitable for those readers whose profundity was superior to entertainment and whose spiritual maturity was more apparent than their wit or learning:

. . . words easy to be understood do often hit the mark, when high and learned ones do only pierce the air. He also that speaks to the weakest, may make the learned understand him; when he that striveth to be high, is not only for the most part understood but of a sort, but also many times is neither understood by them nor by himself.[65]

The Preface to *Grace Abounding* also states the virtue of plainness and simplicity for solemn purposes:

I could have enlarged much in this my Discourse of my Temptations and Troubles for Sin; as also, of the merciful Kindness, and Working of God with my Soul: I could also have stepped into a Stile much higher than this, in which I have here discoursed, and could have adorned all things more than here I have seemed to do; but I dare not: God did not play in tempting of me; neither did I play, when I sunk as into a bottomless Pit, when the Pangs of Hell caught hold upon me; wherefore I may not play in relating of them, but be plain and simple, and lay down the thing as it was: He that liketh it, let him receive it; and he that does not, let him produce a better. Farewell.[66]

By simplicity Bunyan referred to that plain and relatively unmetaphorical style which he preferred for exhortation and for addressing those who required no adornment. His recognition of the need for two methods was founded upon the practice of the Saviour, who, he said, had used parables to reach the emotions of the people, but had appealed by directness and simplicity to the understandings of the disciples.[67]

The last conspicuous example of Bunyan's familiar style is *A Book for Boys and Girls*, 1686, a collection of unpretentious verses, by which the author hoped to enlarge the bounds of holiness by folly.[68] To avoid misunderstanding of his intention, Bunyan devoted his Preface to the ironic praise of frivolity, that subtle means of awakening the immature and the obstinate, and to securing himself from the imputation of childishness. He had designed this book of crude and homely emblems to appeal directly to children and to shame those adults whom the despair and effort of the ministry had failed to disturb. Since both children and childish adults were addicted to the sports of immaturity, Bunyan had supplied them with appropriate toys:

> Wherefore good Reader, that I save them may,
> I now with them, the very Dottril play.

The abandonment of gravity had an illustrious precedent; for

> Paul seem'd to play the Fool, that he might gain
> Those that were Fools, indeed. . . .

This extraordinary and almost impious statement, which is, however, an ingenious explanation of the perplexing character of Paul, served to establish the necessary precedent. "I could, were I so pleas'd use higher Strains," Bunyan said; but as careless as Paul of his reputation among the wise and the profane, he resolutely condescended to the catching of girls and boys:

> To shoot too high doth but make Children gaze,
> Tis that which hits the man, doth him amaze.
> And for the Inconsiderableness
> Of things, by which I do my mind express;
> May I by them bring some good thing to pass . . .
> I have my end, tho I my self expose
> To scorn. . . .

Bunyan's "Homely Rhimes" on pigs, frogs, and flyspecks are drawn from barnyard, home, and countryside, and couched in an inelegant idiom. The refined editors, who preserved the seemliness of the eighteenth century by the omission or the correction of these imperfect verses,[69] revealed both their ignorance of the popular method and their contempt for the Saviour, to whose example, in his thirty-first emblem, Bunyan had devoutly attributed the familiar quality of his eloquence.

Two years before the publication of this book for the young and the foolish, whose capture he had planned by means of homeliness and irony, Bunyan had cast his net for women and children in the second part of *Pilgrim's Progress*. For their enticement he had introduced the agreeable machinery of connubial, domestic, and infantile deportment, such as the nuptials of Mercy, the gratifying increase of the faithful by her industrious parturition, and the indigestion and relief of Matthew.[70] But this tender audience was equally fascinated by Bunyan's riddles, proverbs, catechisms for the young, and emblems of instructive beasts.[71] The "book of the creatures" had been opened by the diligent iconographer of Bedford, who looked with devotion upon stone and fish, pondered the symbolic inclination of the Deity, and wisely concluded that there was nothing on earth but had "some spiritual mystery in it." [72] "It is the wisdom of God," he said, "to speak to us, ofttimes by trees, gold, silver, stones, beasts, fowls, fishes, spiders, ants, frogs, lice, dust, etc." [73] Upon this celestial mystery and the habit of the Creator, Bunyan based the ministerial conduct of his Interpreter, who instructed the travelers of *Pilgrim's Progress* by emblems of dust, raindrops, and unobjectionable animals. The Interpreter had enlightened Christian, not by abstractions of doctrine, but by symbols; and for the inferior capacities of the women and children, this skillful minister displayed emblematic objects of a more homely variety, the muckraker, the spider, the comfortable hen, and the robin. "I chose, my Darlings," said he, "to lead you into the Room where such things are, because you are Women, and they are easie for you." [74] The popular and familiar method of the Interpreter was that of his creator, who had devised this gifted character, as he had his critical prefaces, in commentary upon his art.

Though ignorant of the advice of Horace, Bunyan gained the world as he dedicated his later years to the mixture of the useful and the sweet. He also knew, however, the power of the useful without the admixture of the sweet. Upon these two methods, which served in turn to present the same subject in *The Holy City* and *The Holy War*, Bunyan relied for the expansion of the theocratic church by the valuable increment of men, children, women, and fools. Bunyan's two-handed engine was the sword of the word, but in the light of his preference and later practice, better had it been called the hook.

CHAPTER IX

SWEETNESS AND LIGHT

Whereby 'tis plain thy light and gifts
Are all but plagiary shifts.
Hudibras, I, iii, 1327.

In their hospitality to the Spirit the gifted continuously discovered a sensation of exquisite pleasure and the conviction that their words were those of their celestial Guest. Concerning the favorite residence of the Holy Spirit we may accept the assurances of His hosts, but that His manifest presence and the oracular privilege which it conferred account, as they claimed, for the whole character of their literary work and that their ignorance or avoidance of literary tradition was perfect, we may be permitted to express a reluctant doubt. As John Bunyan shared the pretensions of his colleagues and rivals, so he also incurs the incredulity of the skeptical mind, which must regard the conformity of his writing to the fashions of his day as too strange to admit the easy explanation of coincidence. Of Bunyan's comparative illiteracy, which occasioned the scorn of the cultured and his own social discomfort, there can be no doubt; but that Bunyan was not as illiterate as he himself or his clerical enemies insisted is equally certain. A reputation of gifted ignorance was fostered by Bunyan, encouraged by his admiring contemporaries, and preserved by godly critics of later times,[1] who sought to increase the wonder of his work by the legend of its immaculate conception. But the patient industry of modern scholars has made it almost impossible to receive this pretty fable.

The contemporary biographers of John Bunyan unanimously celebrated his inspiration, his illiteracy, and the meagerness of his library.[2] One who had visited Bunyan in prison reported with satisfaction the sole and irreproachable dependence of that saint upon Fox's *Acts and Monuments* and the Scriptures.[3] It was natural to suppose that the example of the martyrs, the assistance of the sacred text, and the influence of its adorable Author were sufficient to enable Bunyan to draw excellent things from his own bowels. Swift's image of the spider and the bee was partially anticipated in support of this opinion by Ebenezer Chandler and John Wilson, who said of their departed friend: "Like the Spider, all came from his own Bowels; what the Spirit of God gave in to him, by Prayer and Study, that he freely gave out, and communicated to others. . . ."[4] The piety which animated these commentators prevented their observation of Bunyan's greater resemblance to the bee in its agreeable task of culling the materials for sweetness and light from the flowers.

Bunyan himself immodestly maintained the honey and wax of his works to be not the spoil of literary blossoms, but the surprising product of his bowels. To indicate his affection for spiders, to create the impression that his writings were spun of inspiration and the Scriptures, he continually deplored the works of man and bee. The Holy Ghost, he said, brooded over the illiterate and breathed upon them, who, thus inflated, spoke to the admiration of the wise and the good:

> 'Twas he who with his cloven tongues of fire
> Made all those wise ones of the world admire,
> Who heard his breathing in unlearned men.[5]

The Baptist enthusiast, however, depended less upon illumination from above than through the Scriptures. Bunyan devoted part of his Preface to *The Holy City*, which we have observed to resemble the millenarian tracts of his predecessors, to the claim of scriptural inspiration and literary innocence:

. . . had it not been for the Bible, I had not only not thus done it, but not at all. Lastly. I do find in most such a spirit of whoredom and idolatry concerning the learning of this world, and wisdom of the flesh, and God's glory so much stained and diminished thereby; that had I all their aid and assistance at command, I durst not make use of ought thereof, and that for fear lest that grace, and these gifts that the Lord hath given me, should be attributed to their wits, rather than the light of the Word and Spirit of God: Wherefore "I will not take" of them "from a thread even to a shoe-latchet,—lest they should say, We have made Abram rich." Ge. xiv. 23. . . . I honour the godly as Christians, but I prefer the Bible before them; and having that still with me, I count myself far better furnished than if I had without it all the libraries of the two universities. Besides, I am for drinking water out of my own cistern.[6]

Grace Abounding, another traditional work, contains a similar statement.

I never endeavoured to, nor durst make use of other mens lines, Rom. 15.18. (though I condemn not all that do) for I verily thought, and found by experience, that what was taught me by the Word and Spirit of Christ, could be spoken, maintained and stood to, by the soundest and best established Conscience; and though I will not now speak all that I know in this matter; yet my experience hath more interest in that Text of Scripture, Gal. 1. 11, 12. than many amongst men are aware.[7]

He said in *Solomon's Temple*: "I have not for these things fished in other men's waters; my Bible and Concordance are my only library in my writings."[8] And he added elsewhere:

I have presented thee with that which I have received from God; and the holy men of God, who spake as they were moved by the Holy Ghost, do bear me witness. Thou wilt say all pretend to this. Well, but give me the hearing, take me to the Bible . . . I have not writ at a venture, nor borrowed my doctrine from libraries. I depend upon the saying of no man.[9]

A prejudice in favor of the spiritual and the wise restraint of prudence made Bunyan averse to the mention of books or authors, whose earthly character could not but repel a favorite of the Holy Ghost, and whose names might occasion doubt concerning the heavenly origin of his Muse. To avoid the contamination of the Beast, to defend the honor of the Spirit, and to show by silence his contempt and independence of all earthly corroboration or material, Bunyan also refrained from citing sources and authorities.[10] The spiritual integrity of his sixty works could not be injured, however, by the casual mention of a dozen men: John Fox, Luther, Tindall, Campian, Ainsworth, Owen, Baxter, Jessey, Dent, Bayley, Samuel Clarke, and the author of *Francis Spira;* nor by even more casual references, apparently at second hand, to Machiavelli, Origen, Cranmer, and the Koran; nor by the detestable names of his controversial enemies. That Bunyan was also acquainted with Hobbes' *Leviathan* is apparent from a hitherto unnoticed allusion to that book during the progress of his discouragement of Edward Fowler: "but having overthrown the foundation, and broken the head of your Leviathan; what remains falleth of itself. . . ."[11] The ambiguity of this reference is removed by the pained and tragical response of Dr. Fowler: "Reader, canst thou fancy the Design of Christianity to be another Leviathan? or rather art thou able to retain any tolerable opinion of that man that calls it so, and represents it as such a piece of monstrous Devilism?"[12] Of these writers and books, though Bunyan admitted the influence of several upon his thought and development, and sometimes quoted *Francis Spira,* Fox, or Jessey, he credited only Samuel Clarke with any considerable contribution to his work. If we accept the inconspicuous evidence of Bunyan's citations, we are forced to confess his unfamiliarity with literature and to admire the fortunate receptacle of brightness from the air.

The number and the emphasis of his protestations, as well as the implication of his silences, make it necessary to conclude that Bunyan believed, or at least wished to have it believed, that his works were produced mysteriously in ignorance and disdain of carnal tradition by the sole assistance of God and the Scriptures. This conclusion was that of his friends and successors, Chandler and Wilson, who attributed his writings to the influence of the Lord:

For Humane Learning, it's true, he had none; but let it not be therefore said, that what was done by him, is not worth our Time or Pains to read: For as Conversion-work, or the New Birth, is not of Blood, nor of the Will of the Flesh, nor of the Will of Man, but of God; so the Author's Knowledge, and insight into Gospel Mysteries, was given to him by God himself; we don't say, by immediate Inspiration, but by Prayer and Study, without any other external Helps.[13]

But during the lifetime of Bunyan other men presumed to doubt the purity of our author's inspiration. Against the insinuations of these skeptical or impious men Bunyan issued the indignant Postscript to *The Holy War*:

> Some say the Pilgrims Progress is not mine,
> Insinuating as if I would shine
> In name and fame by the worth of another,
> Like some made rich by robbing of their Brother.
> Or that so fond I am of being Sire,
> I'le father Bastards: or if need require,
> I'le tell a lye in Print to get applause.
> I scorn it; *John* such dirt-heap never was,
> Since God converted him. Let this suffice
> To shew why I my *Pilgrim* Patronize.
>
> It came from mine own heart, so to my head,
> And thence into my fingers trickled;
> Then to my Pen, from whence immediately
> On Paper I did dribble it daintily.
>
> Manner and matter too was all mine own,
> Nor was it unto any mortal known,
> 'Till I had done it. Nor did any then
> By Books, by wits, by tongues, or hand, or pen,
> Add five words to it, or write half a line
> Thereof: the whole, and ev'ry whit is mine.
>
> Also for *This,* thine eye is now upon,
> The matter in this manner came from none
> But the same heart, and head, fingers and pen,
> As did the other. Witness all good men;
> For none in all the world without a lye,
> Can say that this is mine, excepting I.
>
> I write not this of any ostentation,
> Nor 'cause I seek of men their commendation;
> I do it to keep them from such surmize,

As tempt them will my name to scandalize.
Witness my name, if Anagram'd to thee,
The Letters make, *Nu hony in a B.*

To these extremities of rhetoric Bunyan was driven for the disinfection of his Muse from a suspicion which may be imputed less to the spleen than to the acquaintance of his critics with similar allegories. The reputation of inspired illiteracy which Bunyan had cultivated excited a skeptical interest in his literary accomplishment, which, if all he said were true, appeared little short of miraculous; for the impiety of the critical had permitted their recollection of many sermons and works of fiction which might have served as Bunyan's sources. The numerous readers of Bernard's *Isle of Man* must have recognized with pleasure or astonishment the origin of Mr. Worldly Wiseman and Lord Willbewill; and the allegorical themes of city and pilgrimage were familiar to the auditors of sermons and the consumers of tracts. Even Bunyan's poetical defense of his originality might have provoked the intolerant smile of the cynical; for this composition is the more remarkable for the resemblance of its concluding couplet, in which Bunyan gave the qualities of the spider to the bee, to several anagrams of Abraham Cheare, the Baptist poet, from whom Bunyan was to borrow the first line of a later effusion.[14]

The labor of recent scholars has supported the insinuations of the skeptical. The indebtedness of Bunyan to Richard Bernard has been exposed to our admiration, the allegorical pilgrimage has been pursued from the Middle Ages to the sermons and tracts of the seventeenth century, Bunyan's acquaintance with the popular romance has been demonstrated, and it has been shown with the assistance of science and industry that Bunyan may or may not have read *The Faerie Queene*.[15] These useful labors, which have centered in *Pilgrim's Progress*, have shown that, though Bunyan was unfamiliar at first hand with the works of the Middle Ages, he knew and used the little-known descendants of these works, the tracts, sermons, and romances of the seventeenth century, which carried their traditional freight to his notice. The ingenious speculations of Mr. Gerald Owst have been valuable in suggesting the sermons of Bunyan's time as the principal source of his similitudes.[16] Though much remains to be done to substantiate this theory, which would require the examination of all the sermons of the century as well as the resurrection of that pulpit oratory which failed to attain even the obscure permanence of print, the available evidence points to the correctness of Mr. Owst's assumption. Apparently at the impulse of the Spirit, Bunyan condescended to employ and to imitate for his imperishable works the materials of pamphlets, which are now as remote as they were once familiar, and of oral sermons, which are now, perhaps, recorded only in heaven. The extent and the nature of Bunyan's reading are suggested by his occasional, vague, and often deprecatory references to ballads, newsbooks, romances, fables, pamphlets, commentaries, sermons, emblems, and characters.[17] He confessed his acquaintance with the books of the Ranters and the Sabbatarians; [18] his use of metrics and the conceit attests his knowledge of contemporary verse; and the resemblance of his sermons in title, subject, and structure to those of his contemporaries reveals his studious interest in tractarian literature.

To discover the reason for his claim of illiteracy and to illustrate the nature and variety of the mechanick preacher's reading, we shall devote ourselves to the investigation of the apparent sources in the literature of Bunyan's time of three of his works, *Mr. Badman, The Holy War,* and *A Book for Boys and Girls,* which have recommended themselves to our notice because of their obvious dependence upon carnal traditions, because little of the evidence has been previously observed, and, inasmuch as the pursuit of literary influences is as repugnant to our temper as foreign to our interest, because three is a convenient number.

The Life and Death of Mr. Badman, Presented To the World

in a Familiar Dialogue Between Mr. Wiseman, and Mr. Atten-tive, 1680, which reveals Bunyan's practice of reworking the materials of pamphlet literature, is a combination of two popular literary types: the dialogue on moral problems and the story of divine judgments. For the conversation between Mr. Wiseman and Mr. Attentive, Bunyan had many precedents in the work of pious authors, who had resorted to dialogue in the effort to be amusing as well as instructive. But his immediate inspiration, as John Brown and Professor James Blanton Wharey have pointed out,[19] appears to have been Arthur Dent's *Plaine Mans Pathway to Heaven . . . Set forth Dialogue-wise, for the better understanding of the simple,* one of the few books with which Bunyan confessed his acquaintance. This edifying debate between Theologus and his friends concerned pride, dress, worldliness, covetousness, Sabbath breaking, games, mocking the ministry, swearing, drunkenness, and profane literature. Mr. Wiseman's capacity included and his eloquence illumined these doubtful problems, which were, however, too familiar to saints to have required the suggestion of Dent. But Bunyan was influenced by Dent's use of moral dialogue. And to Dent's book Bunyan was further indebted for his fortunate discovery of the Muck-raker, who had served Dent as the symbol of covetousness years before he resumed that function in *Pilgrim's Progress*: "The gripple mucke-rakers had as leeve part with their bloud, as their goods. They will pinch their own backs and bellies, to get their god, into their chests."[20]

Bunyan's dialogue differs from Dent's in having a central character, Mr. Badman, in whom every sin is united. For this unamiable person Bunyan may have drawn upon his experience with Mr. Wildman, of Bedford meeting, as Mr. G. B. Harrison has felicitously suggested;[21] but he appears also to have been stimulated by the newsbooks and broadsides devoted to the lives and deaths of rogues both real and exemplary, and decorated with cuts significant of the rake's discreditable progress.[22] There is seeming reference to this kind of literature in Bunyan's prefatory statement that he had presented the whole career of Mr. Badman "set forth as in Cutts."[23] Another and more congenial variety of the rogue story, that of the theological eccentric, seems also to have interested Bunyan. The account in *Mr. Badman* of the dubious individual of Oliver's days, who told his Miss to say she was with child by the Holy Ghost, reflects the tractarian accounts of the Ranters, who habitually fathered their children upon the Spirit or even more impiously claimed for themselves the character and fertility of God the Father.[24]

For the origin of Bunyan's principal theme, however, we must turn to the popular stories of divine judgments, which the saints collected and admired in imposing anthologies. Of the many collections those by Samuel Clarke, Thomas Beard, and Henry Burton were the most popular.[25] Clarke's *Mirrour or Looking-Glass Both for Saints and Sinners* expanded with each successive edition, gradually absorbed the materials of Burton and Beard, and became at last an encyclopedia for saints. In addition to several hundred folio pages of judgments, drawn from both ancient and modern history, from polite literature and observation, this incomparable volume contained all that the pious man need know of geography, history, and exegesis. Reference was so greatly facilitated by the classification of judgments under the appropriate headings of drunkenness, profanity, persecution, Sabbath breaking, pride, and the like, that the inquisitive reader could consult at will the tragical history of Christopher Marlowe, the blasphemer, or of Heliogabalus, whose use of food and love had been incorrect. The compendious work of Samuel Clarke was all that could be desired for a pleasant evening over geography and sin.

From the 1671 folio of this work Bunyan borrowed seven stories of divine judgments for *Mr. Badman*.[26] A desire to inform others of this edifying collection or a feeling that the great collector's fame among the saints made silence futile may account for Bunyan's mention of Clarke and, what is more astonishing, his inclusion of several page references to Clarke's book. Save for a few inconsiderable variations in spelling, punctuation, and vocabulary, these seven stories are faithfully reproduced in *Mr. Badman.* Seven more were attributed by Bunyan to his own experience or to local tradition; of these, the two stories of informers, whose wretched fates resemble that of a Bedfordshire informer mentioned in *A true and Impartial Narrative,* 1670, are apparently factual, although it must be remarked that judgments against persecutors had occupied the attention of most collectors, including Clarke.[27] The six stories for which Bunyan failed to account either in Clarke or in local tradition are of a type common to the collections. The stories of N. P., the swearer, of Edward of the blind alehouse, of the barber who cut his own throat, and of John Cox who perished disagreeably amid his own viscera, have not yet been traced to the anthologies from which they undoubtedly come.[28] Such tales of disturbing diseases and complicated disembowelments were as usual in the collections as those of drunkards who fell from horses; and each of Bunyan's stories contains the customary details, so essential to the suspension of disbelief, of name, place, and date.[29] Bunyan's reference to "my Author" in his story of Old Tod indicates its source in a printed work;[30] but the remaining story, which he attributed only to an unnamed "Relator," we have pursued successfully, by the assistance of chance, to its obscure original. The melancholy tale of Dorothy Mately, who sank into the earth and was seen no more, was taken almost verbatim from a collection of prodigies and judgments, *Mirabilis Annus,* 1661, by Bunyan's friend Henry Jessey, who had been assisted in the labors of compilation by George Cockayne.[31] Of the twenty judgments included in *Mr. Badman,* seven were frankly attributed to Clarke, seven to observation or rumor, and six, for which no definite source is given, were taken beyond doubt from anthologies or other tracts. In effect, *Mr. Badman* is but another of these popular collections, each of which had found its material in earlier books. And the catalogue of Mr. Badman's vices, which were illustrated by these stories, as well as the nature of his conduct, were determined largely by the usual classification and material of the anthologies. Mr. Badman took to drink and fell from his horse after the model of representative men, embalmed for the terror of the unregenerate and the pleasure of the good, in innumerable judgment books.

Mr. Badman not only contains a collection of these tales, but represents in both its plot and conclusion an interesting variety of divine judgment. At the end of his book Bunyan said that the quiet death of his villain was as much a sign of heavenly retribution as the violent fate of other sinners; that a quiet death was God's way of indicating His judgment upon those whose hearts He had hardened and whom in His inscrutable wisdom He had preserved from a spectacular destiny.[32] From this statement it is clear that the entire book is an elaboration of the judgment tale, with a new and subtle variation upon the usual ending of these instructive histories. The collectors of coarse and disgustful judgments, who were perturbed by the numerous failures of divine justice, preferred to ignore rather than to explain the frequent and mysterious neglect of the Lord. But Bunyan ingeniously discovered the peaceful death of a sinner to be not a fault of justice but the evidence of a celestial severity beyond that of common judgments and a paradox for the consolation of the hopeful.

The Holy War, as Professor James Blanton Wharey has excellently observed, owes much to Bernard's *Isle of Man;* and we have labored to indicate its debt to Fifth Monarchy literature. Bunyan also found encouragement and possibly material for *The Holy War* in two allegories of spiritual conflict by Benjamin Keach, *War with the Devil,* which we have already mentioned, and *The Glorious Lover,* 1679.[33] The influence of Milton's *Paradise Lost,* which Bunyan imitated at either first or second hand, and the contribution of the literature of trial scenes can be demonstrated. Concerning Hobbes and *The Holy War* it is impossible to descend much below the dangerous altitude of a conjecture, which, however, the indulgence of the reader may permit us to make in a modest footnote.[34]

The machinery of devils, which affected the reader of Bunyan's allegory with a pleasing confusion of pity and fear, the conduct and the oratorical temper of these degraded beings, and the alternate scenes of heaven and hell, suggest at once the elevated conceptions of Milton's mind. In their "now ragged and beggarly guise," a luster visibly impaired, the fallen angels of *The Holy War* arose in turn amid the discomforts of hell to debate a variety of plots, favored at last the use of guile, and intrusted their wicked purpose to the ingenuity of Diabolus, whose rhetoric was equal to the enticement of Mansoul, by a specious promise of knowledge and liberty, into the gluttonous consumption of a fruit. Meanwhile among the ornaments of heaven, Shaddai and Emanuel pondered redemption, despatched in vain a formidable force of men against the bad angels, and finally saw the wisdom of Emanuel's own participation.[35] The subsequent plots in hell of the fallen but ambitious angels are called "consults," a term which Milton had used to distinguish infernal debate.[36] These similarities, not to include the Ptolemaic astronomy, the classical mythology, and a possible reference in Bunyan's Preface to Milton's thoughts upon the population of the moon and stars,[37] indicate the acquaintance of John Bunyan with the plot and matter of *Paradise Lost*. Had Bunyan's literary isolation been as complete as he claimed, he could still have learned of this epic through Whitelock's minister, George Cockayne, or through John Owen, both of whom had secluded themselves in the agreeable retreat of Bunhill, near the fanatical burying ground and the residence of John Milton.[38]

But the problem of Bunyan's indebtedness to *Paradise Lost* is unfortunately complicated by the Miltonic character of Benja-

min Keach's *Glorious Lover*, 1679, a Baptist epic, which, nevertheless, cannot be denied to possess something of grandeur in
both manner and invention. Each of the sixteen books of this
poetical history of the redemption is preceded by an argument
in prose. As Keach justly observed and as his elegant allusions to
"Adamantine Chains" and "Ophirs Mines" sufficiently testify,
his Muse was "rais'd beyond a vulgar flight." These fine words,
as well as the allegory of Sin and Death, also serve to suggest the
suspicious intimacy of his Muse with her celestial colleague of
Paradise Lost. Our admiration is increasingly excited by the
"consultations" in hell of Benjamin Keach's devils, Apollyon,
Belzebub, Satan, and Lucifer, as they agitated the ruin of Jesus
in protracted and Miltonic oration.[39] These infernal conclaves
and the personification of Will and Conscience could have supplied Bunyan with material for *The Holy War.* His long rivalry
with Keach for the Baptist laurels supports this inference; but
though Bunyan knew Keach's work, *The Holy War* is closer in
its sequences and details to *Paradise Lost* than to *The Glorious
Lover,* which may have served Bunyan best by directing his attention to Milton.

The trial scenes, which are conspicuous in both *Pilgrim's
Progress* and *The Holy War,* furnish the clearest evidence of
Bunyan's unacknowledged debt to literary tradition. For many
years it had been customary for writers of pamphlets to employ
the device of a trial, in which the odious tenets of their enemies
were confuted by a judicial decision, and the characters of the
wicked secured by extinction from further menace to the truth.
The defendants were occasionally accused of moral impropriety
as in Bernard's *Isle of Man,* but as the literary inquisition grew
in favor, they were condemned more commonly for sectarian or
political crimes. Some authors elevated these judicial scenes to
the dignity of a whole tract; but others preferred to use them for
the dramatic illustration of an argument. The elements of these
trials were constant: in each the judicial process begins with the

cry of *O-yes;* the indictment is read by the clerk; the judge and
jury are named; and the culprit's plea of innocence is recorded.
At this point the prisoner usually denies the name under which
he has been indicted, protesting, for example, that his real name
is not Good old Cause but Rump. After he has been intimidated
into silence, witnesses for the prosecution, but rarely for the
defense, are called, and the biased jury invariably affirms his
guilt, which is reviewed by the judge and punished by the severe
penalty of imprisonment, banishment, or death. The trial of
Flora or May games by Thomas Hall is the record of moral indignation; but the trials of the Anabaptist and the lay preacher by
the same author are distinguished by a sectarian animosity like
those of Benjamin Keach, who subjected the Great Whore and
the Quaker to the justice of a Baptist tribunal. The arraignment
of the Presbyterian by Richard Overton for intolerance before
the judicial liberality of Mr. Trueth-and-peace, Gaffer Christian,
and Mr. Gods-vengeance of the Town of Impartiality, revealed,
despite the specious insinuations of Sir Simon Synod, the character and guilt of the accused; and the trial, conviction, and condemnation of Popery by an anonymous saint in 1680 were expe-
dited by the testimony of Sir Naked Truth and Sir Constant
Patience.[40] The trial scenes of *The Holy War* conform in their
religious, moral, social, and political implications, in judicial
procedure, and even in the allegorical names of the characters
to this established literary tradition, and afford unmistakable
evidence of their author's familiarity with pamphlet literature.

That poetical triumph *A Book for Boys and Girls,* 1686, also
reveals Bunyan's dependence upon the literary forms and usages
of his time. In this work the genius of Bunyan employed but
enriched the materials and followed the traditions of Baptist
poets and other writers who tirelessly issued verses, stories,
primers, catechisms, emblems, and fables for the consumption
of a youthful audience.

By 1686 Baptist poetry had been well established by the work of Benjamin Keach, Abraham Cheare, Anna Trapnel, and John Bunyan, whose *Profitable Meditations* had assured the existence, and whose subsequent labors had improved the luster of the twice-watered muse. His own practice and the example of other Baptists provided Bunyan in 1686 with the assurance for a more than middle flight. Though Bunyan's *Book for Boys and Girls* was justified and influenced, perhaps unconsciously, by this orthodox poetry for the mature, its immediate inspiration appears to have been a volume of verses for children written by the Baptist fuller Abraham Cheare.[41] These pretty but sometimes ominous songs had been printed in 1673 with a collection of cautionary tales by Henry Jessey, who, like James Janeway, had endeavored to appeal by prose to the undeveloped conscience.[42]

By 1686 an abundance of irreproachable literature had been furnished for this purpose. The desire to inform the infant mind had directed men of several sects into the production of catechisms, of which we possess examples by George Fox, John Worthington, the Presbyterians, and John Bunyan in the second part of *Pilgrim's Progress*.[43] The primer and the ABC of pedagogical sectarians had led the infant steps of original sinners from the alphabet, through the syllables to useful words like Nebuchadnezzar or predestination, to the Lord's prayer, and often to selections, for the practice of reading, from easy expositions of doctrine or the simpler abuse of the Papist. Works of this variety, combining the functions of alphabets, spellers, dictionaries, first readers, anthologies, and guides to opinion, had been produced by John Owen, Benjamin Keach, and Benjamin Harris.[44] The example of these men, whom Bunyan knew, had its effect on his *Book for Boys and Girls,* which is at once an alphabet, a reader, and a guide to doctrine. At the beginning of this work he placed an ABC, not on the scale of the primer, but more elaborate than the common hornbook since it was augmented by tables of names and numbers after the example of Keach; and he designed the poems to fill the office of first reader.

The impatient Muse of John Bunyan soared, however, not only above the pedestrian levels of pedagogy but also above the illiberal confines of sectarian poetry. His heavenly guide, who must also have assisted Benjamin Keach, had profitably observed the variety of stanzaic forms, the artifice of couplets, the similes, refrains, antitheses, conceits, and traditional subjects of contemporary verse, and even the baroque adornment which distinguished the work of a Giles Fletcher or a Crashaw.[45] The principal object of her contemplation, however, was the emblem, which contributed to the character of *A Book for Boys and Girls*. Of the seventy-four poems in this book most resemble the popular emblem in their formal division into two parts, description and moral, and in their subjects, the candle, the hourglass, the egg, the rose bush, the boy and the butterfly, and the child with the bird. These conventional materials appear in the collections of Quarles, Wither, and the other emblematists, but the engravings, which normally accompanied their philosophic verses, are wanting, for reasons of economy, in the collection of John Bunyan. His emblems of beasts, the snail, the mole, the swallow, the fish, the frog, the swine, the cuckoo, the hen, and the inconsiderable pismire, though of inferior elegance, are of greater interest:

IX. *Upon the Bee.*

The Bee goes out and Honey home doth bring;
And some who seek that Hony find a sting.
Now wouldst thou have the Hony and be free
From stinging; in the first place kill the Bee.

Comparison.

This Bee an Emblem truly is of sin
Whose Sweet unto a many death hath been.
Now would'st have Sweet from sin, and yet not dye,
Do thou it in the first place mortifie.

As the emblem of the spider in the second part of *Pilgrim's Progress* illustrates Bunyan's devotion to that curious beast, whose ugliness and venom, as he ingenuously confessed, put him in mind of the saint,[46] so this poetical emblem expresses Bunyan's unconquerable antipathy to the bee, with its produce of sweetness if not light, and by a resemblance to the bestiary provokes the question of origin. The medieval book of beasts, which had supplied the friar with oratorical embellishment, was closed to Bunyan; but the tradition of moral zoölogy had reached him through the inconspicuous channels of the sermon, the broadside, and the emblem. The occurrence of animal emblems in Bunyan's sermon *Resurrection of the Dead,* 1665, as well as much later in *Seasonable Counsel,* suggests what our search has as yet been unable to confirm, the common use of such emblems by preachers of the seventeenth century in their oral and probably in their written sermons.[47] Euphuistic and purely decorative animal lore from Pliny does appear in published sermons, and the conservatism of the preacher seems also to have preserved the materials and method of the bestiary. But the broadsides and often the title-pages of the seventeenth century employed the animal emblem;[48] and the collections of emblems, which represent an unbroken tradition from the early sixteenth century, presented the medieval zoo to the admiration of Bunyan. Though Bunyan habitually named the Bible as the source as well as the justification of this imagery, his frequent use of the term *emblem*[49] to describe it and the form of his verses point to his acquaintance with the poetical emblem of his day. The emblematists of the Renaissance, who were intrusted with the tradition of the bestiary, preferred to ascribe their ethical analysis of beasts to the learning of Pliny and other classical authorities; but the inspiration if not the immediate source of their work was medieval. Of these men Geffrey Whitney issued in 1586 his emblems of the crocodile, beaver, elephant, scarab, dolphin, sow, ostrich, and pelican.[50] Francis Quarles was ignorant or negligent of bestial creatures; but George Wither, an edition of whose book appeared one year before *A Book for Boys and Girls,*[51] carried on the tradition with moral comments upon the crocodile, salamander, gryphon, pelican, and elephant of earlier collections, together with many kindlier animals, such as the pig, the bee, the squirrel, the fowl, the spider, and the snail. Bunyan also pondered the meaning of bees, spiders, pigs, and snails, as well as that of flint, music, and candles, which had previously occupied the attention of Wither. Though the division of Bunyan's verses, save for the heading *Comparison* which may owe something to the fable,[52] is that of Wither, and though the two writers introduced their collections with strangely similar prefaces,[53] there is little indication that Bunyan found more than encouragement and example for his homelier rhymes in the poetry of Wither. There is every reason to suppose, however, that Bunyan had read George Wither or one of the many other emblematists.

The hunting of literary sources, though commonly a harmless pastime, is also a mystery, hardly susceptible of perfect solution; and when the silence of the investigated author provokes the ingenuity of the critic, the latter may incur the peril which he had destined for his quarry. But the investigation by many competent scholars of the allegorical sources of *Pilgrim's Progress* has demonstrated beyond reasonable doubt the dependence of that book upon tradition; and our less ambitious inquiry into the emblem, the trial scene, the divine judgment, and other matters, has revealed the effect upon Bunyan's work of other contemporary influences. Except for an occasional phrase, the name of a character, or an isolated passage, such as the episode of Dorothy Mately in *Mr. Badman,* Bunyan appears, however, to have refrained from direct appropriation. It must be concluded that Bunyan was well read, particularly in pamphlet literature, and that his works reflect the literary traditions of his time. It is now possible to affirm, what we had made bold to suspect, the true affinity between John Bunyan and the industrious bee.

We are now at last obliged to confront the pretensions of John Bunyan to freedom from worldly influence and to dependence only upon the Scriptures and the Holy Ghost. If examined in the light of his evident indebtedness to carnal tradition, Bunyan's protestations might excite the suspicions of the skeptical, but they can serve only to stimulate the studious and the devout to the discovery of a comfortable explanation. Bunyan may, perhaps, have remained unconscious of the influence which his reading had upon his work. Since his claims appear to be sincere, we might suppose his belief in the literary operation of the Spirit to have been sufficient to obscure from himself the vagaries of his pen;[54] for as we are aware, the depths of the pious mind are profound, its intricacies Minoan. It is possible that his definition of unoriginality was too narrow to include his practices. But it is more reasonable as well as more flattering to the intelligence of John Bunyan to credit him with motives of policy. The most orthodox saints have generously condoned and, not infrequently, have condescended to illustrate the use of pious deception for the defense of the Almighty and the advancement of His reputation.

This reasonable explanation is supported by the evidence of history. The tracts of the lay preachers, who diligently imitated each other and their superiors,[55] advance with considerable candor the claim of inspiration and originality. Matthew Coker, the prophet of Lincoln's Inn, said of one of his compositions: "In all which prophesie, there is not one sentence of my own invention. . . . I wrote it by the immediate and sudden impulse of Gods Spirit."[56] Edward Burrough and T. Tany were raised, they said, by inspiration above a carnal reliance upon books; and Henry Clark condemned the clergy who, when they preached or wrote, "have it not by Revelation from Jesus Christ, but from the Letter, and by works of other men, their own study and imaginations, which comes out of the bottomless Pit."[57] These uneducated but literate men, whose ignorance of books was less than they or the clergy pretended, were driven by the scorn of the wicked and the admiration of the redeemed to adopt the doubtful arguments of obscurantism. The enthusiast, who appeared to speak with the tongue of God, was compelled by the character of his office to maintain his spiritual distinction by denying the influence of man. The simple audience of the inspired would have turned in sorrow from the impolitic prophet whose admission of literary assistance had proved the imperfection of his gift.

To maintain his professional repute and the legend of his gift, John Bunyan wisely announced the literary aid of the Holy Ghost and concealed by silence and the boast of illiteracy the carnal sources of his work. There was reason for this care; for his reputation as an enthusiast had been endangered by those critics whose doubts had "scandalized" his name and driven him in defense of his gift to the dubious refuge of an anagram.[58] The choice of this unfortunate image of honey and bees, which discloses what he had endeavored to conceal, illustrates the agitation of the suspected prophet. In another passage which we have already quoted Bunyan admitted the professional necessity of neglecting, or if we may add what he could not be expected to say, of appearing to neglect the influence of books: "I durst not make use of ought thereof, and that for fear lest that grace, and these gifts that the Lord hath given me, should be attributed to their wits, rather than the light of the Word and Spirit of God. . . ."[59] That the Spirit maintained a residence within John Bunyan we may allow for the encouragement of piety and for want of contrary evidence; but that the literary work of this favored saint owed its form and substance to his ghostly tenant we must decline to believe. Reason and history compel us to ascribe the literary pretensions of John Bunyan to prudence and policy. The gift which was his distinction must serve as his excuse. Unless Bunyan's claim of literary innocence is interpreted as politic, the traditional character of his work would suggest the Holy Spirit's unoriginality; but reason recoils from this dangerous and ignoble inference.

BAD EMINENCE

Triumphant laurels seemed to grow
No where so green as on his brow.
Hudibras, I, iii, 297.

Whether the delectable fancies of Bunyan's muse were the effect of an "excellent Operation of the special Grace of God in him, and the gift of Utterance," as Charles Doe, the devout comb-maker of Southwark, believed, or the less mysterious product of industry, imitation, and wit, they secured for our author the pleasures and the penalty of fame. From the indigent obscurity of his origin the labors of pen and pulpit raised Bunyan to the eminence of popular success;[60] and the last decade of his life was a continual triumph, sweetened by the applause of the faithful, superior to the disdain of the obstinate, and immune from the diligence of constables. His asperity was mitigated by the conveniences of life; and with their success, his writing and preaching improved in mellowness and even in urbanity. Innumerable men, together with their wives and children, purchased or read his books and attended his sermons not only in the counties but in the great metropolis. When he preached in London, the house could contain neither the multitude nor the enthusiasm of his auditors; three thousand came to hear him at a town's end meeting-house, "so that half were fain to go back again for want of room, and then himself was fain at a back-door to be pull'd almost over people to get up stairs to his Pulpit"; and, what is hardly credible, twelve hundred appeared at seven o'clock in the morning of a working day in the dark winter time to admire his eloquence.[61]

In London, where he was a frequent visitor, Bunyan occupied the open-communion pulpits of Stephen More, John Gamman, and Pinners' Hall.[62] The respectability which attached to an invitation to preach at Pinners' Hall, the conspicuous center of dissenting oratory, had rendered the honor, as Walter Wilson observed, the object of sectarian ambition.[63] Though the Baptist pulpit had been closed to Bunyan by his toleration of sprinkling, the open-communion churches welcomed the celebrated saint, and it is probable that he also preached in the liberal Independent churches of John Owen, George Cockayne, Anthony Palmer, George Griffith, Richard Taylor, and Matthew Mead, with all of whom Bunyan's meeting was on terms of tender intimacy.[64] The metropolitan triumph which Bunyan enjoyed in these penultimate years had been anticipated in Bedford by the spontaneous tribute he received from the faithful at the dedication in 1672 of a more elegant and capacious edifice for the worship of God, a barn which had been legally acquired by the generous contributions of his flock.[65]

The eagerness with which the saints of London came to Bunyan's sermons must be ascribed not only to his abilities in the pulpit and to the distinction of martyrdom, which he gracefully supported, but to the success of his books, which had imparted to the once obscure mechanick the attractiveness of the famous author. "His Works being here before him, made him the better accepted," said one of his nameless biographers; and Charles Doe, who had heard that the eminent writer sometimes came to London, went to hear him "because of his Fame, and I having read some of his Books. . . ."[66] His printed works, at one time merely the literary extension of his oral preaching, had opened new and splendid opportunities, upon which the ingenious evangelist seized, for the exercise of his gifts and piscatory arts; with the acquisition of fame, his bait was fresh, his rivers new.

By 1692, according to Charles Doe, about one hundred thousand copies of *Pilgrim's Progress* had been sold; it had been translated into foreign tongues, and had surpassed by ninety thousand copies the combined sale of Benjamin Keach's two most popular allegories.[67] Bunyan's great work had achieved the honor of numerous imitations; envious publishers had issued spurious tracts in his name; and his own publisher had earned the flattering name of "Nathaniel (alias Bunyan) Ponder."[68] Even Bunyan's lesser works "sold admirably well," to the spiritual enlargement of many, including Charles Doe, who was filled one day with the peculiar love of God as he stood on his stair-head, "and about the middle of the Stairs," he said, "I reckoned, that to Sell Books was the best I could do, and by that time I came to the bottom, I concluded to sell Mr. Bunyan's, and so began to Sell books, and have Sold about 3000 of Mr. Bunyan's. . . ."[69]

The elect distinguished Bunyan's name by the addition of those pleasing adjectives, celebrated, famous, and eminent. Though his admiring audience was composed largely of the vulgar, Bunyan's fame was not unknown to more illustrious men. King Charles is reputed to have expressed his astonishment over the equanimity with which John Owen could hear a tinker preach, and Anthony Wood was aware of Bunyan's success.[70] There is little evidence to indicate the approval of any but pious contemporaries, but from the ranks of the wicked and the gently reared came occasional references to Bunyan, which show, if not affection, at least the extent of his repute. Tom Brown, the journalist, reported an imaginary debate in hell between a shoemaker, James Nayler, the Quaker, and Bunyan the tinker.[71] The sectarian bays, which Bunyan gratefully wore, may have obscured his vision by their inclination upon his brows or by the luxuriance of their foliage; for in the Preface to the second part of *Pilgrim's Progress* he claimed for his Muse not only the attention but the adulation of the upper as well as the lower orders, of brave gallants and gentlewomen as well as saints, Frenchmen, and the wild Irish. Bunyan's boast of the universal esteem in which his Pilgrim was held by men of all ranks is of less value as an indication of the character of his audience than of the magnitude of his pride.

Pride was the last infirmity of popular preachers, who often confessed to it, invariably fought it, and sometimes succumbed. Their gifts, the evident favor of the Spirit, and the admiration of the public, tested the humility and tried the endurance of these fortunate men. John Tombes devoted a monitory volume to the error of glorying in gifted men.[72] The odious decline of John Child, the friend of Bunyan, was ascribed by himself and by Benjamin Keach, who was not untouched by the same failing, to the sin of pride. Of Child Keach said, "being much followed wherever he preached, both in the City and Countrey, yet he seemed to be of a haughty Spirit, loving Applause and Popularity, which it may be feared was the Cause of his Fall."[73] Bunyan continually warned the gifted against the exaltation to which they were prone, against the flattery of an audience, and against the pride of being "enabled with expressions."[74] That he himself had experienced and struggled against the infirmity of gifted men, is evident from his ingenuous confession in *Grace Abounding:*

I have also, while found in this blessed Work of Christ, been often tempted to pride and liftings up of Heart; and though I dare not say, I have not been affected with this, yet truly the Lord of his precious mercy hath so carried it towards me, that for the most part I have had but small joy to give way to such a thing: for it hath been my every days portion to be let into the evil of my own heart, and still made to see such a multitude of Corruptions and Infirmities therein, that it hath caused hanging down of the head under all my Gifts and Attainments; I have felt this Thorn in the Flesh (2 *Cor.* 12. 8, 9,) the very mercy of God to me. . . . This consideration therefore, together with some others, were, for the most part, as a Maul on the head of Pride, and desire of vain-glory: What, thought I, shall I be proud because I am a sounding Brass? . . . . This shewed me too, that gifts being alone, were dangerous, not in themselves, but because of those evils that attend them that have them, to wit, pride, desire of vain glory, self-conceit, &c. all which were easily blown up at the applause, and commendation of every unadvised Christian. . . .[75]

In the Valley of Humiliation Apollyon confronted Christian with the accusation of pride: "thou art inwardly desirous of vain Glory," said the fiend, "in all that thou sayest or doest"; to which Christian replied: "All this is true . . . these infirmities possessed me in thy Country, for there I suck'd them in, and I have groaned under them, being sorry for them, and have obtained Pardon of my Prince."[76] To the end of his days Bunyan was compelled to contemplate within himself the penalty which the gift entailed; at times the antidote of humility, as in the Preface to the second part of the *Progress,* proved ineffectual; and in the obituary, composed by George Cockayne, Bunyan's inclination to this ministerial sin and his untiring struggle against it were mentioned: "The truth is, as himself sometimes acknowledged, he always needed the thorn in the flesh . . . lest, under his extraordinary circumstance, he should be exalted above measure; which perhaps was the evil that did more easily beset him than any other."[77]

The success of his gift had atoned, however, for years of mockery and oppression, and had given to Bunyan a measure of earthly happiness.[78] He had arrived at the Land of Beulah, mounted upon a Baptist Pegasus, which, though led to the still waters, had been allowed to remain undipped. But mounted upon his fleshly horse one day, the celebrated itinerant caught a sweating distemper, descended to preach an eloquent sermon on John 1: 13, and presently expired at the house of a pious grocer of Holborn. The remains of John Bunyan were interred amid great applause in Tindall's Burying Ground, better known as Bunhill Fields.

APPENDIX

APPENDIX

STRANGE & TERRIBLE NEWES
FROM CAMBRIDGE

Now Alas what hope,
Of converting the Pope . . . .
A Relation of a Quaker, 1659.

The sectarian heat of the summer of 1659 in Cambridge, the irreligious conduct of a witch, and the chagrin of an alleged horse contributed to Bunyan's controversial career a hitherto neglected episode. The two surviving pamphlets which contain the details of this unfortunate history were mentioned by the Quaker bibliographer Joseph Smith, and one was known to the Rev. George Offor, who dismissed with contempt what he thought repugnant to the fame of his hero.[1] That these pamphlets have escaped all recent notice by Bunyan's biographers is probably to be attributed rather to the decency than to the negligence of these excellent men. But a regard for the truth, however unpleasant, has compelled the consideration, in the obscurity of an appendix, of a subject which illustrates the character of John Bunyan.

The spiritual elevation of Daniel Angier's barn, to which an inscrutable providence had directed Bunyan in May, 1659, had been impeded not only by the objections of the Rev. Thomas Smith and other clergymen, but by the competitive ministrations of the Quakers, who since 1653 had incessantly dispelled the darkness of Cambridgeshire. These ambassadors of the Spirit had entered college quadrangles to deplore the synagogues of Satan; and in 1659, when the conviction of the mayor's wife had secured her husband's complaisance, a Quaker was moved by the Lord to discard his garments and, to the confusion of the profane, to pace naked through the streets of Cambridge. During this very year George Whitehead and Alderman Blackley, enduring the martyrdom of refuse, mops, and domestic vessels of convenience with which the students and the Rev. Thomas Smith endeavored to embarrass them, were busy in the university town.[2] If he were to extend the work of salvation beyond the decent but limited confines of Daniel Angier's barn, Bunyan saw the necessity of destroying or at least of discrediting these attractive rival itinerants with whom for several years his relations had been difficult.

In July, 1659, about a month before the Whitehead-Fox dispute with Smith,[3] Bunyan saw his opportunity in the tears of the unfortunate Margaret Pryor, who had been temporarily transformed into a horse two years earlier by the witchcraft of Widow Morlin, a Quakeress of the vicinity. Since the affection of Quakers for horses was a matter of common knowledge in 1659,[4] and since the witchcraft of the former was universally recognized, this Quakeress was indicted by the grand jury and brought to trial before Judge Windham at the midsummer assizes at Cambridge. A devotion to justice or a desire to make the most of a sectarian scandal led two enemies of the Quakers to express their condemnation of this witch in print; one of them was the anonymous author of *Strange & Terrible Newes from Cambridge,* and the other John Bunyan.

The Quakeress was acquitted, but on August 8, 1659 Alderman Blackley, one of the leading resident Quakers of Cambridge, published *A Lying Wonder Discovered*[5] in order to expose the wickedness of the enemy. It is chiefly to this tract that we owe our knowledge of the unhappy affair and of Bunyan's part in it. According to Blackley, Margaret Pryor, a woman of lewd deportment, had attended Quaker meetings for a time without becoming a member of the society, but had subsequently returned to the established church, whose priest or another interested person had persuaded her to invent her dubious story.[6] Margaret Pryor, said Blackley,

hath brought a slander upon some of them called Quakers, in accusing one of them with bewitching her into a Mare, and saying that two of the Quakers did ride upon her when she was a Mare, four miles from the place where she lived, to a banquet, she said, they were at, which thing she having wickedly muttered abroad, some in their hatred against the people of God did instigate the woman to proceed against these whom she thus accused, (as she confessed) to have them Indicted for witches, which was nigh two years after the time that she said she was so ridden.

After withdrawing her charges against William Allen,[7] one of the Quaker equestrians, Margaret Pryor had reaffirmed before the court her accusation of Widow Morlin, who on November 20, 1657[8] had taken her out of bed from her husband in the night, "put a bridle into her mouth, and transformed her into a bay Mare, and rode upon her to Maddenly House, where she said they hung her on the latch of the door, and that they went in to the Feast, where she said they had Mutton, Rabbets and Lamb." The skepticism of the judge, who had suspected conspiracy, was equaled by the acuteness of Blackley, who did not fail to notice the enormities and inconsistencies of Margaret

Pryor's story. In answer to the judge's question whether her hands and feet had not been sore or dirty, she had replied, only her hind feet; whereas, remarked Blackley, in a horse the front feet become more tender. How they could have had lamb in November when it is out of season, or how she, a mare, and presumably a vegetarian while in that condition, could distinguish meats was beyond Blackley's understanding and apparently beyond that of the jury, who had acquitted the accused widow in fifteen minutes.

Strange & Terrible Newes from Cambridge[9] appeared shortly after this trial in the belated effort to keep the scandal fresh. The unknown author of this six-page news pamphlet, careless with his details, rendered the name of Margaret Pryor incorrectly as Mary Philips, a discrepancy upon which Blackley seized together with certain others between this account and the testimony of Mistress Pryor before the court. From the "priest-like language" of this tract[10] Blackley conjectured that it had been composed by a local cleric; but it is probable from the nature of its errors that it had been hastily compiled by a London newswriter. The increasing menace of geomancy, pyromancy, necromancy, and the indecency of the Quakers[11] occupied the main attention of the author, who left only a page and a half for the affair at Cambridge. The mushroom growth of witches in his day, he said, proceeded from the Prince of Darkness,

. . . as manifestly appears in the case of Mary Philips, who falling from the Church of England, entered into the Society of Robert Dickson, and Jane Cranaway, two unrefined Quakers; but after some few weeks expired, she declined their ways, utterly renouncing them, and detesting their actions; insomuch, that they adjudged her to be in a Reprobate Condition, and not worthy of an Earthly Being; but rather a transfiguration from the Glorious Image she was created in; which (poor Soul) she was soon divested of, even in the Night, as she betook her self to rest with her Husband, being bewitched or inchanted out of the Room where she lay, and transformed into the perfect shape of a Mare, and so rid from Dinton to a Town within four miles of Cambridge, where a Company of seeming Quakers were met: But upon the aforesaid Inchanting-Witches alighting off, and hanging the Bridle upon the Pails, the snaffle (or Bitt) came out of her mouth, and miraculously she appeared in her created Form and Likeness, to the great astonishment of the Neighbors, who beheld this unexpected change with abundance of admiration; and upon the Womans declaring of her self, and the state of her Condition, she went along with some Officers to the Meeting, and coming into the Room, she pointed to the two Quakers, saying, This is the Man and Woman that bewitcht me: Whereupon they were apprehended, and carryed before a justice, who committed them to safe Custody, there to remain till the Assises, which on Thursday last began at Cambridge, and on Friday they were brought to Trial, where the Woman that was bewitcht made Oath against them, and shewed her hands and feet, which were lamentably bruised, and changed as black as a Coal, her sides being also exceedingly rent and torn, just as if they were spur-gal'd, and her smock all bloudy: Evident signs of her sad sufferings; yet utterly denied by the prisoners, who at last were cleared, notwithstanding the Grand Jury finding the Bill of Indictment.

The evident misrepresentations of this account deserved the reasonable rebuke of Alderman Blackley, who said:

. . . its a great disgrace and shame to Priests professors and Schollars, that such grosse dirty stuffe should ever be reported or given credit to by them in Cambridge, or elsewhere; for beside the falshood of this report, see how grosse it is to tell of *the Womans sides being rent and torne and her smock being bloody,* who also told us, *that her smock was all on a muck sweat, with their riding on her,* as if when she was a mare or a horse (as is reported) she could wear her smock; what, can a horse be ridden in a woman's smock? Oh! grosse delusion and folly, that ever Cambridge should be so dishonoured, as to have such newes as these proceeding from any of the learned in it. . . .

A comparison of Blackley's report of *Strange & Terrible Newes* with the original indicates the scrupulous accuracy of the alderman. His reliability would appear from this to have been as great in his account of Bunyan's tract, for knowledge of which, in the absence of the original, we must rely entirely upon *A Lying Wonder Discovered.* Even the extensive search which led to the discovery of *Strange & Terrible Newes* failed to disclose a copy of Bunyan's tract. The difficulty of the search for this lost tract is increased by our ignorance of its title, which, however, from Blackley's allusive description we may conjecture to be: *A Paper touching Witchcraft given forth to your wonderment.* But whether it was signed with Bunyan's full name, or his initials, or whether it was published anonymously, it is now impossible to determine. We know that it was similar in nature and parallel in intention to *Strange & Terrible Newes,* but published in all probability just before the trial. Since both *Strange & Terrible Newes* and *A Lying Wonder Discovered* are short news pamphlets, one of six and one of seven pages, it is probable that Bunyan's tract was of similar form; but it may have been a broadside. It is easier to account for the disappearance of these emphemeral sheets than for their preservation, which usually owes itself to the piety or the eccentricity of a reader and to the particular benevolence of time. *A Lying Wonder Discovered* survived in a collection of his own works made by George Whitehead, who, together with several other Quakers, had attested to the accuracy of the alderman. This tract is now to be found in the Friends' House Library with Whitehead's inscription on the title: "This Paper should not be reprinted amonge myne—G.W." A copy of Bunyan's lost tract may be discovered in a garret or catalogued obscurely in a library.[12]

Bunyan chose to forget this casual production of his youth, and, unaffected by the pride of authorship, to maintain so complete a silence upon the subject that not even Charles Doe, his friend and first bibliographer, had heard of it when some forty years later he compiled a list of his hero's works. But upon the evidence of Blackley and Whitehead, who were in a position to know the pursuits of Bunyan in Cambridge, this lost work must be added to the Bunyan bibliography together with a *Concordance* and *A Christian Dialogue,* two other works of his which have failed to survive in a single copy.[13]

Bunyan had interviewed the victim of Widow Morlin, and apparently had encouraged her to seek legal redress; but unlike the author of *Strange & Terrible Newes,* he was accurate in his details even to the correct rendition of names. After an account of Mistress Pryor's story of the feast of mutton, Blackley says:

This is like John Bunions Relation, who saith, that she (the said Pryor) said she could see who they were a feasting, that they, as they sate at the table, did shine so bright as if they had been Angels; and that she heard them at the feast talk of Doctrine, which was a shame for him to have uttered, that a horse could understand what was like Angels, or understand Doctrine; Ye may see John Bunions faith, what he hath believed and published to make people wonder at such Lies . . . moreover Jo. Bunion saith in his Paper, that she (the said Pryor) told him that she was a bay horse, and yet she told the Judge that she was a Mare.

Returning to Bunyan after a review of *Strange & Terrible Newes,* Blackley continued:

And now to thee John Bunion who goes up and down to preach and lookest upon thy self higher then the Priests and many others, In that thou hast also dispersed a paper abroad against the Quakers, of what the said Margaret Pryor said to thee of her being a horse & ridden upon, thou hast shamed thy self in believing such lyes which thou hast given forth, to render the innocent odious, and to make people wonder like the beast, with thy lying wonder; and thou callest the woman Good-wife Pryor (who hath pretended she was bewitched) and thou saist, she was Rid; what, thou a preacher to the people and so given over to believe lyes, and false dreams which thou hast told, like the false prophets whom God was against! Jer. 23. 32. and thus thou hast slandered the Quakers from the report of a wicked lewd woman, who in the envy and delusion of the devil, hath gon about to vindicate her fals dreams and slanders whereby to murther the innocent; and hast not thou been an incourager of her in this horrible wickednesse, in giving such credit to her, and getting her lyes to publish? And what, will John Bunions hearers own him in such reports as these? who hath believed that a woman through witchcraft may be made a horse? which is such a foolish and unsavoury thing, as we never have read of, that ever was acted among all the Magicians or witches of Egypt . . . .

But I hope few will believe such grosse delusions as this, which John Bunion, and other professors and Priests have believed and reported. . . . And we know that these slanders against the Quakers are much manifest in Cambridgeshire to be false, though some of the Priests and John Bunion in his witchcraft doth seek to delude and make people wonder, with such prophane and vaine bablings against the innocent.[14]

The evidence of Blackley, upon which our knowledge of Bunyan's pamphlet must rest for the present, is corroborated by a Quaker broadside of 1670, *A Testimony from the People of God, Called Quakers, Against Many Lying and Slanderous Books,*[15] which shows that eleven years later Bunyan's early tract was still remembered with displeasure:

... and formerly another railing, slanderous, and lying Pamphlet of one Bunions, the Tinker, and another, called, News from *Cambridge,* where the Judgments of God were seen upon the woman, who was a drunken Sot, and the ground of that scandalous Book; who afterwards hanged her self. All which lying and slanderous Books we testifie against; for by Printing their Lyes and Slanders they think to render us odious to the World, and to set the Magistrates against us, and the rude Multitude upon us . . . .

In justification of Bunyan's evident desire to have the widow destroyed by fire or rope as a witch, it must be said that he was a Baptist and the widow a Quaker; that he was an evangelist and the Quakers his rivals; and that only a few years earlier he himself had been accused of witchcraft by the Friends.[16] It must also be remembered that a belief in witches, whom he had denounced in May, 1659 in *The Doctrine of the Law and Grace Unfolded* and was to condemn in many another tract,[17] was one which he shared with Sir Thomas Browne, the affable Cambridge Platonists, and many other excellent men. Moreover, his pamphlet on Quaker witchcraft conformed to the common tradition of his day, which saw the printing of many tracts of this variety. There is, for example, the curious account of Mary White, who, after attending the meetings of Edward Burrough, "sometimes blared like a calf and sometimes did clasp her Legs about her Neck," and who, after she had somewhat recovered her composure, brought charges of witchcraft, at the instigation of a local minister, against the Quakers.[18] These reports of Quaker enchantments had been so frequent that both Richard Farnworth and George Fox were compelled in defense of their sect to issue denunciations of an art for which, they said, they had no love.[19] It would be incorrect to apply modern considerations of sportsmanship or ancient ideals of chivalry to the criticism of Bunyan, who, like any other lay preacher, gratefully accepted such opportunities as the Lord provided for the advancement of the truth. Both custom and the temper of his time plead Bunyan's blamelessness.

NOTES

NOTES

In the notes all citations of *Pilgrim's Progress*, *The Holy War*, *Mr. Badman*, *Grace Abounding*, and *Relation of Imprisonment*, unless otherwise noted, refer to the two-volume Cambridge University Press edition of Bunyan's major works, 1905 and 1907, edited by John Brown. (See Bibliography.) For *Profitable Meditations* the first, and for *A Book for Boys and Girls* a facsimile of the first edition have been used since these books do not appear in Bunyan's collected works. For all other tracts by Bunyan the three-volume edition of George Offor, Glasgow, 1853, has been cited; short titles are followed by volume and page, e.g., *Few Sighs from Hell*, III, 698. Unless otherwise indicated by the name of the library in parentheses all tracts by other men are to be found in the British Museum. Thomason tracts are followed by their press marks, e.g., E. 632 (14); 669. f. 13 (12).

CHAPTER I

1. The supposed ambiguity of Bunyan's position on the sacrament of baptism has caused many to prefer to call him a Congregationalist without sectarian affiliation, e.g., Gerhard Thiel, *Bunyans Stellung innerhalb der religiösen Strömungen seiner Zeit*, Breslau, 1931, pp. 87 ff. There can be little quarrel with this preference since it is quiet and harmless, but the arguments and the evidence of those who claim Bunyan for the Baptists are stronger, e.g., W. T. Whitley, "The Bunyan Christening," *Transactions of the Baptist Historical Society*, London, Baptist Union, II (1910-11), 253 ff. Mr. Whitley uses evidence which Herr Thiel ignored. Bunyan believed in adult baptism, but tolerated paedobaptists in his congregation. See *Heavenly Footman*, III, 383.

2. For the Baptists see Whitley, *A History of British Baptists*, London, Charles Griffin, 1923. All Baptists after 1640 believed in dipping adults, but some tolerated the sprinkling of infants. The Particular Baptists separated in 1633. See Champlin Burrage, *The Early English Dissenters in the Light of Recent Research*, Cambridge University Press, 1912, Vol. I, chaps. 9-13.

3. William C. Braithwaite, *The Beginnings of Quakerism*, London, Macmillan, 1923.

4. Rufus M. Jones, *Studies in Mystical Religion*, London, Macmillan, 1909, pp. 467 ff.

5. Hastings, *Encyclopedia of Religion and Ethics*.

6. Louise Fargo Brown, *The Political Activities of the Baptists and Fifth Monarchy Men in England During the Interregnum*, Washington, American Historical Association, 1912.

7. Burrage, *op. cit.* Contains a valuable critical bibliography of works on the separatists.

8. A good statement of the unimportance of sectarian boundaries is to be found in Hermann Weingarten, *Die Revolutionskirchen Englands*, Leipzig, Breitkopf und Härtel, 1868, chap. 6, pp. 102 ff. This work is still of value as a general survey of the sectarian revolution, particularly in that it is without religious bias.

9. Richard Hubberthorn, *A True Testimony of Obedience to the Heavenly Call*, 1654, E. 731 (13), pp. 4, 5, 6.

10. Thomas Crosby, *The History of the English Baptists, From the Reformation to the Beginning of the Reign of King George I*, London, Printed for, and Sold by, the Editor, 1738-40 (Union Theological Seminary), II, 185-208; III, 143-47; IV, 268-79. Whitley, *History of Baptists*, pp. 132-33, 137 ff., 177-78. D. Neal,

History of the Puritans, New York, 1844, II, 383-86. For Keach's works see Whitley, *A Baptist Bibliography*, London, Kingsgate Press, 1916. Life of Keach in *D. N. B.*

11. For accounts of the itinerant of the Quakers and the Baptists see: Henry Clark, *A Description of the Prophets, Apostles, and Ministers of Christ, and Also of those called Ministers of England*, London, Printed for Giles Calvert, 1655, E. 861 (8), (Quaker) ; Edward Burrough, Epistle to the Reader, in George Fox, *The Great Mistery of the Great Whore Unfolded*, London, Printed for Tho. Simmons, 1659, (Quaker) ; John Spittlehouse, *An Explanation of the Commission of Jesus Christ; In relation to the Gifts, Call, Mission, Qualification, Work and Maintenance of his Ministers*, London, Printed by J. C., sold by Rich. Moone, 1653, E. 713 (15), (Baptist) ; Thomas Grantham, *Christianismus Primitivus: or, the Ancient Christian Religion*, London, Printed for Francis Smith, 1678, (Baptist). *The Journal* of George Fox is an excellent account of the life of the itinerant, as is George Whitehead, *The Christian Progress of that Ancient Servant and Minister of Jesus Christ, George Whitehead. Historically Relating His Experience, Ministry, Sufferings, Trials and Service, in Defence of the Truth*, London, Printed by the Assigns of J. Sowle, 1725: An everyday experience: "Others of them threw Dirt and Eggs (thought rotten) at me, whereby my Head and Face were greatly daubed, yet I went on declaring the Truth." Cf. Robert Barclay, *The Inner Life of the Religious Societies of the Commonwealth*, London, Hodder and Stoughton, 1876: an excellent but partisan account of the itinerant ministry. (Quaker.)

12. Hubberthorn, *The Immediate Call to the Ministry*, London, Printed for Giles Calvert, 1654, E. 812 (13), pp. 2-3.

13. "Francis Howgil's Testimony Concerning Edward Burrough," in Edward Burrough's *The Memorable Works Of a Son of Thunder and Consolation*, 1672.

14. Laurence Clarkson, *The Lost Sheep Found: or, The Prodigal returned to his Fathers house, after many a sad and weary Journey through many Religious Countreys*, London, Printed for the Author, 1660, pp. 12-15, 21.

15. *Mercurius Cambro-Britannicus, or, News from Wales, Touching The Glorious and Miraculous Propagation of the Gospel in those parts*, London, 1652, E. 674 (25), pp. 4, 6, 10. *Strena Vavasoriensis, A New-Years-Gift for the Welch Itinerants, Or a Hue and Cry after Mr. Vavasor Powell*, Printed by F. L., 1654, E. 727 (14), pp. 5, 6.

16. *A Relation of a Disputation Between Dr. Griffith and Mr. Vavasor Powell*, London, Printed by M. S., and are to be sold by Livewell Chapman, 1653, E. 686 (1), p. 10.

17. Crosby, *History of Baptists*, London, 1738-40, I, 217-19, 373, 378; III, 6. Anthony Wood, *Athenae Oxonienses*, London, 1721, II, 473. *The Life and Death of Mr. Vavasor Powell*, 1671, pp. 10-11, 107-8, 123. John Griffith and Edward Allen, *Vavasoris Examen, & Purgamen: or, Mr. Vavasor Powells Impartiall Triall*, London, Printed for Thomas Brewster and Livewell Chapman, 1654, E. 732 (12) ; and *passim* in the works cited in note 15.

18. *Strena Vavasoriensis*, p. 27.

19. *The Baptist Quarterly*, New Series, III (July, 1927), 316, 319, 320. For John Donne see Samuel Palmer, *The Nonconformist's Memorial*, London, Printed for W. Harris, 1775, I, 223. Gibbs and Dell will be discussed later.

20. *Grace Abounding*, pp. 18, 58, 82, 87-88, on his early itinerancy.

21. John Jukes, *A Brief History of Bunyan's Church, Compiled, Chiefly, from its own records*, London, Partridge and Oakey, 1849, pp. 24-26. Among the subordinate preachers were John Fenn, Oliver Scott, Luke Ashwood, Thomas Cowper, Edward Dent, Edward Isaac, and Nehemiah Cox. The church sent John Wilson to be pastor of the meeting at Hitchin, p. 27. The Bedford congregation held

meetings at Gamblingay, Cotton End, Kempston, Hanes, and many other nearby places, *(Church Book)*. Cf. John Brown, *John Bunyan His Life, Times, and Work*, London, Hulbert, 1928, pp. 212-17; *Transactions of Baptist Historical Society*, I (1908), 165-66. Bunyan's influence extended over Toft, Gamblingay in Cambridgeshire; Keysoe, Turvey, Pavenham, Stevington, Oakley, Stagsden, Kempston, Goldington, Cardington, Cranfield, Hanes, Maulden, Edworth, Blunham in Bedfordshire; Newport Pagnell and Olney in Bucks; and Kimbolton in Huntingdonshire. His influence was informal since the association was voluntary.

22. The office of "messenger" is described in Grantham's *Christianismus Primitivus: or, the Ancient Christian Religion*, London, Printed for Francis Smith, 1678, Book IV, Treatise V, pp. 152 ff. *The Church Book* of the Bedford meeting frequently refers to the emissaries it sent out to visit other meetings as messengers.

23. *The Continuation of Mr. Bunyan's Life*, in *Grace Abounding*, 7th ed., 1692, p. 180.

24. Life of Bunyan, in *Pilgrim's Progress*, Part III, 1700, pp. 33-35; *ibid.*, 1693, pp. 31, 37, 38, 40. William Urwick, *Nonconformity in Hertfordshire*, London, Hazell, Watson, and Viney, 1884, pp. 208-13. *The Baptist Quarterly*, I (1922-23), 74-76; III (Oct. 1927), 364-68.

25. *Grace Abounding*, pp. 91-94; *Instruction for Ignorant*, II, 679; *Treatise of Fear of God*, I, 476; *Saint's Privilege*, I, 678; *Confession of Faith*, II, 594; *Mr. Badman*, pp. 76, 137-39: Badman is a slanderer of innocent ministers. G. B. Harrison, editor, *The Narrative of the Persecution of Agnes Beaumont in 1674*, London, Constable, 1929.

26. *Paul's Departure*, I, 734.

27. *Grace Abounding*, pp. 96, 98: Bunyan says that he foresaw his imprisonment but regarded it as a cross which must not be shirked; in *Relation of Imprisonment*, pp. 105-6, he says that he went to preach on the day of his seizure knowing he would be arrested, but went to preserve his reputation, to encourage weak brethren, and out of the feeling that God had selected him to be the "forlorn hope" of that district, to be the first to have the honor of suffering for the gospel; cf. *Differences in Judgment*, II, 618. He could easily have avoided arrest as he did in his later years. In *Pilgrim's Progress*, Part II, p. 390, Bunyan praises Faithful's martyrdom as an aid to the cause. The best study of Bunyan's trials and imprisonments is Whitley's "Bunyan's Imprisonments," *Transactions of Baptist Historical Society*, London, VI (1918-19), 1-24.

28. *Seasonable Counsel*, II, 710-37 on the call to martyrdom; Bunyan warned the eager against inviting martyrdom unless one had a definite call from God by a powerful impulse at heart; God appointed all martyrs and martyrdom was a special dignity of which few were counted worthy. Charles Doe ascribed Bunyan's fame and success partly to his long imprisonment: Doe, "Reasons why Christian People should Promote by Subscriptions the Printing in Folio the Labours of Mr. John Bunyan," in 1692 folio of Bunyan's works.

29. Most of the Quakers produced accounts of their trials and imprisonments: e.g., Humphrey Smith, *Something further laid open of the cruel Persecution of the People called Quakers By the Magistrates and People of Evesham*, London, 1656, E. 863 (7). Cf. the similar Baptist accounts, e.g., Thomas Delaune, *A Narrative of the Tryal and Sufferings of Thomas Delaune, for Writing, Printing and Publishing a late Book, Called, A Plea for the Non-Conformists*, London, Printed for the Author, 1683. See *Life and Death of Mr. Vavasor Powell*, 1671, pp. 123-89, "His Sufferings and Imprisonments," written, however, by his followers.

30. *Grace Abounding*, pp. 94 ff., "A brief Account of the Authors Imprisonment."

31. This work was left in manuscript until 1765.

32. *Prison Meditations*, 1665, I, 63*ff. The spiritual comfort of his martyrdom was considerable.

33. Burrough, Epistle, in Fox's *Mistery of Great Whore*, 1659. John Toldervy, *The Foot out of the Snare, or, A Restoration of the Inhabitants of Zion into their Place*, London, Printed for Thomas Brewster, 1655, E. 861 (13).

34. Lodowick Muggleton, *A True Interpretation of All the Chief Texts, and Mysterious Sayings and Visions opened, of the whole Book of the Revelation of St. John*, London, Printed for the Author, 1665, p. 196 and Epistle: "by the Revelation of the Spirit of Faith, I shall open the meaning of Johns words."

35. Thomas Greene, *An Alarm To the False Shepheards*, London, Printed for Robert Wilson, 1660.

36. *The Divell in Kent, or His strange Delusions at Sandwitch*, London, 1647, E. 401 (14), pp. 1-2.

37. James Hunt, *The spirituall Verses and Prose of James Hunt, which shall be plainly showne, God hath lighted my Candle within his glorious Throne*, 1648, E. 476 (38), p. 2.

38. Burrough, *op. cit.*

39. Samuel Butler frequently commented upon the gift in *Hudibras:* "Some call it gifts, and some new-light;/ A lib'ral art, that costs no pains/ Of study industry, or brains. . . ." (*Hudibras*, I, i, 482); "Whate'er men speak by this new light,/ Still they are sure to be i' th right./ 'Tis a dark-lanthorn of the spirit,/ Which none see by but those that bear it"; (*Hudibras*, I, i, 503; cf. I, i, 515).

40. Henry More, *Enthusiasmus Triumphatus*, in *A Collection Of Several Philosophical Writings*, 2d ed., London, Printed for William Morden, 1662, pp. 2, 12, 15. Cf. Meric Casaubon, *A Treatise Concerning Enthusiasme, As it is an Effect of Nature: but is mistaken by many for either Divine Inspiration, or Diabolical Possession*, London, Printed by R. D., 1655, E. 1452 (2).

41. *The Autobiography of Richard Baxter*, edited by J. M. Lloyd Thomas, London, Dent, 1925, pp. 179, 237. But Baxter's deprecation of the gift was an imperfect carminative for the Quakers and the Baptists.

42. Daniel Featley, *The Dippers dipt. Or, The Anabaptists Duck'd and Plung'd Over Head and Eares, at a Disputation in Southwark*, London, Printed for Nicholas Bourne, and Richard Royston, 1645, E. 268 (11), p. 31.

43. Edward Fowler, *Libertas Evangelica: Or, A Discourse of Christian Liberty*, London, Printed for Richard Royston, 1680, pp. 212-14.

44. Thomas Hall, *The Pulpit Guarded with XVII Arguments*, London, Printed by J. Cottrel, for E. Blackmore, 1651, E. 628 (4), pp. 6-7; William Erbury, *An Olive-leaf*, London, Printed by J. Cottrel, 1654, E. 726 (5). Though an enthusiast himself, Erbury opposed the millenarian enthusiasm of Vavasor Powell and Rogers, of whom he asked, "Are you the Prophets of the Lord as Jeremiah was, or are ye Ministers of the Gospel, as Paul?" (p. 2). The distinction between minister and prophet is indicated in this question.

45. George Griffith, *A Bold Challenge of an Itinerant Preacher Modestly Answered By a Local Minister*, 1652, E. 667 (7).

46. E.g., the dispute between Hall, Presbyterian, and Collier, the Baptist: Thomas Collier, *The Pulpit-Guard Routed*, London, Printed for the Author, sold by Giles Calvert, 1651, E. 641 (22). Collier defended reliance upon dreams, visions, and the gift and claimed that he himself was a "partaker in a measure of the Heavenly Gift."

47. Humphrey Ellis, *Pseudochristus: Or, A true and faithful Relation of the Grand Impostures . . . Lately spread abroad and acted in the County of*

Southampton, by William Frankelin and Mary Gadbury, and their Companions. The one most blasphemously professing and asserting himself to be The Christ, The Messiah . . . The other as wickedly professing and asserting her self to be the Spouse of Christ, called The Lady Mary . . . Together with the Visions and Revelations, to which they did pretend . . . As also their Examinations and Confessions before the Justices of the Peace, their Imprisonment, and their Tryal, London, Printed for Luke Fawn, 1650, E. 602 (12).

48. *The Declaration of John Robins, the false Prophet, otherwise called the Shakers God,* London, Printed by R. Wood, 1651, E. 629 (13). *All the Proceedings at the Sessions Of the Peace holden at Westminster, on the 20. day of June, 1651. against Thomas Tydford, Elizabeth Sorrell etc.,* London, Printed by Thomas Harper, 1651, E. 637 (18).

49. John Deacon, *The Grand Impostor Examined: Or, The Life, Tryal, and Examination of James Nayler,* London, Printed for Henry Brome, 1656, E. 896 (2): Nayler's excuse was, "I ought not to slight anything which the Spirit of the Lord moves."

50. *False Prophets Discovered,* London, Printed for I. W., 1642, E. 138 (4); Walter Gostelo, *The coming of God in Mercy, in Vengeance; Beginning With fire, to Convert or Consume, at this so sinful City London,* London, Printed for the Author, 1658, E. 1833 (1). John Toldervy, *Foot out of the Snare,* 1655, E. 861 (13).

51. *Divine Fire-Works, or, Some Sparkles from the Spirit of Burning in this dead Letter. Hinting What the Almighty Emanuel is doing in these Whipping Times. And In this His day which burns as an Oven,* 1657, 669. f. 20 (45).

52. G. B. Harrison, editor, *The Church Book of Bunyan Meeting, 1650-1821,* a reproduction in facsimile, London, J. M. Dent, 1928. Bunyan's gifts were debated and approved by the church before his election as chief elder, p. 50; the gifts of other preachers also examined and approved, pp. 2-4, 23, 48, 51. Cf. Jukes, *Brief History of Bunyan's Church,* 1849, pp. 10, 25-26; *Grace Abounding,* pp. 82-83; *Relation of Imprisonment,* pp. 115, 118, where Bunyan refers to his possession of the gift. George Fox commented skeptically upon Bunyan's claim to the gift: "John Burton saith John Bunian is furnished with spiritual gifts, which gifts the Ministers of Christ must have whether learned or unlearned; as to humane, and John Bunians preaching he saith is not by humane art. . . ." Fox, *The Great Mistery of the Great Whore Unfolded,* 1659, p. 208; Burton had commended Bunyan's gift in the preface to *Some Gospel Truths,* II, 141.

53. *Light for Them,* I, 421-22; *Solomon's Temple,* III, 466, 467, 468, 481; *Saint's Knowledge,* II, 22; *Pharisee and Publican,* II, 225; *Vindication of Gospel Truths,* II, 177, 178, 208; *Doctrine of Law and Grace,* I, 537; *Holy City,* III, 400, 435; *Seventh Day Sabbath,* II, 381; *Some Gospel Truths,* II, 145, 152.

54. *Relation of Imprisonment,* p. 115.

55. *Grace Abounding,* pp. 12, 20-21, 64; *Treatise of Fear of God,* I, 476; *Greatness of Soul,* I, 110. Cf. *The Life and Death of . . . Mr. Hanserd Knollys,* London, Printed for John Harris, 1692, pp. 10, 15; Knollys also heard voices and received direct communications from God.

56. *Forest of Lebanon,* III, 532; *Some Gospel Truths,* II, 148.

57. *Relation of Imprisonment,* pp. 118, 123, 124.

58. *Ibid.,* p. 115.

59. *Pilgrim's Progress,* Part I, p. 243; Weingarten is correct in interpreting the *Progress* as the richest summary of the enthusiasm of the period, as the best picture of the inner life of the saints; in this book Bunyan presented the life, emotions, and ideals of the enthusiast. Hermann Weingarten, *Die Revolutionskirchen Englands,* 1868, pp. 273-77.

60. Burrough, Epistle, in Fox's *Great Mistery of the Great Whore*, 1659, pp. 12-15.

61. Bunyan also described the preacher and his functions in: *Solomon's Temple*, III, *passim*, pp. 466-509; *Building, Nature, Excellency of the House of God*, II, 581-84; *Greatness of Soul*, I, 143; *Case of Conscience*, II, 663-64.

CHAPTER II

1. Many of these ministerial biographies, which appear to have been written shortly after the deaths of their subjects and circulated in manuscript among the devout, are conveniently collected in Samuel Clarke, *The Lives of Thirty Two English Divines, Famous in their Generations for Learning and Piety*, in *A General Martyrologie*, 3d ed., London, Printed for William Birch, 1677. Life of eminent convert: Thomas Taylor, *A Profitable Memoriall of the Conversion, Life, and Death of Mistris Marie Gunter, set up as a Monument to be looked upon both by Protestants and Papists*, in *Three Treatises*, London, Printed for John Bartlet, 1633. Treatises of spiritual experience: Thomas Goodwin, *A Childe of Light Walking in Darkness: or A Treatise Shewing The Causes, by which, The Cases, wherein, The Ends, for which God leaves his children to distresse of conscience. Together With Directions how to walke, so as to come forth of such a condition*, London, Printed for R. Dawlman, 1643; Richard Sibbes, *The Bruised Reede and Smoaking Flax*, London, 1630, (all but last in Union).

2. That the autobiographies of the Catholic saints such as Augustine and Teresa had any direct influence upon the lay preachers is doubtful. A translation of Augustine's *Confessions* appeared, however, in 1660, E. 1755 (2), and Bunyan's friend John Simpson, who did not write an autobiography, mentioned Augustine's *Confessions* in his *Perfection of Justification maintained*, 1648, E. 1133, Epistle. Arise Evans mentioned St. Paul as his model, as did Francis Bampfield, and in clear imitation of the history of Paul, Lodowick Muggleton called his autobiography *The Acts*. Bunyan cited Acts 22 as the model for his autobiography, *Grace Abounding*, p. 5.

3. See Daniel Featley, *The Dippers dipt*, 1645, p. 204. Featley says that all devisers of new religions must claim inspiration and communion with angels in order to secure their tenets from the test of examination. When haled before the court in New England, Wm. Robinson, Quaker, wanted to read "A Declaration of my Call" to establish his divine commission. Marmaduke Stephenson, *A Call from Death to Life*, (1660), Edinburgh, Aungervyle Society, 1886, p. 358.

4. Arise Evans, *An Eccho To the Voice from Heaven. or A Narration of the Life, and manner of the special Calling, and Visions of Arise Evans*, Printed for the Author, 1652, E. 1304 (2).

5. Nicholas Smith, *Wonderfull Prophecyes Revealed to Nicholas Smith Shoemaker, Living at Tillington neer Petworth in Sussex . . . Manifested unto me Nicholas Smith . . . by a Spirit from God; and am now come up to London to doe the Work I am commanded*, London, 1652, E. 683 (5). Convincing as this evidence was, the skeptical *Perfect Nocturnall*, Dec. 1-8, 1652, E. 683 (20), said in the course of a mock testament of an ox, "I give my Braines to Prophet Smith the inspired Cobler, That he may have the wit to be Chancellor of Bedlam."

6. James Hunt, *A Sermon Gathered And set forth by that Divine Spirit which God hath given to me*, 1648, E. 448 (14).

7. Richard Coppin, *Truth's Testimony . . . With The Authors Call and Conversion to the truth*, London, Printed for Giles Calvert, 1655, E. 829 (8).

8. Francis Howgill, *The Inheritance of Jacob Discovered. After his Return out of Aegypt: And the Leading of the Lord to the Land of promise, declared, and*

some information of the way thither, London, Printed for Giles Calvert, 1656, E. 869 (3). George Whitehead, *Jacob found in a desert Land: or, A Recovery Of the Lost out of the Loss,* London, Printed for Giles Calvert, 1656, E. 889 (1). Years later in *The Christian Progress of that Ancient Servant and Minister of Jesus Christ, George Whitehead,* London, Printed by the Assigns of J. Sowle, 1725, Whitehead again told the story of his conversion and ministry, but like Fox's *Journal* this second work is a memoir rather than propaganda for his ministry.

9. Whitehead, *Jacob found in a desert Land,* pp. 8-9.

10. Richard Farnworth, *The Heart Opened by Christ; or, The Conditions of a troubled Soul that could find no true Rest, Peace, Comfort, nor satisfaction in any thing below . . . God,* 1654, E. 745 (7). Richard Hubberthorn, *The Immediate Call To the Ministry,* London, Printed for Giles Calvert, 1654; *A True Testimony of Obedience to the Heavenly Call,* (1654), E. 731 (13). Geotge Rofe, *The Righteousness of God to Man . . . With A true Declaration how I lived before I knew the truth, and how I came to know the truth, and overcame deceit,* London, Printed for Giles Calvert, 1656, E. 885 (3). Thomas Zachary, *A Word to all those who have bin convinced of the Truth,* N. D., (c. 1659), p. 4., "An Account of my own Condition." Anne Wentworth, *A Vindication of Anne Wentworth,* 1677. Isaac Pennington, *Babylon the Great described, with some plain Queries further to discover her,* London, Printed for Lodowick Lloyd, 1659, E. 770 (2), Preface. Several of Pennington's other works recount his spiritual experiences, e.g., *A Voyce out of the thick Darkness,* London, Printed by John Macock, 1650, E. 597 (7), p. 18, "The Sence of A Poor shattered Soul Concerning His Loss." While not strictly parallel to the other ministerial autobiographies in that it was written before the author had attained certainty, this work is similar to them in its subjective analysis.

11. John Crook, *A short History of the Life of John Crook, Containing Some of his Spiritual Travels and Breathings after God, in his Young and Tender Years: Also an Account of various Temptations wherewith he was Exercised, and the Means by which he came to the Knowledge of the Truth,* London, Printed and Sold by T. Sowle, 1706.
The posthumous publication of this work, like that of Fox's *Journal,* puts it in the category of memoirs, apart from the average enthusiastic autobiography published during the author's lifetime. But in every way other than intention both works are like the other autobiographies.

12. Edward Burrough, *A True Description of my Manner of Life, Of what I have been in My Profession of Religion unto this very Day: and What I am at Present, by the Grace of God,* London, Printed for Robert Wilson, 1663.

13. Burrough, "A Warning from the Lord to the Inhabitants of Underbarrow . . . With the manner of my passage through the dark World," 1654, in *Works,* 1672.

14. Muggleton, *The Acts of the Witnesses of the Spirit. By Lodowick Muggleton: One of the Two Witnesses and True Prophets of the only High, Immortal, Glorious God, Christ Jesus,* London, 1699, (posthumous, but he published an earlier autobiography). Muggleton and John Reeve, *A transcendent Spiritual Treatise upon several heavenly doctrines,* (1656). The first part is a brief autobiography by Muggleton. Laurence Clarkson, *The Lost Sheep Found: or, The Prodigal returned to his Fathers house, after many a sad and weary Journey through many Religious Countreys,* London, Printed for the Author, 1660; *The Right Devil Discovered,* London, Printed for the Author, sold by Francis Cossinet, 1659, Introduction.

15. Clarkson, *The Lost Sheep Found,* pp. 37-38.

16. Muggleton, *The Acts of the Witnesses,* p. 81.

17. Coppin, *Truth's Testimony . . . With The Authors Call and Conversion to the truth*, London, Printed by Giles Calvert, 1655, E. 829 (8). George Foster, *The Sounding of the Last Trumpet*, 1650, E. 598 (18). For Coppe see *infra*, Chap. V.

18. Joseph Salmon, *Heights in Depths and Depths in Heights. Wherein is discovered how the author hath been acted in and redeemed from, the unknown paths of darkness*, London, Printed by Tho. Newcomb, 1651, E. 1361 (4).

19. William Kiffin, *Remarkable Passages in the Life of William Kiffin: written by himself, and edited from the Original Manuscript by William Orme*, London, Printed for Burton and Smith, 1823.

20. *The Life and Death of Mr. Henry Jessey, Late Preacher of the Gospel*, 1671. Jessey's short spiritual autobiography occupies pp. 25-31. *The Life and Death of . . . Mr. Hanserd Knollys . . . Written with his own Hand to the Year 1672 and continued in General, in an Epistle by Mr. William Kiffin*, London, Printed for John Harris, 1692.

21. Thomas Crosby, *History of Baptists*, IV, 268.

22. *The Life and Death of Mr. Vavasor Powell . . . Wherein his Eminent Conversion, Laborious, Successful Ministry . . . are faithfully Recorded for Publick benefit*, 1671. "Mr. Powel's Account of his Conversion and Ministry" occupies pp. 1-19; his diary, pp. 56 ff; the rest is devoted to accounts of his life by friends. Powell, Knollys, and Jessey, saw no objection to publishing the spiritual experiences of others, especially of their own converts. To this form of advertising they were not averse. Knollys edited the experiences of Katherine Sutton in 1663, and the others brought out similar works. The very fact that all three published the experiences of others while leaving their own unpublished suggests the presence of a common restraint, probably social.

23. Bampfield, *A Name, an After-one; or A Name, New One, In the Later-Day-Glory: or, An Historical Declaration of the Life of Shem Acher . . . relating to his more thorow lawful Call to the Office and Work of the Ministry*, London, Printed for John Lawrence, 1681.

24. Anna Trapnel, *A Legacy for Saints; Being Several Experiences of the dealings of God with Anna Trapnel, In, and after her Conversion (written some years since with her own hand)*, London, Printed for T. Brewster, 1654, E. 806 (1); *The Cry of a Stone*, London, 1654, E. 730 (3), pp. 3-14.

25. Trapnel, *A Legacy for Saints*, pp. 54-64. She continues: "And these cruel Rulers had no patience to hear, but pulled me off my pillow, and rung me by the nose, and caused my eye-lids to be pulled up, but no harm I felt, nor nothing interrupted me. . . . But my dear friends, if Christ's eye ravisheth, I must sing." Samples of her extempore verse and song taken down on the spot by admirers are printed in *The Cry of a Stone*.

26. *Grace Abounding*, p. 12.

27. *Ibid.*, p. 67.

28. In *Christ as an Advocate*, I, 160, Bunyan said: "The best saints are most sensible of their sins, and most apt to make mountains of their mole hills."

29. Nathaniel Bacon, *A Relation Of the fearful Estate of Francis Spira, In the Year 1548*, London, Printed for Nathaniel Brook, 1668. There had been many previous editions of this popular book. Color is given to the hypothesis that Spira influenced Bunyan by his echoing of Spira's wish that he could be a devil in hell to torment rather than to be tormented, *Grace Abounding*, p. 9.

30. A consideration of the involved psychology of conversion is beyond the province of this chapter, which deals merely with the ministerial capitalization of the phenomenon. Of the many excellent treatises on the psychology of religion William James's *The Varieties of Religious Experience*, 13th ed., London, Long-

mans, Green, 1907, is still the best. James devoted considerable attention both to Calvinistic or unhealthy-minded conversion, and to the case of Bunyan. Of the recent works on the subject Alfred Underwood's *Conversion: Christian and Non-Christian*, New York, Macmillan, 1925, contains in Part II, especially chap. 14, a useful summary of the later conclusions. James B. Pratt's *The Religious Consciousness*, New York, Macmillan, 1924, is valuable for its analysis of the conversion of Bunyan, pp. 140-45. Bunyan's conversion was of the standard Calvinistic variety, the "passive" type which could find unification of self only in the abdication of self. James and Pratt call Bunyan psychopathic, a diagnosis which, while reasonable from the evidence at hand, ignores the probability that Bunyan was exaggerating his symptoms for purposes of ministerial propaganda. The treatises of Starbuck, Coe, Leuba, may also be consulted with profit.

31. *Come and Welcome*, I, 285-86. His main intention in this passage is to console those who had had a mild conversion.

32. *Jerusalem Sinner*, I, 79-81.

33. *Christ a Complete Saviour*, I, 224. Cf. Zeph. Smith, *The Skillfull Teacher. In a Sermon*, London, Printed for John Rothwell, 1648, E. 467 (8): "A Man that hath had the Pox or the Plague, and recovered it, can experimentally tell what it is. So they that have seen the plague of a hard heart, the plague-sore of sinne, they can best declare to others the bitternesse of it." p. 23. This sermon emphasizes the need of a severe conversion for the minister. Cf. Burton's preface to Bunyan's *Some Gospel Truths*, II, 140-41, where Bunyan is commended as a minister for having experienced the temptations of Satan.

34. *Grace Abounding*, p. 81. This section comprises pp. 81-88.

35. *Ibid.*, p. 83.

36. *Ibid.*, pp. 83-84, 87, 88.

37. Henry Jessey, *The Exceeding Riches of Grace Advanced By the Spirit of Grace, In an Empty Nothing Creature*, (viz.) *Mris Sarah Wight*, 6th ed., London, Printed by J. M. for Henry Cripps, 1652, E. 1307 (2). Vavasor Powell, *Spiritual Experiences Of Sundry Beleevers. Held forth by them at severall solemne meetings*, 2d ed., London, Printed for Robert Ibbitson, 1653, E. 1389. John Toldervy, *The Foot out of the Snare . . . Being A Brief Declaration of his entrance into that Sect, Called . . . Quakers . . . With the manner of his Separation from them*, London, Printed for Tho. Brewster, 1656, E. 861 (13). Charles Doe, *A Collection of Experience of the Work of Grace: (Never before Printed.) or the Spirit of God working upon the Souls of several Persons . . .*, London, Printed for Charles Doe, 1700, (Bodleian). Samuel Petto, *The Voice of the Spirit . . . To which is added Roses from Sharon or sweet Experiences reached out by Christ to some of his beloved ones in this Wildernes*, London, Printed for Livewell Chapman, 1654, E. 1500 (2). Jane Turner, *Choice Experiences of the kind dealings of God before in, and after Conversion*, London, Printed by H. Hils, 1653, Introduction by John Spilsbury.

38. Richard Baxter, *A Treatise of Conversion*, London, Printed for Nevil Simmons, 1657, E. 920 (2); *Directions and Perswasions To a Sound Conversion*, London, Printed for Nevil Simmons, 1658, E. 1717. A. Palmer, *The Gospel New-Creature*, London, Printed for Edward Brewster, 1658, E. 1826 (2).

39. Benjamin Keach, *War with the Devil: or the Young Mans Conflict with the Powers of Darkness . . . and the Nature of true Conversion . . . chiefly intended for the Instruction of the Younger sort*, 4th ed., London, Printed for Benjamin Harris, 1676. Keach's *The Glorious Lover*, 1679, contains an account of conversion, pp. 149 ff. His *Progress of Sin*, 1684, chap. 5, pp. 99-131, deals popularly with conversion. T. S.'s *Youth's Tragedy*, 4th ed., 1672, and his *Youth's*

Comedy, 1680, deal largely with conversion. Bunyan's *Mr. Badman* corresponds to T. S.'s *Youth's Tragedy,* the monitory tale of one who failed to achieve conversion.

40. *Grace Abounding,* Preface, pp. 4-5. He was following the example of Paul, Acts 22, in recounting his conversion.

41. *Heavenly Footman,* III, 389.

42. In the following places Bunyan outlined the process of conversion, often giving brief résumés of his own experiences, sometimes merely listing the requirements, or giving advice on the conduct of the sufferer: *Some Gospel Truths,* II, 167; *Few Sighs from Hell,* III, 719-22; *Doctrine of Law and Grace,* I, 505, 541-43, 545, 548-50, 562, 565-66; *Justification by Faith,* II, 298; *Confession of Faith,* II, 599; *Light for Them,* I, 434-35; *Saved by Grace,* I, 339; *Come and Welcome,* I, 268-71; *Pharisee and Publican,* II, 251-52; *Acceptable Sacrifice,* I, 699-700; *Last Sermon,* II, 756; *Exposition of Genesis,* II, 418-20; *Christ a Complete Saviour,* I, 209, 214, 227.

43. In *Pilgrim's Progress* Christian's critics think he is suffering from "some frenzy Distemper," and recommend carnal physic and bed, Part I, p. 143; Mr. Badman's physician, another representative of the naturalistic classes, diagnosed Badman's fears as the result of fever, p. 146. These passages are Bunyan's ironic answers to the naturalists. In his tracts he also impugned the naturalistic diagnosis of melancholy, and insisted upon sickness as the condition preparatory to grace, e.g., *Come and Welcome,* I, 278-79, 282; *Doctrine of Law and Grace,* I, 555; *Justification by Imputed Righteousness,* I, 325; *Acceptable Sacrifice,* I, 718. For his descriptions and recommendations see: *Pharisee and Publican,* II, 275; *Treatise of Fear of God,* I, 450, 452-53, 476; *Pilgrim's Progress,* Part I, p. 268; *Jerusalem Sinner,* I, 102-3, 90-93, 96; *Christ a Complete Saviour,* I, 209, 224. In view of the exuberance of the desires aroused by such description of thorough conversion, Bunyan found it necessary to warn novices that sometimes conversion was unattended by the expected horrors. He urged them not to be disappointed if God denied them the ordeal of a first-class conversion. Sometimes conversions were mild, and, he added tactfully, he would have preferred a mild one himself. *Come and Welcome,* I, 285-86. The mild conversion of Mercy and others in the second part of the *Progress* is part of his effort to console the weak for their unimpressive showing.

44. *Jerusalem Sinner,* I, 93-95.

45. *Grace Abounding,* pp. 10, 41. Martin Luther, *A Commentarie upon the Epistle of S. Paul to the Galathians,* London, Printed by George Miller, 1635. In this work Luther outlines salvation by faith. Arthur Dent, *The Plaine Mans Pathway to Heaven,* 18th ed., London, Printed for Geo. Latham, 1622. One of the earliest popularizations of conversion; see pp. 23, 30-31.

46. *Acceptable Sacrifice,* I, 716.

47. *Building, Nature, Excellency of the House of God,* II, 582.

48. In *Grace Abounding,* p. 28, Bunyan says: "I found my self as on a miry Bog, that shook if I did but stir."

49. In *Grace Abounding,* p. 34: "And despair would hold me a Captive there." The psalmist's image of the Valley of the Shadow of Death was frequently used in tracts on spiritual experience to indicate backsliding, e.g., Sibbs, *The Returning Backslider,* London, Printed for George Edwards, 1639, To the Reader; Goodwin, *A Childe of Light Walking in Darkness,* London, Printed for R. Dawlman, 1643, p. 3, (both in Union). Bunyan took his Valley of the Shadow from this usage of contemporary authorities to illustrate his own spiritual decline.

50. *Pilgrim's Progress,* Part I, pp. 256-63. This is an experience-meeting on the

road between Christian and Hopeful. In his autobiography John Crook tells what pleasure he had in recounting and listening to accounts of conversion. *A short History of the Life of John Crook*, 1706, p. 17. Experience-meetings are mentioned in Doe's *A Collection of Experience*, 1700, pp. 21, 25.

51. T. S. (Thomas Sherman), *The Second Part of the Pilgrims Progress, From This present World of Wickedness and Misery, to An Eternity of Holiness and Felicity. Exactly Described under the Similitude of a Dream*, London, Printed by T. H. over against the Poultry, 1682. In the Author's Apology: "I have endeavoured to supply a fourfold Defect, which I observe, the brevity of that discourse necessitated the Author into: First their is nothing said of the State of Man in his first Creation: Nor Secondly, of the Misery of Man in his Lapsed Estate before Conversion. Thirdly, a too brief passing over the Methods of Divine Goodness, in the Convincing, Converting, and Reconciling of Sinners to himself. . . ."

52. *Pilgrim's Progress*, Part II, pp. 293 ff., 320-21, 362-65.

53. *Ibid.*, p. 311.

54. *Ibid.*, pp. 367, 383, 402.

55. *Jerusalem Sinner*, I, 69, 77. Commentaries on his success as an evangelist: *Some Gospel Truths*, Preface, II, 141; Thomas Paul, *Some Serious Reflections*, 1673, pp. 36-37; Chandler and Wilson, Preface to 1692 folio of Bunyan's Works.

56. *Grace Abounding*, p. 88. Cf. pp. 83, 87.

CHAPTER III

1. George Griffith, *A Bold Challenge of an Itinerant Preacher Modestly Answered*, 1652, E. 667 (7). *A Welsh Narrative . . . Containing a Narration Of the Disputation Between Dr. Griffith and Mr. Vavasor Powell, neer New-Chappell in Montgomery-shire, July 23, 1652*, London, Printed by A. M. for John Browne, 1653, E. 675 (10). *A Relation of a Disputation Between Dr. Griffith and Mr. Vavasor Powell*, London, Printed by M. S., sold by Livewell Chapman, 1653, E. 686 (1). Cf. the dispute between Walter Rosewell and Richard Coppin: Walter Rosewell, *The Serpents Subtilty Discovered, Or a True Relation of what passed in the Cathedrall Church of Rochester, Between divers Ministers and Richard Coppin*, London, Printed by A. M. for Jos. Cranford, 1656.

2. *Grace Abounding*, p. 86. He admitted, however, that it pleased him to contend for justification by faith.

3. E.g., Richard Baxter in the midst of controversy deplored contention as the scab of the church: *More Proofs of Infants Church-membership*, London, Printed by N. Simmons, 1675, pp. 185 ff.

4. *Heavenly Footman*, III, 383; *Holy City*, III, 419; *Holy Life*, II, 537-38; *Pharisee and Publican*, II, 219. In his license to preach, 1672, he called himself "congregationalist," not Baptist.

5. The meaninglessness of this desire for unity and deprecation of sectarianism is shown by the fact that William Kiffin, a most intolerant Baptist, shared it: *A Sober Discourse of Right to Church-Communion*, London, Printed for Enoch Prosser, 1681, p. 2. William Allen, Anglican ex-Baptist, made the same wish in *A Perswasive to Peace and Unity*, 1680. Peace and unity meant peace and unity under the author's sect.

6. *Grace Abounding*, p. 18.

7. Allusions to the Ranters, mostly directed against the Quakers and antinomians occur in many of Bunyan's works. E.g., *Some Gospel Truths*, 1656, II, *passim*; *Vindication of Gospel Truths*, 1657, II, 182-83; *Few Sighs from Hell*, 1658, III, 724; *Doctrine of Law and Grace*, 1659, I, 569; *Resurrection of Dead*,

1665, II, 106; *Holy City*, 1665, III, 440; *Light for Them*, 1675, I, 423; *Heavenly Footman*, 1698, III, 383. In *Mr. Badman*, pp. 58-59, the story of the child by the Holy Ghost, there is allusion to the claims of John Robins and other Ranters. See *A List of Some of the Grand Blasphemers and Blasphemies*, London, Printed by Robert Ibbitson, 1654.

8. *Grace Abounding*, p. 39; *Doctrine of Law and Grace*, I, 549.

9. Jeremiah Ives, *The Quakers Quaking*, London, Printed for R. Moon, 1656, E. 883 (3). Matthew Caffyn, *The Deceived and deceiving Quakers discovered*, London, Printed for Francis Smith, 1656, E. 873 (2). James Nayler, *The Light of Christ*, London, Printed for Giles Calvert, 1656, E. 877 (1). John Gilpin, *The Quakers Shaken: Or, A Fire-brand snatch'd out of the Fire*, Gateside, Printed by S. B., 1653. Cf. the stories of Toldervy and Jane Turner. A convenient list of oral disputations between Baptists and Quakers by Arthur S. Langley appears in *Transactions of Baptist Historical Society*, VI (1918-19), 216 ff. Cf. W. T. Whitley, *A Baptist Bibliography* under years 1653 ff.

10. William C. Braithwaite, *Beginnings of Quakerism*, pp. 175, 333; John Brown, *John Bunyan*, pp. 105-6. John Crook, *A short History of the Life of John Crook*, London, 1706, pp. 27, 39-49; *A Declaration of the people of God in scorn called Quakers to all Magistrates and People*, London, Printed for Thomas Simmons, 1659.

11. *Some Gospel Truths*, II, 163; *Vindication of Gospel Truths*, II, 201, 210. Edward Burrough, "The True Faith of the Gospel of Peace," 1656, in *Works*, 1672, pp. 151-52; *Truth (the Strongest of all) Witnessed forth*, London, Printed for Giles Calvert, 1657, pp. 42, 53-55. For Anne Blaykling, a boisterous, and vehement person, see Braithwaite, *Beginnings of Quakerism*, pp. 93, 295, 345, 346; and Richard Hubberthorn, *The Immediate Call to the Ministry . . . With a true Declaration of the persecution of Richard Hubberthorne . . . Ann Blayling, by Will Pickering, who is Mayor of Cambridge*, London, Printed for Giles Calvert, 1654, E. 812 (13), pp. 1-4. Her name occurs in various spellings.

12. *Vindication of Gospel Truths*, II, 182. In *Some Gospel Truths*, II, 163 Bunyan admitted that many were falling from the faith. Cf. *Vindication*, II, 177.

13. Burrough, "The True Faith of the Gospel of Peace Contended for, in the Spirit of Meekness; and the Mystery of Salvation (Christ within the Hope of Glory) Vindicated in the Spirit of Love, Against the secret opposition of John Bunyan a professed Minister in Bedfordshire," (Sept. 6, 1656, Thomason) in *Works*, 1672. *Vindication of Gospel Truths*, II, 181. For Burrough's career see: Francis Howgill, "Testimony Concerning Edward Burrough," in *Works*, 1672; *A True Description of my Manner of Life*, 1663; *A Visitation & Warning Proclaimed And An Alarm Sounded in the Popes Borders*, London, Printed for Thomas Simmons, 1659. Burrough had not met Bunyan, but he was in Bedfordshire in February, 1657, Braithwaite, *op. cit.*, p. 345. The contemporary allusions to the Bunyan-Burrough dispute show it to have taken its place in the public consciousness: Thomas Collier, *A Looking-Glasse for the Quakers*, London, Printed for Thomas Brewster, 1656, E. 896 (11), pp. 4, 9; Richard Blome, Appendix to Thomas Smith, *A Gagg for the Quakers*, 1659, p. 15; Thomas Underhill, *Hell broke loose: or An History of the Quakers*, London, Printed for Simon Miller, 1659, E. 770 (6), pp. 19-20.

14. *Vindication of Gospel Truths*, probably Jan., 1657.

15. Burrough, *Truth (the Strongest of all) Witnessed forth in the Spirit of Truth, against all Deceit: And Pleading in Righteousnesse its owne cause, to the understanding of the Simple, against a very great number of lyes, slanders, perverting of the Scriptures, contradictions and false damnable doctrines, held forth*

*by the Independants. And In particular by one John Bunion, (one of Gogs Army)
in two severall Bookes put forth by him, against the despised scattered People
called Quakers,* London, Printed for Giles Calvert, 1657, (May 5, Thomason),
E. 910 (3).

16. George Fox, *The Great Mistery of the Great Whore Unfolded: and Antichrists Kingdom Revealed unto Destruction. In Answer to many False Doctrines
and Principles which Babylons Merchants have traded with, being held forth by
the professed Ministers, and Teachers, and Professors in England . . . in this
Answer to . . . Anabaptists, Independents, Presbyters, Ranters,* London, Printed
for Tho. Simmons, 1659, pp. 8-13, 205-11.

17. William Penn, *The Sandy Foundation Shaken: or, Those so generally
believed and applauded Doctrines Of One God, subsisting in Three distinct and
separate Persons, The impossibility of God's pardoning sinners without a plenary
satisfaction, The justification of impure persons by an imputative Righteousness,
Refuted,* London, 1668. *Justification by Faith,* II, 297, 333. See Bunyan's allusion
to Penn's "satisfactionists," *Israel's Hope,* I, 613-14; Penn, *Sandy Foundation,* p.
31. Later allusions to the Quakers: *Doctrine of Law and Grace,* I, 562-63, 569;
Resurrection of Dead, II, 106 (not by name); *Justification by Faith,* II, 292; *Differences in Judgment,* II, 641; *Light for Them,* I, possible allusion in title and p. 436;
Saved by Grace, I, 348 (not by name); *Strait Gate,* I, 389; *Come and Welcome,*
I, 258 (not by name); *Seventh Day Sabbath,* II, 362; *Pharisee and Publican,* II,
228; *Justification by Imputed Righteousness,* I, 321; *Christ a Complete Saviour,*
I, 221; *Heavenly Footman,* III, 383.

18. Bunyan was indicted at the assizes at Eaton, Feb., 1658, *Church Book,* p.
20; the incumbent at Eaton, at whose request Bunyan was probably indicted was
Thomas Becke, Presbyterian, Whitley, *Transactions of Baptist Historical Society,*
Vol. VI (1918-19), p. 3. Bunyan's attitude toward and troubles with the clergy
in these early years are mentioned in *Grace Abounding,* pp. 11, 86-88; *Doctrine
of Law and Grace,* I, 496; *Vindication of Gospel Truths,* II, 197; *Few Sighs from
Hell,* III, 674, 699, 716, 721.

19. Life of Bunyan in *Pilgrim's Progress,* Part III, 1700, p. 27. In *Come and
Welcome,* I, 278, Bunyan mentions people who, like this student, came to flout
and jeer but were brought under grace. Doe, "The Struggler," in 1692 folio of
Bunyan's works.

20. John Peile, *Biographical Register of Christ's College, 1505-1905,* Cambridge, University Press, 1910, I, 468.

21. The account of this dispute is to be found in: Smith, *A Letter Sent To Mr.
E. of Taft, Four miles from Cambridge, To which no Answer hath been returned,
May, 1659,* an appendix to Thomas Smith, *The Quaker Disarm'd, or A True
Relation Of a Late Publick Dispute Held At Cambridge By Three Eminent
Quakers, against One Scholar of Cambridge. With A Letter in Defence of the
Ministry, And Against Lay-Preachers. Also Several Queries proposed to the Quakers
to be answered if they can.* London, Printed by J. C. and are sold neer the Little
North-Door of S. Pauls Church, 1659. The copies in the British Museum and
Friends' Library are imperfect, the B. M. copy lacking most of *A Letter Sent
To Mr. E.,* and the Friends' copy badly shaved in the margin to the injury of
the text.

22. Smith probably was familiar with *Enthusiasmus Triumphatus* by Henry
More, whom he appears to have known. Bunyan's defense against the charges of
enthusiasm and madness appears in *Christ a Complete Saviour,* I, 230; *Come
and Welcome,* I, 278: "Is any merry? Let him sing psalms," said Bunyan in answer
to the charge of melancholy.

23. The Smith-Bunyan debate was typical of the encounters between the clergy and the unlearned dissenters. The same points had been raised by Featley against Kiffin: Featley, *The Dippers dipt*, 1645, pp. 1-22.

24. For Smith's dispute with the Quakers see: Smith, *The Quaker Disarm'd*; George Whitehead, *The Christian Progress of that Ancient Servant and Minister of Jesus Christ, George Whitehead*, 1725, pp. 163-68; Smith's letter of Dec. 4, 1659 to Williamson, secretary of the Polyglot Bible board, in *Calendar of State Papers, Domestic, 1659-60*, p. 276. It was probably in answer to Smith's syllogistic attack that George Fox wrote his deprecation of logic, rhetoric, etc., *A Primer for the Scholars and Doctors of Europe, But especially to them in and about the (called) Two famous Universities in England*, London, Printed for Thomas Simmons, 1659. Smith did not take the advice of the broadside, *A Gagge for Lay-Preachers*, July 5, 1652, 669. f. 16 (57), which urged the clergy to avoid useless debates with the illiterate.

25. Life of Denne in *D.N.B.* Cf. Pease, *The Leveller Movement*, pp. 280-82. Thomas Crosby, *History of the English Baptists*, London, 1738-40, I, 221, 297-306.

26. Henry Denne, *The Quaker No Papist, in Answer to the Quaker Disarm'd. or, A brief Reply and Censure of Mr. Thomas Smith's frivolous Relation of a Dispute held betwixt himself and certain Quakers at Cambridge*, London, Printed by Francis Smith, 1659, (Oct. 16), E. 1000 (13). Denne devoted his Preface to a defense of Bunyan.

27. Smith, *A Gagg for the Quakers, with an Answer to Mr. Denn's Quaker no Papist*, London, Printed by J. C., 1659, E. 764 (2). Blome described this dispute in *The Fanatick History*, London, Printed for J. Sims, 1660, E. 1832 (2), Lib. II, chap. 8, cf. pp. 181-84, 189. Whitehead and Fox answered Smith's pamphlets. Smith appears to have known both Worthington and Cudworth besides More: Peile, *Biographical Register of Christ's College*, I, 468.

28. In this period his chief controversial production was an attack on Common Prayer, *I will Pray with the Spirit*, 1663, answered rather belatedly in 1700 in *Liturgies vindicated by . . . the very texts of scripture urged against them by John Bunyan and the dissenters*; no copy known; see Whitley, *Baptist Bibliography*, p. 135.

29. Biography of Fowler in *D.N.B.* Anthony Wood, *Athenae Oxonienses*, London, 1721, Vol. II, 1029-30.

30. [Edward Fowler], *The Principles and Practices, Of certain Moderate Divines of the Church of England*, London, Printed for Lodowick Lloyd, 1670, (Union).

31. John Tulloch, *Rational Theology and Christian Philosophy in England in the Seventeenth Century*, 2d ed., Edinburgh, Wm. Blackwood, 1874, II, 34-44, 437-39.

32. Fowler, *The Design of Christianity; or A plain Demonstration and Improvement of this Proposition, Viz. That the enduing men with Inward Real Righteousness or True Holiness, was the Ultimate End of our Saviour's Coming into the World, and is the Great Intendment of His Blessed Gospel*, London, Printed by E. Tyler and R. Holt for R. Royston, Bookseller to the King's most Excellent Majesty, and Lodowick Lloyd, 1671.

33. *Defence of the Doctrine of Justification by Faith*, II, 323.

34. [Fowler], *Dirt wip't off: or A manifest Discovery of the Gross Ignorance, Erroneousness and most Unchristian and Wicked Spirit of one John Bunyan, Lay-Preacher in Bedford, Which he hath shewed in a Vile Pamphlet Publish't by him, against The Design of Christianity. Written for the disabusing of those*

poor deluded people that are followers of him, and such like Teachers, and to prevent their farther deluding of others, and poisoning them with Licentious and destructive Principles, London, Printed by R. N. for Richard Royston, 1672.

35. In his *Libertas Evangelica: or, A Discourse of Christian Liberty*, London, Printed for Richard Royston, 1680, p. 159, Fowler said, "The Antinomians (not to make worse of them than they are) tell us, that they do not deny the Obligation of Christians to the performance of the Duties required by the Moral Law, but 'tis only Love, Gratitude and ingenuity that can oblige them." Since Bunyan was the most annoying antinomian Fowler knew, this passage is in a sense an allusion to him.

36. I.e., John Worthington, *A Form of Sound Words: or, A Scripture-Catechism ... Very useful for Persons of all Ages and Capacities as well as Children*, London, Printed for R. Royston, 1673, (imprimatur Nov. 8, 1672). In his Preface to this work Fowler alluded to those who grossly misunderstood the gospel despite their loud profession of it. This book, he said, was written in easy words "for the sake of the ignorant" and for those of the "lowest capacities." At the end Fowler's *Dirt wip't off* is advertised. Fowler may have had Bunyan in mind in his preface.

37. Baxter had raised a mild objection to Fowler's use of the word "only": *How Far Holiness is the Design of Christianity*, Printed for Nevill Simmons, 1671, (Union). Cf. Baxter's account of Fowler and his *Design in Reliquiae Baxterianae*, London, Printed for T. Parkhurst, etc., 1696, Part III, p. 85. Cf. John Dunton, *The Life and Errors of John Dunton*, London, Printed for S. Malthus, 1705, p. 445. Fowler, he said, was "tender, mild, compassionate," an enemy to persecution, and by his piety, learning, and moderation, a great honor to the church.

38. *Advice to Sufferers*, II, 718.

39. *Light for Them*, I, 408-9, 414, 421, 423, 429-34.

40. There is, however, possible allusion to the Quakers in the last paragraph and in the title.

41. *Israel's Hope Encouraged*, I, 611, 613, 615, 616-18.

42. *Ibid.*, 616.

43. E.g., Bunyan wrote *Christ as an Advocate*, 1688, in answer to an Anglican sermon he had heard. The clergyman had said: " 'See that your cause be good, else Christ will not undertake it,' " I, 159-60; *Strait Gate*, 1676, I, 388-89; *Exposition of Genesis*, 1692, II, 427; *Justification by Imputed Righteousness*, 1692, I, 317, 320-21; *Seasonable Counsel*, 1684, II, 712-13; *Saints' Knowledge*, 1692, II, 32; *Christ a Complete Saviour*, 1692, I, 210, 221; *Pharisee and Publican*, 1685, II, 236, 241-42, 276; since Fowler had compared Bunyan to the Pharisee, it is possible that the Pharisee in this tract was intended in many ways to embody Fowler; *Mr. Badman*, pp. 143-44; *Holy War*, pp. 367, 386, 421-22, a general attack upon "scepticism" or latitudinarianism; Lord Willbewill wanted to be free, i.e., free will, pp. 202-3.

44. See Underhill, *Confessions of Faith*, London, Printed for Hanserd Knollys Society, 1854. On June 25, 1672 Bunyan's congregation ordered a brief confession of faith to be drawn up by the elders and gifted brethren. On Aug. 29, 1672 this was still under discussion, *Church Book*, pp. 52-53. This desire for a confession may have come from the idea of supporting their leader in his controversy with the Baptists.

45. In the fellowship of Ralpho, the Baptist, and Hudibras, the Presbyterian, despite their differences over circumstantials, Samuel Butler seems to have been indicating open communion.

46. Whitley has shown in "The Bunyan Christening," *Transactions of Baptist Historical Society*, II (1910-11), that Bunyan did not have his infant son bap-

tized in 1672, removing a fancied inconsistency on the part of the Bedford Baptist which had troubled many. Bunyan was a firm believer in adult baptism, though tolerant of paedobaptism.

47. For the troubles with Henry Forty, a strict Baptist, and Francis Holcroft, of Cambridge, for the temporary division in the Bedford church created by Nehemiah Cox, and the cordial relationship with the Independent open-communion churches of Cockayne, Owen, Anthony Palmer, and others, see *Church Book*, 1670-74, pp. 32, 34, 36, 37, 46, 50, 54, 55, 57, 58, 61, 71; and *Transactions of Baptist Historical Society*, I (1908-9) , 248; Vol. II (1910-11), 260. For Holcroft see Edmund Calamy, *A Continuation of the Account of the Ministers . . . Ejected and Silenced*, London, 1727, I, 118-19.

48. *Differences in Judgment*, II, 616-18, 640.

49. Before this quarrel reached print Bunyan had had a conference with Danvers and had spoken in Baptist pulpits, though he had denied the Baptists like privilege in his. Thomas Paul, *Some Serious Reflections*, 1673, pp. 59-61; Bunyan, *Differences in Judgment*, II, 619, 640-41. Most of the above information about the preliminaries of this dispute is to be found *passim* in the pamphlets of Paul, Danvers, Denne, and Bunyan, for which see *infra*.

50. *Differences in Judgment*, II, 640-42.

51. *Peaceable Principles*, II, 655-56.

52. Paul and Kiffin, *Some Serious Reflections On that Part of Mr. Bunion's Confession of Faith: Touching . . . Communion with Unbaptized Persons*, London, Printed for Francis Smith, 1673, (Bodleian). One of Bunyan's early biographers speaks of those of Bunyan's persuasion who "appeared in the Front of those that oppressed him" and for whom Bunyan piously prayed: *The Continuation of Mr. Bunyan's Life*, in *Grace Abounding*, 7th ed., 1692, p. 184. For Kiffin see: *Remarkable Passages in the Life of William Kiffin*, edited by Wm. Orme, 1823. Life in *D.N.B.* And the satiric *The Life and Approaching Death of William Kiffin, Extracted out of the Visitation Book By A Church Member*, London, Printed for Thomas Bateman, 1659, E. 1017 (4) . Cf. Crosby, *History of Baptists*, 1738-40, II, 184; III, 3-6.

53. For Jessey's open-communion belief see *The Life and Death of Mr. Henry Jessey*, 1671, pp. 86-88. On May 29, 1674 Bunyan's church sent in vain a letter on open communion to the church formerly under Jessey. *Church Book*, pp. 55-58. Under the persuasion of Kiffin and Forty, Jessey's church had abandoned open communion for strict communion. *Transactions of Baptist Historical Society*, I (1908-9) , 248; II (1910-11) , 260. Cf. Crosby, *History of Baptists*, London, 1738-40, III, 100; Walter Wilson, *History and Antiquities of Dissenting Churches*, 1808, I, 50.

54. John Denne, *Truth outweighing Error: Or, An Answer To A Treatise lately published by J. B. Entituled, A Confession of his Faith*, London, Printed for the Author, and sold by F. Smith, 1673, (Bodleian).

55. *Peaceable Principles*, II, 648-49. This tract is in answer to Paul's lost work. On p. 650 Bunyan refers to "P. 4 of your first," indicating that Paul wrote two tracts against him.

56. Henry Danvers, *A Treatise of Baptism . . . And, A brief Answer to Mr. Bunyan about Communion with Persons Unbaptized*, London, Printed for Francis Smith, 1673, (Bodleian) . That Danvers also had replied to Bunyan's *Confession* is clear from his statement in his *Treatise of Baptism*, "I took myself concerned, having briefly hinted to his former, to give some short answer to this also," appendix, p. 41.

57. The Baptists had prevented John Owen from contributing a preface to

Bunyan's preceding work, *Peaceable Principles*, II, 649. See *ibid.*, 655-57 for Bunyan's dismissal of the opinions of Baxter, Thomas Lamb, and William Allen, cited by Danvers, and of a certain Mr. Dan, who appears to have joined the fray.

58. The Baptists made two more attacks on Bunyan: Denne, *Hypocrisie Detected, or Peaceable and True Principles as so pretended by John Bunyan, tryed and found False and Unsound*, 1674, (no copy known). Kiffin, *A Sober Discourse of Right to Church-Communion. Wherein is proved . . . That no Unbaptized person may be Regularly admitted to the Lords Supper*, London, Printed by George Larkin, for Enoch Prosser, 1681. Without mentioning Bunyan, this work answers all his arguments. Orme also believed this work to be an answer to Bunyan, *Life of Kiffin*, p. 128. In 1677 the Baptist *Confession*, however, expressed Bunyan's point of view, a victory for open communion: *Transactions of Baptist Historical Society*, I (1908-9), 248. Bunyan's subsequent allusions to this dispute: *Holy Life*, II, 538; *Saved by Grace*, 1675, I, 359-60; *Strait Gate*, 1676, I, 388; *Solomon's Temple*, 1688, III, 524-25; *Building, Nature, Excellency of House of God*, 1688, II, 589.

59. *Grace Abounding*, p. 86.

60. With the exception of his occasional references to the Socinians, e.g., his *Of the Trinity and a Christian*, 1692, and his infrequent references to other sects.

61. Mr. K. did not live in Bedford. His paper was probably in MS. Cf. Bunyan's remarks on women: *Exposition of Genesis*, 1692, II, 429, 438-39. His distaste for female activities may possibly be traced to the Quaker toleration of such doings. See *Case of Conscience*, II, 664, where he refers to women's desires as Quakerish. Cf. Robert Barclay, *Inner Life*, 1876, pp. 442-43.

62. *Case of Conscience*, II, 674.

63. Bunyan preached his *Greatness of the Soul* in Pinners' Hall, 1682; and his friendship with Anthony Palmer, Matthew Mead, and John Owen, who were connected with Pinners' Hall, was intimate as the *Church Book* shows. See Wilson, *The History and Antiquities of Dissenting Churches and Meeting Houses, in London, Westminster, and Southwark*, London, 1808, II, 249-55. From 1680-81 until 1684 Pinners' Hall had been let on Saturdays to Bampfield. Whitley, *The Baptists of London*, London, Kingsgate Press, 1928, p. 119.

64. *Advice to Sufferers*, II, 734; *Light for Them*, I, 421. Doe, "Reasons why Christian People should Promote by Subscriptions," p. 6., in 1692 folio of Bunyan's works.

65. *Strait Gate*, 1676, I, 388-89.

66. *Come and Welcome*, 1678, I, 258.

67. *Heavenly Footman*, 1692, III, 384-85.

68. *Pilgrim's Progress*, Part I, pp. 222-28; Part II, p. 384. Much of the description of By-ends appeared for the first time in the second edition.

69. Fowler, *Design of Christianity*, 1671, p. 2; cf. "by-end" in *Treatise of Fear of God*, 1679, I, 465.

70. Fowler, *Design of Christianity*, 1671, p. 242.

71. *Justification by Faith*, II, 322. Cf. *Strait Gate*, I, 388-89 where the latitudinarian in the sketch for *P. P.* is also called a weathercock. *Justification by Faith*, II, 314.

72. *Paul's Departure*, I, 727: "It is an uncomely thing for any man in his profession to be in and out with the times." By-ends' descent from "a waterman, looking one way, and rowing another," p. 223, might suggest to the fanciful an allusion to John Taylor the water-poet, who in Bunyan's youth was one of the chief enemies of the sectarians, but the phrase was proverbial at the time.

73. *Pilgrim's Progress*, Part I, p. 225.

74. *Justification by Faith*, II, 313-14.

75. *Ibid.*, 324.

76. *Ibid.*, 293.

77. *Pilgrim's Progress*, Part I, pp. 244-45, 263-68, 279. Cf. John W. Draper, "Bunyan's Mr. Ignorance," in *Modern Language Review*, Cambridge, University Press, XXII (1927), 14-21. Mr. Draper considers Ignorance an embodiment of the bourgeois sentimentalism which resulted in the opinions of Shaftesbury. It is true that Ignorance represents the bourgeois disciple of natural religion, and if he is approached through a knowledge of Shaftesbury alone, this is a sufficient explanation, but to the student of the seventeenth century he is that variety of bourgeois naturalist known as the Latitudinarian.

78. *Pilgrim's Progress*, Part I, p. 244; *Justification by Faith*, II, 293.

79. *Pilgrim's Progress*, Part I, p. 266.

80. *Loc. cit.* The Quakerish sentiments of Ignorance indicate what Bunyan had called Fowler's "Papistical Quakerism." His contempt for revelation proves that Ignorance is not a Quaker.

81. *Pilgrim's Progress*, Part I, p. 279.

82. *Ibid.*, pp. 150-56. Mr. Wiseman first appears in the second edition.

83. *Ibid.*, pp. 169-70.

84. *Ibid.*, pp. 241, 242.

85. *Pilgrim's Progress*, Part II, pp. 367-69.

86. *Pilgrim's Progress*, Part I, pp. 201-10. Bunyan's attacks on the talkative: *Doctrine of Law and Grace*, 1659, I, 514-15; *Saved by Grace*, 1675, I, 350; *Strait Gate*, 1676, I, 369, 373, 377. Bunyan considered the Quakers mere talkers, verbal hypocrites: *Vindication of Gospel Truths*, 1657, II, 183. He confessed to having once been a talker himself: *Grace Abounding*, p. 16.

87. *Pilgrim's Progress*, Part I, pp. 245, 269-70.

88. John Child challenged Bunyan to dispute in 1676: John Child, *A moderate message to Quakers, Seekers, and Socinians . . . Three questions offered to be disputed with John Bunion before any publique audience either in city or countrey*, 1676, (Friends' Library copy cannot be found). After Child's suicide comparisons between Child and Spira were common, e.g., *A Warning from God to all Apostates; or, The Nature, great Evil, and Danger of Apostacy discovered. Wherein the fearful States of Francis Spira and John Child are compared; the latter whereof, under dismal Despair, hang'd himself, Octob.* 13, 1684, London, Printed for Christopher Hussey, 1684. Child told Keach just before he killed himself that he had needlessly provoked disputes, and out of pride had endeavored to run down all men in disputes against free grace in favor of Arminianism; he had written a book against the Baptists, attacking their ministers "because some of them were not learned men, I mean with the Knowledge of Tongues." His challenge to Bunyan may have involved free will or Bunyan's ignorance. Benjamin Keach, *A Trumpet Blown in Zion*, London, 1694, pp. 48-50. Cf. *Israel's Hope*, 1692, I, 580, 583; *Holy Life*, 1684, II, 523. For Child see also Crosby, *History of the Baptists*, London, 1738-40, II, 384.

89. *Pilgrim's Progress*, Part I, pp. 252-53.

90. *Pilgrim's Progress*, Part II, p. 286.

91. T. S., *The Second Part of the Pilgrims Progress*, London, Printed by T. H. over against the Poultry, 1682, pp. 115-16, on general call.

92. *Pilgrim's Progress*, Part II, p. 335.

93. *Ibid.*, pp. 343, 373-74.

94. *Ibid.*, p. 322.

95. *Ibid.*, p. 295.

96. *Confession of Faith*, II, 610.

97. *Differences in Judgment*, II, 630.

98. *Pilgrim's Progress*, Part II, pp. 379-82.

99. *Ibid.*, pp. 382, 393-94, 395.

100. *Ibid.*, p. 373.

101. For the debates in 1674 and 1690 over singing psalms see *Church Book*, pp. 55, 75, 76, 77C. Cf. John Jukes, *A Brief History of Bunyan's Church*, London, Partridge and Oakey, 1849. Gerhard Thiel, *Bunyans Stellung innerhalb der religiösen Strömungen seiner Zeit*, 1931, pp. 104-5. A good discussion of the sectarian controversy over singing appears in Robert Barclay, *The Inner Life of the Religious Societies of the Commonwealth*, London, 1876, pp. 451-58.

102. *Solomon's Temple*, 1688, III, 496; *Light for Them*, 1675, I, 424; in *The Holy War* the saints sang psalms, p. 378. In *Treatise of Fear of God*, 1679, I, 473, Bunyan quoted the Sternhold and Hopkins version of the 128th Psalm. *Pilgrim's Progress*, Part II, p. 335. See *Transactions of Baptist Historical Society*, VI (1918-19), 277: "Bunyan advocated singing in 1688."

103. Henry S. Burrage, *Baptist Hymn Writers*, Portland, Maine, 1888, pp. 27-28. For Keach see pp. 30-31. Cf. John Julian, *A Dictionary of Hymnology*, London, John Murray, 1892, p. 193 for Bunyan, p. 610 for Keach. For Powell see Crosby, *History of the Baptists*, London, 1738-40, I, 378, 380; for Baptist conference on singing, III, 266-71. The song from *Pilgrim's Progress* "Who would true Valour see," ("He who would valiant be") with changes and additions is also used today as a hymn in Anglican churches. It appears as Hymn 402, p. 324 in *The English Hymnal*, Oxford, Clarendon Press, N. D. Only a few of the songs of *Pilgrim's Progress* are suitable for use as hymns. Many are too occasional in character. But all were intended as propaganda for pious song.

104. *Pilgrim's Progress*, Part II, p. 396.

CHAPTER IV

1. Daniel Featley, *The Dippers dipt. Or, The Anabaptists Duck'd and Plung'd Over Head and Eares, at a Disputation in Southwark*, London, Printed for Nicholas Bourne and Richard Royston, 1645, E. 268 (11), To the Reader.

2. *The Lay-Divine: or, The simple House-preaching Taylor*, London, Printed for W. Ley, 1647, E. 386 (5), p. 2.

3. E. Pagitt, *Heresiography*, London, Printed by M. Okes, 1645, E. 282 (5), p. 37: "The Anabaptists are all Preachers, every man at his pleasure taketh upon him to be the Lords Embassadour: as John Becold the Taylor of Leyden . . . and hence have our Coblers, Shoomakers, Ostlers, &c. learnt to take upon them this divine calling."

4. For a good account of the rise of the lay preachers and of the social position of the Baptists see: W. T. Whitley, *A History of British Baptists*, London, 1923, pp. 68-73, 95-97, 152-53.

5. John B. Marsh, *The Story of Harecourt*, London, 1871, p. 181, quoted from *S. P. D.*, Dec. 18, 1681.

6. *The Baptist Quarterly*, III (July 1927), No. 7, p. 319.

7. John Brown, *John Bunyan*, p. 203.

8. *A true and Impartial Narrative of Some Illegal and Arbitrary proceedings . . . against several innocent and peaceable Nonconformists in and near the Town of Bedford*, 1670. In this tract names are followed by occupations.

9. E.g., *Mercurius Aulicus*, Aug. 21-28, 1649, E. 572 (2); *A Paire of Spectacles for the Citie*, 1647, E. 419 (9); *Mercurius Elencticus*, Aug. 27-Sept. 3, 1649, E. 572 (15); Thomas Wilson, *A Sermon on the Martyrdom of King Charles I*, London, Printed by Walter Davis, 1682, pp. 18 ff.

10. John Taylor, *A Swarme of Sectaries*, 1641, E. 158 (1).

11. E.g., *Mercurius Democritus,* Aug. 17-24, 1653, E. 711 (14); *A Perfect Diurnall,* April 1-8, 1649, E. 534 (25).

12. *New Preachers New,* 1641, E. 180 (26).

13. *The Brownists Synagogue or a late Discovery of their Conventicles,* 1641, E. 172 (32). *Tub-preachers overturn'd or Independency to be abandon'd and abhor'd as destructive to the Magestracy and Ministry . . .,* London, Printed for George Lindsey, 1647, E. 384 (7). Cf. *These Trades-men are Preachers in and about the City of London. Or a Discovery of the Most Dangerous and Damnable Tenets that Have Been Spread Within this Few yeares: By many Erronious, Hereticall and Mechannick spirits,* 1647, 669. f. 11 (6).

14. Taylor, *A Swarme of Sectaries,* 1641, E. 158 (1). Cf. Thomas Edwards, *Gangraena: Or a Catalogue and Discovery of many of the Errours, Heresies, Blasphemies and pernicious Practices of the Sectaries of this time,* London, Printed for Ralph Smith, 1646, E. 323 (2); Part II, 1646, E. 338 (12); Part III, 1646, E. 368 (5). Edwards makes frequent mention of mechanicks and their attacks upon learning.

15. *A New Directory: Compiled by these most grave, venerable and Orthodox Divines: Videlicet. Wyat the Cobler, Ford the Trumpetter, Dupper the Cow-Keeper, Bulcher the Chicken-man, Patience the Taylor, &c. Wherein it doth appeare, that manuall practitioners may very probably be, and produce the best proficients in Divinity,* 1647, E. 406 (15). Cf. Taylor, *A Tale In a Tub or, A Tub Lecture As it was delivered by My-heele Mend-soale, an Inspired Brownist, and a most upright Translator. In a meeting house neere Bedlam, the one and twentieth of December, Last,* London, 1641, E. 138 (27).

16. [Nathaniel Ward], Theodore de la Guarden, *Mercurius Anti-mechanicus. Or The Simple Coblers Boy. With his Lap-full of Caveats (or Take heeds) Documents, Advertisements and Praemonitions to all his honest fellow-tradesmen-Preachers, but more especially a dozen of them, in or about the City of London . . . .,* London, Printed for John Walker, 1648, E. 470 (25).

17. *The Discovery of a Swarme of Separatists, or A Leathersellers Sermon,* London, Printed for John Greensmith, 1641, E. 180 (25).

18. Taylor, *A Swarme of Sectaries, and Schismatiques: Wherein is discovered the strange preaching (or prating) of such as are by their trades Coblers, Tinkers, Pedlers, Weavers, Sow-gelders, and Chymney-Sweepers,* 1641, E. 158 (1). Cf. *A Gagge for Lay-Preachers,* 1652, 669. f. 16 (57); Humphrey Brown, *The Ox Muzzled and Ox-ford Dried,* London, Printed for John Stephenson, 1649, E. 587 (4), p. 24: "By the Laws of the Land a person occupying the craft of a Butcher, may not use the Occupation of a Tanner; and a Brewer may not deal in the Occupation of a Cooper; yet now any base Mechanick may use or rather abuse, the office of a preacher . . . ." Taylor gives the gist of How's *Sufficiencie of the Spirits Teaching,* which was printed posthumously in 1645.

19. John Milton, *Considerations Touching the likeliest means to remove hirelings out of the church,* 1659. William Walwyn, *A Prediction of Mr. Edwards His Conversion,* London, Printed for G. Whittington, 1646, E. 1184 (5). Cf. Gerrard Winstanley, *The Breaking of the Day of God,* London, Printed for Giles Calvert, 1648, pp. 13, 59, 72-73, 120. R. Lawrence, *The Wolf Stript of his Sheeps Clothing,* London, 1647, E. 386 (10).

20. Roger Williams, *The Hireling Ministry None of Christs, Or A Discourse Touching the Propagating the Gospel of Christ Jesus,* London, 1652, p. 11.

21. Biography in *D.N.B.;* Crosby, *History of Baptists,* 1738-40, I, 323-33; *Gangraena,* III, 45, 63; *A Paire of Spectacles for the Citie,* 1647, pp. 5-6.

22. William Dell, *The Stumbling Stone, or, A Discourse touching that offence*

which the World and Worldly Church do take against Christ Himself ... *Wherein the University is reproved by the Word of God,* London, Printed by R. W. for Giles Calvert, 1653, E. 692 (1).

23. Similar ideas occur throughout Dell's work, e.g., *Several Sermons and Discourses of William Dell,* London, Printed for Giles Calvert, 1652, E. 645 (4), pp. 6, 16-18, 54, 64, 66, 73, 76-78, 85-86, 115, 197, 212, 219. Dell continued his championship of mechanicks in: *The Tryal of Spirits Both in Teachers and Hearers,* London, Printed for Giles Calvert, 1653, E. 723 (4); *A Plain and Necessary Confutation of Divers Gross and Anti-christian Errors, Delivered* ... *by Sydrach Simpson, Master of Pembroke Hall,* London, Printed for Giles Calvert, 1654, E. 723 (4). Simpson had entered the debate in defense of learning.

24. Joseph Sedgwick, *A Sermon, Preached at St. Marie's in the University of Cambridge May 1st, 1653. or, An Essay to the discovery of the Spirit of Enthusiasme and pretended Inspiration, that disturbs and strikes at the Universities,* London, Printed for Edward Story, 1653, E. 699 (2). See in particular pp. 6, 50.

25. *Mercurius Elencticus,* Feb. 6-13, 1649, E. 542 (13).

26. Dell, *Tryal of Spirits,* Preface.

27. Brown, *John Bunyan,* pp. 117-18, from House of Lords MSS, June 20, 1660.

28. Samuel Butler, *Hudibras,* I, ii, 335-45, 359-60, 535.

29. E.g., *Mercurius Fumigosus,* March 21-28, 1655, E. 830 (26), p. 339: "Broom-men, Dray-men, Tinkers, Porters, and the meanest Mechanicks." *Mercurius Pragmaticus,* June 5-12, 1649, E. 559 (13): "Base Brewers, Tinkers ... Mechanick Slaves." *Mercurius Elencticus,* May 21-28, 1649, E. 556 (19): "Some Coblers, Tinkers, Broom-men, stinking-Jaylors,/ Trim Button-makers, Bakers, Tapsters, Taylors/ ... And all of them brim-full of Revelations." *Englands Murthering Monsters,* (c. 1650), Lutt. II. (70): "Tinker and Tailor ... Think they can preach profound as any Doctor." *The Glory of the English Nation,* London, Printed for W. Bucknel, 1681, Lutt. II. (91). *The Loyal Health,* London, Printed for A. Banks, 1682, Lutt. II. (96). W. Winstanley, *The Muses Cabinet,* London, Printed for F. Coles, 1655, E. 1479 (5), p. 14.

30. E.g., Bunyan's license to preach at the house of Josias Roughead, shoemaker, 1672, and his will, 1685: John Jukes, *A Brief History of Bunyan's Church,* 1849, p. 23; Offor, I, lxi, lxxii. The MS inscription on the verso of A2, p. 4, of the British Museum copy of Bunyan's *Profitable Meditations,* 1661, which Brown read as: "A Brasher now in prison in Bedford, 1664," appears rather to be: "A Brassier now in prison . . . ."

31. Life of Bunyan, in *Grace Abounding,* 7th ed., 1692, p. 180; Life of Bunyan, in *The Pilgrim's Progress,* Part III, 1693, p. 37: on leaving prison, "he resolved, as much as possible, to decline Worldly business, and give himself wholly up to the service of God." Chandler and Wilson, To the Reader, in 1692 folio of Bunyan's Works: the "Calling that he was instructed in, and did in the Morning of his dayes follow . . . ."

32. Certain passages in Bunyan's works seem to imply that he did not approve, in his later years, of the combination of trade and preaching: *Exposition of Genesis,* II, 494: Bunyan disapproved of Noah's becoming a farmer because this secular occupation interfered with his activities as a preacher; *Solomon's Temple,* III, 473: Bunyan cited the lilies of the field as examples to ministers, advising them, like the Quakers, to let God provide for them. These passages appear to imply that he ceased his tinkering in his later years.

33. Thomas Hall, *The Pulpit Guarded with XVII Arguments Proving the Unlawfulness* ... *of suffering Private persons to take upon them Publike Preaching,* London, Printed by J. Cottrel, for E. Blackmore, 1651, E. 628 (4), pp. 23,

25. Cf. John Drew, *A Serious Addresse to Samuel Oates,* London, Printed for John Bartlet, 1649, E. 549 (16). For a mechanick defense see: Jeremy Ives, *Confidence Encountred: or, A Vindication of the Lawfulness of Preaching without Ordination,* London, Sold by Dan White, 1658, E. 936 (1), p. 14.

34. Hall, *The Collier in his Colours,* London, 1652, E. 658 (5*); Thomas Collier, *The Pulpit-Guard Routed, In Its Twenty Strong-Holds,* London, Sold by Giles Calvert, 1651, E. 641 (22); *Gangraena,* II, 148.

35. Hall, *The Font Guarded With XX Arguments,* London, Printed for Thomas Simmons, 1652, E. 658 (5).

36. Edmund Chillenden, *Preaching Without Ordination or, A Treatise proving the lawfulnesse of all Persons, of what Degree, Ranke, or Trade soever, being inabled with sufficient guifts and qualifications from God by his Spirit, to preach . . . .,* London, Printed for George Whittington, 1647, E. 405 (10).

37. *Ibid.,* pp. 6-7. Chillenden was answered by Filodexter Transilvanus, *Church-Members Set in Joynt,* London, Printed for Edmund Paxton, 1648, E. 422 (3). There are many other attacks upon and defenses of mechanicks, ignorance, and learning: e.g., by Jeffrey Watts, E. 921 (1); R. Boreman, E. 681 (10); H. Thurmin, *A Defence of Humane Learning in the Ministry,* Oxford, Printed for Rich. Davis, 1660; David Bramley, E. 374 (2); D. Lupton, E. 1331 (3); Ellis Bradshaw, E. 571 (13); John Martin, E. 1592 (2); Matthew Poole, E. 952 (2); Edward Waterhouse, *An humble Apologie for Learning and Learned Men,* London, Printed for M. Bedell, 1653, E. 1237 (1), pp. 95, 103.

38. *A Relation of the Imprisonment of Mr. John Bunyan,* p. 107.

39. *Ibid.,* p. 108.

40. *Ibid.,* pp. 110-11. Bunyan called Foster's attention to God's choice of the foolish and the base and to His rejection of the wise and mighty.

41. *Ibid.,* pp. 117-18. Bunyan cited Peter 4: 11 and Acts 18 on the preaching of the gifted.

42. According to Francis Howgill, Edward Burrough was "a man of no great Learning in natural Tongues," in "Francis Howgil's Testimony Concerning Edward Burrough," in Burrough's *Works,* 1672.

43. Thomas Smith, *A Letter Sent to Mr. E. of Taft, Four Miles from Cambridge.* In *The Quaker Disarm'd or A True Relation of a Late Publick Dispute Held at Cambridge . . . With a Letter in Defense of the Ministry, and Against Lay-Preachers,* London, Printed by J. C., 1659 (Friends' Library.) Smith was connected with Christ's College to which Sedgwick, who had attacked Dell, belonged. It was a matter of pride to Bunyan's friends that in his disputes with scholars he argued plainly, and by Scripture, "without Phrases and Logical Expressions." Life of Bunyan in *Grace Abounding,* 7th ed. 1692, pp. 186-87.

44. Smith feared social chaos and the end of learning if tinkers were allowed to preach, *ibid.,* section 37. Every enemy of the mechanicks feared a recurrence of Münster and John of Leyden: e.g., Pagitt, *Heresiography,* 1645, pp. 4, 43-44; *Mercurius Melancholicus,* Sept. 4, 1649, E. 405 (24): "Heavens keepe him from a Revelation; for I never thinke of that Taylor, but I remember the Cobler of Amsterdam, who by his forgeries and Revelations became King of Munster"; Richard Blome, *The Fanatick History,* London, Printed for J. Sims, 1660, E. 1832 (2). To the shocked conservatives the mechanicks were so many fully charged Leyden jars.

45. Edwards, *Gangraena,* I, 182.

46. Henry Denne, *The Quaker No Papist,* London, Printed and sold by Francis Smith, 1659, E. 1000 (13).

47. Fowler, *Dirt wip't off,* London, 1672. Attacks on Bunyan's ignorance: pp.

54, 57; for Bunyan's attack on Fowler's dependence on authorities see: *Justification by Faith,* II, 294, and cf. pp. 284, 291, 307 for attacks on Fowler's heathen learning.

48. Kiffin and Thomas Paul, *Some Serious Reflections On that Part of Mr. Bunion's Confession of Faith,* London, Printed for Francis Smith, 1673, p. 1: "Should all of your rank, take occasion to tell the World what they do, and do not believe or practice, it might give them more imployment than they can or need to attend . . . neither should I have medled with the controversie at all, had I found any, of parts, that would divert themselves from more weighty occasions, to take notice of you . . . ."

49. *Differences in Judgment,* 1673, II, 617-18. Paul and John Denne mocked Bunyan's ignorance of Latin, logic, grammar, and good usage, in the effort to demonstrate his illiteracy: *Peaceable Principles,* II, 653; John Denne, *Truth outweighing Error,* 1673, *passim.*

50. Charles Doe, "The Struggler," in Bunyan's Works, 1692, folio. Cf. Doe, "Reasons why Christian People should Promote by Subscriptions the Printing in Folio the Labours of Mr. John Bunyan," in Bunyan's Works, 1692 folio, p. 4. Cf. Life of Bunyan, in *Pilgrim's Progress,* Part III, 1693, p. 8. That Doe, a comb-maker, had also felt the disdain showered upon mechanicks is evident from an MS inscription on the verso of title of his *A Collection of Experience,* 1700, (Bodleian): the writer took it as a symptom of pride "that such a pittiful mechanic as the generallity of people take a combmaker to be should be the collectour and Authour of such Elaborate tracts thus seeking to get a name above his degree, like the protestant footman that wrote against the papists . . . . Or, to judge as charitably as we can is not the true and real cause, self interest, our author by this practice hoping to sell as many thousand combs as he did of John Bunyans books . . . ."

51. Ebenezer Chandler and John Wilson, "To the Serious Judicious, and Impartial Reader," in Bunyan's Works, 1692 folio. For Chandler see Wilson, *History of Dissenting Churches in London,* 1808, I, 178, and *Church Book,* pp. 75, 77C.

52. *Some Gospel Truths,* 1656, II, 140-41.

53. Life of John Gibbs, *The Baptist Quarterly,* III (July, 1927) , pp. 316-20.

54. Life of Carpenter, *D.N.B.* Richard Carpenter, *The Anabaptist Washt and washt, and shrunk in the washing: Or, a Scholasticall Discussion of the much agitated Controversie concerning Infant-Baptism; Occasioned by a Publike Disputation, Before a great Assembly of Ministers, and other Persons of worth, in the Church of Newport-Pagnell, Betwixt Mr. Gibs Minister there, and the Author,* London, Printed by William Hunt, 1653, E. 1484 (1).

55. *Few Sighs from Hell,* 1658, III, 672-73. In 1669 Brother Whitbread raised an objection in the Bedford meeting to mechanick preaching and desired a regular minister such as Brother Burton had been. Bunyan was sent to admonish him, and the church said: "We know not what you meane by an able pastor; we have sch as we hope, the Holy Ghost hath made overseers, and guides among us, to feed us in ye word, and doctrine, to whom that title of pastor belongeth, as well as of bishops, and ministers." *Church Book,* pp. 31, 32, 35.

56. *Few Sighs from Hell, loc. cit.,* and Chandler, *op. cit.*

57. Williams, *op. cit.,* p. 11.

58. Samuel How, *The Sufficiencie of the Spirits Teaching without humane learning. Or a Treatise tending to prove Human-learning to be no helpe to the spiritual understanding of the Word of God,* 1645, E. 25 (16) .

59. John Spencer, *A Short Treatise Concerning the lawfullnesse of every mans exercising his gift as God shall call him thereunto,* London, Printed for John Spencer, 1641, E. 172 (4) . Cf. Lodowick Muggleton's attack upon learning, learned

men, lawyers, physicians, in *A True Interpretation of All the Chief Texts . . . of Revelation,* 1665, pp. 177, 179, 231. Cf. the long deprecation of learning and universities by James Hunt, the warrener, in *The Spirituall Verses and Prose of James Hunt,* 1648, pp. 1, 5, *passim.* Cf. the defense of mechanicks by Benjamin Keach, the tailor, during his trial, Thomas Crosby, *History of Baptists,* II, 192, 198; after 1688, however, Keach became more respectable with success and joined Kiffin and Knollys in the endeavor to make the ministry more reputable by fixed maintenance and the abolishment of mechanick preaching, Crosby, *op. cit.,* IV, 292-97.

60. *Some Gospel Truths,* II, 145. Cf. *The Declaration of John Robins,* London, Printed by R. Wood, 1651, p. 6: "I have receiv'd the inspiration of the Holy Ghost, and have had great things revealed to me . . . .As for humane learning I never had any; my Hebrew, Greek, and Latine, comes by inspiration." Cf. Anna Trapnel, *The Cry of a Stone,* 1654, p. 42:

For human Arts and Sciences, because you doat on them, Therefore the Lord wil others teach whom you count but Lay-men	Christs Scholars they are perfected with learning from above, To them he gives capacity to know his depths of love.

61. *Case of Conscience,* II, 661.

62. *Pilgrim's Progress,* Part II, p. 343.

63. *Doctrine of Law and Grace,* I, 495. Cf. Bunyan's contemptuous allusions to learning, libraries, degrees, and worldly knowledge: *Few Sighs from Hell,* III, 716, on Plato and Aristotle; *Holy Life,* II, 536-37; *Barren Fig Tree,* III, 569; *Holy War,* pp. 196-97; *Come and Welcome,* I, 255, 275-76; *Christ a Complete Saviour,* I, 238; *Mr. Badman,* p. 44; *Justification by Faith,* II, *passim.*

64. *Holy City,* III, 397-99.

65. How, *The Sufficiency of the Spirits Teaching,* London, Sold by William Marshall, 1692, T. 370 (4). Bunyan's friend Charles Doe also published How's tract: Doe, *A Collection of Experience,* 1700, p. 57.

66. Whitley, *History of British Baptists,* p. 140. "The Hubbard-How-More Church," in *Transactions of Baptist Historical Society,* III (1910-11), 31 ff.

67. *Transactions of Baptist Historical Society,* III (1910-11), p. 51.

68. *Solomon's Temple,* III, 471: "True, the men were but mean in themselves; for what is Paul or what Apollos, or what was James or John? Yet by their call to that office they were made highest of all in the church. Christ did raise them eighteen cubits high . . . ." *Light for Them,* I, 429; *Holy Life,* II, 527; *Pilgrim's Progress,* Part II, p. 377. The consideration that the apostles were also ignorant, says one of Bunyan's early biographers, was of weight with him when he was first asked to preach: Life of Bunyan, in *Pilgrim's Progress,* Part III, 1693, p. 28.

69. *Saved by Grace,* I, 346.

70. *Vindication of Gospel Truths,* II, 201.

71. *The true and perfect Speech of John James, A Baptist, and a Fifth-Monarchy-man . . . at Tyburn,* London, Printed for George Horton, 1661, p. 5.

72. Abraham Cheare, *Words in Season,* London, Printed for Nathan Brookes, 1668, Post-Script, p. 239. Cf. Jacob Bauthumley, *The Light and Dark Sides of God,* London, Printed for William Learner, 1650, E. 1353 (2), Epistle: "And however my person, and parts be meane in the Worlds Eye, and so may cast an odium upon the things that I hold forth; yet I shall runne the hazard in that kinde, and leave the Lord to gaine his own Honour and Glory in it; as seeing by sweet experience, it is one of his greatest designes in the World, to confound the high and mighty things thereof, by the most meane and contemptible." Cf.

Winstanley, *The Mysterie of God*, 1648, p. A2: "when some of you sees my name subscribed to this ensuing Discourse, you may wonder at it, and it may be despise me in your heart, as David's Brethren dispised him . . . but know that Gods works are not like mens, he doth not always take the wise, the learned, the rich of the world . . . but he chuses the dispised, the unlearned, the poor . . . ."

73. *Grace Abounding*, pp. 7-8. Cf. *Treatise of Fear of God*, I, 490: "And here the poor Christian hath something to answer them that reproach him for his ignoble pedigree, and shortness of the glory of the wisdom of the world. True, may that man say, I was taken out of the dunghill, I was born in a base and low estate, but I fear God. I have no worldly greatness, nor excellency of natural parts, but I fear God . . . he is the man of many, he is to be honoured of men: though this, to wit, that he feareth the Lord is all that he hath in this world. He hath the thing, the honour, the life, and glory that is lasting: his blessedness will abide when all men's but his are buried in the dust in shame and contempt." Cf. *Christ a Complete Saviour*, I, 229; *Treatise of Fear of God*, I, 470, 480; *Solomon's Temple*, III, 509; *Desire of Righteous*, I, 757; *Holy Life*, II, 547; *Greatness of Soul*, I, 146-47; *Saint's Knowledge*, II, 34.

74. *Few Sighs from Hell*, III, 674, and note by Offor.

75. Title-page, *Doctrine of Law and Grace*, 1659; Cf. his citation of I Pet. 2:4, "Disallowed indeed of men, but chosen of God, and precious," after his name on title of *Justification by Faith*.

76. In Bunyan's works, as in those of the Quakers (*passim*), such expressions are common: e.g., *Strait Gate*, I, 376, the saints are "a company of poor sorry people in the world, very inconsiderable, set by with nobody"; *Forest of Lebanon*, III, 517, the church "however contemned by men, was highest perfection . . . how base and how low soever in the judgment of the world." *Christ as Advocate*, I, 163, "True the church and saints are despicable in the world."

77. John Crook, *A short History of the Life of John Crook*, London, Printed by T. Sowle, 1706, p. 27. Cf. Mary Penington, *Some Account of Circumstances in the Life of Mary Penington*, London, 1821, pp. 31-32. Cf. Thomas Zachary, *A Word To all those who have bin convinced of the Truth*, 1659.

78. Thomas Lamb, *Truth prevailing against the fiercest Opposition*, London, Printed by G. Dawson, sold by Francis Smith, 1655, p. a. Lamb conformed in 1659.

79. *Pilgrim's Progress*, Part I, pp. 270-71; *Come and Welcome*, I, 276-77, 288; *Strait Gate*, I, 370, 389: "Do not despise me, but hear me"; *Heavenly Footman*, III, 379.

80. *Pilgrim's Progress*, Part I, pp. 143-45, 198-200, 214-15, 270-71; Faithful's encounter with Discontent, p. 198, is of similar significance. Cf. *Doctrine of Law and Grace*, I, 565, "Shall I now be ashamed of the cause, ways, people, or saints of Jesus Christ?"

CHAPTER V

1. Gerrard Winstanley, *An Appeal To the House of Commons*, 1649, E. 564 (5), pp. 6-7, 8, 11.

2. *The mournfull Cryes of many thousand Poore Tradesmen*, 1647, 669. f.11 (116).

3. James E. T. Rogers, *A History of Agriculture and Prices in England*, Oxford, Clarendon Press, 1887, V, 12, 103, 204 ff., 656, 664 ff.; *Six Centuries of Work and Wages*, London, W. S. Sonnenschein, 1884, pp. 6, 392-93, 428, 431-33, 463-64. George Unwin, Introduction to *Richard Baxter's Last Treatise*, Man-

chester, University Press, 1926, pp. 5-11. Ephraim Lipson, *The Economic History of England*, London, A. & C. Black, 1931, II, "Age of Mercantilism," *passim*, and chap. 3, pp. 371-433.

4. John Cook, *Unum Necessarium: or, The Poore Mans Case*, London, Printed for Matthew Walbanke, 1648, E. 425 (1). Peter Chamberlen, *The Poore Mans Advocate*, London, Printed for Giles Calvert, 1649, E. 552 (1). Samuel Richardson, *The Cause of the Poor Pleaded*, London, Printed for Livewell Chapman, 1653, E. 703 (9). Thomas Lamb, *An Appeal to the Parliament concerning the Poor*, London, Printed for Robert Wilson, 1660. Reprinted in *Baptist Quarterly*, I (1922-23), 128 ff.

5. Richard Baxter, *The Poor Husbandman's Advocate To Rich Racking Landlords*, 1691, printed from the MS and edited with introductions by Frederick J. Powicke and George Unwin as *The Reverend Richard Baxter's Last Treatise*, Manchester, University Press, 1926, pp. 20, 24.

6. *The Moderate*, Sept. 11-18, 1649, E. 574. The newspapers of this period are full of accounts of starvation, rioting, uprisings of laborers, attacks by farmers on excise men, high prices, and the decay of trade.

7. *The Husbandmans Plea Against Tithes*, London, 1647, E. 389 (2).

8. *The mournfull Cryes of many thousand Poore Tradesmen, who are ready to famish through decay of Trade, Or the warning Teares of the Oppressed*, 1647, 669. f. 11 (116).

9. *Englands Troublers Troubled, Or the just Resolutions of The plainemen of England, Against the Rich and Mightie: by whose pride treachery and wilfulness, they are brought into extream necessity and misery*, 1648, E. 459 (11), pp. 5, 6, 7-10.

10. Winstanley's tracts are to be found in the Thomason collection and in the Seligman collection at Columbia University. For discussions see Lewis H. Berens, *The Digger Movement*, London, 1906; Gooch and Laski, *English Democratic Ideas*, 1927, pp. 181-91.

11. Thomas Carlyle, *The Letters and Speeches of Oliver Cromwell*, edited by S. C. Lomas, London, Methuen, 1904, II, 343. Cromwell condemned "levelling" as making "the tenant as liberal a fortune as the landlord . . . a pleasing voice to all Poor Men, and truly not unwelcome to all Bad Men."

12. See Theodore Calvin Pease, *The Leveller Movement*, Washington, American Historical Association, 1916, pp. 217, 242-44, 265-66, 306.

13. Thomas Edwards called the sectarian revolt of the forties not a matter of conscience but a faction which drafted "needy, broken, decaid men, who know not how to live." *Gangraena*, II, 185. Richard Blome had an eye on England when he said that German anabaptism had been "embraced by a multitude that groaned under miserable bondage . . . the lower sort of people being bred in an ancient hatred against Superiors, imbraced that doctrine greedily." *The Fanatick History*, London, Printed for J. Sims, 1660, E. 1832 (2), pp. 5, 7-36.

14. Gerald R. Owst, *Literature and Pulpit in Medieval England*, Cambridge, University Press, 1933, chap. 6, p. 287 ff.

15. Lilburne was converted to Quakerism by "a contemptible yet spiritually knowing . . . Shoomaker": *The Resurrection of John Lilburne*, London, Printed for Giles Calvert, 1656, E. 880 (2).

16. Winstanley, *A New-yeers Gift for the Parliament and Armie*, London, Printed for Giles Calvert, 1650, E. 587 (6), pp. 37, 43; *A Watch-word to the City of London, and the Armie*, London, Printed for Giles Calvert, 1649, p. A2.

17. Winstanley, *The Mysterie of God, Concerning the whole Creation*, 1648, pp. 5, 44-66, and *passim; The Breaking of the Day of God*, London, Printed for

Giles Calvert, 1648, pp. A3, A4, 14, 41, 45, 76, 122; *The Saints Paradise*, London, Printed for G. Calvert, 1658, E. 2137 (1).

18. Richard Hubberthorn, *The Immediate Call To the Ministry of the Gospel*, London, Printed for Giles Calvert, 1654, E. 812 (13), pp. 4-5.

19. *Baxter's Last Treatise*, Manchester, 1926, pp. 48, 52. Cf. Baxter, *The Poor Man's Family Book*, London, Printed for Nevill Simmons, 1674, pp. 89-103 for his humanitarian support of the oppressed tenant.

20. *The Ranters Last Sermon . . . delivered in an Exercise neer Pissing-Conduit*, London, Printed by J. C., 1654, E. 808 (1), p. 4.

21. Thomas Crosby, *History of Baptists*, London, 1738-40, I, 224.

22. Abiezer Coppe, *A Fiery Flying Roll: A Word from the Lord to all the Great Ones of the Earth: Being the last Warning Piece at the dreadful day of Judgement*, London, 1649, E. 587 (13); Abiezer Coppe, *A Second Fiery Flying Roule: To All the Inhabitants of the Earth; specially the rich ones*, 1649, E. 587 (14).

23. Coppe, *A Second Fiery Flying Roule*, p. 9.

24. *Loc. cit.*

25. *An Order of Parliament that all copies of the book entitled "A Fiery Flying Roll" by Abiezer Coppe, shall be seized and burnt*, London, Printed by Edward Husband and John Field, 1650, 669. f. 15 (10). Cf. Whitelock, Jan. 14, 1650, p. 438.

26. *The Weekly Intelligencer*, Oct. 1-8, 1650, E. 614 (5), p. 16.

27. Coppe, *Copp's Return to the wayes of Truth*, London, Printed by Tho. Newcomb, 1651, E. 637 (4).

28. For mechanick Ranters see: *The Ranters Ranting*, London, Printed by B. Alsop, 1650, E. 618 (8).

29. Joseph Salmon, *A Rout, A Rout: Or some part of the armies Quarters Beaten Up*, London, Printed by T. N., 1649, E. 542 (5), p. A2; *Heights in Depths and Depths in Heights*, London, Printed by Tho. Newcomb, 1651, E. 1361 (4), Preface, and pp. 18-19.

30. Jacob Bauthumley, *The Light and Dark sides of God*, London, Printed for William Learner, 1650, E. 1353 (2), pp. A2, 9.

31. Richard Coppin, *Divine Teachings . . . Being some sparks of that Glory that shines and dwels in Richard Coppin*, London, Giles Calvert, 1649, E. 574 (5); *A Hint of the Glorious Mystery of Divine Teachings*, London, Printed for Giles Calvert, 1649, T. 370 (3); *Saul Smitten For Not Smiting Amalek*, London, Printed by William Larner and Richard Moon, 1653, E. 711 (8).

32. George Foster, *The Pouring Forth of the Seventh and Last Viall Upon all Flesh and Fleshliness, Which will be a Terror to the Men that have Great Possessions*, 1650, T. 370 (17), pp. A2, A3, 9, 12, 13.

33. Foster, *The Sounding of the Last Trumpet: Or, Severall Visions, declaring the Universall overturning and rooting up of all Earthly Powers in England*, 1650, E. 598 (18), p. 17, cf. pp. 11, 19, 46; Foster hoped for relief in the Fifth Monarchy, p. 39.

34. T. Tany, *Theauraujohn High Priest to the Jewes, His Disputive Challenge to the Universities of Oxford and Cambridge*, 1652, E. 656 (10), pp. 1, 3, 6.

35. Edward Ellis, *A Sudden and Cloudy Messenger*, 1649, T. 370 (5).

36. Lodowick Muggleton, *The Acts of the Witnesses of the Spirit*, 1699, pp. 110-13, 153-54, 157 ff.; *A True Interpretation of All the Chief Texts . . . of the whole Book of the Revelation*, 1665; attacks on the learned and mighty, on lawyers, etc., pp. 177, 179, 231, 228.

37. Laurence Clarkson, *The Generall Charge Or, Impeachment of High-*

Treason, London, 1647, E. 410 (9) ; *The Lost Sheep Found,* 1660, pp. 7, 31, 49.

38. There is no adequate account of the social and economic revolt of the Quakers. The best discussions are Gooch and Laski, *English Democratic Ideas,* pp. 228-38; Eduard Bernstein, *Cromwell and Communism, Socialism and Democracy in the great English Revolution,* Translated by H. J. Stenning, London, Allen & Unwin, 1930, chap. 16, pp. 225 ff.—often incorrect and too little acquainted with the tracts but strong on Marxism.

39. For Quaker social radicalism, their knowledge of Lilburne, and the charges of leveling made against them, see: James Nayler, *Saul's Errand to Damascus,* London, Printed for Giles Calvert, 1653, E. 689 (17), p. 30; Hubberthorn, *The Horn of the He-goat broken,* London, Printed for Giles Calvert, 1656, E. 883 (2) , p. 10; Joseph Kellet, *A Faithful Discovery of a treacherous Design of Mystical Antichrist,* London, Printed for Thomas Brewster, 1653, E. 699 (13), p. 42; Blome, *The Fanatick History,* 1660, *passim.*

40. Edward Burrough, *A Word of Reproof,* London, Printed for Thomas Simmons, 1659, pp. 71-77; for his enmity to corruption in the great and mighty see his Preface to Fox's *Great Mistery of the Great Whore,* 1659, p. 12.

41. For the radicalism of the Quakers see: Hermann Weingarten, *Die Revolutionskirchen Englands,* Leipzig, 1868, pp. 240 ff.

42. Nayler and George Fox, *Saul's Errand to Damascus,* London, Printed for Giles Calvert, 1653, E. 689 (17) , p. 29.

43. James Parnell, *A Shield of the Truth, or The Truth of God cleared from Scandals,* London, Printed for Giles Calvert, 1655, E. 829 (11), p. 21: "And he [Satan] calls this Manners and Breeding, and who can honour him the most, and exalt him the highest, those he saith is the best bred, and of the best breeding, and those he calls Noblemen and Gentlemen, and the other he calls Yeomen and Common people, and Inferiors." Cf. pp. 22-26.

44. *Ibid.,* p. 27. Today in France communists insist upon *tu* for all men, and have discarded *monsieur* for *camarade,* as the Quakers used *friend;* communists today dislike elegant dress. As to hats Parnell said: "If a poor man come before a rich man . . . the poor man must stand with his hat off before him, and that is called honour and manners." *Loc. cit.*

45. Nayler, *Deceit Brought to Day-Light in Answer to Thomas Collier,* London, Printed for Giles Calvert, 1656, p. 6.

46. Richard Farnworth, *The Pure Language of the Spirit of Truth,* London, Printed for Giles Calvert, 1655, E. 829 (5), p. 6.

47. E.g., John Harwood, *A Warning from the Lord to the Town of Cambridge,* 1655, E. 853 (20). Fox, *The Trumpet of the Lord Sounded,* London, Printed for Giles Calvert, 1654, E. 732 (23) , pp. 13-14. Parnell, *The Watcher,* London, Printed for Giles Calvert, 1655, E. 845 (18), pp. 12-13.

48. Hubberthorn, *A True Testimony of the zeal of Oxford-Professors,* London, Printed for Giles Calvert, 1654, E. 806 (8).

49. Nayler, *Behold you Rulers, and hearken proud Men and Women,* London, Printed for Thomas Simmons, 1660, T. 377 (3) , p. 6. Many of the tracts of James Nayler, George Fox, Edward Burrough, Francis Howgill, James Parnell, and Richard Hubberthorn contain passages of social and economic significance.

50. Nayler, *A Few Words occasioned by a Paper lately Printed, Stiled A Discourse concerning the Quakers,* 1654, E. 731 (23) , pp. 21-22.

51. Owst, *Literature and Pulpit in Medieval England,* 1933.

52. William Tomlinson, *Seven Particulars, Containing as followeth, I. Against Oppressors . . .,* London, Printed for Giles Calvert, 1657, p. 1; see pp. 1-5.

53. See the statements of this essential brotherhood of the radical sects: Clark-

son, *Lost Sheep Found*, 1660, pp. 39-40; Burrough, "An Answer to a Declaration of the People called Anabaptists," 1659, in *Works*, 1672, pp. 616-18.

54. See also John Spencer, *The Spirituall Warfare*, London, 1642, E. 145 (10), pp. 5, 6. Benjamin Keach, *The Travels of True Godliness*, London, Printed for John Dunton, 1684, pp. 23-56, 70-85; but Keach also condemned the ungodly poor, and felt that the middle classes were perhaps the best.

55. *Strena Vavasoriensis*, 1654, pp. 20, 27; *Mercurius Cambro-Britannicus*, 1652, pp. 6, 7; *The Baptist Quarterly*, III (July 1927), 318; John Gibbs, *Several Divine Treatises*, London, Printed for J. Blare, 1704, p. 6.

56. William Erbury, *The Grand Oppressor, Or, The Terror of Tithes*, London, Printed for Giles Calvert, 1652, E. 671 (13), pp. 2-3; cf. pp. 4-6, 14, 15; *A Scourge for the Assyrian, the Great Oppressor*, London, Printed for Giles Calvert, 1652, pp. 40-42, on the Fifth Monarchy as relief for the poor.

57. William Dell, *Right Reformation*, 1646, in *Several Sermons*, London, Printed for Giles Calvert, 1652, E. 645 (4), pp. 112, 115-16, 125, *The Increase of Popery in England*, London, Printed for Richard Janeway, 1681, pp. 3, 8. See Henry Lawrence's charge of leveling against Dell: *A Plea for the Use of Gospell Ordinances*, London, Printed for Livewell Chapman, 1652, E. 654 (2), p. A2.

58. Life of Bunyan, in *Pilgrim's Progress*, Part III, 1693, p. 5.

59. *Relation of Imprisonment*, p. 129. Judge Twisdon told Bunyan's wife that she made poverty her cloak, pp. 127, 129. John Owen commented upon Bunyan's poverty and the difficulty poor men found in getting justice: John Asty, *Memoirs of the Life of Dr. Owen*, in *A Complete Collection of the Sermons Of the Reverend and Learned John Owen*, London, Printed for John Clark, 1721, p. xxx.

60. *Relation of Imprisonment*, pp. 114, 128.

61. *Ibid.*, p. 130. Hales advised her to apply for a writ of error as the cheapest way of appeal.

62. Life, in *Grace Abounding*, 7th ed., 1692, p. 188; cf. Life, in *Pilgrim's Progress*, Part III, 1700, p. 35: Bunyan had neither poverty nor riches (in his last years) but God always gave him food convenient.

63. Charles Doe, "Reasons why Christian People . . .," in 1692 folio of Bunyan's works, p. 6.

64. Doe, *op. cit.*, p. 11. John Brown says that Bunyan died possessed of less than one hundred pounds, but how much less is not known. Life, in *Pilgrim's Progress*, Part III, 1700, p. 35: Bunyan refused an offer from a gentleman of London to take his son to apprentice because "God did not send him to advance his Family, but to Preach the Gospel."

65. Rogers, *Work and Wages*, pp. 431-32; *Agriculture and Prices*, V, 204 ff., 664 ff. In *Grace Abounding*, p. 10, Bunyan tells of his extreme poverty at the time of his marriage: "This woman and I . . . came together as poor as poor might be, (not having so much house-hold-stuff as a dish or spoon betwixt us both) . . . ."

66. *Few Sighs from Hell*, III, 674.

67. E.g., Fox, *Christ's Parable of Dives and Lazarus, For all Call'd Christians and others to Consider*, 1677. Baxter, *The Poor Man's Family Book*, 1674, pp. 89 ff. Keach, *A Trumpet Blown in Zion*, London, 1694, p. 70. Foster, *The Pouring Forth of the Seventh and Last Viall . . .*, 1650, pp. 3-4. John Pendarves, *Arrowes Against Babylon*, London, Printed for Livewell Chapman, 1656, p. 28. In the tracts of Lilburne, Winstanley, Walwyn, Nayler, Fox, Farnworth, and Clarkson mention of Dives and Lazarus is common. The friars had used this parable in the same way, Owst, *Literature and Pulpit in Medieval England*,

1933, pp. 297-98, 571. Dives also appears occasionally in the secular literature of Elizabethan times.

68. Benjamin Harris, *The Protestant Tutor*, London, Printed for Ben. Harris, 1679, p. 94.

69. *Few Sighs from Hell*, III, 695. Cf. *Christian Behaviour*, II, 568: "It argueth pride when a reproof or admonition will not down as well from the poorest saint, as the greatest doctor; and it argueth a glory in men." Bunyan hoped the upper classes would forget their prejudice and learn to "condescend to men of low degree."

70. *Few Sighs from Hell*, III, 684-85, 687, 688, 690, 692, 695, 696, 699, 700, 704-5, 708, 711, 718. Cf. *Instruction for Ignorant*, II, 690: "Consider how sweet the thought of salvation will be to thee when thou seest thyself in heaven, whilst others are roaring in hell." *Come and Welcome*, I, 261: "This wicked world thinks that the fancies of a heaven, and a happiness hereafter, may serve well enough to take the heart of such as either have not the world's good things to delight in, or that are fools, and know not how to delight themselves therein." *Greatness of Soul*, I, 147: "God has refused to give his children the great, the brave, the glorious things of this world, a few only excepted, because he has prepared some better thing for them." To felicity with Lazarus Bunyan looked forward, *Grace Abounding*, p. 80; and according to his elegist, "his bless'd soul to Abraham's bosum's fled." *Relation of Imprisonment*, 1765, p. 56.

71. *Few Sighs from Hell*, III, 676.

72. *Ibid.*, 676; preface by Gibbs, 669, 670.

73. *Ibid.*, 698.

74. *Ibid.*, 676.

75. *Ibid.*, 675, 677-78, 686, 690-91.

76. *Ibid.*, 677-78. Fox, *Christ's Parable of Dives and Lazarus*, 1677. *Englands Troublers Troubled*, 1648, pp. 7-10: "Ye are so rich, fat and swoln with wealth, that ye esteem far lesse of plaine men then you do of your horses or doggs which ye feed and pamper; whilst by your means such as we are enforced to starve or begg. But know this, God can pull down your pride like Dives."

77. *Few Sighs from Hell*, III, 677-78, 714.

78. *Ibid.*, 677. The burdens of the tenant were increased by tithes: *The Husbandmans Plea Against Tithes*, 1647: "Tithes have been the cause of depopulation of many Villages in this Kingdom; for the Landlord perceiving that he can make more Rent of his land to grase, then the husbandman can give for it to plow, by reason that the tenth of his Stock is taken from him, and the tenth of his yeers labour every yeer under the name of Tithes; and therefore the Landlord hath let fall, or pulled down his houses, and turned his land to pasture." Dives was also mentioned in this tract. Cf. Hubberthorn, *The Record of Sufferings for Tythes*, 1658, p. 13. Clarkson mentions the oppression of tenants by landlords, *The Right Devil Discovered*, 1659, p. 111. Cf. John Musgrave, *A true Representation of the State of the Bordering Customary Tenants in the North, under an Oppressing Landlord*, 1654, E. 730 (12). For the land tenure of the time see J. L. and Barbara Hammond, *The Village Labourer*, 4th ed., London, Longmans, 1927, pp. 4-8.

79. Lipson, *The Economic History of England*, 1931, II, 406-7; the position of the tenant and the progress of inclosures is discussed, pp. 397-409. John Moore, *The Crying Sin of England, of not Caring for the Poor. Wherein Inclosure, viz. such as doth unpeople Townes, and uncorn Fields, is Arraigned, Convicted, and Condemned by the Word of God*, London, Printed for Anthony Williamson, 1653, E. 713 (7).

80. *To the Parliament . . . The humble Representation and desires of divers Freeholders and others well affected to the Commonwealth of England, inhabiting within the County of Bedford,* London, Printed for Thos. Brewster, 1659, 669. f. 21 (51). A week later an almost identical petition from Hertfordshire appeared.

81. *Few Sighs from Hell,* III, 699, 712, 714. Cf. the implicit hatred of landlords in *Building, Nature, Excellency, of House of God,* II, 579: the church "is rent-free; here the man may dwell That loves his landlord. . . ." The church is for those whom "the lofty of this world disdain" and "the distressed and discontent." pp. 578, 579, 580.

It is possible that the emissaries of the Diggers, who toured Bedfordshire in 1649, preaching their social doctrines, had had some influence in the creation of landlord-tenant consciousness in that district: *The Perfect Diurnall,* April 1-8, 1650, E. 534 (25). The Digger experiment at Wellingborrow near Bedford may also have had some influence.

82. *Few Sighs from Hell,* III, 672.

83. *Profitable Meditations,* 1661, pp. 28 ff., "A Discourse between a Saint in Heaven and a Sinner in Hell, alluding to the 16th of Luke." Cf. "A Discourse between Death and a Sinner":

> "I am the man that hath the World at will,
> Both House and Land, and Chattel very much . . .
> Oh sad! in fire I must have my room." p. 19.

Vindication of Gospel Truths, II, 179; *Greatness of Soul,* I, 107, 116, 136, 141; *Pilgrim's Progress,* Part I, p. 163; *Saved by Grace,* I, 342; *Christ a Complete Saviour,* I, 230; *Mr. Badman,* pp. 9, 147, 174; *Paul's Departure,* I, 741; *Grace Abounding,* p. 80. By coincidence the most malignant royalist of Bedfordshire at this time was Sir Lewis Dyves, variously spelled Dives, and Dyve.

84. *Heavenly Footman,* III, 390, 394. Cf. the remark in John Simpson's funeral sermon, *The Failing & Perishing of Good Men,* 1663: "A Nation is more beholding to the meanest Ketchen-maid in it, that hath in her a spirit of prayer, then to a thousand of the profane swaggering Gentry." The prayers of one godly person "be he a Cobler, or a Tinker, or be she a Kitchin Maid" will prevail over those of the profane, pp. 13-14.

85. Parnell, *The Trumpet of the Lord Blowne. Or, A Blast Against Pride and Oppression,* London, Printed for Giles Calvert, 1655, E. 830 (5), pp. 1, 4, 11-12, and *passim.* Clarkson, *The Right Devil Discovered,* London, Printed for the Author, and sold by Francis Cossinet, 1659, pp. 33, 38, 46, 48, 88-89, 132-33, 91-109, and *passim.*

86. Owst, *Literature and Pulpit in Medieval England,* 1933, pp. 287 ff.

87. Richard H. Tawney, *Religion and the Rise of Capitalism,* New York, Harcourt, Brace, 1926, pp. 9, 10, 18, 19, 31-32, 92, 135-41, 219, 220-25 and *passim.* Tawney rarely penetrates below the middle classes, and he is weakest in the 1640-88 period. His discussion of Bunyan and Baxter is sound.

88. *Mr. Badman,* pp. 5, 7, 162.

89. *Ibid.,* pp. 109-10.

90. *Ibid.,* p. 116.

91. *Ibid.,* p. 117.

92. *Ibid.,* p. 116. Bunyan's protest against mercantile fraud had many parallels in his time and earlier, some, relics of the medieval moral tradition, others, complaints of the oppressed: Tawney, *op. cit., passim;* Lipson, *op. cit.,* II, 421-22, 431-33; Christopher Love, *Scripture Rules to be Observed in Buying and Selling,* 1653; Alexander Parker, *A Call out of Egypt,* London, Printed for Giles Calvert, 1656,

E. 893 (3), p. 37; Burrough, *The Testimony of the Lord Concerning London*, 1657, in *Works*, 1672, p. 200; Farnworth, *An Easter Reckoning*, London, Printed for Giles Calvert, 1653, E. 703 (5) , p. 19; Fox, *The Trumpet of the Lord*, 1654, pp. 4, 12-13; Clarkson, *Right Devil Discovered*, 1659, pp. 36-39, 111; Moore, *The Crying Sin of England*, 1653, p. 22; William Pryor and Thomas Turner *The Out-cries of the Poor, Oppressed, & Imprisoned*, London, Printed for Francis Smith, 1659, E. 1010 (23) , p. 14; Arthur Dent, *The Plaine Mans Pathway to Heaven*, 1622, pp. 180-96.

93. *Mr. Badman*, p. 125. Cf. C. F-G, *Gods Blessing upon the Providers of Corne; and Gods Curse upon the Hoarders*, London, Printed for M. S., 1647, E. 419 (26) .

94. *Mr. Badman*, pp. 116-17.

95. *Treatise of Fear of God*, I, 477; *Holy Life*, II, 529; *Saint's Knowledge*, II, 8.

96. *Christian Behaviour*, II, 566-67; *Treatise of Fear of God*, I, 468, 474, 475, 486; *Greatness of Soul*, I, 105, 107; *Solomon's Temple*, III, 476; *Christ a Complete Saviour*, I, 218-19; *Holy Life*, II, 520; *Exposition of Genesis*, II, 463; *Desire of Righteous*, I, 767, 768; *Barren Fig Tree*, III, 579; *Paul's Departure*, I, 733-36; *Saved by Grace*, I, 349.

97. *Vindication of Gospel Truths*, II, 178, 183, 201, 209, an answer to Burrough's insinuations against Burton; *Solomon's Temple*, III, 473, "Covetousness makes a minister smell frowish"; *Few Sighs from Hell*, III, 699; *Pray with the Spirit*, I, 636; *Antichrist and His Ruin*, II, 78; *Justification by Faith*, II, 313; *Pilgrim's Progress*, Part I, pp. 226-27, 244; *Treatise of Fear of God*, I, 475; *Mr. Badman*, pp. 12, 73, 103, 112.

98. *Mr. Badman*, p. 177.

99. *Holy War*, pp. 343, 350, 397-98, cf. passage on Laodicean church which fell through riches, pp. 397-98; *Greatness of Soul*, I, 132.

100. *Holy War*, p. 398.

101. *Pilgrim's Progress*, Part I, p. 213.

102. *Ibid.*, p. 230. For Demas see Spencer, *The Spirituall Warfare*, 1642, p. 5; Sydrach Simpson, *Two Books of Mr. Sydrach Simpson*, 1658, pp. 211 ff.

103. *Pilgrim's Progress*, Part II, pp. 411-12.

104. *Ibid.*, pp. 314-15. Cf. *Christian Behaviour*, II, 557.

105. E.g., *Saint's Knowledge*, II, 11-12: Providences, he held, were of two sorts: temporal goods, and temporal evils. Those who suffered the evils were better and esteemed of God; *Barren Fig Tree*, III, 579: Peace and prosperity signs of God's wrath; *Mr. Badman*, p. 177. But rather inconsistently he also interpreted the ruin of evil people as a sign of God's displeasure: e.g., *Mr. Badman*, p. 99; *Barren Fig Tree*, III, 580.

106. E.g., *Advice to Sufferers*, II, 699; *Paul's Departure*, I, 735; *Grace Abounding*, title-page; *Christ as an Advocate*, I, 190; *Saved by Grace*, I, 349, 350; *Seasonable Counsel*, II, 719; *Mr. Badman*, p. 100; *Treatise of Fear of God*, I, 473; *Resurrection of Dead*, II, 101; *Pharisee and Publican*, II, 218; *Few Sighs from Hell*, title-page. Cf. Life of Bunyan, in *Pilgrim's Progress*, Part III, 1700, p. 1.

107. Clarkson, *The Right Devil Discovered*, 1659, pp. 73-74. For this imagery see Tomlinson, *Seven Particulars*, 1657, p. 22; Howgill, *This Was the word of the Lord . . . to Oliver Cromwell*, London, 1654, E. 732 (22) . Most Quaker tracts contain this imagery.

108. *Water of Life*, III, 541, 543, 545. Cf. *Pilgrim's Progress*, Part II, p. 345. In his use of the word "steeple" Bunyan is like the Quakers, who always used the word to indicate the established church.

109. *Mr. Badman*, pp. 126-34; *Acceptable Sacrifice*, I, 704; *Treatise of Fear of God*, I, 474.

110. *Christian Behaviour*, II, 567-68.

111. *Mr. Badman*, pp. 130-32; *Barren Fig Tree*, III, 565, 568; *Heavenly Footman*, III, 385; *Holy Life*, II, 519; *Pilgrim's Progress*, Part I, p. 152. Cf. Fox, *The Serious Peoples Reasonings and Speech*, London, Printed for Thomas Simmons, 1659, p. 5, and *passim*.

112. *Greatness of Soul*, I, 110; *Acceptable Sacrifice*, I, 709; *Mr. Badman*, pp. 9, 31, 35, 52, 56, 59, 133-34; *Treatise of Fear of God*, I, 476; *Holy Life*, II, 519.

113. *Exposition of Genesis*, II, 442; *Resurrection of Dead*, II, 102; *Israel's Hope*, I, 588; *Last Sermon*, II, 755. Bunyan made class-conscious distinctions in direct address: he usually addressed men of the upper classes as "sir," those of his own class as "friend": e.g., *Holy City*, III, 397; he addressed Fowler and the hostile reader of his *Confession of Faith* as "sir"; cf. *Pilgrim's Progress*, Part I, 172-73. Bunyan was called "goodman," a male equivalent of goody: *Acceptable Sacrifice*, I, 702; Cobb addressed Bunyan as "neighbor" and "goodman," while Bunyan addressed him as "sir," *Relation of Imprisonment*, pp. 120, 122. Fowler frequently employed the contemptuous *thee* and *thou* in his answer to Bunyan, but not consistently; Evangelist is also addressed as "sir."

114. *Pilgrim's Progress*, Part I, pp. 222-24, 229.

115. *Ibid.*, pp. 217-19.

116. *Pilgrim's Progress*, Part II, p. 300. Cf. *Holy City*, III, *passim*, where the harlot is called a gentlewoman; *Antichrist and His Ruin*, II, 54, where Antichrist is called a gentleman.

117. *Holy War*, pp. 197, 214, 239, 259.

118. The following good or semigood people are called gentlemen: Understanding and Conscience, both of whom were eminent men, pp. 242-43; Mr. Gods-peace, p. 331; Mr. Godlyfear, p. 336; Mr. Experience, p. 317; in *Pilgrim's Progress*, Part II, p. 291, Mr. Sagacity is also called a gentleman.

119. *Holy War*, pp. 262, 285, 333, 348, 358, 416.

120. *Ibid.*, pp. 202-3.

121. *Ibid.*, p. 277. Mr. Wet Eyes is also called a poor man, p. 281, as is Mr. Meditation, who is given all the wealth of rich Mr. Letgoodslip in the final leveling of estates, p. 424.

122. *Ibid.*, pp. 303-4. This passage appears to be based on the trial of Wilfull-will in Richard Bernard's *Isle of Man*, 1627, pp. 178-82; Bernard also had much to say against the gentry, covetousness, and the oppression of the poor, pp. 185 ff.

123. *A Relation of the Imprisonment of Mr. John Bunyan*, London, Printed for James Buckland, 1765, p. 57.

CHAPTER VI

1. For descriptions of the Fifth Monarchy and its government see: William Aspinwall, *A Brief Description of the Fifth Monarchy, or Kingdome, That shortly is to come into the World*, London, Printed for M. Simmons, 1653, E. 708 (8); *An Explication and Application Of the Seventh Chapter of Daniel ... Wherein is briefly shewed The State and Downfall of the four Monarchies*, London, Printed for Livewell Chapman, 1654, E. 732 (2), p. 19; *The Legislative Power is Christ's Peculiar Prerogative. Proved from the 9th of Isaiah*, London, Printed for Livewell Chapman, 1656, E. 498 (4); cf. account of speech by Christopher Feake, John Thurloe, *A Collection of State Papers*, London, 1742, VII, 57-8: "We must allow of noe other government than the government of our Lord God, and Jesus Christ."

2. Edward Gibbon, *Decline and Fall*, London, 1776, I, chap. 15, 471-72. Thomas M. Lindsay, *A History of the Reformation*, New York, Scribner, 1910, II, 438, 444, 458.

3. Louise Fargo Brown, *The Political Activities of the Baptists and Fifth Monarchy Men in England During the Interregnum,* Washington, American Historical Association, 1912. This excellent study has been invaluable during the present investigation; the reader is referred to it for the history of the movement from 1650 to 1660. See also: Gooch and Laski, *English Democratic Ideas in the Seventeenth Century,* Cambridge, 1927, pp. 220-28; "The Fifth Monarchy Movement, 1645-1660," *Transactions of Baptist Historical Society,* II (1910-11), pp. 166 ff.

4. Thurloe, *op. cit.,* VI, 184-85, 187.

5. *A Standard Set up: Whereunto the true Seed and Saints of the most High may be gathered together into one,* 1657, E. 910 (10), (May 17, the manifesto of Venner's first uprising). For the social and economic relief of the oppressed see: Aspinwall, *A Premonition Of Sundry Sad Calamities Yet to Come, Grounded upon an Explication of the twenty fourth Chapter of Isaiah,* London, Printed for Livewell Chapman, 1655, E. 818 (7), pp. 13-14; John Spittlehouse, *The first Addresses to His Excellencie the Lord General, with the Assembly of Elders elected by him . . . Containing Rules & Directions how to advance the Kingdom of Jesus Christ over the face of the whole earth,* London, Printed for J. C. and Richard Moone, 1653, E. 703 (19); *The Prophets Malachy and Isaiah Prophecying,* London, Printed for Livewell Chapman, 1656, E. 888 (2); John Rogers, *Sagrir. Or Doomes-day drawing nigh, With Thunder and Lightning to Lawyers. In an Alarum For New Laws, and the Peoples Liberties from the Norman and Babylonian Yokes. Making Discoverie Of the present ungodly Laws and Lawyers of the Fourth Monarchy, and of the approach of the Fifth; with those Godly Laws, Officers and Ordinances that belong to the Legislative Power of the Lord Jesus,* London, Printed for Giles Calvert, 1654, E. 716 (1); Feake, *The Oppressed Close Prisoner,* London, Printed for L. Chapman, 1655, E. 820 (10); Mary Cary, *The Little Horns Doom & Downfall,* 1651, E. 1274 (1); *The Banner of Truth Displayed,* London, 1656, E. 888 (4); sermon by Feake, Thurloe, V, 755-59.

The Quakers, notably Edward Burrough, had millenarian ideas, as had Gerrard Winstanley. An exaggerated account of the millenarianism of the Quakers appears in Hermann Weingarten, *Die Revolutionskirchen Englands,* 1868, p. 263. Weingarten devotes much attention to the Fifth Monarchy movement, which he considers the unifying principle of the enthusiasts, *passim.*

6. *A Door of Hope: or, A Call and Declaration for the gathering together of the first ripe Fruits unto the Standard of our Lord, King Jesus,* Jan. 6, 1661, E. 764 (7), pp. 4-5, 10 (the manifesto of Venner's second revolt; the author attempts to unite all the discontented factions with the promise of reform of all political, social, and economic abuses).

7. E.g., Aspinwall, *An Explication and Application Of the Seventh Chapter of Daniel,* 1654.

8. E.g., John Canne, *A Voice From the Temple To the Higher Powers,* London, Printed for Matthew Simmons, 1653, E. 699 (16), pp. 1-6; *The Prophets Malachy and Isaiah Prophecying,* 1656.

9. E.g., Aspinwall, *An Explication and Application Of the Seventh Chapter of Daniel,* 1654.

10. E.g., Mary Cary, *The Little Horns Doom & Downfall,* 1651; Canne, *A Voice From the Temple,* 1653.

11. These dates appear in the tracts of Mary Cary, Henry Jessey, Christopher Feake, John Rogers, William Aspinwall, Hanserd Knollys, and others. Feake cautiously dated the kingdom within fifty years of 1654.

12. E.g., Cary, *op. cit.;* Aspinwall, *op. cit.*

13. E.g., Rogers, *Sagrir,* 1654; *The Fifth Monarchy, or Kingdom of Christ in*

opposition to the Beast's Asserted, London, Printed for Livewell Chapman, 1659, E. 993 (31). Typical of the moderate view is the General Baptist Confession of Faith, 1654, reprinted in E. B. Underhill, *Confessions of Faith*, London, Hanserd Knollys Society, 1854, p. 329. Passive suffering until the appearance of Jesus is recommended.

14. *The Banner of Truth Displayed: Or, A Testimony for Christ, and against Anti-Christ*, London, 1656, E. 888 (4), pp. 46-47, 65-66. An immediate insurrection is urged.

15. Feake, *A Beam of Light*, London, Printed for Livewell Chapman, 1659, E. 980 (5). Contains the history of the party. For fuller account see L. F. Brown, *op. cit.*

16. Thomas Carlyle, *The Letters and Speeches of Oliver Cromwell*, edited by S. C. Lomas, London, Methuen, 1904, Speech II, Sept. 4, 1654, II, 348-50; Speech V, II, 528.

17. E.g., Canne, *A Voice From the Temple*, 1653, pp. 5-6. Canne resented comparison with John of Leyden, and denied the parallel between the Fifth Monarchy and Münster.

18. *The Loyal Scout*, July 22-29, 1659, E. 993 (3), p. 108.

19. *C.S.P.D.*, 1660-61, pp. 470-71; *Londons Glory, or The Riot and Ruine Of the Fifth Monarchy Men . . . Being a true and perfect Relation of their desperate and bloody Attempts and Practises in the City of London on Monday, Tuesday, and Wednesday last, Jan. the ninth, 1660*, London, Printed for C. C., 1661, E. 1874 (3).

20. Baptist apologies reprinted in: Thomas Crosby, *History of Baptists*, 1738-40, II, 35-83; Underhill, *Confessions of Faith*, p. 343. In volume E. 1055 of the Thomason collection are several pamphlets of January, 1661 against the Fifth Monarchists. Subsequent Fifth Monarchy terrors: *The Traytors Unvailed, or A Brief and true account of that horrid and bloody designe intended by those Rebellious People, known by the names of Anabaptists and Fifth Monarchy*, 1661, E. 1087 (10), (April 18); *A true Discovery of a Bloody Plot Contrived by the Phanaticks*, London, Printed for John Jones, 1661, E. 1087 (9).

21. E.g., Weingarten, *Die Revolutionskirchen Englands*, 1868, p. 272.

22. Lodowick Muggleton, *A True Interpretation of All the Chief Texts . . . of the whole Book of the Revelation*, London, Printed for the Author, 1665.

23. Henry More, *Apocalypsis Apocalypseos*, London, Printed for J. Martyn, and W. Kettilby, 1680, pp. xxv-xxvii, 249-50; *Paralipomena Prophetica*, London, Printed for Walter Kettilby, 1685, Preface.

24. Richard Baxter, *The Glorious Kingdom of Christ Described*, London, Printed for Thomas Parkhurst, 1691, p. 12. Cf. Baxter, *A Paraphrase on the New Testament*, London, 1695, in which he says he was tempted to omit Revelation upon which he maintained a complete skepticism. Cf. John Tombes, *Saints no Smiters*, London, Printed for Henry Eversden, 1664: Apparently trying to curry favor with Clarendon, this backsliding Baptist insidiously questioned the certainty of the visible kingdom. Cf. ridicule of millennium in *Mene Tekel To Fifth Monarchy, with The Knavery of the Cloak*, London, 1665. For Thomas Beverley's academic chiliasm see collection of his tracts, dating from the eighties and later, in volume 701.i.11 in the British Museum.

25. E.g., Arthur Dent, *The Ruine of Rome, Or, An Exposition upon the whole Revelation*, London, Printed for John Waterson, 1656, E. 1615 (1). An example of the academic and non-Fifth Monarchy interpretation.

26. *Calendar of State Papers, Domestic*: 1660-61, pp. 506, 561, 569; 1661-62, pp. 71, 87, 91, 98, 161, 397, 400, 415, 418; 1663-64, pp. 12, 13, 225, 277-78, 346, 428-29, 507,

554, 603, 621, 678; 1664-65, pp. 44-45, 148, 234, 287, 344; 1666-67, p. 318; 1667-68, pp. 154, 318, 319; 1668-69, pp. 342, 463; 1670, pp. 221, 236, 310; 1671, pp. 356, 357, 375, 386; 1677-78, pp. 386, 388; 1678, pp. 246, 290; 1680-81, pp. 174, 500; 1682, pp. 226, 495, 496. The absence of reports from 1672 to 1677 is probably to be attributed to the period of toleration when informers were inactive.

27. Few of the active millenarians mentioned in the State Papers wrote pamphlets: e.g., Belcher, Palmer, Feake, Thomas Hobson, John James, Helmes, Cockayne, Nathaniel Strange. For Belcher see: *A Narrative; Wherein is faithfully set forth the sufferings of John Canne, . . . John Belcher, . . . called . . . Fift Monarchy Men,* London, 1658; for James see: *The Speech and Declaration of John James, A Weaver . . . to the Fifth-Monarchy-Men,* London, Printed for George Horton, 1661; *The true and perfect Speech of John James, A Baptist, and Fifth-Monarchy-Man,* London, Printed for George Horton, 1661. James, an elder in Peter Chamberlen's Baptist church, was executed for Fifth Monarchy activities. Other silent but active Fifth Monarchy Baptists were Thomas Tillam, George Barret, Richard Adams, who in 1682 had a congregation of three hundred Fifth Monarchists, and John Spencer, the coachman.

28. *The Traytors Unvailed,* 1661; *C.S.P.D.,* 1661-62, pp. 87, 98; 1663-64, p. 678.

29. Knollys, *The Parable of the Kingdom of Heaven Expounded,* London, Printed for Benjamin Harris, 1674; *An Exposition of the Eleventh Chapter of the Revelation,* 1679; *The World that Now is; and the World that is to Come,* London, Printed by Tho. Snowden, 1681; *An Exposition Of the whole Book of the Revelation,* London, Sold by William Marshall, 1689.

30. Henry Danvers, *Theopolis, or the City of God New Jerusalem,* London, Printed for Nathaniel Ponder, 1672. Cf. Edward Bagshaw, *The Doctrine of the Kingdom And Personal Reign of Christ asserted and Explained in An Exposition upon Zach. 14,* 1669; Richard Hayter, *The Meaning of the Revelation,* London, Printed for John Courtney, 1675.

31. W. T. Whitley, *The Baptist Quarterly,* London, I (1922-23), 85-86, quoted from *S.P.D.,* Doc. 55, Vol. 419. *C.S.P.D.,* 1670, p. 239, addenda for 1661 in same vol., p. 661; 1666-67, p. 537; 1675-76, pp. 419, 516; 1676-77, p. 90; 1682, pp. 405, 495, 496. Cf. Crosby, *History of Baptists,* III, 97, an admission of Danvers' Fifth Monarchy principles, but a denial of his practices; Walter Wilson, *History and Antiquities of Dissenting Churches in London,* 1808, I, 393-95, his plotting for Monmouth.

32. *Relation of Imprisonment,* pp. 105, 107.

33. *Ibid.,* pp. 120-21.

34. *Ibid.,* p. 131.

35. *The Church Book of Bunyan Meeting 1650-1821,* edited by G. B. Harrison, reproduced in facsimile, London, J. M. Dent, 1928, p. 23; for Simpson, 1658, p. 21: 1659, p. 23; 1661, p. 25. For Jessey, 1657, p. 19; 1658, p. 21; 1674, p. 55. For Cockayne, 1671, p. 46; 1689, p. 74. The Mr. Rogers who is referred to in 1658 in connection with Jessey and Simpson, p. 21, may be John Rogers, the Fifth Monarchy man.

36. Thurloe, *op. cit.,* Dec. 17, 1655, IV, 321: his violent preaching against the government and his attempts to stir up revolt forced him to hide; p. 343: "John Sympson preaches like any Bedlam." Cf. p. 308 and V, 755-59. Miss Louise Brown has conveniently gathered all the evidence from the State Papers on Simpson, *Baptists and Fifth Monarchy Men,* pp. 22, 49, 52, 67, 82, 94, 104.

37. *The Declaration of Arise Evans . . . touching Mr. Feake, and Mr. Simpson,* London, Printed for G. Convert, 1654, E. 224 (1).

38. *A Declaration of several of the churches of Christ . . . Concerning the Kingly Interest of Christ,* London, Printed for Livewell Chapman, 1654, E. 809 (15).

39. The Bodleian has a folio volume without title-page of her verse: S.1. 42. Th. 1657-58.

40. *C.S.P.D.*, 1661-62, pp. 87, 97, 111, 162.

41. George Cockayne, *Flesh expiring, and the Spirit Inspiring in the New Earth: Or God himself, supplying the room of withered Powers, judging and inheriting all Nations*, London, Printed for Giles Calvert, 1648, E. 473 (37). Life of Cockayne in *D.N.B.* and in John B. Marsh, *The Story of Harecourt Being the History of an Independent Church*, London, Strahan, 1871. For his connections with Bedfordshire and Bunyan see pp. 74, 112, 122-25, 139; Marsh minimizes Cockayne's Fifth Monarchy leanings, saying that informers misunderstood his spiritual aims, pp. 95, 122-24, 130-31, 133. Bunyan died at the home of John Strudwick, grocer, a member of Cockayne's church.

42. L. F. Brown, *op. cit.*, p. 22.

43. Joseph Kellet, *A Faithful Discovery of a treacherous Design of Mystical Antichrist*, London, Printed for Thomas Brewster, 1655, E. 820 (7).

44. William Erbury, *The Bishop of London, The Welsh Curate, and Common Prayer, with Apocrypha In the End*, London, 1652, E. 684 (26).

45. *C.S.P.D.*, 1663-64, p. 678; 1664-65, pp. 44-45; 1666-67, p. 157; 1678, p. 246.

46. *Transactions of Baptist Historical Society*, I (1908-9), p. 247: "In the Bedfordshire district other Mixed Communion churches were growing, which learned to quote Jessey as justifying their practice." Bunyan, *Differences in Judgment*, 1675.

47. Whitley, *History of British Baptists*, pp. 72, 86. In his Preface to Mary Cary's book Jessey said that he had ready for printing an exposition of Revelation and Daniel, and he expressed approval of Mary Cary's millenarian ideas. See account of Jessey's "fanatic" career and "absurd cantings" by the prejudiced Anthony Wood, *Athenae Oxonienses*, London, 1721, I, 238-39; Jessey knew William Dell, II, 514.

48. *An Essay toward Settlement*, Printed for Giles Calvert, 1659, 669.f.21 (73).

49. *Mirabilis Annus, or The year of Prodigies and Wonders*, 1661; *C.S.P.D.*, 1661-62, pp. 159, 173, 608. Bunyan's acquaintance with this radical volume is shown by his theft of a passage from it for his *Mr. Badman*. See *infra*, chap. 9.

50. *C.S.P.D.*, 1660-61, p. 424; 1663-64, pp. 277-78.

51. *The Life and Death of Mr. Henry Jessey*, 1671, p. 92.

52. *C.S.P.D.*, 1667-68, p. 319.

53. Vavasor Powell, *A New and Useful Concordance to the Holy Bible*, London, Printed for Francis Smith, 1673. In Powell's Diary the reference without date to J. B. may mean Bunyan: "I received a special Letter this day, from our dear Brother J. B. which suited much with my condition and judgment. . . ." *The Life and Death of Mr. Vavasor Powell*, 1671, p. 73.

54. *C.S.P.D.*, 1660-61, pp. 123, 130, 135-36, 423, 484; 1661-62, p. 463. Louise F. Brown, *Baptists and Fifth Monarchy Men*, pp. 45-46, 51, 63. Wood, *Athenae Oxonienses*, 1721, II, 476: "a busy-body, pragmatical, bold, and an indefatigable Enemy to Monarchy . . . some held him to be an Anabaptist, others a Fifth Monarchy Man and a Millenary: sure it is he was neither Presbyterian or Independent, but a most dangerous and pestilent Man . . . ." Powell was a friend of Edward Bagshaw the millenarian. *Strena Vavasoriensis*, 1654, pp. 5, 6, 24. Cf. Powell's hymn in *Three Hymnes, or Certain excellent new Psalmes, composed by those three Reverend and Learned Divines. Mr. John Goodwin, Mr. Vavaser Powel, and Mr. Appletree*, London, Printed by John Clowes, 1650, E. 1300 (3). Erbury attacked Powell, Feake, Simpson, and Rogers for their literalistic interpretation of Christ's kingdom: *An Olive-leaf*, London, Printed by J. Cottrel, 1654; *A Call to the Churches; or A Packet of Letters To the Pastors of Wales*, London, 1653, E.

688 (1), p. 35; *The Man of Peace*, London, Printed by James Cottrel, 1654, E. 729 (11).

55. John Owen, *The Advantage of the Kingdom of Christ in the Shaking of the Kingdoms of the World*, Oxford, Printed for Tho. Robinson, 1651, p. 3. Cf. Owen's other millenarian tracts of 1649 and 1652, E. 551 (4) and E. 678 (28). Feake cited Owen's millenarian ideas with approval, *Oppressed Close Prisoner*, 1655, p. 100.

56. William Dell, *Several Sermons and Discourses*, London, Printed for Giles Calvert, 1652, E. 645 (4), *passim; The Increase of Popery in England*, London, Printed for Richard Janeway, 1681, Postscript, pp. 18-19.

57. For Knollys at Pinners' Hall see Crosby, *History of Baptists*, I, 340. For Canne, Jessey, and More see *Transactions of Baptist Historical Society*, I (1908-9), 250; II, (1910-11), 31-36. Bunyan knew More and preached in his church. Bunyan mentions Ainsworth, Canne's predecessor at Amsterdam, *Differences in Judgment*, II, 646.

58. Crosby, *History of Baptists*, II, 185-208 contains full account of Keach's Fifth Monarchy opinions and imprisonment; IV, 313. Keach, *The Child's Delight: Or Instructions for Children and Youth*, 3d ed., London, Printed for William and Joseph Marshall, (c. 1703), pp. 30, 46; *The Display of Glorious Grace: or, the Covenant of Peace*, London, Printed by S. Bridge, 1698, pp. 3-4; *Spiritual Melody, Containing near Three Hundred Sacred Hymns*, Printed for John Hancock, 1691, p. 9; *passim* in his other works.

59. That there was some attempt to arouse interest in the millennium in Bedford is probable from the circumstance that in 1657 the Fifth Monarchy party had an agent in the town, John Child, silk-weaver: Thurloe, VI, 187.

60. *The Humble and Serious Testimony Of many Hundreds, of Godly and well affected People in the County of Bedford, and parts adjacent, Constant Adherers to the Cause of God and the Nation*, April 14, 1657. They wrote "for the love of Christ's Kingdome" and would wait patiently "till God shall appeare againe in his own due time, and shall fulfill his gracious promises, wherein he hath caused us to trust, for the full destruction of Antichrists Kingdome and for the advancing of the Kingdome of Christ, together with the obtaining of our just rights and freedomes in civill things which thereby will undoubtedly accrue to the Nations." See account in Thurloe, VI, 228-30.

61. *Address of the Anabaptist Ministers in London To the Lord Protector*, April 3, 1657, reprinted in Underhill, *Confessions of Faith*, p. 335.

62. Thurloe, *op. cit.*, VI, 185; *D.N.B.*

63. *C.S.P.D.*, 1670, additions for 1661, p. 661; *The last farewell to the Rebellious Sect Called the Fifth Monarchy-Men*, London, 1661; *London's Glory*, E. 1874 (3), p. 14.

64. References to the coming of Christ in Bunyan's earlier works are ambiguous in that they may imply the coming to judgment: e.g. *Some Gospel Truths*, II, 162-66; *Vindication of Gospel Truths*, II, 210-11.

65. *Prison Meditations*, I, stanzas 50, 58.

66. *Holy City*, III, 397-98.

67. *Ibid.*, 398. Henry More attacked enthusiasts who attempted to interpret Revelation with no assistance but inspiration: *Apocalypsis Apocalypseos*, 1680, pp. 249-50; but Bunyan, who had carefully studied previous commentaries, is not to be classed with these inspired critics despite his desire to be.

68. Knollys, *An Exposition of the whole Book of Revelation*, 1689; J. E., *The Prophetical Intelligencer, Shewing The causes why all corrupt Churches of Christendome shall passe away, . . . and that the holy City of the Church of new Jerusalem is now comming down from my God out of Heaven*, London, Printed

by M. Simmons, 1647, E. 404 (19) ; in his attack upon the Fifth Monarchy Thomas Hall selected Rev. 21 as one of the main foundations of the idea and ridiculed the literal interpretation of this text: *Chiliastomastix redivivus, Sive Homesus enervatus. A confutation of the Millenarian Opinion, Plainly demonstrating that Christ will not Reign Visibly and Personally on earth with the Saints for a thousand yeers,* London, Printed for John Starkey, 1657, E. 1654 (2) , pp. 43-45.

69. The editor of John Brown's life of Bunyan believed on the strength of a contemporary catalogue which listed "a book on Revelation 21: v. 10 to v. 5 of chap. 22, by John Bunyan, duod. 1665" that he had discovered a lost work by our author: Brown's *Bunyan,* p. 474. It will not be necessary, however, to add this work to the Bunyan bibliography since it is *The Holy City.*

70. *Holy City,* III, 403.

71. *Ibid.,* 402, 403, 405, 420, 425-26, 427, 428, 444.

72. *Ibid.,* 406, 458.

73. *Ibid.,* 406, 407.

74. *Ibid.,* 409. Cf. Thomas Goodwin, *A Sermon of the Fifth Monarchy,* London, Printed for Livewell Chapman, 1654, E. 812 (9) , To the Reader: "The doctrine of the Saints Reign on Earth is a matter of great Comfort to the People of God . . . . The prayers of the Saints against those that oppresses them, will still bring the vintage of Gods wrath."

75. *Ibid.,* 408-9.

76. *Ibid.,* 428; cf. Danvers, *Theopolis;* Knollys, *Parable of the Kingdom of Heaven,* pp. 68-72.

77. *Holy City,* III, 429.

78. *Ibid.,* 429-30, 433-35.

79. *Ibid.,* 429, 438-39.

80. *Ibid.,* 410. *The Holy City* may have been the book by Bunyan seized by L'Estrange in a raid on Francis Smith's warehouse in 1666. Smith had published several of Bunyan's earlier prison books and published the second edition of *The Holy City.* No publisher's name is given in the first edition though one variant names J. Dover as printer. It is probable that Smith published *The Holy City* in 1665. Francis Smith, *An Account of the Injurious Proceedings of Sir George Jeffreys Knt. Late Recorder of London, Against Francis Smith, Bookseller, Sept. 16, 1680,* London, Printed for Francis Smith, p. 11.

81. *Holy City,* III, 445.

82. *Ibid.,* 430, 444, 445, 446, 447.

83. The few references to the coming of Christ and to the preparations for it during this intermediate period are unimportant and sometimes ambiguous: e.g., *Confession of Faith,* 1672, II, 616; *Light for Them,* I, 428; *Instruction for Ignorant,* II, 686. Bunyan's period of silence coincides with that of the State Papers during the interim of toleration, when there are no reports of millenarian activities.

84. *Solomon's Temple,* III, 507-8.

85. *Antichrist and His Ruin,* II, 58-59: "And as to the saints that would very willingly see her downfall, how often have they been mistaken as to the set time thereof." *Exposition of Genesis,* II, 480-81.

86. *Forest of Lebanon,* III, 527, 536.

87. *Exposition of Genesis,* II, 424, 426, 456.

88. *Ibid.,* 488.

89. *Ibid.,* 456-57.

90. *Antichrist and His Ruin,* II, 79.

91. *Ibid.,* 52-54.

92. *Ibid.*, 59-72.

93. *Antichrist and His Ruin*, II, 67: Bunyan again claimed originality: "I do not question but many good men have writ more largely of this matter: but as I have not seen their books, so I walk not by their rules." Cf. Knollys, *The World that Now is*, pp. 81-91; 13-19 *bis*.

94. *Antichrist and His Ruin*, II, 52, 55-58.

95. *Ibid.*, 45, 47, 48, 51, 72.

96. *Ibid.*, 72-78.

97. *Ibid.*, 61, 72-74.

98. E.g., *Forest of Lebanon*, 1692, *passim*; *Mr. Badman*, pp. 85-87; *Christian Behaviour*, 1663, II, 553; *Resurrection of Dead*, 1665, II, 85; *Pray with the Spirit*, 1663, I, 640.

99. *Seasonable Counsel*, II, 707. Cf. 705, 709, 738, 741.

100. *Forest of Lebanon*, III, 516; *Confession of Faith*, II, 593-94; *Holy City*, III, 410; *Christ as an Advocate*, I, 195; *Water of Life*, III, 556; *Saint's Knowledge*, II, 19; *Relation of Imprisonment*, pp. 124-25.

101. *Strena Vavasoriensis*, 1654, E. 727 (14); *Vavasoris Examen, & Purgamen*, 1654, E. 732 (12).

102. Underhill, *Confessions of Faith* is a handy collection of these documents; cf. Crosby, *History of Baptists*, II, 35-83.

Christopher Feake, the Fifth Monarchist, owned the government as God commanded, but said significantly, "It is one thing to own the government according to God; another to own them as they want to be owned." Feake, *The Oppressed Close Prisoner In Windsor-Castle, His Defiance To The Father of Lyes*, London, Printed for L. Chapman, 1655, E. 820 (10), p. 77.

103. *Confession of Faith*, II, 601. Cf. *Antichrist and His Ruin*, II, 44, 73; *Seasonable Counsel*, II, 692, 705-6, 709-10. The following considerations may also have influenced Bunyan's expressions of loyalty: his belief that persecution was a means of trying and purging the church, and that greater suffering would bring greater reward, *Holy City*, III, 431, *Seasonable Counsel*, II, 725; that persecution was the just desert of the church's laxity and sin, *Holy Life*, II, 513, *Antichrist and His Ruin*, II, 45; that kings were tools in the hand of God for disciplining saints, *Seasonable Counsel*, II, 724, 728, *Saint's Knowledge*, II, 21; that God would fully avenge the wrongs of persecution Himself, *Seasonable Counsel*, II, 737, 739, *Pharisee and Publican*, II, 217.

104. Charles Doe, "The Struggler," in the 1692 folio of Bunyan's works. Doe says that Bunyan hid so successfully and preached so secretly that it pleased the Lord to preserve him out of the hands of his enemies.

105. *The Continuation of Mr. Bunyan's Life*, in *Grace Abounding*, 7th ed., 1692, p. 181.

106. *Seasonable Counsel*, II, 694, 714; *Water of Life*, III, 547; *Christ a Complete Saviour*, I, 226.

107. *Seasonable Counsel*, II, 709.

108. See "Militant Baptists 1660-72," *Transactions of Baptist Historical Society*, I (1908), 148 ff: "Most of the Baptists were pronounced republicans," who saw no more harm in plotting insurrection than the royalists had under Cromwell. The radical Baptists carried into action the convictions of the moderate.

109. *Saved by Grace*, I, 341; *Antichrist and His Ruin*, II, 77; *Holy City*, III, 446; *Treatise of Fear of God*, I, 481; *Forest of Lebanon*, III, 520-21; *Seasonable Counsel*, II, 709, 712; *Strait Gate*, I, 371; in *Antichrist and His Ruin*, II, 43-44 Bunyan's picture of Artaxerxes, the ideal king, who gave his subjects liberty of worship, is in obvious contrast to Charles.

110. *The Continuation of Mr. Bunyan's Life*, in *Grace Abounding*, 7th ed., London, 1692, p. 181. This biographer also credits Bunyan's "piercing Wit" with having penetrated the motives behind James' declaration of liberty of conscience. Cf. Life of Bunyan, in *Pilgrim's Progress*, Part III, 1693, pp. 39, 40; and life in 1700 edition of this work, p. 34. Bunyan is reported to have approved of the abolition of the test and penal laws, probably out of the willingness to profit by any concessions of the Beast: William Page, editor, *The Victoria County History of Bedford*, London, Archibald Constable, 1908, II, 59. See the discussion of John Eston's letter on the attitude of the Bedford dissenters toward the repeal of the test act, Brown, *John Bunyan*, pp. 349-53. This passage is a good discussion of the political situation at Bedford; several members of Bunyan's conventicle were named for office as favoring repeal; their motives, however, are obscure.

111. Printed conveniently in John Brown's *Bunyan*, p. 93.

112. Although Brown cast doubt upon the signature, holding that it must have been that of another John Bunyan, our Bunyan, as Mr. Frank Harrison has pointed out in his notes to Brown, is the only one who was associated with the other signers. *Ibid.*, p. 122.

113. *The Humble and Serious Testimony Of many Hundreds, of Godly and well affected People in the County of Bedford, and parts adjacent, Constant Adherers to the Cause of God and the Nation*, April 14, 1657. Thurloe, VI, 228-30.

The Church Book records the agitation of the meeting at the threat of Cromwell's assumption of monarchy, their prayers for the nation in the troubled times before the Restoration, and their hope that God might influence the new governors. These carefully discreet passages show the distress of the meeting upon each threat of the return of monarchy and their desire to continue the work of God, or commonwealth principles, in the nation: in March and April, 1657, they sought God about the affairs of the nation and in May gave thanks for Cromwell's rejection of the crown, p. 18; in Aug., 1657 they prayed at the suggestion of brother Jessey, the Fifth Monarchist, p. 19; in Oct., 1657, Dec., 1657, Feb., 1658, April, 1658 they sought God about the affairs of the nation and about the carrying on of His work in the nation (i.e., Fifth Monarchy), pp. 19, 20; in Oct. and Dec., 1659, just before the Restoration, they prayed fervently for the nation and God's work, pp. 23, 24; in Oct., 1660 they prayed God to direct their governors, and in Aug., 1661 they mentioned the increase of their troubles, p. 25. After this there is a complete silence on political affairs for many years.

114. *The Serious Attestation of many Thousands, Religious and well disposed People, living in London, Westminster, Borough of Southwark, and parts adjoyning*, March 26, 1657. A protest against "arbitrary power" and praise of the Leveller agreements.

115. *A True Narrative Of The Manner of the taking of Sir George Booth, On Tuesday Night last, at Newport-Pannel . . . With his Speech to Mr. John Gibbs, the Minister of the Town*, London, Printed for Thomas Richardson, 1659, E. 995 (4). "Life of John Gibbs" in *The Baptist Quarterly*, III (July, 1927), 316-20.

Henry Denne, *The Levellers Designe Discovered: Or the Anatomie of the late unhappie Mutinie*, London, Printed for Francis Tyton, 1649, E. 556 (11).

116. "Militant Baptists, 1660-72," in *Transactions of Baptist Historical Society*, I (1908-9), 148 ff. The conventicles of Marsden, Tillam and others were hotbeds of conspiracy. While not all conventicles were seditious, most were animated by hatred of the government. Cf. *C.S.P.D.*, 1660 ff. under headings, "Anabaptist" and "Fanatic." Francis Smith, Bunyan's publisher, professed commonwealth principles.

117. *Church Book,* pp. 28, 29: Brother Merrill "began in an obscure way to charge the Church with rebellion, and also with taking some portions of scripture, that made for their purpose, and refusing the other," and accused it of having a hand in the blood of the king and of disobedience to the government. The church professed surprise at these charges.

A true and Impartial Narrative of Some Illegal and Arbitrary proceedings by certain Justices of the Peace and others, against several innocent and peaceable Nonconformists in and near the Town of Bedford, upon pretence of putting in execution the late Act against Conventicles, Together With a brief Account of the late sudden and strange Death of the Grand Informer, and one of the most malicious Prosecutors against these poor people, Printed in the year, 1670.

118. E.g., Keach, *Distressed Sion Relieved . . . A Poem . . . Wherein are Discovered the Grand Causes of the Churches Trouble and Misery under the late Dismal Dispensation,* London, Printed for Nath. Crouch, 1689.

119. Keach, *The Travels of True Godliness From the Beginning of the World to this present Day; in an apt and pleasant Allegory,* London, Printed for John Dunton, 1684, Chap. 8, pp. 113 ff., 117-19, 130-31.

120. Coppin, *Truth's Testimony,* 1655, pp. 17-18. Coppin practiced the obliquity he recommended: *Saul Smitten For Not Smiting Amalek . . . Being an Allegorical Allusion to the present passages of the Times,* London, Printed by William Larner and Richard Moon, 1653, E. 711 (8). But his title gave his intention away.

121. Rogers, "Epistle," John Canne, *The Time of the End,* London, Printed for Livewell Chapman, 1657, p. A3 verso.

122. Baxter, *A Paraphrase on the New Testament, Second Edition, To which is added at the End, Mr. Richard Baxter's Account of his Notes on some particular Texts for which he was Imprisoned,* London, Printed for T. Parkhurst, 1695. *Reliquiae Baxterianae,* 1696, Appendix VIII, pp. 123 ff: "The general defence of my Accused Writings, called Seditious and Schismatical."

123. Roger L'Estrange, *Considerations and Proposals In Order to the Regulation of the Press: Together with Diverse Instances of Treasonous, and Seditious Pamphlets, Proving the Necessity thereof,* London, Printed by A. C., 1663, p. 10.

124. *Exposition of Genesis,* II, *passim;* Aspinwall, Arise Evans, and most other saints also believed that the Bible was a political allegory.

125. Nimrod was the usual symbol for Charles II among the Baptists. In 1682 Marsden's conventicle sang a political hymn of hate on the subject of Nimrod: Marsh, *The Story of Harecourt,* London, 1871, pp. 164-65. The Fifth Monarchists used Cain and Nimrod as symbols of the earthly governor, e.g., *A Door of Hope,* 1661, p. 1; Canne, *The Time of the End,* 1657, Epistle. Nimrod was Erbury's symbol of the oppressor and absolute monarch: Erbury, *The Man of Peace,* London, Printed by James Cottrel, 1654, E. 729 (11), pp. 5-6. Cain is the symbol of the persecutor in F. E., *Christian Information Concerning these Last times,* London, 1664, p. 13. The Quakers used Cain for the same purpose: *Cains Off-spring Demonstrated . . . in a bitter Persecution . . . at Newark,* London, Printed for Thomas Simmons, 1659, p. 6.

126. *Exposition of Genesis,* II, 420, 437, 442-46, 447, 452.

127. *Ibid.,* 466-74.

128. *Ibid.,* 454, 460-61, 489.

129. *Pilgrim's Progress,* Part II, pp. 332-33, 357-58, 378. Cf. Greatheart's millenarian battle against the ten-horned beast of Rev. 17:3, *ibid.,* p. 389.

130. *Exposition of Genesis,* II, 497.

131. *Loc. cit.*

132. *Exposition of Genesis,* II, 465.

CHAPTER VII

1. Richard Heath, "The Archetype of 'The Holy War,' " in *The Contemporary Review,* New York, LXXII, (1897), 105. Cf. Heath, "The Archetype of the 'Pilgrim's Progress,' " *ibid.,* LXX, (1896) , 541.

2. John Brown, *John Bunyan,* p. 311. For Newport Pagnell see: George Lipscomb, *The History and Antiquities of the County of Buckingham,* London, J & W. Robins, 1847, IV, 282.

3. Gerald R. Owst, *Literature and Pulpit in Medieval England,* Cambridge, 1933, pp. 79-86, 97-98, 109. Professor William Haller of Barnard College informs me that the imagery of the siege was common in sermons before 1640.

4. T. S. (Thomas Sherman) , *The Second Part of the Pilgrim's Progress,* 1682, Author's Apology. James B. Wharey, *A Study of the Sources of Bunyan's Allegories,* Baltimore, J. H. Furst, 1904. Richard Bernard, *The Isle of Man; or, The Legall Proceeding in Man-shire against Sinne. Wherein, by way of a continued Allegorie, the chiefe Malefactors disturbing both Church and Common-Wealth, are detected and attached; with their Arraignment, and Judiciall triall* . . . 4th ed., London, Printed for Edward Blackmore, 1627. Bernard was one of many preachers who used the imagery of the town.

5. *Building of House of God,* II, 579, 581. The term "holy war" had been used by John Rogers, the Fifth Monarchist, to refer to the establishment of Christ's kingdom, *Sagrir,* 1654, p. A3.

6. *Holy City,* III, 405, 411, 421, 422; *Holy War,* p. 321; *Forest of Lebanon,* III, 525, 527. The idea of Mansoul as a composite man came from the idea of Christ as a composite man, *Antichrist and His Ruin,* II, 45-46.

7. *Holy City,* III, 454; *Holy War,* p. 379.

8. *Holy War,* pp. 328-29. For the white linen dress of the millennial saints see: Mary Cary, *Little Horns Doom,* p. 179; *The Prophets Malachy and Isaiah Prophecying,* p. 10. In the latter the spotting of these robes, such as occurs during the defection of Mansoul, indicates turning from Christ. Cf. *Forest of Lebanon,* III, 527. In *Pilgrim's Progress,* Part I, p. 276, Part II, p. 292, white robes and the tree of life appear in heaven as they do in the Holy City which is heaven on earth.

9. *Holy City,* III, 439-40.

10. Benjamin Keach, *The Progress of Sin; or the Travels of Ungodliness . . . In an apt and Pleasant Allegory: Together with The great Victories he hath obtained . . . As also, The Manner of his Apprehension, Arraignment, Tryal, Condemnation and Execution,* London, Printed for John Dunton, 1684, chaps. 9-11, pp. 186 ff. Chap. 10 is entitled "A Compendious Description of Mount Zion the City of God, that is now, and always hath been Besieged by the Powers of Darkness." His city is based on Rev. 21, etc., and its charter, government, laws, defense, are closely modeled upon Mansoul's. In his *War with the Devil,* 4th ed., 1676, Keach occasionally employed the imagery of the fight for a city to illustrate his moral allegory, but without any suggestion of the millennium.

11. *Holy City,* III, 403, 421, 424, 427, 441; *Exposition of Genesis,* II, 466; *Barren Fig Tree,* III, 562; *Some Gospel Truths,* II, 160; *Resurrection of Dead,* II, 92.

12. Henry Jessey, *Miscellanea Sacra: or, Diverse necessary Truths,* London, Printed for Livewell Chapman, 1665, p. 16, "Rules about the Literal and Mystical Sense."

13. E.g., In the capacity of Adam, Mansoul is described as pure before its fall; whereas the allegory of conversion required Mansoul's impurity at this stage before rebirth.

14. Keach attempted a many-layered allegory of the moral conflict within the

individual, the history of the church and the millennium, and the course of biblical history. The effect is confusing.

15. *Holy War*, pp. 199, 207.

16. *The Continuation of Mr. Bunyan's Life*, in *Grace Abounding*, 7th ed., 1692, p. 181, (quoted in Chapter VI).

17. Brown, *John Bunyan*, chap. 14, "Mansoul and the Bedford Corporation," pp. 311, 315-24. For the date of publication of *The Holy War* see Arber, *Term Catalogues*.

18. William Page, editor, *The Victoria County History of Bedford*, London, Constable, 1908, II, 57-59 on the new-modeling of Bedford. Cf. Henry Hallam, *The Constitutional History of England*, New York, Harper, 1847, pp. 486-87.

19. *Holy War*, pp. 204-06, 212-13, 217. Bunyan cautioned in his Preface against attempting to explain his allegory without consulting his marginal key because "In mysteries men soon do lose their way," p. 187. His verbal marginal key refers usually to his allegory of conversion, but occasionally also to his subsidiary themes; his marginal textual citations, however, supply the key to his subsidiary themes. These citations will be noted when they are important.

20. *Holy War*, pp. 208, 211, 212, 213. In Keach's *Progress of Sin*, Apollyon uses play-books and songs against the "paper-enemy" or the propaganda of the saints, p. 22. *The Phanatiques Creed, or a Door of Safety*, 1661, pp. 12-13, advocated the prohibition of preaching and the censorship of the press to crush Fifth Monarchy activities. This tract was an answer to *A Door of Hope*, 1661, which contains a picture of Restoration wickedness similar to that in *The Holy War*. Cf. Roger L'Estrange, *Considerations and Proposals In Order to the Regulation of the Press*, 1663. L'Estrange seized one of Bunyan's books in 1666.

21. The name Emmanuel occurs only twice in the Bible, Isa. 7: 14 and Matt. 1: 23. For the millenarian use of the name see: John Canne, *Emanuel, or God With Us*, London, Printed by Matthew Simmons, 1650, E. 614 (11); William Pryor and Thomas Turner, *The Out-cries of the Poor, Oppressed, & Imprisoned*, London, Printed for Francis Smith, 1659, E. 1010 (23), p. 12. In *Pilgrim's Progress*, Part I, pp. 183, 240, the Delectable Mountains, which appear to represent the Fifth Monarchy, are called Immanuels Land. This land is located near the gate of the celestial city, is supervised by shepherds or ministers, and is common to all pilgrims. But this conception of Immanuels Land is more pastoral than municipal and is intended merely to suggest felicity on earth, not the character of the Holy City.

22. William Smith, *Dictionary of the Bible*, edited by H. B. Hackett, New York, Hurd & Houghton, 1869. Bunyan knew that the Shaddai of the Hebrew text appears as the Almighty in the King James version as his marginal note at the first mention of Shaddai shows, *Holy War*, p. 189.

23. Bunyan said in *Antichrist and His Ruin*, II, 62-63, that when only wicked men were left in Babylon and had complete control of her "hold" and "castle," the time was at hand for the appearance of Christ. Cf. *Forest of Lebanon*, III, 521, on the dragon breaking into the church, and the resulting necessity of a holy war.

24. *Holy War*, p. 210.

25. *Ibid.*, p. 267.

26. *Holy War*, pp. 274, 283, 315-16. Diabolus is described by the citation of two millenarian texts, Rev. 20: 1, 2 and Rev. 9:9, on binding in chains for 1,000 years, and sounding of fifth trumpet, *Holy War*, pp. 193, 215. Like Danvers, *Theopolis*, p. 36, Bunyan interpreted the chains figuratively as symbols of the domination of godliness. The citation of Isa. 33: 24 imparts a millenarian tone to Emanuel's victory, p. 290.

27. *Holy War*, pp. 293, 295, 297-300, 300. Cf. *Holy City*, III, 412: God will encamp around the city to defend it, Zec. 9: 8.

28. *Holy War*, pp. 319, 323, 329-31. Cf. *Holy City*, III, 403: "Out of the church that is now in captivity, there shall come a complete city, so exact in all things, according to the laws and liberties, privileges and riches of a city, that she shall lie level with the great charter of heaven." Members of the church in captivity will rule the new city.

29. This interval may be intended to represent the millennium, condensed for purposes of art or in the interests of the main theme of conversion. *Holy War*, p. 331.

30. *Holy City*, III, 448-49; *Holy War*, p. 332. *Holy City*, III, 426: Bunyan says the saints of the Holy City would still be imperfect though free for a time from Satan.

31. *Holy War*, pp. 332, 397: in latter place see citation of Rev. 3: 17 on luke-warm Laodiceans.

32. *Holy City*, III, 401.

33. *Ibid.*, 447.

34. *Forest of Lebanon*, III, 521.

35. *Holy War*, pp. 366-68. Cf. this dragon, *Holy City*, III, 401. The other Doubters are also characterized by texts from Revelation.

36. *Holy War*, p. 387; the two and a half years may refer to the two and a half years of backsliding during his own conversion, *Grace Abounding*, p. 62. Cf. *Holy City*, III, 401: they shall tread under foot her "city constitutions, her forts and strength, her laws and privileges for a long time." To Bunyan the killing of the witnesses was their political subjection, the loss of their "visible church-state": *Antichrist and His Ruin*, II, 65-68. See *loc. cit.* for his statement of doubt as to how long this three and a half years would last. Canne and Aspinwall shared Bunyan's opinions on these points. Cf. Keach, *Progress of Sin*, p. 190, for parallel killing of the "witnesses."

37. *Holy War*, p. 398.

38. *Ibid.*, p. 402.

39. *Ibid.*, pp. 428, 429. Isa. 33: 17 is cited p. 426, on king in his beauty.

40. *Antichrist and His Ruin*, II, 52, 65-68.

41. E.g., Cary, *Little Horns Doom*, pp. 171, 176-84. *Holy War*, p. 410.

42. *Holy War*, p. 415.

43. In *Holy City*, III, 402, 405, 456, Bunyan called the millennium putting the church "into her primitive state" and "former glory." This idea of a millennial return to the primitive church was common among the Quakers.

44. Charles H. Firth, *Cromwell's Army*, London, 1902, pp. 43-45, 57, 70-71, 121-22, 150, 173, 278, 289, 291, 313 ff., 330, 331, 335, 341, 408, 409 ff. Compare *Holy War*, pp. 218, 220, 222-24, 234, 246, 250, 259, 286, 288, 292-93, 400.

45. *Holy War*, pp. 191, 250, 380, 399; cf. Firth, pp. 26, 102, and "Reformado" in *N.E.D.*

46. For the millenarian characteristics of the short parliament see: Samuel R. Gardiner, *History of the Commonwealth and Protectorate*, London, Longmans, 1903, II, 268-340.

47. On the offer of the crown see: Firth, *The Last Years of the Protectorate*, London, Longmans, 1909, I, 128-98.

48. John Spittlehouse, *A Warning-Piece Discharged*, London, Printed for Richard Moone, 1653, E. 697 (11). The following works treat of the materialistic backsliding of Cromwell: Christopher Feake, *The Oppressed Close Prisoner*, 1655, pp. 43-48; *A Beam of Light*, 1659; Canne, *The Time of the End*, 1657, pp. 48-53; *A Door of Hope*, 1661, p. 3: "the wicked Apostacy of O. C."; *A Standard Set up,*

1657, pp. 6-9; Powell, *A word for God, or a testimony on truth's behalf, from several churches . . . against wickedness in high places,* 1655, in John Thurloe, *A Collection of State Papers,* IV, 380-84; cf. Spittlehouse's warning to Cromwell to continue the work he had begun: Spittlehouse, *The first Address to His Excellencie the Lord General, with the Assembly of Elders elected by him . . . Containing Certain Rules & Directions how to advance the Kingdom of Christ,* London, Printed for J. C. and Richard Moone, 1653, E. 703 (19). Cf. Weingarten on Cromwell's apostasy, *Revolutionskirchen Englands,* pp. 134, 182, 251; p. 274, Weingarten recognized the political allusion to Charles in Bunyan's *Holy War.*

49. *Some Gospel Truths,* II, 163.

50. Keach's city in *The Progress of Sin* also fell through carnal security, apostasy, and backsliding, pp. 164, 190, 198, 218, 221.

51. Lukewarmness, backsliding, and the ineffectuality of the preachers are discussed as signs of the coming of Christ in *Antichrist and His Ruin,* II, 45, 59-72; *Holy Life,* II, 509, 534, 539, 540, 543. Hanserd Knollys had the same idea.

52. *Antichrist and His Ruin,* II, 67. The impatience of the inhabitants over the delay of Emanuel was that of the Restoration saints over Christ's coming, *Solomon's Temple,* III, 507-08.

53. For the theocratic ideals of the saints see: Robert Barclay, *The Inner Life of the Religious Societies of the Commonwealth,* 1876, pp. 486-89, 494-95. Cf. Richard Tawney, *Religion and the Rise of Capitalism,* 1926, on the theocratic tendency of Calvinism, pp. 115, 118, 119, 131.

54. *The Church Book* reveals the use of excommunication as a disciplinary weapon and the control of the meeting over the entire life of each member, *passim.*

55. Feake, *The Oppressed Close Prisoner,* 1655, p. 105.

56. Aspinwall, *An Explication and Application of Dan. 7,* 1654, p. 36; cf. Aspinwall, *The Legislative Power is Christ's,* 1656, p. 30.

57. Thurloe, *op. cit.,* IV, 348.

58. For a bibliography of these trial scenes see *infra* Chapter IX.

59. Firth also interprets these trial scenes literally as manifestations of puritan intolerance, "Bunyan's Holy War," in *The Journal of English Studies,* I (1913), pp. 143-44.

60. James Park, *False Fictions and Romances Rebuked: In Answer to Pretended Matter Charged against the Quaker, in a Book, Intituled, The Progress of Sin,* London, 1684, p. 9. The treatment of the Quakers in the New England theocracy is significant: see Marmaduke Stephenson, *A Call from Death to Life, Being An Account of the Sufferings of Marmaduke Stephenson, William Robinson and Mary Dyer, in New England, 1659,* London, 1660, reprinted Edinburgh, Aungervyle Society, 1886, pp. 46-49.

61. *Holy War,* p. 239. Aspinwall took pains to decry the common impression that it was unsafe to have no laws but Christ's and none but godly judges: *An Explication and Application of Dan. 7,* pp. 19-20.

62. *Holy War,* pp. 260, 300, 301-14, 319, 366, 376, 417, 418-23, 424-25; cf. *Pilgrim's Progress,* Part II, pp. 331-32 on burning of Timorous and Mistrust through the tongue, like Nayler, for having impeded Christian. Saints in power were severe.

63. For the destruction of the wicked by preaching and disputation see: *Antichrist and His Ruin,* II, 48-51; *Forest of Lebanon,* III, 521. Carnal weapons are deplored.

64. *Holy War,* pp. 217-18, 219, 220. In *Holy City* Bunyan said some of the preachers during the millennium would be "sons of thunder," an idea of which this character Boanerges is apparently the fruit, III, 435.

65. *Holy War,* pp. 212-15, 221-23, 225. Cf. *Holy City,* III, 410.

66. *Holy War,* pp. 227, 229, 230, 231; cf. pp. 283-84.

67. *Holy War,* p. 232. In *Holy City,* III, 445, the saints also play "gunshot" upon the Beast "by the Word and Spirit of God."

68. *Holy War,* pp. 234, 235, 238, 240-44; the preaching witnesses are considered "tormentors" by the Beast in *Antichrist and His Ruin,* II, 69-72; in this same tract Bunyan foresaw the fall of Antichrist by internal division, II, 56.

69. *Holy War,* pp. 245-46, 247, 248, 251, 262, 263, 264-65, 268, 269. Cf. *Holy City,* III, 406 on Lord's coming to relieve Antichristian siege by power of the word; *Antichrist and His Ruin,* II, 47-48, 51 on sword of word, 72, on Christ's action through instruments; *Holy City,* III, 428. The Reformades, who took a conspicuous part in the action, *Holy War,* p. 263, are probably the "messengers" who coördinated the activities of Baptist churches. *The Church Book* mentions them frequently. Cf. Samuel Butler, *Hudibras,* III, ii, 91: "Reformed t' a reformado saint,/ And glad to turn itinerant,/ To stroll and teach from town to town . . . ."

70. Bunyan's expectation of the conversion and aid of kings would appear from this to be merely politic in *Antichrist and His Ruin,* II, 61-62; *Holy City,* III, 445-47. In the obscurity of allegory Bunyan could tell the truth about kings.

71. *Holy War,* pp. 299, 322, 323, 329, 337-40, 362-63, 364, 373, 376, 378, 401, 414. Cf. *Holy City,* III, 413-14; *Seasonable Counsel,* II, 712-13.

CHAPTER VIII

1. Gerald R. Owst, *Literature and Pulpit in Medieval England,* Cambridge, 1933: on homely and familiar analogies, pp. 24 ff.; on allegorical elaboration of imagery, pp. 56 ff.; on the medieval character of the seventeenth-century sermon, p. 98; on Bunyan's reflection of this tradition, p. 109; on *exemplum* and illustration, pp. 149, 189 ff.

2. *Seventh Day Sabbath,* II, 361. Cf. *Instruction for Ignorant,* II, 675, "a plain and easy dialogue, fitted to the capacity of the weakest." His usual audience was the poor and the ignorant, and the price of his books was purposely kept low, *Seventh Day Sabbath, loc. cit.* Keach's and probably Bunyan's books were distributed by hawkers to this audience, Thomas Crosby, *History of Baptists,* IV, 279.

3. Several rhetorics guided the higher ministry, e.g., John Prideaux, *Sacred Eloquence: Or, the Art of Rhetorick, As it is Layd down in Scripture,* London, Printed by W. Wilson, for George Sawbridge, 1659, E. 1790 (2). See Caroline F. Richardson, *English Preachers and Preaching 1640-1670,* New York, Macmillan, 1928, a discussion chiefly devoted to the rhetorical usages of the respectable pulpit, and to the rhetorical training of the clergy.

4. For the development of the popular style during the Civil Wars see William Haller, *Tracts on Liberty,* New York, Columbia University Press, 1934, I, 6, 12, 31, 53, 78, 80. According to John Dunton the popular style was marked by plainness, easiness, and adaptation to its audience. Of Keach he said: "He's a popular Preacher, and (as appears by his awakeing Sermons) understands the Humour and Necessity of his Audience." Dunton, *The Life and Errors of,* London, Printed for S. Malthus, 1705, pp. 233, 236. Cf. the discussions of popular vs. academic manners by Robert Barclay, *The Inner Life of the Religious Societies of the Commonwealth,* London, 1876, pp. 150-55, 161, 383. The latter two references concern the methods of Henry Denne and the Quakers.

5. Roger L'Estrange, *Considerations and Proposals In Order to the Regulation of the Press,* London, Printed by A. C., 1663, p. 10.

6. Richard Baxter, *The Poor Man's Family Book*, London, Printed for Nevill Simmons, 1674, To the Reader.

7. Praise-God Barebones, *A Discourse Tending To Prove the Baptisme In, or under The Defection of Antichrist to be the Ordinance of Jesus Christ*, London, Printed by R. Oulton & G. Dexter, 1642, E. 138 (23).

8. Edward Fowler, *The Principles and Practices, Of certain Moderate Divines of the Church of England*, London, Printed for Lodowick Lloyd, 1670, p. 104, a plea for an easy and intelligible pulpit style and an attack on pedantic wit and ornament.

9. Abraham Wright, *Five Sermons, In Five several Styles; or Waies of Preaching*, London, Printed for Edward Archer, 1656, E. 1670 (1), Epistle to the Reader.

10. John Tombes, *Anthropolatria; or The Sinne Of glorying in Men, Especially In Eminent Ministers of the Gospel*, London, Printed by G. Miller for John Bellamy, 1645, E. 282 (13), pp. 12-16.

11. *Strena Vavasoriensis, A New-Years-Gift for the Welch Itinerants*, London, Printed by F. L., 1654, E. 727 (14), pp. 7-8.

12. *The Life and Death of Mr. Vavasor Powell*, 1671, pp. 108-9.

13. *Few Sighs from Hell*, III, 672-73.

14. Ebenezer Chandler and John Wilson, "To the Serious Judicious and Impartial Reader," in 1692 folio of Bunyan's works.

15. Charles Doe, *A Collection of Experience of the Work of Grace*, London, Printed for Cha. Doe, a Comb-maker in the Burrough, 1700, p. 52. Cf. Doe, "Reasons why Christian People should Promote by Subscriptions the Printing in Folio the Labours of Mr. John Bunyan," in 1692 folio of Bunyan's works: "Many thousands had the Soul-benefit and Comfort of his Ministry to astonishment, as if an Angel or an Apostle had touch'd their Souls with a Coal of holy Fire from the Altar."

16. Epitaph, in *A Relation of the Imprisonment of Mr. John Bunyan*, 1765, p. 57.

17. *The Continuation of Mr. Bunyan's Life*, in *Grace Abounding*, 7th ed., London, 1692, p. 181. In *Grace Abounding*, p. 83, Bunyan said that people flocked to hear him for a variety of reasons, many apparently out of curiosity.

18. See *supra*, note 19 in Chap. III, for account of his conversion of Cambridge student.

19. Epitaph, *Relation of Imprisonment*, 1765, p. 57.

20. *Jerusalem Sinner*, 1688, I, 79.

21. *Solomon's Temple*, 1688, III, 466.

22. See *supra*, Chap. IV.

23. *Jerusalem Sinner*, I, 98.

24. *Acceptable Sacrifice*, 1689, I, 707; cf. story of senile lady who mentioned Christ and a pitcher, *ibid.*, I, 702.

25. *Advice to Sufferers*, 1684, II, 733.

26. E.g., *Come and Welcome*, 1678, I, 282, 283.

27. *Christ a Complete Saviour*, 1692, I, 220; cf. another example of what Bunyan calls the "metaphor of gleaning," *Strait Gate*, I, 380: "It is the devil and sin that carry away the cart-loads, while Christ and his ministers come after a gleaning."

28. *Pharisee and Publican*, 1685, II, 252.

29. *Advice to Sufferers*, 1684, II, 702.

30. For the elaboration of metaphor through an entire sermon cf. Thomas Porter, M.A., *Spiritual Salt*, London, Printed for Ralph Smith, 1651, E. 629 (14); William Gurnall, *The Christian in Compleat Armour*, London, Printed for Ralph Smith, 1655, E. 824 (1); Faithful Teate, *A Scripture-Map of the Wilderness of Sin*,

And Way to Canaan, London, Printed for G. Sawbridge, 1655, E. 839 (1). The latter two indicate the probable source of *Pilgrim's Progress* in the imagery of sermons.

31. *Christ as an Advocate,* I, 190.

32. *Water of Life,* III, 539, 542, 543, 558. A typical doctor's bill is to be found in the British Museum, 669. f. 20 (41) ; cf. the advertisement of Salvator Moretto, 1647, E. 526 (19) ; other medical advertisements are to be found in the newspapers, e.g., *The Publick Adviser,* Sept. 14-21, 1657, E. 925 (11), and in the Baptist paper *The Faithful Scout, passim.* Benjamin Keach elaborated the metaphor of the curative water of life in *The Progress of Sin,* 1684, pp. 214-15. Bunyan's last sermon, which exists only in the notes of one of his hearers, is the elaboration of the metaphor of children, of which he said, "I will give you a clear description of it under one similitude or two." *Last Sermon,* 1689, II, 756. The outstanding example of Bunyan's medical similitude occurs in *Jerusalem Sinner,* I, 75-76, "But we will follow a little our metaphor."

33. *Relation of Imprisonment,* 1765, p. 57.

34. Incidental dialogue: "Ay, that is well for you, Paul; but what advantage have we thereby? Oh, very much, saith he. . . ." *Jerusalem Sinner,* I, 77; "Sinner, turn, says God. Lord, I cannot tend it, says the sinner. Turn or burn, says God. I will venture that, says the sinner. Turn, and be saved, says God. I cannot leave my pleasures, says the sinner: sweet sins, sweet pleasures, sweet delights, says the sinner," *Saved by Grace,* 1675, I, 352. Cf. *Acceptable Sacrifice,* 1689, I, 710. Colloquialism: "there is never a barrel of better herring, but that the whole lump of them are, in truth, a pack of knaves," *Israel's Hope,* I, 619; "The Son of God will put his shoulder to the work," *Light for Them,* I, 408. Cf. *Come and Welcome,* I, 282, 285; *Water of Life,* III, 544. John Brown has made a convenient list of Bunyan's colloquialisms in his life of Bunyan, p. 436.

35. *Water of Life,* III, 540-41.

36. *Desire of Righteous,* I, 749.

37. In *Christ as an Advocate,* I, 161, he used analogy "to bring this down to weak capacities"; In *Israel's Hope,* I, 580, he used "a plain similitude" as an illustration; in *Saint's Knowledge,* II, 17, he said Christ condescended to weak capacities by the use of similitudes.

38. *Solomon's Temple,* III, 491.

39. *Ebal and Gerizim,* III, 744.

40. *Exposition of Genesis,* II, 421, 423, 462, 492; *Forest of Lebanon,* III, 515, 523; *Holy City,* III, 409, "These words are the metaphor by which the Holy Ghost is pleased to illustrate the whole business. Indeed similitudes, if fitly spoke and applied, do much set off and out any point. . . ."; *Holy City,* III, 424, "Yet consider that these are but metaphorical and borrowed expressions, spoken to our capacities. . . . You know it is usual for the Holy Ghost in Scripture to call the saints sheep, lambs, heifers, cows, rams, doves, swallows, pelicans, and the like . . . all of which are but shadowish and figurative expressions even as this. . . ."; cf. *Holy City,* III, 420, 421, 427, 437, 451. Cf. comments on similitudes of Paul and Christ: *Resurrection of Dead,* II, 91; *Exposition of Genesis,* II, 485; *Barren Fig Tree,* III, 562; *Few Sighs from Hell,* III, 674; *Some Gospel Truths,* II, 142, 159, "Now let me give you a similitude, for it is warrantable; for both Christ and his apostles did sometimes use them, to the end, souls might be better informed"; *Strait Gate,* I, 366, 367; *Heavenly Footman,* III, 382; *Pilgrim's Progress,* Part II, p. 366, on metaphor of music, "I make bold to talk thus Metaphorically, for the ripening of the Wits of young Readers, and because in the Book of the Revelations, the Saved are compared to a company of Musitians."

41. Keach and Thomas Delaune, *Tropologia: A Key to open Scripture-Metaphors. Book I. Containing Sacred Philology, or, The Tropes in Scripture . . . Book II & III. Containing a Practical Improvement . . . of Several of the most Frequent and Useful Metaphors, Allegories, and Express Similitudes, of the Old and New Testament,* London, Printed by J. R. and J. D. for Enoch Prosser, 1682, Book II, pp. 112, 203, 319. Bunyan's occasional comments on metaphor, e.g., *Water of Life,* III, 540-41, resemble Keach's prefatory discussion of allegory and tropes.

42. Metaphors are much less frequent in Keach's sermons than in Bunyan's. For his occasional metaphors see Keach, *The Display of Glorious Grace: or, the Covenant of Peace, Opened. In Fourteen Sermons,* London, Printed by S. Bridge, 1698, pp. 277-80; *A Trumpet Blown in Zion, or an Allarm in God's Holy Mountain: Containing An Exposition of that Metaphorical Scripture Matth. III. 12.,* London, 1694. Cf. Crosby's statement that Keach preached without embellishment, *History of Baptists,* IV, 305.

43. *Saint's Knowledge,* II, 16. Cf. *Pharisee and Publican,* II, 276: "They that use high and flaunting language in prayer, their simplicity and godly sincerity is to be questioned." In *Light for Them,* I, 392 he commends simplicity and plainness to express sincerity in critical times; *Doctrine of Law and Grace,* I, 495, on his plain and homely style; *Relation of Imprisonment,* p. 115, he decried "elegant" words without spirit, implying that elegance was incompatible with spirit; *Saint's Knowledge,* II, 11, 22; *Justification by Faith,* II, 323.

44. Keach, *The Display of Glorious Grace,* 1698, To the Reader, p. iii; *Tropologia,* To the Reader in both Book I and Book II on human vs. divine eloquence.

45. *Book for Boys and Girls,* No. 59, "Upon a Skilful Player on an Instrument": The minister "So skilfully doth handle evr'y Word; And by his Saying, doth the heart so reach, That it doth sigh before the Lord." Cf. *Holy Life,* II, 521, during a condemnation of those who relied merely upon rhetoric, he said, "the noise and sound of the word . . . [has] some kind of musicalness in it, especially when well handled and fingered by a skilful preacher."

46. See section on his preaching, *Grace Abounding,* pp. 83-88. Cf. *Treatise of Fear of God,* I, 474: "I have endeavoured with words as fit as I could to display it in its colours before thy face."

47. *Grace Abounding, loc. cit.*

48. *Solomon's Temple,* III, 472.

49. *Jerusalem Sinner,* I, 69.

50. *Pilgrim's Progress,* Part I, p. 137.

51. Doe, T. S., and the author of the life of Bunyan in *Pilgrim's Progress,* Part III, 1693, p. 38, refer to the *Progress* as a tract.

52. Doe, "The Struggler," in 1692 folio of Bunyan's works. Cf. life in *Pilgrim's Progress,* Part III, 1693, p. 38: in the *Progress* are such "Lively Representations of things Figured out to the mind, that it cannot but be very pleasing and delightful, as well as profitable, to a Godly Life."

53. Arthur Dent, *The Plaine Mans Pathway to Heaven,* 18th ed., London, 1622; Dent, *The Opening of Heaven Gates, Or The ready way to everlasting life. Delivered in a most familier Dialogue, between Reason and Religion, touching Predestination,* London, Printed for John Wright, 1617; *A Pastime for Parents,* London, Printed for Thomas Man, 1612, a catechism for children.

54. T. S., *Youths Tragedy, A Poem: Drawn up by way of a Dialogue . . . For the Caution, and direction, of the Younger Sort,* 4th ed., London, Printed for John Starkey and Francis Smith, 1672; *Youth's Comedy, or the Souls Tryals and Triumph: A Dramatick Poem . . .,* London, Printed for Nath. Ponder, 1680.

William Balmford, *The Seaman's Spiritual Companion: Or Navigation Spiritual-ized*, London, Printed for Benj. Harris, 1678.

55. T. S., *The Second Part of the Pilgrim's Progress*, The Authors Apology.

56. *Profitable Meditations, Fitted to Mans Different Condition, In a Conference Between Christ and a Sinner*, London, Printed for Francis Smith, (1661) , (British Museum) . This work is not included in Offor's collected edition. Cf. Preface of Keach, *War with the Devil*, 4th ed., London, Printed for Benjamin Harris, 1676, one of the verse allegories preceding *Pilgrim's Progress:*

> One Reason, Reader, of this Mode or Style,
> Is, that it might with honest craft beguile
> Such curious Fancies who had rather chose
> To read ten lines in Verse, than one in Prose.

Cf. Keach, *The Glorious Lover. A Divine Poem*, 1679: Preface, "A Verse may catch a wandring Soul, that flies/Profounder Tracts. . . ." Similar prefaces on the evan-gelistic virtues of poetry occur in T. S., *Youth's Comedy*, 1680; Keach, *Spiritual Melody*, 1691. Cf. George Herbert's "A Verse may find him, who a Sermon flies."

57. In the Conclusion to *Profitable Meditations*, p. 31, Bunyan again pleaded with the reactionary: "Slight it not for its method, so as to Reject it." Keach's "Vindication of this Book" in *War with the Devil* also reveals a struggle with Bap-tist conservatives:

> . . . because that at this day,
> All Poetry there's many do gain-say;
> And very much condemn, as if the same,
> Did worthily deserve, reproach and blame.
> If any Book in Verse, they chance to spy,
> A way Prophane, they presently do cry:

Keach insisted that verse was as sacred as prose, that its use had been sanctioned by David, and that it showed direct inspiration.

58. Cf. Keach, *The Travels of True Godliness . . . in an apt and pleasant Alle-gory*, 5th ed., London, Printed for John Dunton, 1684, Epistle to the Reader: "In this Tract . . . I hope none will be offended, because True Godliness is here presented in an Allegory, sith the Holy Scriptures abound with them, and so fully justifie our practice herein." *The Progress of Sin*, 1684, Preface: "I have in it made use of the same Method I did before, viz. Presenting all I have said, Allegori-cally; which Jesus himself much delighted in, and made use of; for all he spoke unto the Multitude, was by Parables, &c. And indeed, had I not warrant from Gods Word thus to write, I should not presume so to do." The Preface to the spurious Part III of *Pilgrim's Progress*, 1693, contains a commendation of the expository value of allegory, but no apology. By that time the conservative appear to have yielded or expired.

59. *Pilgrim's Progress*, Part II, p. 286.

60. *Pilgrim's Progress*, Part I, p. 280.

61. T. S., *The Second Part of the Pilgrim's Progress*, The Authors Apology.

62. *Pilgrim's Progress*, Part I, Preface. The "dialect" of Sherman's first para-graph shows the point of Bunyan's pride in his own style, and also the ground of Sherman's objection to Bunyan's levity and homeliness: "The Spring being far advanced, the Meadows being Covered with a Curious Carpet of delightful Green, and the Earth Cloathed in Rich and Glorious Attire, to Rejoyce and Tri-umph for the Return of her Shining Bridegroom: The Healthful Air rendered

more Pleasing and Delightful by the gentle Winds then breathed from the South, impregnated with the Exhilerating Fragrency of the Variety of Flowers and Odoriferous Plants over which they had passed; and every blooming Bush, and Flourishing Grove plentifully stored with Winged Inhabitants . . . ." This is Sherman's improvement upon Bunyan's style. T. S., *The Second Part of the Pilgrim's Progress,* p. 1.

63. *Mr. Badman,* pp. 3, 10; *Holy War,* p. 183.

64. *Solomon's Temple,* III, 492, on spoons for spoon-feeding those who could not stand meat and had to be dandled. In his letter in *The Church Book,* John Gifford recommended an adaptation of manner to the capacity of the audience, milk for babes and meat for the strong. Bunyan was following the precept of his old guide.

65. *Holy City,* Epistle to Four Sorts of Readers, III, 397-99.

66. *Grace Abounding,* p. 6. Cf. William Penn, *No Cross, no Crown,* 1669, Preface: "My matter, stile and method speak not the least premeditation or singularity, but that simplicity and truth which plainly show the affectionate sincerity of my heart . . . ." Matthew Coker, *A Prophetical Revelation Given from God himself unto Matthew Coker,* 1654: "And thus I have in an homely and plain stile declared my selfe to the poorest and simplest, as well as the richest and wisest of men. . . ." *The Life and Death of Mr. Henry Jessey,* 1671: Jessey is said to have preached "in that plain simple style, and dress, which . . . the World calls foolishness," and he is said to have disapproved of garnishing his sermons with neatness and art as a hindrance to converting work, p. 34. Cf. John Asty, *Memoirs of the Life of Dr. John Owen,* in Owen's *Sermons,* London, Printed for John Clark, 1721, p. v: Owen laid aside all affectation of pomp and humane learning to preach the gospel "in all plainness and simplicity, which is the peculiar excellency of an evangelical minister."

67. *Exposition of Genesis,* II, 485.

68. *A Book for Boys and Girls; or, Country Rhymes for Children,* 1686, a facsimile of the first edition, with introduction by John Brown, London, Elliot Stock, 1889. This work is not reprinted fully in Offor's collected edition.

69. For a discussion of the eighteenth-century efforts to make Bunyan elegant see John Brown's introduction to *Book for Boys and Girls,* 1889, pp. xii-xvii.

70. The Preface to Part II of the *Progress* shows his intention of including material profitable for young and old; he introduced Mercy to appeal to girls. Since even children had liked the first part, he included matter for them in the second. *Pilgrim's Progress,* Part II, pp. 284-88. Henry Jessey and Abraham Cheare among the Baptists had preceded Bunyan in writing for children. Concerning the indigestion of Matthew, *Pilgrim's Progress,* Part II, p. 343: Matthew was given pills. A remedy of the day was known as Matthew's pills; when overcome in the pulpit, Vavasor Powell took one of "Mathews pills," and presently died. *Life and Death of Mr. Vavasor Powell,* 1671, p. 190. Matthew, however, survived.

71. *Pilgrim's Progress,* Part II, pp. 318, 338, 340, 344-47, 375-76.

72. *Treatise of Fear of God,* I, 460. Cf. *Resurrection of Dead,* 1665, II, 110-12, Bunyan's bestiary; *Pilgrim's Progress,* Part II, pp. 344-45. In *The Quaker Disarm'd,* 1659, Thomas Smith said that he heard Bunyan preaching on the book of the creatures: "By the book of the creatures, he said, he meant this or that cup of bear, or pot of wine whereby a man is drunk, the timber in the wall, &c." Even in 1659 Bunyan was preaching concretely by examples.

73. *Solomon's Temple,* III, 500.

74. *Pilgrim's Progress,* Part I, pp. 159 ff., Part II, pp. 315-17. The shepherds in

Pilgrim's Progress, Part II, p. 396, who represent ministers, also taught by emblems. In *The Holy War* Emanuel also entertained and instructed the townsmen with riddles and metaphors, and taught them to interpret allegory, *Holy War,* p. 298.

CHAPTER IX

1. E.g., George Offor, Introduction to *Pilgrim's Progress,* III, 29-55; after listing previous allegories, he concluded that Bunyan had no literary sources; cf. his *Memoir of Bunyan,* I, lxvii. Cf. F. J. Furnivall, editor, *Deguilleville's Pilgrimage of the Life of Man,* E.E.T.S., London, K. Paul, Trench, etc., 1899-1904. pp. liii-lxii; after a review of the evidence of Bunyan's indebtedness to previous allegories, the writer of the Preface concluded that Bunyan was influenced by nothing but his own life and the Bible.

2. His biographer in *Grace Abounding,* 7th ed., 1692, p. 181, says, for example, that many who heard Bunyan preach "wondered as the Jews did at the Apostles (viz) whence this Man should have these things, perhaps not considering that God more immediately assists those that make it their business industriously and chearfully to labour in his Vineyard."

3. *The Life and Death of Mr. John Bunyan,* in *Pilgrim's Progress,* Part III 4th ed., London, Printed by W. Onley, for J. Back, 1700, p. 29. Cf. similar account by Hearn, quoted in John Brown, *John Bunyan,* p. 358.

4. Ebenezer Chandler and John Wilson, "To the Serious Judicious, and Impartial Reader," 1692 folio of Bunyan's works.

5. *Building, Nature, Excellency of the House of God,* II, 581.

6. *Holy City,* III, 398.

7. *Grace Abounding,* p. 86. His texts are significant: Rom. 15: 18: "For I will not dare to speak of any of those things which Christ hath not wrought by me . . . ."; Gal. 1:11, 12: "But I certify you, brethren, that the gospel which was preached of me is not after man. For I neither received it of man, neither was I taught it, but by the revelation of Jesus Christ."

8. *Solomon's Temple,* III, 464.

9. *Light for Them,* I, 392.

10. To the innumerable citations with which Edward Fowler had supported his tract Bunyan displayed a contemptuous indifference: "It matters nothing to me, I have neither made my creed out of them, nor other, than the holy scriptures": *Justification by Faith,* II, 294. Cf. *Seventh Day Sabbath,* II, 364, 373: "I know not what our expositors say of this text"; *Antichrist and His Ruin,* II, 67; *Christ a Complete Saviour,* I, 238.

11. *Justification by Faith,* II, 319.

12. Edward Fowler, *Dirt wip't off,* 1672, p. 16; cf. p. 70. Fowler's indignation was the greater because he had devoted himself in 1670 to the repudiation of Hobbes with whom many appear to have confused the Latitudinarians: *The Principles and Practices, Of certain Moderate Divines of the Church of England,* London, Printed for Lodowick Lloyd, 1670, pp. 13-14, (Union).

13. Chandler and Wilson, *op. cit.*

14. Cheare's verses are printed in *A Looking-Glass for Children,* by Henry Jessey (3d ed., London, Printed for Robert Boulter, 1673) ; from Cheare's introductory verse, "Go little Book . . . ." Bunyan appears to have taken his "Go, now my little Book" at the beginning of the second part of the *Progress.*

15. E.g., James Blanton Wharey, *A Study of the Sources of Bunyan's Allegories,* Baltimore, J. H. Furst, 1904.

Harold Golder, *The Chivalric Background of Pilgrim's Progress*, 1925, in *Harvard University Summaries of Theses*, Cambridge, University Press, 1928; apparently Dr. Golder has published from time to time sections of this interesting dissertation in scholarly magazines: e.g., "Bunyan and Spenser," PMLA, XLV (March, 1930), 216-37; "Bunyan's Valley of the Shadow," *Modern Philology*, XXVII (Aug., 1929), 55-72; "Bunyan's Giant Despair," *Journal of Eng. and Germanic Phil.*, XXX (Oct., 1931), 361-78; "Bunyan's Hypocrisy," *North American Review*, CCXXIII (1926), 323-32. The last concerns Bunyan's condemnation of the romances to which he was indebted.

16. Gerald R. Owst, *Literature and Pulpit in Medieval England*, Cambridge, 1933, pp. 97-109. Many sermons and other tracts employ the imagery of the journey, way, spiritual armor, weapons, hills, valleys, etc., e.g., Thomas Taylor, *The Pilgrim's Profession*, in *Three Treatises*, London, Printed for John Bartlet, 1633, pp. 99-155; Henry Nicholas, *Terra Pacis. A True Testification Of The Spiritual Land of Peace (which is the Spiritual Land of Promise, and the holy City of Peace, or the heavenly Jerusalem) and of the holy and spiritual People that dwell therein, as also of the walking in the Spirit, which leadeth thereunto*, London, Printed for Samuel Satterthwaite, 1649, (both in Union). Cf. other works, note 30, Chap. VIII, *supra*.

17. E.g., *Few Sighs from Hell*, III, 711; *Christian Behaviour*, II, 552, 556; *Mr. Badman*, pp. 42-43, 161; *Holy War*, p. 386; *Pilgrim's Progress*, Part II, p. 332; *Greatness of Soul*, I, 147; Cf. Bunyan's imitation of Shakespeare in "Who would true valour see," *Pilgrim's Progress*, Part II, p. 405.

18. E.g., *Light for Them*, I, 430; *Differences in Judgment*, II, 624; *Christian Behaviour*, II, 549; *Grace Abounding*, pp. 18, 41; *Forest of Lebanon*, III, 512, 524; *Jerusalem Sinner*, I, 81-82; *Seventh Day Sabbath*, II, 369; *Holy War*, p. 183.

19. John Brown, *John Bunyan*, p. 306; cf. Prefatory Note in Brown's edition of *Mr. Badman* and *The Holy War*, Cambridge University Press, 1905. Wharey, "Bunyan's Mr. Badman," in *Modern Language Notes*, XXXVI (Feb., 1921), 65-79. In the Preface to the first part of *Pilgrim's Progress* Bunyan testified to his awareness of the dialogue tradition: "I find that Men (as high as Trees) will write Dialogue-wise." p. 139.

20. Arthur Dent, *The Plaine Mans Pathway to Heaven. Wherein every man may clearely see whether hee shall bee saved or damned. Set forth Dialogue-wise, for the better understanding of the simple*, 18th ed., London, Printed for Geo. Latham, 1622, p. 91. Offor says that Bunyan owned the 1625 edition, III, 45.

21. G. B. Harrison, *John Bunyan: A Study in Personality*, London, Dent, 1928. Mr. Harrison was anticipated by Brown, *John Bunyan*, pp. 305-06. For Wildman see *Church Book*.

22. E.g., *The Young-Man's Warning-Piece. Or, The Extravagant Youths Pilgrimage and Progress in this World*, Printed for P. Brooksby, 1682, a broadside with cuts; *A Looking glass for a Drunkard*, London, Printed for W. Whirwood, (c. 1674); *The English Villain: Or the Grand Thief, Being A full Relation of the desperate Life and deserved Death of that most notable Thief and notorious Robber, Richard Hanam*, London, Printed for John Andrews, 1656, E. 1645 (3).

23. *Mr. Badman*, p. 5.

24. *Mr. Badman*, pp. 58-59. Taylor, *Ranters of both Sexes, Male and Female . . . Wherein John Robins doth declare himself to be the great God of Heaven . . . and that his wife is with childe with Jesus Christ*, Printed for John Hammon, 1651, E. 629 (15); *The Ranters Monster: Being a true Relation of one Mary Adams . . . blasphemously affirming, That she was conceived with child by the Holy Ghost*, London, Printed for George Horton, 1652, E. 658 (6); *A List of some of*

the Grand Blasphemers and Blasphemies, London, Printed by Robert Ibbitson, 1654.

25. Samuel Clarke, *A Mirrour or Looking-Glasse Both for Saints and Sinners: Wherein, By many memorable Examples is set forth, as Gods exceeding great mercies to the one, so his severe judgements upon the other,* London, Printed for John Bellamy, 1646, E. 1104; 2d ed., 1654; 4th ed., 1671. Thomas Beard, *The Theatre of Gods Judgements: Revised, and augmented. Wherein is represented the admirable justice of God against all notorious sinners,* London, Printed by Adam Islip, for Michael Sparke, 1631. Henry Burton, *A Divine Tragedie Lately Acted, or A Collection of sundrie memorable examples of Gods judgments upon Sabbath-breakers, and other like Libertines, in their unlawful Sports,* 1641, E. 176 (1). The judgments against cat-players and bell-ringers which appear in this book, pp. 8, 14, or in another similar collection, may have been the cause of Bunyan's terror while indulging in these vices. Lewis Bayly, *The Practise of Pietie,* 3d ed., London, Printed for John Hodgets, 1613; pp. 548-55, judgments against Sabbath breakers; Bunyan had read this book. Laurence Price, *A Ready way to prevent Sudden Death,* London, Printed for William Gilbertson, 1655, E. 1478 (3). *The Ranters Monster,* 1652, E. 658 (6), pp. 6, 7. John Fox's *Book of Martyrs* contains judgments. Divine judgments were sometimes used as exempla in sermons of the seventeenth century.

26. Clarke, *A Mirrour, or Looking-Glass,* 4th ed., London, Printed by Thomas Milbourn for Robert Clavel, 1671. In the Preface to *Mr. Badman,* p. 3, Bunyan says that one may see his hero "as in a glass," in apparent allusion to the title of Clarke's book or to the many similar titles. The seven stories from Clarke in *Mr. Badman* appear, pp. 60, 142, 154, 155; in Clarke, 1671, pp. 12, 41, 148, 149; Clarke, 1654, p. 212; Clarke, 1646, p. 107; several also occur in Beard, pp. 147, 187, 192, 372, 557.

27. "A true Relation of the sudden and strange Death of one Feckman, a malicious Persecutor of the good People at Bedford," p. 12, in *A true and Impartial Narrative of Some Illegal and Arbitrary proceedings by certain Justices of the Peace and others, against several innocent and peaceable Nonconformists in and near the Town of Bedford,* 1670. John Brown, *John Bunyan,* p. 211, traces Bunyan's story of the informer W. S. to an actual event at Bedford. Clarke, *A Looking-glass for Persecutors: Containing Multitudes of Examples of God's Severe, but Righteous Judgments, upon bloody and merciless Haters of his Children in all Times, from the beginning of the World to this present Age,* London, Printed for William Miller, 1674. No modern instances.

28. *Mr. Badman,* pp. 37, 38, 168.

29. E.g., Clarke, ed. 1646, pp. 41 ff., 58 ff., 95 ff. Ulcers, intestines, rots, scabs, tumors are the staple of these stories as of Bunyan's. The saints were excellent pathologists. Bunyan's prefatory statement, pp. 10-11, that he would conceal the names of those whose fate he recounted is the usual one in these collections; cf. Beard, pp. 316-17, and *passim.* There can be no doubt of the truth of Bunyan's assertion, p. 170, that he could have collected hundreds of such stories; for they were one of the most popular varieties of saintly literature: e.g., *A Looking glass for a Drunkard,* London, (c. 1674); *A Timely Warning to Drunkards,* London, Printed for J. Coniers, 1673; *Divine Examples of God's Severe Judgments upon Sabbath-Breakers, In their unlawful Sports,* London, Printed for T.C., 1672.

30. *Mr. Badman,* p. 26. In his Preface Bunyan said, while explaining his use of index hands: "All which are things either fully known by me, as being eye and ear-witness thereto, or that I have received from such hands, whose relation as to this, I am bound to believe," p. 6.

31. *Mr. Badman*, p. 37. [Henry Jessey], *Mirabilis Annus, or The year of Prodigies and Wonders, being a faithful and impartial Collection of several Signs that have been seen in the Heavens, in the Earth, and in the Waters; together with many remarkable Accidents and Judgments befalling divers Persons*, 1661, Sec. xxv, p. 82. Another but slightly different version of the same story appears in *Two most Strange Wonders; The One Is a true Relation of an Angel appearing to Mr. James Wise . . . The Other Being a most fearful judgment which befell Dorothy Mately of Ashover*, Printed for W. Gilbertson, 1662. Jessey produced two other books of prodigies and judgments: *Mirabilis Annus Secundus; Or, The Second Year of Prodigies*, 1662; *The Lords Loud Call to England; Being a True Relation of some Late, Various, and Wonderful Judgments*, London, Printed for L. Chapman and Francis Smith, 1660, E. 1038 (8). For Cockayne and Jessey see Marsh, *Story of Harecourt*, 1871, p. 98.

32. *Mr. Badman*, pp. 171 ff.

33. By far the most likely immediate source of Bunyan's personification of the faculties of the soul and of his allegory of conversion is Benjamin Keach, *The Glorious Lover*, London, Printed for Christopher Hussey, 1679, pp. 190 ff. Keach was indebted to Bernard as Bunyan also was. The imagery of a fight for an allegorical city appears frequently in Keach's *War with the Devil*; in his subsequent books Keach was influenced by Bunyan's *Holy War*. Other works contain similar ideas, e.g., Joshua Sylvester, "Auto-machia or self-civil war," a poem of the "Holy War" within the soul, reflecting the medieval psychomachia; Henry Carpenter, *The Deputy Divinity*, London, Printed for N. Webb, 1657, expository but personifying Conscience and other faculties; T. S., *Youths Tragedy*, 1672, internal conflict with use of military imagery, and personification of Will and Conscience, p. 15. Bunyan's book reflects the still current tradition of the psychomachia as Owst points out. For the relationship between Keach and Bunyan see W. T. Whitley, *History of British Baptists*, 1923, pp. 138-40.

34. We have already noted that Bunyan knew of *Leviathan*. Since *The Holy War* represents the Fifth and *Leviathan* the Fourth Monarchy, it is possible that Bunyan intended his book to be a millenarian antidote to Hobbes, as Richard Baxter had intended his theocratic *Holy Commonwealth* as a counter-*Leviathan*: Baxter, *A Holy Commonwealth, or, Political Aphorisms, Opening The true Principles of Government . . . And directing the Desires of sober Christians that long to see the Kingdoms of this world, become the Kingdoms of the Lord, and of his Christ*, London, Printed for Thomas Underhill, 1659, (Union), pp. 190, 213, 216. Baxter was a theocrat without being a millenarian; his plan is presented as a substitute for those of the Fifth Monarchists, Harrington, and Hobbes, p. 223, yet his Utopia resembles Mansoul. The preface of *The Holy War* contains a passage which may refer to Hobbes:

> Some will again of that which never was,
> Nor will be, feign, (and that without a cause)
> Such matter, raise such mountains, tell such things
> Of men, of Laws, of Countries, and of Kings:
> And in their Story seem to be so sage,
> And with such gravity cloath ev'ry Page,
> That though their Frontice-piece say all is vain,
> Yet to their way Disciples they obtain.
>
> *Holy War*, p. 183.

The resemblance between the frontispieces of *The Holy War* and of *Leviathan* is so striking as to lead to the belief that Bunyan intended his as a reference to that of Hobbes, as sardonically appropriate for his rival Utopia. The attack upon Mansoul by the Doubters confirms this supposition; for the Doubters were not only the latitudinarians and Fowler but also Hobbes with whom Bunyan had classed Fowler.

35. *Holy War*, pp. 190-95, 210-11, 217, 248-49, 354-57. The indebtedness of Bunyan to Milton was suggested by Edmund A. Knox, *John Bunyan in Relation to his Times*, London, Longmans, 1928, p. 107.

36. *Holy War*, pp. 210, 245. This noun was not uncommon at the time; it was often used to refer to councils of the Jesuits, *N.E.D.*

37. *Paradise Lost*, viii, 145-58; *Holy War*, Preface, p. 187:

> Count me not then with them that to amaze
> The people, set them on the stars to gaze,
> Insinuating with much confidence,
> That each of them is now the residence
> Of some brave Creatures; yea, a world they will
> Have in each star, though it be past their skill
> To make it manifest to any man . . . .

But this may be a reference to John Wilkins's *Discovery of a World in the Moone*, or to the speculations of the Royal Society. Bunyan's friend John Owen knew Wilkins; and Bunyan detested natural science. In *The Holy War* Bunyan mentions "Primum mobile," the spheres, the poles, and the four points of the heavens; Milton may have been the cause of his interest in celestial mechanics. Allusions to Mors, Cerberus, and the Eumenides, Alecto, Megaera, Tisiphone (whom Bunyan ignorantly made male devils), pp. 193, 345, 353, 369, betoken a new knowledge at second hand of the classics. Milton mentions Megaera alone, *Paradise Lost*, x, 560; but Richard Overton's *New Lambeth Fayre*, London, Printed by R. O. and G. D., 1642, E. 138 (26), mentions all the furies. Bunyan had acquired his Ptolemaic and classical lore from Milton or from the pamphlets of the time; and since this knowledge is new in his work, it is possible that *Paradise Lost* had stimulated him.

38. John B. Marsh, *Story of Harecourt*, London, 1871, p. 161.

39. Keach, *The Glorious Lover, A Divine Poem, Upon the Adorable Mystery of Sinners Redemption*, London, Printed for Christopher Hussey, 1679, pp. 103-7, 114 ff., 209 ff.

40. Trial scenes occur in the following works: *The Arraignment of the Anabaptists Good Old Cause, With the manner and proceedings of the Court of Justice Against him. Also the names of the Jury and Witnesses that came in against him, With the Sentence of Death pronounced by the Judge before his Execution*, London, Printed by John Morgan, 1660, E. 1017 (32); *The Tryal, Conviction, and Condemnation of Popery, For High Treason, in Conspiring the Death, Ruine, and Subversion of Christianity. Who upon full Evidence was convicted, and received Sentence accordingly*, London, Printed for Richard Janeway, 1680; [Overton], *The Arraignment of Mr. Persecution. Presented to the Consideration of the House of Commons, and to all the Common People of England. By Yongue Martin Mar-Priest*, Europe, Printed by Martin Claw-Clergie, Printer to the Reverend Assembly of Divines, and are to be sould at his Shop in Toleration Street, at the Signe of the Subjects Liberty, right opposite to Persecuting Court, 1645, E. 276 (23). Thomas Hall, *The Font Guarded With XX Arguments*, London, Printed for Thomas Simmons, 1652, E. 658 (5), pp. 73-86, a trial of the Anabaptist; *The Pulpit Guarded with XVII Arguments*, London, Printed for E. Blackmore, 1651, E. 628 (4), pp. 29-38, the trial of the lay preacher; *Funebria Florae, The Downfall*

of May-Games, London, Printed for Henry Mortlock, 1660, E. 1035 (7), pp. 18-30. Keach, *Sion in Distress: or, the Groans of the Protestant Church*, 2d ed., London, Printed for Enoch Prosser, 1681, (1st ed. 1666), pp. 88-112, the trial of the Whore or Roman Church; reprinted in Keach's *Distressed Sion Relieved*, London, Printed for Nath. Crouch, 1689, p. 130; Keach, *The Progress of Sin; or the Travels of Ungodliness . . . As also, The Manner of his Apprehension, Arraignment, Tryal, Condemnation and Execution*, London, Printed for John Dunton, 1684, pp. 224-72; Keach, *The Glorious Lover*, 1679, pp. 92-103, the trial of the soul before the bar of Jehovah without jury.

41. Cheare's verses, which are printed in Jessey's book, mentioned *infra* note 42, inspired Bunyan by their intention rather than by their substance or form.

42. Jessey, *A Looking-Glass for Children*, London, Printed for Robert Boulter, 1673. James Janeway, *A Token for Children*, London, Printed for T. Norris, (1672); literature for children had appeared much earlier, e.g. Francis Cokayne, *Divine Blossomes. A Prospect or Looking-Glass for Youth*, London, Printed for E. Farnham, 1657, E. 1652 (1).

43. George Fox, *A Catechisme for Children*, London, Printed for Giles Calvert, 1657, E. 1667 (3); John Worthington, *A Form of Sound Words*, London, Printed for R. Royston, 1673; Fowler had called Bunyan's attention to this work; *A Catechisme for Young Children. Appointed by Act of the Church and Council of Scotland*, 1641; see E. B. Underhill, *Confessions of Faith*, p. xv; several catechisms appear in vol. 3505.c.17 in B.M. Frequently catechisms, the commandments, and even alphabets were versified to tempt the young: T. D., *Zions Song For Young Children, or A Catechism in Verse*, London, Printed by Jane Bell, 1650, E. 1379 (1); John Chishull, *A Brief Explication of the Ten Commandments; Intended for a help to the Understanding and Memories of Children*, London, 166(?); Robert Port, *An Holy Alphabet for Young Christians*, London, Printed by G. Dawson, 1658, E. 1548 (3); in his first poem Bunyan also versified the commandments.

44. William Orme, "Life of John Owen," in Owen's *Works*, London, Printed for Richard Baynes, 1826, I, 225. Owen's primer has been lost. Keach, *The Child's Delight: Or Instructions for Children and Youth Wherein All the chief Principles of the Christian Religion are Clearly (though briefly) Opened . . . Together With many other things, both Pleasant and Useful, for the Christian Education of Youth . . . teaching to Spell, Read, and cast Accompts, With a short Dictionary interpreting hard Words and Names*, 3d ed., London, Printed for William and Joseph Marshall, (c. 1703), 1st ed., 1664; see Thomas Crosby, *History of Baptists*, II, 185-208, III, 146. Benjamin Harris, *The Protestant Tutor. Instructing Children to Spel and read English, and Grounding them in the True Protestant Religion*, London, Printed for Ben. Harris, 1679.

45. For Fletcherian imagery see *Building, Nature, Excellency of House of God*, 1688, II, 580-81: "His eyes are like the doves which waters wet," etc. For conceit see: *Book for Boys and Girls*, p. 68: "Now let the Physick be the Holy Word," etc.

46. *Pilgrim's Progress*, Part II, p. 316.

47. *Resurrection of Dead*, II, 110-12; *Seasonable Counsel*, II, 738. In the Preface to *Book for Boys and Girls* Bunyan cited the example of the Bible in teaching moral lessons by "inconsiderable" things such as swallows, cuckows, ants, and the ass. Professor William Haller of Barnard College informs me that animal emblems were common in spiritual literature before 1640.

48. E.g., John Tustin, *Tustin's Observations, or, Conscience Embleme; The Watch of God, similized by the Wakefull Dog*, 1646. A broadside.

49. *Holy War*, p. 385; *Pilgrim's Progress*, Part II, pp. 318, 332; *Seasonable Counsel*, II, 738; *Greatness of Soul*, I, 147. Emblems appear frequently in the *Progress* especially in the scenes at the Interpreter's House.

50. Geffrey Whitney, *A Choice of Emblems, and other Devises, For the most parte gathered out of sundrie writers, Englished and Moralized,* Leyden, Printed for Christopher Plantyn, 1586. A few animal emblems appear in the earlier *Emblems d'Alciat de nouveau Translatez en Francois,* Lyon, Chez Guill. Roville, 1549.

51. George Wither, *A Collection of Emblemes, Ancient and Moderne,* London, Printed by A.M. for Robert Milbourne, 1685. The collections of John Hall, 1658, and Edmund Arwaker, 1686, have no animals. Both Wither and Quarles were popular among the sectarians; Bunyan's friend John Gibbs, for example, cited Quarles with approval.

52. Bunyan's use of a heading for the conclusion of his verses suggests the influence of the rhymed versions of Aesop, which ordinarily employed the word *Moral* for this purpose. Many of these fables, which also concern the beaver, the fly, and other beasts, differ in no way from the emblem. Since Aesop in Latin was used to exercise the perseverance of the seventeenth-century schoolboy, it is possible that Bunyan intended his versified primer as a more godly substitute for the heathen fabulist among those whose station had denied them the classical languages. Among the versified fables the most similar to Bunyan's emblems are: Leonard Willan, *The Phrygian Fabulist: or, The Fables of Aesop: Extracted From the Latine Copie, and Moraliz'd,* London, Printed for Nicholas Bourn, 1650, E. 1371 (1); John Ogilby, *The Fables of Aesop Paraphras'd in Verse: Adorn'd with Sculpture,* London, Printed by Thomas Roycroft, 1665; *The Fables of Esop in English,* London, Printed for Abell Roper, 1658, E. 1889, (a prose version with cuts); in 1692 L'Estrange's fables appeared; Aesop was read by the sectarians as we know from Keach's mention of the fables in *Travels of True Godliness,* 1684, p. 202. For the influence of fables and the bestiary tradition upon children's literature of this period see: F. J. Harvey Darton, *Children's Books in England,* Cambridge, University Press, 1932, pp. 11-19, 28-30, 53-67; Keach, Cheare, and Bunyan are discussed.

53. The Preface to Wither's *Collection of Emblemes,* 1685, is almost identical in substance and tone with Bunyan's Preface to *A Book for Boys and Girls.* Wither also said that he intended his emblems as "play-games," hobby horses, and rattles to attract those of meaner capacity, who, in love with folly, scorned higher things.

54. *Advice to Sufferers,* II, 734: "'take no thought how or what ye shall speak: for it shall be given you in that same hour what ye shall speak.' Mat. x. 19. I have often been amazed in my mind at this text, for how could Jesus Christ have said such a word if he had not been able to perform it?"; *Forest of Lebanon,* III, 532 and *Water of Life,* III, 558: "it is not ourselves that speak, but the Lord that speaketh in us," he quotes from Fox; and of the Holy Spirit he says, "It will make you speak well."

55. Benjamin Keach is an example.

56. Matthew Coker, *A Prophetical Revelation Given from God himself unto Matthew Coker of Lincoln's-Inne,* London, Printed by James Cottrel, 1654, E. 734 (7), Epistle.

57. Henry Clark, *A Description of the Prophets, Apostles, and Ministers of Christ,* 1655, p. 5. Edward Burrough, Epistle to the Reader, in Fox, *The Great Mistery of the Great Whore,* 1659, p. 24, cf. pp. 4, 8, 9. T. Tany, *Theauraujohn, His Aurora,* 1655, E. 853 (26), Preface: "I am not book-learned, but I am heartknowledged by divine inspiration." Cf. Abraham Cheare, *Words in Season,* London, Printed for Nathan Brookes, 1668, in which the editor claims Cheare was merely the scribe of God, who delivered to him what he set down, and rejoices that Cheare had never been disadvantaged by academical education, that all he wrote was by inspiration. Anna Trapnel, *Voice For the King of Saints and Nations,*

London, 1658, T. 370 (7) ; she claims all her poems to be directly inspired and pure automatic writing. Henry More discussed the claims of these prophets, who may be called Holy Ghost writers, in *Enthusiasmus Triumphatus*, ed. 1662, pp. 11-13.

58. Epilogue to *Holy War:*

> "Witness my name, if Anagram'd to thee,
> The Letters make, *Nu hony in a B.*"

59. *Holy City,* III, 398.

60. Charles Doe, "Reasons why Christian People should Promote by Subscriptions the Printing in Folio the Labours of Mr. John Bunyan," in 1692 folio of Bunyan's works, sections 2, 6, 30: "He became thus able and excellent a Minister by a great degree of Gospel-Grace bestowed upon his own Soul, more than probable for that very end; for that God wrought him from a very great profane Sinner, and an illiterate poor Man, to this profound understanding the true or genuine Spiritual Meaning of the Scriptures, whereby he could experimentally preach to Souls with Power, and Affection, and Apostolical Learning, the true Nature of the Gospel. . . ." "And lastly, (Pardon me, if I speak too great a Word, as it may seem to some to be born,) All things considered, that is, his own former Profaneness, Poverty, Unlearnedness, together with his great Natural Parts, the great change made by Grace, and his long Imprisonment, and the great Maturity in Grace and Preaching he attained to; I say, our deceased Bunyan hath not left in England, or the World, his Equal behind him, as I know of."

61. Doe, "The Struggler," in 1692 folio. Cf. "An Account of the Life and Actions of Mr. John Bunyan," in *Pilgrim's Progress,* Part III, 1693, pp. 30, 38, on his success as a writer and preacher and the applause of the public.

62. Whitley, *A History of British Baptists,* 1923, pp. 140-41: his popularity despite the antipathy of the strict Baptists, is the best proof of Bunyan's appeal. Cf. "An Account of the Life and Actions of Mr. John Bunyan," 1693, p. 40: Bunyan preached several times in London, particularly in Southwark where he had an audience of about five hundred; "The Life and Death of Mr. John Bunyan," in *Pilgrim's Progress,* Part III, 4th ed., 1700, p. 34: he went to London once a year to preach in several places especially in Southwark near the Faulcon; "The Continuation of Mr. Bunyan's Life," in *Grace Abounding,* 7th ed., 1692, p. 181: "When he was at leisure from Writing and Teaching, he often came up to London, and there went among the Congregations of the Non-conformists, and used his Talent to the great good liking of the Hearers, and even some to whom he had been misrepresented, upon the account of his Education, were convinced of his Worth and Knowledge in Sacred things."

63. Wilson, *The History and Antiquities of Dissenting Churches and Meeting Houses, in London, Westminster, and Southwark,* London, 1808, II, 249-55. Bunyan's friends John Owen, Matthew Mead, and Anthony Palmer also preached in Pinners' Hall.

64. *Church Book, passim.*

65. "The Continuation of Mr. Bunyan's Life," 1692, p. 180: at the opening of the new meeting house in Bedford, "the place was so thronged, that many was constrained to stay without, though the House was very spacious, every one striving to partake of his Instructions, that were of his perswasion; and show their good will towards him, by being present at the opening of the place . . . ." Cf. J. Brown, *John Bunyan,* pp. 215-16.

66. "An Account of the Life and Actions of Mr. John Bunyan," 1693, p. 39: this biographer continues: "for not only the Ignorant, but even the Learned

approved and the rather admired them [his works], because he was a Man of
no Learning, as to School matters." Doe, *A Collection of Experience*, 1700, p. 52;
this was in 1684, at Mr. Moore's meeting in a private house during the persecution.

67. Doe, "The Struggler." John Dunton, *The Life and Errors of John Dunton*,
London, Printed for S. Malthus, 1705, p. 236. Cf. publisher's advertisement in
"The Labours of John Bunyan, Author of the Pilgrim's Progress," in 1692 folio.
The popularity of Bunyan's *Progress* is shown by the depositions of booksellers
from 1690-97: see *The Year's Work in English Studies*, Oxford, University Press,
IX (1930), p. 255.

68. Brown, *John Bunyan*, chap. 19, pp. 439 ff., a good account of the imitations, the parodies, and the reception of the *Progress;* Dunton, *op. cit.,* p. 437.

69. Doe, *A Collection of Experience*, 1700, p. 57. In the margin of the Bodleian
copy is a MS note in a contemporary hand: "to sell such lying books is the
Devil's work."

70. Orme, "Memoirs of Owen," in *Works of John Owen*, 1826, I, 305: Owen
replied to his sovereign, "Had I the tinker's abilities, please your Majesty, I
would most gladly relinquish my learning." Anthony Wood, *Athenae Oxonienses*,
London, 1721, II, 1030, in life of Edward Fowler: "The said John Bunyan, who is
reported to have been a Tinker in Bedford, was Author of several useful and
practical Books . . . ." Crosby, *History of Baptists*, II, 92: "the famous Mr. John
Bunyan"; for other seventeenth- and eighteenth-century allusions to Bunyan
see John Brown, *John Bunyan*, pp. 444, 462.

71. Tom Brown, *Letters from the Dead to the Living*, in *Amusements Serious
and Comical and Other Works*, ed. by Arthur L. Hayward, London, Routledge,
1927, p. 399: a shoemaker had "such an assurance of his parts, as to challenge
Bunyan the tinker to chop logic with him; and Nayler the quaker, who was of
a principle between both, was thought the best qualified person in all hell for
an impartial moderator. But your nimblechopped pupil was too cunning for the
Pilgrim author, as a fox is for a badger, so that at last the shoemaker got his ends,
and left the poor tinker without one argument in his budget."

72. John Tombes, *Anthropolatria; or The Sinne of glorying in Men, Especially
In Eminent Ministers of the Gospel*, London, Printed for John Bellamy, 1645, E.
282 (13). Cf. John Spencer, *The Spirituall Warfare*, London, 1642, p. 5, on being
exalted by gifts and the dangers incurred by gifted ministers, who must fight
themselves.

73. Keach, *A Trumpet Blown in Zion*, 1694, pp. 48, 50. Several preachers confessed to a ruling sin against which they struggled; Powell's was wrath: *The Life
and Death of Mr. Vavasor Powell*, 1671, Preface.

74. *Pray with the Spirit*, I, 631; *Israel's Hope*, I, 589; *Justification by Imputed
Righteousness*, I, 331; *Holy Life*, II, 517, 525, 531; *Christian Behaviour*, II, 566,
567; *Acceptable Sacrifice*, I, 704-05; *Heavenly Footman*, III, 386-87.

75. *Grace Abounding*, pp. 89-91. Paul, Kiffin, and John Denne accused Bunyan
of wishing "to be thought some body," of writing, disputing, and suffering
martyrdom for the sake of popular applause and fame: "Ask your heart whether
popilarity, and applause of variety of professors, be not in the bottom of what
you have said; that hath been your snare." Paul and Kiffin, *Some Serious Reflections*, 1673, pp. 58, 60; Denne, *Truth outweighing error*, 1673, p. 12; Paul's lost
attack on Bunyan contained five pages on Bunyan's pride, *Peaceable Principles*,
II, 648; Bunyan's denials and responses occur in *Differences in Judgment*, II, 618,
640, 641. Charges of pride were constantly made against the sectarians; Baxter
answered them in *Reliquiae Baxterianae*, 1696, Part III, p. 105.

76. *Pilgrim's Progress*, Part I, pp. 186-87.

77. George Cockayne, *A Preface to Reader*, Sept. 21, 1688, in Bunyan's *Acceptable Sacrifice*, I, 685. Bunyan's contemporary biographers emphasize his modesty and humility out of a natural desire to whiten the departed brother.

78. The following verses from an elegy on Bunyan might refer to his final earthly felicity rather than to his translation to heaven:

> By many storms and tempests now at last,
> Our Bunyan on a blessed shore is cast;
> And having reach'd that harbour of delight,
> It argues that he steer'd his course aright . . .
> And though his education small, I'll say,
> He was a light that burned in his day.

An Elegy On the Death of the worthy and pious Mr. John Bunyan, in *A Relation of Imprisonment*, 1765, pp. 53-55; one of his biographers says of Bunyan's later years: "he lived in much Peace and quiet of Mind." "The Continuation of Mr. Bunyan's Life," 1692, p. 180.

APPENDIX

1. George Offor, *Memoir of John Bunyan*, in *Works of Bunyan*, I, xliv-xlvi. Joseph Smith, *Bibliotheca Anti-Quakeriana; or, A Catalogue of Books Adverse to the Society of Friends*, London, Joseph Smith, 1873; this work is a supplement to Smith's *A Descriptive Catalogue of Friends' Books*, London, Smith, 1867. I am indebted to Smith for my knowledge of the existence of these tracts. In his *Bibliography*, First Series, p. 72, W. C. Hazlitt, erroneously attributed *Strange & Terrible Newes* to Bunyan.

2. *The First New Persecution; or, A True Narrative of the Cruel usage of two Christians, by the present Mayor of Cambridge*, London, Printed for Giles Calvert, 1654, E. 725 (19). William Sympson, *From One who was moved of the Lord God to go a sign among the Priests & Professors*, London, Printed for Thomas Simmons, 1659. Edward Sammon, *A Discovery of the Education of the Schollars of Cambridge; by Their Abominations and wicked Practices acted upon, and against, the Despised People, in scorn Called Quakers*, London, Printed for Giles Calvert, 1659. Thomas Smith, *A Letter Sent to Mr. E. of Taft, Four miles from Cambridge*, in *The Quaker Disarm'd*, London, Printed by J. C., 1659.

3. T. Smith, *The Quaker Disarm'd*, 1659. Richard Blome, *Questions propounded to George Whitehead and George Fox, who disputed by turns against one University-Man in Cambr. Aug. 29, 1659*, in T. Smith, *A Gagg for the Quakers*, London, Printed by J. C., 1659, E. 764 (2). George Whitehead, *The Christian Progress of that Ancient Servant and Minister of Jesus Christ, George Whitehead*, London, Printed by the Assigns of J. Sowle, 1725, pp. 163-68, (Columbia University).

4. Among the current stories of Quakers and horses was one dated May 20, 1659: *A Relation of a Quaker, That to the Shame of his Profession, Attempted to Bugger a Mare near Colchester*, 669. f. 21 (35):

> Help Woodcock, Fox, and Nailor.
> For Brother Green's a Stalion,
> Now Alas what hope,
> Of converting the Pope,
> When a Quaker turns Italian.

Richard Blome, who was aiding Thomas Smith against the Cambridge Quakers, made charges similar to this against Hugh Bisbroun: Blome, *Questions propounded to George Whitehead*, in T. Smith, *A Gagg for the Quakers*, 1659. In 1659 the grave charge of intimacy between Quakers and horses was favored by controversialists; always sensitive to the trend of the times, Bunyan provided his harmless variation upon the theme.

5. James Blackley, *A Lying Wonder Discovered, and The Strange and Terrible Newes from Cambridge proved false. Which false News is published in a Libel, Concerning a wicked slander cast upon a Quaker, but the Author of the said Libel was ashamed to subscribe his name to it. Also This contains an answer to John Bunions Paper touching the said imagined witchcraft, which he hath given forth to your wonderment (as he saith) but it is also proved a Lye and a slander by many credible witnesses hereafter mentioned*, London, Printed for Thomas Simmons at the Bull and Mouth near Aldersgate, 1659, (Aug. 8, 1659; copy in Friends' House).

6. In a petition of Quaker women against tithes and learning, dated July, 1659, the second name of the Cambridgeshire section is that of Widow Prior. If this is Margaret Pryor, it would prove that she was still considered a member of the society contrary to Blackley's assertion that the Friends had disowned her; but our Margaret Pryor was not a widow unless her husband had died after 1657: *These several Papers was sent to the Parliament the twentieth day of the fifth Moneth, 1659. Being above seven thousand of the Names of the Hand-Maids and Daughters of the Lord*, London, Printed for Mary Westwood, 1659, p. 37; Richard Blome mentioned this petition.

7. William Allen, a friend of Blackley's, was one of the leading Quakers of Cambridge. He is mentioned by Thomas Smith as having had a part in the Fox-Whitehead dispute of August. Blome's Appendix to Smith's *Gagg for the Quakers*, 1659, adds the information that Allen claimed infallibility and perfection. He was a barber-surgeon and an itinerant preacher, Braithwaite, pp. 295-96, 383-84.

8. The text has 1659, an obvious misprint.

9. *Strange & Terrible Newes from Cambridge, Being A true Relation of the Quakers bewitching of Mary Philips out of the Bed from her Husband in the Night, and transformed her into the shape of a Bay Mare, riding her from Dinton, towards the University. With the manner how she became visible again to the People in her own Likeness and Shape, with her sides all rent and torn, as if they had been spur-gal'd, her hands and feet worn as black as a Coal, and her mouth slit with the Bridle Bit. Likewise, her Speech to the Scholars and Countreymen, upon this great and wonderful Change, her Oath before the judges and justices, and the Names of the Quakers brought to Tryal on Friday last at the Assises held at Cambridge. With the judgment of the Court. As also, the Devils snatching of one from his Company, and hoisting of him up into the Air, with what hapned thereupon*, London, Printed for C. Brooks, and are to be sold at the Royal Exchange in Cornhill, 1659, (British Museum).

10. By priestlike language Blackley referred to the inflated style of the opening: "As the Wings and Motion of Time, are usher'd into the Universe with various Changes; so is the Creature transformed daily from his Rational Intellects, to an irrational sensuality of Dumb Creatures. O monstrous! What Christians become Beasts; what a sad Age do we live in?"

11. E.g., "A high-flown Spirit, on Sabbath day last was sevennight, took the impudence to pull down his breeches on the Communion Table, and laid there his most odious and nasty burden: But observe and tremble at the Divine Vengeance; he was suddenly tormented with the griping in his guts; and lamentably

roaring out, died within the space of an hour or two." There are several divine judgments in this tract.

12. *Strange & Terrible Newes* was discovered, after considerable search and despair, catalogued strangely and terribly in the British Museum under Mary Philips. The press mark is 719.g.75.

13. See Frank M. Harrison, *A Bibliography of the Works of John Bunyan*, Oxford, The Bibliographical Society, 1932, p. 26. There is no mention in this bibliography of Bunyan's lost tract on witches, but two other lost works are mentioned. Apparently there is still another lost tract from the same year, 1659, which Harrison has also failed to notice; in William London's *A Catalogue of New Books, By way of Supplement to the former. Being Such as have been Printed from that time, till Easter-Term, 1660*, London, Printed by A. M. and are to be sold by Luke Fawn, and Francis Tyton, 1660, (May 31), E. 1025 (17), a work called *On the Covenant* is ascribed to Mr. Bunnian, whose *Few Sighs from Hell* and *Doctrine of Law and Grace* are also listed. This unknown work is not described nor is the full title given, but it was apparently a production of 1659. Unless the bibliographer made an error of ascription, this work must also take its place among Bunyan's lost works. It is, of course, possible that it was in an appendix to this tract that Bunyan wrote of the Cambridge witches.

14. Blackley, *Lying Wonder*, pp. 3-4, 7, 8.

15. *A Testimony from the People of God, Called Quakers, Against Many Lying and Slanderous Books, and a Ballad lately published in Envy and Malice, to render the said People odious, and accusing them of things they are clear of. From the People of God, called Quakers, and is to go abroad in all Cities, Towns, and Countries where those lying Pamphlets and Ballads have been spread*, London, the 11th of the 2d Moneth, 1670, (British Museum, 1876. b. 6 (13).

16. *Some Gospel Truths*, II, 163; *Vindication of Gospel Truths*, II, 201.

17. *Doctrine of Law and Grace*, I, 536; *Differences in Judgment*, II, 635; *Pilgrim's Progress*, Part I, p. 228; *Treatise of Fear of God*, I, 446; *Mr. Badman*, p. 36; *Holy War*, p. 326; *Holy Life*, II, 513-14; *Book for Boys and Girls*, No. 65, "Upon our being afraid of the Apparition of Evil Spirits"; *Instruction for Ignorant*, II, 678; *Water of Life*, III, 558.

18. *Quakers Are Inchanters, and Dangerous Seducers Appearing in their Inchantment of one Mary White At Wickham-skeyth in Suffolk*, London, Printed by T. M. for Edward Dod, 1655; John Gilpin's *The Quakers Shaken*, 1653, also makes charges of witchcraft against the Quakers. For other similar accusations see Braithwaite, *The Beginnings of Quakerism*, pp. 53, 67, 220, 487.

19. Richard Farnworth, *Witchcraft Cast out from the Religious Seed and Israel of God*, London, Printed for Giles Calvert, 1655, E. 829 (12); George Fox, *A Declaration of the Ground of Error*, London, Printed for Giles Calvert, 1657, E. 916 (4), pp. 13-41.

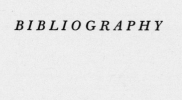

BIBLIOGRAPHY

BIBLIOGRAPHY

This bibliography contains the secondary and more or less recent works which have been found useful or interesting and the editions of Bunyan's works which have been employed. Since the seventeenth-century pamphlets and other books of that period are cited fully in the notes, and since most are listed in the bibliographies mentioned below, it has been thought best to omit them from this bibliography. The Index will facilitate reference to the bibliographical notes. The biographies of Bunyan which add nothing to the work of John Brown and the scholarly or other discussions of Bunyan which do not concern the present investigation have also been omitted.

I. BIBLIOGRAPHIES

Fortescue, G. K., Catalogue of the Pamphlets, Books, Newspapers, and Manuscripts . . . Collected by George Thomason, 1640-1661. London, British Museum, 1908.

Gillett, Charles Ripley, Catalogue of the McAlpin Collection of British History and Theology. New York, Union Theological Seminary, 1930.

Harrison, Frank Mott, A Bibliography of the Works of John Bunyan. Oxford, Bibliographical Society, 1932.

Smith, Joseph, Bibliotheca Anti-Quakeriana; or, A Catalogue of Books Adverse to the Society of Friends. London, Joseph Smith, 1873.

———A Descriptive Catalogue of Friends' Books. London, Joseph Smith, 1867.

Whitley, W. T., A Baptist Bibliography. 2 vols., London, Kingsgate Press, 1916.

II. THE WORKS OF BUNYAN

Bunyan, John, A Book for Boys and Girls; or, Country Rhymes for Children. 1686. A facsimile of the first edition with Introduction by John Brown. London, Elliot Stock, 1889.

Grace Abounding and The Pilgrim's Progress. Edited by John Brown. Cambridge, University Press, 1907.

Mr. Badman and The Holy War. Edited by John Brown. Cambridge, University Press, 1905.

Profitable Meditations, Fitted to Mans Different Condition, In a

Conference Between Christ and a Sinner. London, printed for Francis Smith, 1661.

The Works of John Bunyan. Edited by George Offor. 3 vols., Glasgow, Blackie, 1853.

III. OTHER WORKS

Baptist Historical Society, Transactions of. London, Baptist Union, 1908 ff.

Baptist Quarterly. New Series, London, Baptist Union, 1922 ff.

Barclay, Robert, The Inner Life of the Religious Societies of the Commonwealth. London, Hodder and Stoughton, 1876.

Berens, Lewis H., The Digger Movement. London, Simpkin, Marshall, etc., 1906.

Bernstein, Eduard, Cromwell and Communism, Socialism and Democracy in the Great English Revolution. Translated by H. J. Stenning. London, Allen & Unwin, 1930.

Blunt, John Henry, Dictionary of Sects, Heresies, Ecclesiastical Parties. Philadelphia, Lippincott, 1874.

Braithwaite, William C., The Beginnings of Quakerism. London, Macmillan, 1923.

Brook, Benjamin, The Lives of the Puritans. London, James Black, 1813.

Brown, John, John Bunyan, His Life, Times, and Work. Revised by Frank Mott Harrison. London, Hulbert, 1928.

Brown, Louise Fargo, The Political Activities of the Baptists and Fifth Monarchy Men in England during the Interregnum. Washington, American Historical Association, 1912.

Burrage, Champlin, The Early English Dissenters in the Light of Recent Research. Cambridge, University Press, 1912.

Burrage, Henry S., Baptist Hymn Writers. Portland, Maine, Brown, Thurston, 1888.

Calamy, Edmund, A Continuation of the Account of the Ministers . . . Ejected and Silenced. London, printed for R. Ford, 1727.

Calendar of State Papers, Domestic.

Carlyle, Thomas, The Letters and Speeches of Oliver Cromwell. Edited by S. C. Lomas. London, Methuen, 1904.

Cathcart, William, The Baptist Encyclopaedia. Philadelphia, Everts, 1881.

Clark, Henry W., History of English Nonconformity. London, Chapman and Hall, 1911.

Crosby, Thomas, The History of the English Baptists, From the Reformation to the Beginning of the Reign of King George I. London, printed for the editor, 1738-40.

Darton, F. J. Harvey, Children's Books in England. Cambridge, University Press, 1932.

Dictionary of National Biography.

Draper, John W., Bunyan's Mr. Ignorance. *Modern Language Review,* XXII (1927), 14-21.

Firth, Charles H., Bunyan's Holy War. *Journal of English Studies,* I (1913), No. 3, 143-44.

———Cromwell's Army. London, Methuen, 1902.

———The Last Years of the Protectorate. London, Longmans, 1909.

Furnivall, F. J., editor, Deguilleville's Pilgrimage of the Life of Man. London, E. E. T. S., Paul, Trench, etc., 1899-1904.

Gardiner, Samuel R., History of the Commonwealth and Protectorate. London, Longmans, 1903.

Golder, Harold, "The Chivalric Background of Pilgrim's Progress," 1925. Harvard University Summaries of Theses. Cambridge, Harvard University Press, 1928.

———Bunyan's Hypocrisy. *North American Review,* CCXXIII (1926), 323-32.

———Bunyan and Spenser. *Publication of the Modern Language Association,* XLV (March, 1930), 216-37. Other articles on Bunyan by Dr. Golder have appeared in various scholarly publications.

Gooch, G. P., and H. J. Laski, English Democratic Ideas in the Seventeenth Century. Cambridge, University Press, 1927.

Griffith, Gwilym O., John Bunyan. London, Hodder and Stoughton, 1927.

Hallam, Henry, The Constitutional History of England. New York, Harper, 1847.

Haller, William, Tracts on Liberty. New York, Columbia University Press, 1934.

Hammond, J. L., and Barbara Hammond, The Village Labourer. 4th ed., London, Longmans, 1927.

Harrison, G. B., editor, The Church Book of Bunyan Meeting 1650-1821. A reproduction in facsimile, London, Dent, 1928.

———editor, The Narrative of the Persecution of Agnes Beaumont in 1674. London, Constable, 1929.

———John Bunyan: A Study in Personality. London, Dent, 1928.

Hastings, James, Encyclopedia of Religion and Ethics. New York, Scribner, 1908-27.

Heath, Richard, The Archetype of "The Holy War." *The Contemporary Review*, LXXII (1897), 105.

James, William, The Varieties of Religious Experience. 13th ed., London, Longmans, 1907.

Jones, Rufus M., Studies in Mystical Religion. London, Macmillan, 1909.

Jukes, John, A Brief History of Bunyan's Church, Compiled, Chiefly, from its own records. London, Partridge and Oakey, 1849.

Julian, John, A Dictionary of Hymnology. London, John Murray, 1892.

Knox, Edmund A., John Bunyan in Relation to His Times. London, Longmans, 1928.

Lindsay, Thomas M., A History of the Reformation. New York, Scribner, 1906-10.

Lipscomb, George, The History and Antiquities of the County of Buckingham. London, J. & W. Robins, 1847.

Lipson, Ephraim, The Economic History of England. 2 vols., London, A. & C. Black, 1931.

Marsh, John B., The Story of Harecourt Being the History of an Independent Church. London, Strahan, 1871.

Neal, Daniel, History of the Puritans. New York, Harper, 1843-44.

Owst, Gerald R., Literature and Pulpit in Medieval England. Cambridge, University Press, 1933.

Page, William, editor, The Victoria County History of Bedford. London, Constable, 1908.

Palmer, Samuel, The Nonconformist's Memorial. London, printed for W. Harris, 1775.

Pease, Theodore Calvin, The Leveller Movement. Washington, American Historical Association, 1916.

Peile, John, Biographical Register of Christ's College, 1505-1905. Cambridge, University Press, 1910.

Pratt, James B., The Religious Consciousness. New York, Macmillan, 1924.

Richardson, Caroline F., English Preachers and Preaching, 1640-1670. New York, Macmillan, 1928.

Rogers, James E. T., Six Centuries of Work and Wages. London, W. S. Sonnenschein, 1884.

———A History of Agriculture and Prices in England. Oxford, Clarendon Press, 1887.

Smith, William, Dictionary of the Bible. Edited by H. B. Hackett. New York, Hurd and Houghton, 1869.

Southey, Robert, The Life of John Bunyan. London, John Murray, 1844.

Tallack, William, George Fox, The Friends, and The Early Baptists. London, Partridge, 1868.

Tawney, Richard H., Religion and the Rise of Capitalism. New York, Harcourt, Brace, 1926.

Thiel, Gerhard, Bunyans Stellung innerhalb der religiösen Strömungen seiner Zeit. Breslau, 1931.

Thurloe, John, A Collection of State Papers. Edited by Thomas Birch. London, 1742.

Trevelyan, George M., England under the Stuarts. New York, Putnam, 1930.

Tulloch, John, Rational Theology and Christian Philosophy in England in the Seventeenth Century. 2d ed., Edinburgh, Blackwood, 1874.

Underhill, E. B., Confessions of Faith. London, printed for Hanserd Knollys Society, 1854.

Underwood, Alfred, Conversion: Christian and Non-Christian. New York, Macmillan, 1925.

Unwin, George, Introduction to The Reverend Richard Baxter's Last Treatise. Manchester, University Press, 1926.

Urwick, William, Nonconformity in Hertfordshire. London, Hazell, Watson, & Viney, 1884.

Weingarten, Hermann, Die Revolutionskirchen Englands. Leipzig, Breitkopf und Härtel, 1868.

Wharey, James B., A Study of the Sources of Bunyan's Allegories. Baltimore, J. H. Furst, 1904.

———Bunyan's Mr. Badman. *Modern Language Notes,* XXXVI (February, 1921), 65-79.

Whitley, W. T., A History of British Baptists. London, Charles Griffin, 1923.

———The Baptists of London. London, Kingsgate Press, 1928.

Wilson, Walter, The History and Antiquities of Dissenting Churches and Meeting Houses, in London, Westminster, and Southwark. London, 1808.

Wood, Anthony, Athenae Oxonienses. London, 1721.

INDEX

INDEX